Making and Shaping the Law of Armed Conflict

THE LIEBER STUDIES

The Lieber Studies is the flagship publication of the Lieber Institute for Law and Warfare. It is designed to provide scholars, practitioners, and students with in-depth and critical analysis of the most challenging legal issues related to warfare in the 21st Century. Established by the Department of Law of the United States Military Academy at West Point, the mission of the Lieber Institute is to foster a deeper understanding of the complex and evolving relationship between law and warfare in order to educate and empower current and future combat leaders. It does so through global academic engagement and advanced interdisciplinary research. As such, it lies at the crossroads of scholarship and practice by bringing together scholars, military officers, government legal advisers, and members of civil society from around the world to collaboratively examine the role and application of the law of armed conflict in current and future armed conflicts, as well as that of other regimes of international law in situations threatening international peace and security.

Lieber Institute for Law and Warfare
The Lieber Studies

Volume 10

Making and Shaping the Law of Armed Conflict

General Editors
Professor Michael N. Schmitt
Professor Sean Watts

Managing Editor
Professor Robert Lawless

Volume Editors
Professor Sandesh Sivakumaran
Captain Christian R. Burne

OXFORD
UNIVERSITY PRESS

OXFORD
UNIVERSITY PRESS

Oxford University Press is a department of the University of Oxford. It furthers the University's objective of excellence in research, scholarship, and education by publishing worldwide. Oxford is a registered trade mark of Oxford University Press in the UK and certain other countries.

Published in the United States of America by Oxford University Press
198 Madison Avenue, New York, NY 10016, United States of America.

Library of Congress Cataloging-in-Publication Data
Names: Sivakumaran, Sandesh, editor. | Burne, Christian R., editor.
Title: Making and shaping the law of armed conflict /
edited by Sandesh Sivakumaran and Christian R. Burne.
Description: New York : Oxford University Press, 2024. |
Series: Lieber studies series | Includes bibliographical references and index.
Identifiers: LCCN 2023056783 (print) | LCCN 2023056784 (ebook) |
ISBN 9780197775134 (hardback) | ISBN 9780197775141 (epub) |
ISBN 9780197775158 | ISBN 9780197775165
Subjects: LCSH: War (International law) | International humanitarian law. |
Non-state actors (International relations)
Classification: LCC KZ6385 .M3375 2024 (print) | LCC KZ6385 (ebook) |
DDC 341.6—dc23/eng/20231214
LC record available at https://lccn.loc.gov/2023056783
LC ebook record available at https://lccn.loc.gov/2023056784

DOI: 10.1093/oso/9780197775134.001.0001

MIX Paper FSC FSC® C183721

Printed by Integrated Books International, United States of America

CONTENTS

TABLE OF CASES

International Cases

Eritrea-Ethiopia Claims Commission

European Court of Human Rights

Extraordinary Chambers in the Courts of Cambodia

Inter-American Commission on Human Rights

International Court of Justice

International Criminal Court

International Criminal Tribunal for the former Yugoslavia

International Criminal Tribunal for Rwanda

Permanent Court of International Justice

Special Court for Sierra Leone

National Courts

Belgium

Canada

Germany

Israel

South Africa

Sweden

United Kingdom

United States

TABLE OF TREATIES

Hague Conventions and Regulations

Other Treaties

Other Instruments

CONTRIBUTORS

Martha M. Bradley is Associate Professor in the Department of Public Law, Faculty of Law, and University of Johannesburg.

Christian R. Burne is a captain in the United States Army Judge Advocate General's Corps and an Assistant Professor of Law at the United States Military Academy.

Katharine Fortin is Associate Professor at the Netherlands Institute of Human Rights, Utrecht University, and a member of the Montaigne Centre for Rule of Law and Administration of Justice.

Ezequiel Heffes is the Director of Watchlist on Children and Armed Conflict in New York.

Jean-Marie Henckaerts is Head of Unit, Commentaries Update Unit, Legal Division, and International Committee of the Red Cross.

Yousuf Syed Khan is a Senior Lawyer with Global Rights Compliance.

Michael W. Meier is the senior civilian adviser to the Army Judge Advocate General on matters related to the Law of Armed Conflict.

Michael N. Schmitt is the G. Norman Lieber Distinguished Scholar at West Point's Lieber Institute; Professor of Public International Law at the University of Reading (UK); and Professor Emeritus and Charles H. Stockton Distinguished Scholar-in-Residence at the United States Naval War College.

Yahli Shereshevsky is a Senior Lecturer at the Faculty of Law, University of Haifa.

Sandesh Sivakumaran is Professor of International Law at the University of Cambridge; Director of the Lauterpacht Centre for International Law; Fellow of St Edmund's College, Cambridge; and was the 2022 Lieber Scholar at the Lieber Institute for Law and Warfare, United States Military Academy.

Alessandra Spadaro is Assistant Professor of Public International Law at Utrecht University, where she is also a Member of the Montaigne Centre for Rule of Law and Administration of Justice.

Rebecca Sutton is Senior Lecturer in International Law, School of Law, University of Glasgow.

Jeroen Van Den Boogaard serves as Legal Counsel, Ministry of Foreign Affairs, The Netherlands, and Lecturer in International Humanitarian Law, University of Amsterdam.

Gus Waschefort is Associate Professor at Essex Law School and Human Rights Centre, and Barrister at Guernica 37 Chambers, London.

Sean Watts is a Professor in the Department of Law at the United States Military Academy at West Point, where he co-directs the Lieber Institute for Law and Warfare.

PART ONE

Introduction

1

Making and Shaping the Law of Armed Conflict: An Overview

SANDESH SIVAKUMARAN* AND CHRISTIAN R. BURNE**

I. RATIONALE FOR THE VOLUME

The making and shaping of the law of armed conflict is one of the most important topics to which those who study and practice this field may devote themselves. Almost every legal question involves aspects of law-making and shaping, be it identification of a rule, interpretation of that rule, or determination of the rule's scope of application. All who operate in this space—whether academic or practitioner, policy maker or legal adviser—must appreciate and understand the forces, factors, and actors which converge to make and shape the ever-developing law of armed conflict.

Disputes over the substance of the law are not infrequently also disputes over the making of the law. Consider the regulation of non-international armed conflicts. Given the paucity of conventional law, considerable attention has been paid to the state of customary international law. This in turn has given rise to debates over the methodology for identifying rules of customary international

* Sandesh Sivakumaran is Professor of International Law, University of Cambridge; Director of the Lauterpacht Centre for International Law; and Fellow of St Edmund's College, Cambridge, and was the 2022 Lieber Scholar at the Lieber Institute for Law and Warfare, United States Military Academy.

** Christian R. Burne is a captain in the United States Army Judge Advocate General's Corps and an Assistant Professor of Law at the United States Military Academy.

Sandesh Sivakumaran and Christian R. Burne, *Making and Shaping the Law of Armed Conflict: An Overview* In: *Making and Shaping the Law of Armed Conflict*. Edited by: Sandesh Sivakumaran and Christian R. Burne, Oxford University Press.
 DOI: 10.1093/oso/9780197775134.003.0001

humanitarian law.[1] Or take the issue of whether so-called "war-sustaining" objects can lawfully be targeted. That involves interpretation of Article 52(2) of Additional Protocol I and its customary equivalent.[2] A similar issue arises in relation to the debates surrounding the meaning of the phrase: "Civilians shall enjoy the protection afforded by this Section, unless and for such time as they take a direct part in hostilities."[3] The substantive question is, at the same time, a question of interpretation and raises, among other considerations, the weight to be given to International Committee of the Red Cross (ICRC) interpretations of the law.[4] At a structural level, there are also questions as to what constitutes a gap in the law as opposed to deliberate silence[5] and what weight should be given to attempts to fill gaps in the law, such as through expert manuals.

A related set of issues, already apparent from the previous paragraph, concerns actors. A range of actors are involved in the making and shaping of international humanitarian law (IHL). As the principal actors in the international community, States play the dominant role. A host of other well-known actors also play a role, including the ICRC, international courts and tribunals, domestic courts, and expert groups. Cutting across these actors are regional and other alignments, causing both convergence and divergence of views, and exhorting disparate levels of influence. For example, the views of States and other actors of the Global North tend to elicit greater focus than those of other regions. In addition to these well-known actors, other entities, such as commissions of inquiry, trainers of IHL, and non-State armed groups also engage with IHL. The role they play in making and shaping the law, if any, is also deserving of consideration.

1. *Cf.* Customary International Humanitarian Law (Jean-Marie Henckaerts & Louise Doswald-Beck eds., 2005); John B. Bellinger III & William J. Haynes II, *A US Government Response to the International Committee of the Red Cross Study* Customary International Humanitarian Law, 89 International Review of the Red Cross 443 (2007); Jean-Marie Henckaerts, *Customary International Humanitarian Law: A Response to US Comments*, 89 International Review of the Red Cross 473 (2007).

2. Protocol Additional to the Geneva Conventions of 12 August 1949, and Relating to the Protection of Victims of International Armed Conflicts, June 8, 1977, 1125 U.N.T.S. 3 [hereinafter Additional Protocol I].

3. Additional Protocol I, art. 51(3). *See also* Protocol Additional to the Geneva Conventions of 12 August 1949, and Relating to the Protection of Victims of Non-International Armed Conflicts, art. 13(3), June 8, 1977, 1125 U.N.T.S. 609.

4. *See, e.g.*, International Committee of the Red Cross, Interpretive Guidance on the Notion of Direct Participation in Hostilities under International Humanitarian Law (2009). *Cf.* W. Hays Parks, *Part IX of the ICRC "Direct Participation in Hostilities" Study: No Mandate, No Expertise, and Legally Incorrect*, 42 New York University Journal of International Law and Politics 769 (2010).

5. *See* Sean Watts, *The Updated First Geneva Convention Commentary, DOD's Law of War Manual, and a More Perfect Law of War: Part III*, Just Security (Sept. 16, 2016), https://www.justsecurity.org/32989/updated-geneva-convention-commentary-dods-law-war-manual-perfect-law-war-part-iii/.

International humanitarian law does not exist in isolation. Today, it is well recognized that there is a close, if sometimes difficult, even controversial, relationship between IHL and international human rights law and an even closer relationship between IHL and international criminal law. These relationships have given rise to international human rights law and international criminal law mechanisms interpreting and applying IHL. The impact that these mechanisms and their interpretations have on the development of IHL also warrants consideration.

Despite the importance of the subject, until recently there were relatively few in-depth treatments of the topic. There were extended analyses of aspects of the issue, including customary IHL,[6] judicial development of IHL,[7] military manuals,[8] expert manuals,[9] the role of the ICRC,[10] and the impact of international criminal law mechanisms.[11] But there were few extended analyses of the subject as a comprehensive whole. That position changed during the course of preparation of the present volume. There are now two recent, important works on the subject,[12] which the present volume stands alongside.

II. TERMINOLOGY

A word or two is in order on definitional matters. Despite differences in emphasis or connotation, the terms "law of armed conflict," "international humanitarian law," and the "law of war" are used interchangeably throughout the volume, unless individual chapter authors indicate otherwise.

The phrase "making and shaping" is used deliberately. The terms are intended to capture the full spectrum of activities, from creation of the law through to shaping the discourse, and from interpretation to acting as a catalyst and putting the issue on the agenda of the international community. Use of the terms also avoids some

6. *E.g.*, Perspectives on the ICRC Study on Customary International Humanitarian Law (Elizabeth Wilmshurst & Susan Breau eds., 2007).

7. *E.g.*, Shane Darcy, Judges, Law and War: The Judicial Development of International Humanitarian Law (2014); sharon weill, The Role of National Courts in Applying International Humanitarian Law (2014).

8. *E.g.*, National Military Manuals on the Law of Armed Conflict (Nobuo Hayashi ed., 2d ed. 2010).

9. *E.g.*, Anton Petrov, Expert Laws of War: Restating and Making Law in Expert Processes (2020).

10. *E.g.*, Humanizing the Laws of War: the Red Cross and the Development of International Humanitarian Law (Robin Geiß, Andreas Zimmermann, & Stefanie Haumer eds., 2017).

11. *E.g.*, Darcy, *supra* note 7.

12. Law-making and Legitimacy in International Humanitarian Law (Heike Krieger & Jonas Püschmann eds., 2021); *How International Humanitarian Law Develops*, 104 International Review of the Red Cross 1507 (2022).

of the constraints or intellectual baggage that comes with terms of art such as "sources" (and its association with Article 38 of the Statute of the International Court of Justice) or "development" (and its narrative of progress). Again, this is subject to more specific definitions or understandings used by authors in their individual chapters.

III. STRUCTURE AND CHAPTERS

The volume is divided into five parts. Part Two considers foundational materials. It commences with Jean-Marie Henckaerts' engaging chapter entitled "Where Vienna and Geneva Meet: Treaty Interpretation and the Geneva Conventions." Drawing on his wealth of experience, most recently as Head of the Commentaries Update Unit at the Legal Division of the ICRC, although writing here in his personal capacity, Henckaerts explores the important topic of interpreting the 1949 Geneva Conventions. He situates treaty interpretation against other methods of keeping IHL treaties up to date and takes the reader meticulously through the 1969 Vienna Convention on the Law of Treaties rules on treaty interpretation and their application to the Geneva Conventions. In doing so, the chapter identifies contested issues and points of interest and provides illustrations from the ICRC's updated commentaries.

In her tour de force, Katharine Fortin discusses the transformative force that is customary international law. She explores understandings of customary international law over the years, dissects the entanglements between treaty law and customary international law, and analyzes the role that custom has played in the making and shaping of international humanitarian law. The chapter goes on to identify and unpack certain puzzling features of custom and thoughtfully engages with how custom might develop in the future. As the chapter demonstrates, "the story of the role of custom in the making and shaping of international humanitarian law is interwoven with the story of the role of international humanitarian law in the making and shaping of custom."[13]

Jeroen van den Boogaard takes us through an important, foundational topic, yet one that has received relatively little attention: the identification of the principles of international humanitarian law. Critiquing the principles that are currently used by many armed forces, van den Boogaard helpfully distinguishes between foundations, principles, and rules and explains the differences and relationships between them. Taking a "functional" approach, he proposes a new framework of IHL principles, one which, as he explains, can be used both for educational purposes as well as for operational guidance during armed conflict.

Michael W. Meier thoughtfully explores the role of soft law and its impact on international humanitarian law. Meier asks, "Soft Law: What Is It Good For?" The chapter not only addresses the contested nature of soft law and distinguishes

13. Page 38.

between different types of soft law but also analyzes why States and other actors turn to soft law and, importantly, considers how to measure the effectiveness of soft law. These issues are expertly explored with reference to the Montreux Document on Pertinent International Legal Obligations and Good Practices for States related to Operations of Private Military and Security Companies during Armed Conflict, the Political Declaration on Strengthening the Protection of Civilians from the Humanitarian Consequences Arising from the Use of Explosive Weapons in Populated Areas, and the Tallinn Manuals.

Part Three of the volume shifts to the topic of actors and influences. It spotlights the role of specific actors in the making and shaping of the law and explores the influence of closely related bodies of law.

Drawing on his leading roles in the drafting of four expert manuals, Michael N. Schmitt provides an engaging insider's account of expert manuals. Schmitt explores how manuals can influence States' understandings of international law. He helpfully identifies three types of influence: the identification of a (usually customary) rule, the interpretation of a rule, and the identification of interpretative issues. He also identifies factors which affect the influence of expert manuals. Despite his own, enormously influential, work on expert manuals, Schmitt cautions that expert manuals are not necessarily a positive phenomenon, and their proliferation may well be suboptimal for international law.

Sandesh Sivakumaran considers the contribution of the ICRC to the development of international humanitarian law. He analyzes the ICRC's role in the drafting of the Geneva Conventions, its contributions to the interpretation of treaty law, and its role in the identification of customary IHL. The ICRC's work in this area is contextualized with the work of other actors, such as States, National Red Cross and Red Crescent Societies, and experts. He also demonstrates how the ICRC has acted as a catalyst for the formation and publication of States' views on various legal issues.

The role of domestic courts in the development of international law is taken up by Yahli Shereshevsky. He identifies and expertly analyzes two issues which have largely been unaddressed in the scholarship on the topic, namely, the fusion of international law and domestic law and the lack of IHL expertise on the part of domestic judges. Shereshevsky identifies three types of fusion: the application of international law by domestic courts, the application of domestic law doctrines when deciding matters of international law, and situations when the legality of a measure under international law depends on appropriate regulation under domestic law. He demonstrates the link between direct application of domestic law and lack of IHL expertise on the part of domestic courts, examines the general expertise of domestic courts, and explains what all this means for the development of IHL by domestic courts.

Martha M. Bradley considers the role of international criminal tribunals in the development of the law of armed conflict. She identifies instances of positive development on the part of international criminal tribunals, forensically exploring the contribution of the International Criminal Tribunal for the former Yugoslavia (ICTY) to the definition of non-international armed conflict and of the International Criminal Tribunal for Rwanda (ICTR) to the definition of rape. Noting that not all instances of development are positive, the chapter also explores difficulties with two aspects of the *Ntaganda* case, namely, on the issue of intraparty protection and on the meaning of "attack." Bradley rightly cautions against judicial activism and reminds us of the proper relationship between international humanitarian law and international criminal law.

In her thoughtful chapter, Alessandra Spadaro discusses the role of human rights mechanisms in shaping international humanitarian law. After exploring notions of "shaping" and helpfully distinguishing between process and outcome, Spadaro identifies the various roles that different human rights mechanisms have played in the shaping of international humanitarian law, as well as some of their limitations. The chapter then turns to "new avenues" for shaping IHL, revealing the impact the Human Rights Council and its special rapporteurs and independent investigations have had on shaping the IHL (and IHRL) obligations of armed groups parties to non-international armed conflicts.

Drawing on his experience at a number of UN mandated mechanisms, although writing in his personal capacity, Yousuf Syed Khan considers the application and interpretation of the law of armed conflict by the UN Independent Impartial Commission of Inquiry on the Syrian Arab Republic and by the UN Commission on Human Rights in South Sudan. Identifying IHL issues which the UN investigative mechanisms were the first to consider, Khan demonstrates the impact the interpretations and findings have had on IHL-related discourse. He goes on to explore how UN mechanisms with a mandate to support criminal accountability share their findings and underlying evidence with (quasi-)judicial bodies, thus indirectly shaping and influencing the law.

Drawing on his vast experience of armed groups, Ezequiel Heffes considers the impact of non-State armed groups (NSAG) on the making and shaping of the law of armed conflict. Distinguishing between "domestic" law-making activities, such as NSAG codes of conduct, and "quasi-international" activities, such as special agreements, UN action plans, and Geneva Call Deeds of Commitment, Heffes expertly demonstrates how NSAGs "shape the legal landscape."[14] He argues that NSAG do so by bringing into force international obligations that would not otherwise be applicable and by influencing the view that international human rights law is applicable to NSAGs.

Part Four turns to an examination of different "spaces" in the making and shaping of the law. Gus Waschefort explores the role of regionalism in the development of the law of armed conflict. He explores issues of regionalism in the development of the conventional as well as customary law of armed conflict. In a powerful challenge to many an orthodox view, he casts doubt on the purported "super universality" of the law of armed conflict, instead seeing it as a more recent construction and inter alia as a way to "redeem the Eurocentric history of the development of modern LOAC, while staying the course that had been set by the

14. Page 249.

West."[15] Waschefort calls for "increased accommodation of regional approaches and perspectives in the making and shaping of LOAC as a regime of universal application,"[16] arguing that this will enhance its legitimacy, expand ownership, and insulate it from the dangers of developing competing regional regimes.

In a highly original chapter, Rebecca Sutton asks us to broaden our gaze beyond those who are traditionally considered to make and shape IHL and the settings in which the law is traditionally seen as being made and shaped. She argues that the law "can be found in very different kinds of settings and that it is being constituted and reconstituted on a daily basis by those we might not tend to think of as legal actors."[17] Drawing on empirical research in the Central African Republic and in civil-military training sites, Sutton explores how the principle of distinction circulates through the Pedagogical, Kinetic, and Intellectual realms. She demonstrates that, "[a]s differently situated actors enact, engage with, and contest IHL rules, they individually and collectively forge IHL's (multiple) meaning(s)."[18]

The final part, Part Five, takes a different tack. Whereas the other chapters focus primarily on making and shaping the law, Sean Watts turns his attention to "unmaking" the law. He notes perceptively that, much like the present volume itself, the focus of most efforts is on making the law, with far less attention devoted to issues of unmaking. In his chapter, Watts explores what is meant by unmaking; analyzes different types of unmaking, such as repeal, revocation, and abandonment; and expertly makes the case for paying greater attention to issues of unmaking and adopting a more rigorous approach to unmaking issues.

IV. THEMES

Chapter authors were deliberately not asked to draft their chapters around a single, unifying theme. Instead, the authors were left to write freely on relatively broad topics with the intention of seeing what unifying themes, if any, would arise. Most of the chapters were discussed at the annual workshop of the Lieber Institute for Law and Warfare at the United States Military Academy, West Point, New York, in November 2022. A number of themes emerged during workshop discussions and come through in the volume.

The first theme is the role of States in making the law and the need to disaggregate the notion of the State. Different branches of the State (legislature, executive, judiciary) contribute to the making of the law in different ways. Furthermore, it is not just top-level officials who contribute to law-making and shaping; the everyday official also plays a role. One branch of the State—the judiciary—is analyzed

15. Page 290.

16. Page 272.

17. Page 300.

18. Page 300.

by Shereshevsky, who also considers the implications of the domestic legal framework for the law of armed conflict. Analyzing the role of States in making the law from a different angle, it is important to consider *which* States are included and, importantly, (consciously or subconsciously) excluded in references to "States" (Waschefort). When it is said that "States say this" or "State practice is that," what is actually the case is that *some* States say this or *some* State practice is that. The States in question tend to be mainly Western States, with the practices of States from the Global South often overlooked or ignored.

A second theme is the role of actors other than States in *shaping* the law. A number of chapters discuss the host of actors other than States which play an influential role in shaping the law. These include the ICRC (Sivakumaran), expert groups (Schmitt), trainers (Sutton), international human rights law mechanisms (Spadaro), international criminal law mechanisms (Bradley), commissions of inquiry (Khan), and armed groups (Heffes). A number of factors make these entities more or less influential in shaping the law, including, importantly, expertise and different types of expertise (Shereshefsky, Bradley, Khan, Spadaro) and reception of their outputs by States and other actors (Schmitt, Sivakumaran).

Third, the chapters demonstrate that the making and shaping of the law is dynamic and interactive (Henckaerts, Fortin), not static or siloed. There is interaction *between* actors (Sivakumaran, Schmitt, Sutton, Khan), between sources (Fortin, van den Boogaard, Meier), and between bodies of law (Spadaro, Bradley, Fortin), as well as between actors and sources (Henckaerts) and between actors and bodies of law (Bradley).

Fourth, norms have multiple and parallel lives. There is the public life of a norm as well as an invisible life outside of the public gaze. Insofar as the public life is concerned, norms exist on the books and in the field. They circulate between the Pedagogical, Kinetic, and Intellectual realms (Sutton). They might also operate differently in different spaces, such as in territory controlled by the State as compared to territory under the control of a non-State armed group (Heffes).

Readers will no doubt identify other themes as they progress through the chapters.

V. A WORD OF THANKS

Many hands were involved in "making and shaping" this tenth volume of the Lieber Studies series. We are first grateful for the work that each chapter author has contributed. This volume would not exist without their willingness to share their impressive talents, and it was a pleasure to work with each of them. Naturally, all views are those of the chapter authors alone. We are also grateful to our colleagues at the Lieber Institute for Law and Warfare and the United States Military Academy Department of Law for hosting a terrific workshop, as well as for their support in the preparation of the present volume.

PART TWO

Foundational Materials

2

Where Vienna and Geneva Meet: Treaty Interpretation and the Geneva Conventions

JEAN-MARIE HENCKAERTS*

I. INTRODUCTION: THE IMPORTANCE OF TREATY INTERPRETATION

This chapter deals with the application of the 1969 Vienna Convention on the Law of Treaties[1] (hereinafter Vienna Convention) to the interpretation of the 1949 Geneva Conventions[2] and with the importance of treaty interpretation for making and shaping international humanitarian law (IHL). It is written against the background of the author's work on updating the Commentaries on the

*Jean-Marie Henckaerts is Head of Unit, Commentaries Update Unit, Legal Division, International Committee of the Red Cross (ICRC). This chapter is based on a presentation given at the Lauterpacht Centre for International Law on May 6, 2022. It was revised for the Lieber Workshop and has benefited from feedback received during the workshop. The author wishes to thank his colleagues Heleen Hiemstra, Kubo Mačák, and Ellen Policinski for their input, as well as Christina Grisewood for editorial assistance. All opinions are personal and do not necessarily reflect those of the ICRC.

1. Vienna Convention on the Law of Treaties, May 23, 1969, 1155 U.N.T.S. 331.

2. Convention (I) for the Amelioration of the Condition of the Wounded and Sick in the Armed Forces in the Field, Aug. 12, 1949, 6 U.S.T. 3114, 75 U.N.T.S. 31; Convention (II) for the Amelioration of the Condition of the Wounded, Sick, and Shipwrecked Members of Armed Forces at Sea, Aug. 12, 1949, 6 U.S.T. 3217, 75 U.N.T.S. 85; Convention (III) Relative to the Treatment of Prisoners of War, Aug. 12, 1949, 6 U.S.T. 3316, 75 U.N.T.S. 135; Convention (IV) Relative to the Protection of Civilian Persons in Time of War, Aug. 12, 1949, 6 U.S.T. 3516, 75 U.N.T.S. 287.

Jean-Marie Henckaerts, *Where Vienna and Geneva Meet: Treaty Interpretation and the Geneva Conventions* In: *Making and Shaping the Law of Armed Conflict.* Edited by: Sandesh Sivakumaran and Christian R. Burne, Oxford University Press.
 DOI: 10.1093/oso/9780197775134.003.0002

Geneva Conventions and draws on examples from the updated Commentary on the Third Geneva Convention.[3]

The Vienna Convention is premised on the idea that treaties are living instruments. It is through application and interpretation that the plain words on paper will come to life in practice. If they were not applied, the treaty provisions would remain a dead letter or might fall into desuetude.[4] A treaty's interpretation is particularly important for how the legal rules in the treaty will evolve; how they will be shaped in and by practice. The interpretation of treaties may evolve over time to take account of developments in society, law, and practice. For example, the Vienna Convention requires that the elements of subsequent practice and other relevant rules of international law that may develop after its adoption are taken into account in its interpretation.[5] The ordinary meaning of terms may also change over time. Taking social, legal, and practical developments into consideration in treaty interpretation is a key characteristic of the Vienna Convention's framework and allows treaties to remain relevant. In so doing, the Vienna Convention also strikes a proper balance between stability and change.

Other methods to keep treaties in step with developments in society, law, and practice include adopting new treaties (possibly replacing previous ones), adding protocols, or amending existing treaties. But these have proven more difficult—though not impossible—to achieve in recent decades.[6] Interpretation of existing treaties remains thus of considerable importance.

This chapter will first consider the methods, other than treaty interpretation, to keep treaties in step with developments in society, law, and practice (section II). It will then look at the framework for treaty interpretation (section III). Next, it will examine this framework in detail by looking at the general rule of treaty interpretation (section IV), how the Vienna Convention requires the consideration of subsequent developments in law and practice (section V), and supplementary means of interpretation (section VI). The next section will look briefly at the interpretation of treaties authenticated in several languages, as is the case for the Geneva Conventions (section VII). Finally, the relevance of the interpreter for treaty interpretation (section VIII) and some of the limits of treaty interpretation (section IX) are discussed. The chapter ends with a general conclusion (section X).

3. International Committee of the Red Cross, Commentary on the Third Geneva Convention: Convention (III) relative to the Treatment of Prisoners of War, 2 vols. (2021) [hereinafter "ICRC, Updated Commentary on Geneva Convention III"].

4. On desuetude, *see* Jan Wouters & Sten Verhoeven, *Desuetudo*, version of November 2008, *in* Max Planck Encyclopedia of Public International Law (Rüdiger Wolfrum ed.), http://opil.ouplaw.com/home/EPIL.

5. *See* section V.

6. *See* Cordula Droege & Eirini Giorgou, *How International Humanitarian Law Develops*, 104 International Review of the Red Cross 1798 (2022).

II. METHODS TO KEEP IHL TREATIES UP TO DATE

Updating existing treaties and adding new ones was the process for developing the Geneva regime governing the law of armed conflict until 1949. The 1949 treaties are the fourth iteration of the original Geneva Convention of 1864,[7] which was a single convention designed to protect wounded soldiers in the field. The 1864 Convention was updated in 1906[8] and again in 1929,[9] when a separate convention governing the treatment of prisoners of war[10] was added. These two Conventions were updated in 1949 and joined by an updated convention on warfare at sea (updating the 1907 Hague Convention (X)) and an entirely new convention protecting civilians. These became the current four Geneva Conventions, protecting wounded and sick soldiers in the field, sailors at sea, prisoners of war, and civilians, respectively. The four Conventions are universally ratified.[11] They have not been the subject of an entirely new iteration as in 1906 and 1929. In the absence of a new iteration and with the passage of significant time, the process of interpretation of the existing Conventions becomes a more important tool to allow the Conventions to evolve over time and to adapt to changes in warfare and technology.

Another way to update treaties is by creating "additional" rules. Additional Protocols have been one of the primary techniques for "updating" the Conventions since 1949. Three protocols have been added to the Geneva Conventions in this way: Additional Protocols I and II in 1977 and Additional Protocol III in 2005. The advantage of this system is to preserve the *acquis* of the main Conventions, while States can adhere to the additional rules in the Protocols.[12] To date, however, these Additional Protocols are not yet universally ratified. This means that, depending on which parties to an armed conflict have ratified the Protocols, different regulatory frameworks apply as a matter of treaty law.[13]

7. Convention for the Amelioration of the Condition of the Wounded in Armies in the Field, Aug. 22, 1864, 22 Stat. 940, 129 Consol. T.S. 361.

8. Convention for the Amelioration of the Condition of the Wounded and Sick in Armies in the Field, July 6, 1906, 35 Stat. 1885, 202 Consol. T.S. 144.

9. Convention for the Amelioration of the Condition of the Wounded and Sick in Armies in the Field, July 27, 1929, 75 U.N.T.S. 31.

10. Convention Relative to the Treatment of Prisoners of War, July 27, 1929, 47 Stat. 2021, 118 L.N.T.S. 343.

11. *See* Jean-Philippe Lavoyer, *A Milestone for International Humanitarian Law*, STATEMENT (Sept. 22, 2006), https://www.icrc.org/en/doc/resources/documents/statement/geneva-conventions-statement-220906.htm.

12. Other IHL treaties, including on the protection of cultural property and the regulation or prohibition of certain weapons, have also used this system.

13. However, customary IHL can play a unifying role in this respect. *See* Jean-Marie Henckaerts & Els Debuf, *The ICRC and the Clarification of Customary International Humanitarian Law*, *in* REEXAMINING CUSTOMARY INTERNATIONAL LAW 163–65 (Brian Lepard ed., 2016).

Amendments are another technique to update existing treaties.[14] This has been especially the case in the context of weapons law. Thus, in 1996 an Amended Protocol II to the Convention on Certain Conventional Weapons (CCW) was adopted to set stricter limits on the use of mines, booby-traps, and similar devices than the original Protocol of 1980 had done.[15] In 2001 the CCW itself was amended to extend the scope of application of all the then-existing Protocols (I–IV) to non-international armed conflict, as defined in common Article 3 of the Geneva Conventions.[16] As can be seen, amendments are not common in IHL.

The result of these processes is that the Geneva Conventions of 1949 remain the only universally binding treaties to regulate both international and non-international armed conflicts. Their interpretation is therefore of the utmost importance.

III. THE FRAMEWORK FOR TREATY INTERPRETATION

The four Geneva Conventions were adopted in 1949, in the wake of the Second World War. The Vienna Convention was adopted twenty years later, in 1969. So, the first question is whether the Vienna Convention even applies to the Geneva Conventions. Article 4 on the non-retroactivity of the Vienna Convention provides that it applies only to treaties concluded *after* its entry into force. On that account, the Vienna Convention would not apply to the Geneva Conventions.

However, Article 4 of the Vienna Convention opens by stating that it is "[w]ithout prejudice to the application of any rules set forth in the . . . Convention to which treaties would be subject under international law independently of the Convention." Such rules would include those of customary international law, for example.

And indeed, the Vienna Convention rules on interpretation are accepted as reflecting customary international law. The International Court of Justice (ICJ) has upheld this view on several occasions.[17]

14. On treaty amendments, *see* Vienna Convention on the Law of Treaties, *supra* note 1, arts. 39–40.

15. Protocol on Prohibitions or Restrictions on the Use of Mines, Booby-Traps and Other Devices as Amended on May 3, 1996, 2048 U.N.T.S. 93.

16. Convention on Prohibitions or Restrictions on the Use of Certain Conventional Weapons Which May Be Deemed to Be Excessively Injurious or to Have Indiscriminate Effects as Amended on Dec. 21, 2001, art. 1, 1342 U.N.T.S. 137.

17. *See, e.g.*, Territorial Dispute (Libya v. Chad), Judgment, 1994 I.C.J. Rep. 6 (Feb. 3), ¶ 41; Kasikili/Sedudu Island (Botswana v. Namibia), Judgment, 1999 I.C.J. Rep. 1045 (Dec. 13), ¶ 18; Application of the Convention on the Prevention and Punishment of the Crime of Genocide (Bosn. & Herz. v. Serb. & Montenegro), Merits, Judgment, 2007 I.C.J. Rep. 43 (Feb. 26), ¶ 160; Question of the Delimitation of the Continental Shelf between Nicaragua and Colombia beyond 200 Nautical Miles from the Nicaraguan Coast (Nicaragua v. Colombia), Preliminary Objections, Judgment, 2016 I.C.J. Rep. 100 (Mar. 17), ¶ 33.

Accordingly, we can rely on the Vienna Convention to interpret treaties concluded before 1969, such as the 1949 Geneva Conventions. Such a conclusion is both crucial and useful, not just for the Geneva Conventions but for the many other treaties adopted before 1969. It means that there exists an agreed methodology in international law for interpreting all treaties.

This methodology is set down, in particular, in three articles of the Vienna Convention: a general rule expressed in Article 31; a rule on supplementary means of interpretation in Article 32; and a specific rule in Article 33 related to the interpretation of treaties authenticated in two or more languages, as is the case for the Geneva Conventions (English and French).

We will now examine these three rules in more detail.

IV. THE GENERAL RULE OF TREATY INTERPRETATION

Article 31(1) of the Vienna Convention provides that a treaty must be interpreted "in good faith in accordance with the ordinary meaning to be given to the terms of the treaty in their context and in the light of its object and purpose." This rule of interpretation has different elements, and the interpretation itself must combine all these elements. In other words, the Vienna Convention does not offer a choice between different methods of interpretation, for example a method based on the ordinary meaning only (a literal interpretation) or on the object and purpose only (a teleological interpretation). Rather, it contains one general rule of interpretation that must be applied as a whole.

The exact combination of the elements and the emphasis on one or other element depend on the provision and issue at hand but always need to be applied in good faith.

What follows is a more detailed examination of the different elements in this general rule.

A. Good Faith

Good faith has several meanings in international law. For the purpose of treaty interpretation, it has two prongs.

The first prong is a certain subjective quality, namely, that the interpreter undertakes their task "honestly, without fraud or intent to deceive"[18] or, in other words, in the *absence* of bad faith. An example of good faith can be found in the

18. Richard K. Gardiner, Treaty Interpretation 17 (2d ed. 2015). *See also* Mark E. Villiger, Commentary on the 1969 Vienna Convention on the Law of Treaties 425 (2009) ("Good faith requires the parties to a treaty to act honestly, fairly and reasonably, and to refrain from taking unfair advantage.").

updated commentary on common Article 3 regarding the issue of consent to humanitarian activities in the context of a non-international armed conflict:

> Para. 866 – Common Article 3 states that "[a]n impartial humanitarian body, such as the ICRC [International Committee of the Red Cross], may offer its services to the Parties to the conflict," but does not spell out by whom, nor how, such an offer is to be responded to. In this respect, common Article 3 differs from Article 18(2) of Additional Protocol II, which explicitly addresses the requirement to obtain the consent "of the High Contracting Party concerned" with regard to a particular type of humanitarian activities, i.e. relief actions.[19]
>
> Para. 867 – Despite the silence of common Article 3, it is clear from the logic underpinning international law in general,[20] and humanitarian law in particular, that, in principle, an impartial humanitarian organization will only be able to carry out the proposed humanitarian activities if it has consent to do so.[21]

Although common Article 3 does not refer to consent, the commentary refers to consent as it is mentioned in Article 18 of Additional Protocol II. And as the commentary relies on Additional Protocol II in other places to clarify the content of common Article 3,[22] it could not disregard Additional Protocol II on this topic where it was maybe "inconvenient" because the Protocol explicitly spells out the requirement of consent.

Thus, when an interpreter refers to other international law rules, as required by the Vienna Convention,[23] this must be done in good faith and with reference to all the relevant rules. An interpreter may not pick and choose only those rules that are "convenient" but must refer to all relevant provisions.

The second prong of good faith relates to the task of interpretation itself, i.e., *how* the interpretation is to be undertaken.[24] This involves applying a set of considerations, notably reasonableness, the importance of balancing different treaty elements, and the principle of effectiveness of the treaty.

On effectiveness, the International Law Commission (ILC) stated:

19. Similarly, for international armed conflicts to which Additional Protocol I applies, *see* arts. 70(1) and 81(1) of that Protocol. *See also ICRC Q&A and Lexicon on Humanitarian Access*, 96 International Review of the Red Cross 359 (2014); ICRC, International Humanitarian Law and the Challenges of Contemporary Armed Conflicts 26–30 (2015).

20. This includes a State's sovereign right to regulate access to its territory.

21. ICRC, Updated Commentary on Geneva Convention III, *supra* note 3.

22. *Id.*, ¶¶ 866–67.

23. *See* section V.C.

24. Gardiner, *supra* note 18, at 171.

> When a treaty is open to two interpretations one of which does and the other does not enable the treaty to have appropriate effects, good faith and the objects and purposes of the treaty demand that the former interpretation be adopted.[25]

This principle of effectiveness is also supported by the ICJ, for example in the territorial dispute between Libya and Chad in 1994.[26]

We find an example of this in the commentary on common Article 3 in relation to the application of this provision to armed groups:

> Para. 728 – Common Article 3 requires "a regularly constituted court." If this would refer exclusively to State courts constituted according to domestic law, non-State armed groups would not be able to comply with this requirement. The application of this rule in common Article 3 to "each Party to the conflict" would then be without effect. Therefore, to give effect to this provision, it may be argued that courts are regularly constituted as long as they are constituted in accordance with the "laws" of the armed group. Alternatively, armed groups could continue to operate existing courts applying existing legislation.[27]

The interpretations endorsed in the Commentaries are informed by good faith and considerations that allow the provisions to have their intended effect.

B. The Ordinary Meaning of the Text

According to the Vienna Convention, treaties have to be interpreted in accordance with the ordinary meaning to be given to the terms of the treaty. It further specifies that to determine the ordinary meaning, we must consider the terms of a treaty "in their context and in light of the treaty's object and purpose."[28] These are complementary elements. Indeed, it is impossible to define a treaty term in isolation.

To clarify the ordinary meaning of terms, the Commentary refers to authoritative, standard English and legal dictionaries.[29] For example, Article 38 of the Third Geneva Convention requires "the Detaining Power to *encourage* intellectual,

25. [1966] 2 Yearbook of the International Law Commission 219, ¶ 6.

26. Territorial Dispute case (Libya v. Chad), *supra* note 17, ¶ 51 (In international law, the principle of effectiveness is regarded as "one of the fundamental principles of interpretation of treaties.").

27. ICRC, Updated Commentary on Geneva Convention III, *supra* note 3 (internal citation omitted).

28. Vienna Convention on the Law of Treaties, *supra* note 1, art. 31(1).

29. Such as the *Concise Oxford English Dictionary* or *Black's Law Dictionary*. For example, as the Conventions do not provide a specific definition of "violence" for the purposes of Article

educational and recreational pursuits among prisoners of war." The meaning of the verb "to encourage" is then further clarified in the updated commentary on that provision:

> Para. 2469 – The obligation to "encourage," however, encompasses more than merely allowing activities organized by relief agencies or the prisoners to take place. According to the ordinary meaning of the term, it also means that the Detaining Power must give support to and help or stimulate the practice of the purposeful activities mentioned in the article. The 1929 Convention was "too vague on this point and allowed the Detaining Power to adopt a passive attitude towards these essential activities." (internal citation omitted)

The ordinary meaning of terms refers to the meaning terms have at the time of interpretation. This meaning may evolve, especially as the Geneva Conventions were adopted more than seven decades ago. For example, the term "honour" in Article 14(1) has to be read in a contemporary light.[30] Similarly, today's understanding of mental health and disability has greatly evolved since 1949 and has had an impact on the interpretation of related obligations under the Conventions.[31]

The French version of the Conventions, which is equally authentic, has also consistently been consulted in line with Article 33 of the Vienna Convention. This can help to clarify the terminology of some provisions.[32]

13, which protects prisoners of war from "acts of violence" at all times, the Commentaries use the definition "behaviour involving physical force intended to hurt, damage, or kill." CONCISE OXFORD ENGLISH DICTIONARY 1614 (12th ed. 2011), *cited in* ICRC, UPDATED COMMENTARY ON THE THIRD CONVENTION, *supra* note 3, ¶ 1619. *See also* BRYAN A. GARNER, BLACK'S LAW DICTIONARY 1881 (11th ed. 2019), *cited in* ICRC, UPDATED COMMENTARY ON THE THIRD CONVENTION, *supra* note 3, commentary on art. 13, ¶ 1619. In another instance, "suitable" for the purposes of the Article 51 requirement that prisoners of war be given "suitable working conditions" is defined as "fit and appropriate for the intended purpose." GARNER, *supra*, at 1735, *cited in* ICRC, UPDATED COMMENTARY ON GENEVA CONVENTION III, *supra* note 3, commentary on art. 51, ¶ 2721.

30. For a discussion of the challenges in interpreting this notion, *see* Jemma Arman, *GCIII Commentary: Protecting the Honour of Prisoners of War*, ICRC HUMANITARIAN LAW AND POLICY BLOG (Sept. 3, 2020), https://blogs.icrc.org/law-and-policy/2020/09/03/gciii-commentary-honour-prisoners-of-war/.

31. *See, e.g.*, ICRC, UPDATED COMMENTARY ON GENEVA CONVENTION III, *supra* note 3, ¶¶ 2236–47 (on isolation wards for prisoners of war suffering from "mental disease"), and ¶¶ 2255–62 (on special measures for "disabled" prisoners of war).

32. *See* section VII.

C. Object and Purpose

The Vienna Convention requires that, in addition to the context, treaty terms must also be interpreted in the light of a treaty's object and purpose. However, it does not expressly state how to identify that object and purpose.

The preamble may be a good source of information, but the Geneva Conventions do not contain a substantive preamble because the drafters could not reach agreement on its text. In particular, there was disagreement on the Holy See's proposal that "there should be some reference to the Deity in each Preamble"[33] and on the importance to be given to the punishment of violations of the Conventions.[34] Ultimately, the drafters of the Conventions decided not to include a substantive preamble.[35]

With or without a substantive preamble, we must look at the whole of the treaty and especially the substantive provisions to identify the treaty's object and purpose.[36] The text of the treaty itself, including the title, preamble (if any), headings, and substantive provisions, is the primary resource to determine its object and purpose.[37] The supplementary means of interpretation set down in Article 32 of the Vienna Convention, including the preparatory work,[38] can then be used to confirm that prima facie object and purpose.[39]

On this basis, the Commentary on the Third Geneva Convention identifies the overall object and purpose of the Convention as being "to ensure that prisoners of war are humanely treated at all times, while allowing belligerents to intern captured enemy combatants to prevent them from returning to the battlefield."[40] This balance between humanitarian considerations on the one hand and military necessity on the other hand is reflected throughout the Convention.

As was noted in the preceding quote from the ILC, a treaty can have more than one object and purpose. In this regard, it is submitted that common Article 3

33. *See* II-A Final Record of the Diplomatic Conference of Geneva of 1949 112–14 (1949).

34. *Id.*, at 165.

35. ICRC, Updated Commentary on Geneva Convention III, *supra* note 3, Preamble, ¶¶ 134–39.

36. *See* Mačák & Policinski, *In Pursuit of a Treaty's Soul: A Study of the Object and Purpose of the Fourth Geneva Convention*, 73 Int'l & Comp. L. Quarterly (2024, forthcoming); Villiger, *supra* note 18, at 428, with further references; Gardiner, *supra* note 18, at 217–18.

37. Gardiner, *supra* note 18, at 197.

38. *See* section VI.

39. Isabelle Buffard & Karl Zemanek, *The "Object and Purpose" of a Treaty: An Enigma?*, 3 Austrian Review of International & European Law 311, 333 (1998); Villiger, *supra* note 18, at 428.

40. ICRC, Updated Commentary on Geneva Convention III, *supra* note 3, Introduction, ¶ 89.

provides the Geneva Conventions with an additional object and purpose, namely, protecting persons hors de combat in non-international armed conflict.[41]

One example in the updated Commentary where the object and purpose of the treaty, in addition to State practice, informed the interpretation can be found in the discussion on the geographical scope of application of common Article 3. As is well known, the ordinary meaning of the terms of common Article 3, which refers to armed conflict "occurring within the territory of one of the High Contracting Parties," is not clear and, as noted in the Commentary, can be read in two ways:

> Para. 500 – . . . One reading of this phrase could be that the conflict must occur in the territory of precisely "one" of the High Contracting Parties, thereby limiting the application of common Article 3 to "internal" armed conflicts. However, another reading could put the emphasis on the fact that the conflict must occur in the territory of one of the "High Contracting Parties," thereby merely excluding conflicts which occur on the territory of a State not party to the Geneva Conventions.[42] Common Article 2 likewise contains a reference to the States party to the Geneva Conventions. Viewed in this context, the reference to "High Contracting Parties" in both articles may have been included to avoid any misunderstanding to the effect that the 1949 Geneva Conventions would create new obligations for States not party to them.

To further clarify the meaning, reference is then made to the object and purpose as a first step:

> Para. 501 – The object and purpose of common Article 3 supports its applicability in non-international armed conflict reaching beyond the territory of one State. Given that its aim is to provide persons not or no longer actively participating in hostilities with certain minimum protections during intense armed confrontations between States and non-State armed groups or between such groups, it is logical that those same protections would apply when such violence spans the territory of more than one State. (internal citation omitted)

The commentary continues by examining the drafting history and State practice with regard to different scenarios of non-international armed conflicts taking place beyond the borders of one single State, in particular so-called "cross-border," "spill-over," and "trans-national" armed conflicts.[43]

41. *Id.*, ¶ 90.

42. In this sense, *see, e.g.*, Marco Sassòli, *Transnational Armed Groups and International Humanitarian Law*, HPCR Occasional Paper Series 9 (2006).

43. *See* ICRC, Updated Commentary on Geneva Convention III, *supra* note 3, ¶¶ 503–16.

V. DEVELOPMENTS AFTER THE CONCLUSION OF A TREATY, TO BE TAKEN INTO ACCOUNT WHEN INTERPRETING TREATIES

According to the Vienna Convention, certain developments in law and practice have to be taken into account when interpreting a treaty. These developments are important and allow the interpretation of treaty terms to evolve over time. The requirement to take these developments into account in treaty interpretation allows treaties to be living instruments and keep up with developments, for example in technology.

Article 31(3) of the Vienna Convention lists three types of developments to be taken into account:

- any subsequent agreement between the parties regarding the interpretation of the treaty or the application of its provisions;
- any subsequent practice in the application of the treaty which establishes the agreement of the parties regarding its interpretation; and
- any relevant rules of international law applicable in the relations between the parties.

Taking these developments into account is very important as treaties age, and it may not always be possible to update or amend them accordingly. Thus, in many areas of international law, more and more treaties will be subject to more and more subsequent developments.

A. Subsequent Agreements

The first category, "any subsequent agreement between the parties regarding the interpretation of the treaty or the application of its provisions," has not proved relevant for the Geneva Conventions. The Additional Protocols do not as such constitute "subsequent agreements."[44] They are separate treaties that have not been ratified by all parties to the Geneva Conventions, as Article 31(3)(a) of the Vienna Convention would require. However, this does not exclude that the provisions of the Additional Protocols may be considered in interpreting the Geneva Conventions as other "relevant rules of international law," including as part of customary international law.

By contrast, subsequent practice and other relevant rules of international law do play an essential role in interpreting the Geneva Conventions today.

44. Vienna Convention on the Law of Treaties, *supra* note 1, art. 31(3)(b).

B. Subsequent Practice

Subsequent practice by States in the application of a treaty is an important source of interpretation.[45] This has been particularly pertinent in the update of the ICRC Commentaries on the Geneva Conventions. The original Commentaries were drafted in the light of the preparatory work and previous conflicts, most notably World War II.

Following the Vienna Convention's methodology, the update of the Commentaries now takes into account the way the Conventions have been applied and interpreted by States since their adoption. This is a perspective the original Commentaries could not offer and is endorsed, indeed required, by the Vienna Convention.

The ILC defines subsequent practice under Article 31 as "consist[ing] of conduct in the application of a treaty, after its conclusion, which establishes the agreement of the parties regarding the interpretation of the treaty."[46] It requires "a common understanding regarding the interpretation of a treaty which the parties are aware of and accept."[47] This is generally understood as implying the agreement of *all* parties to the treaty,[48] which is quite difficult to establish for the Geneva Conventions as they have been universally ratified, with 196 States parties.

However, the agreement of all parties does not necessarily mean that there must be practice by all parties as, in some circumstances, silence can constitute acceptance of a subsequent practice.[49] For example, the fact that States generally did not object to the absence of the appointment of Protecting Powers in international armed conflicts since 1982 (Falklands-Malvinas conflict) can be taken as tacit agreement of this practice. Hence, the Commentary concludes that the obligation expressed in common Article 8 (Article 9 in the Fourth Convention) should today be interpreted as optional.[50]

45. According to the ILC, "[s]ubsequent agreements and subsequent practice under article 31, paragraph 3 (a) and (b), being objective evidence of the understanding of the parties as to the meaning of the treaty, are authentic means of interpretation, in the application of the general rule of treaty interpretation reflected in article 31." International Law Commission, *Report on the Work of its Seventieth Session*, ch. IV, sec. E.2, at 23, conclusion 3, UN Doc. A/73/10 (2018) [hereinafter "ILC, *Report on the Work of its Seventieth Session*"].

46. *Id.* at 27, conclusion 4.2.

47. *Id.* at 75, conclusion 10.1.

48. *Id.*, commentary on draft conclusion 10.1, ¶ 2.

49. *Id.*, conclusion 10.2: "The number of parties that must actively engage in subsequent practice in order to establish an agreement under article 31, paragraph 3 (b), may vary. Silence on the part of one or more parties may constitute acceptance of the subsequent practice when the circumstances call for some reaction." *See also* Gardiner, *supra* note 18, at 270 ("[I]t is sufficient if there is practice of one or more parties and good evidence that the other parties have endorsed the practice.").

50. International Committee of the Red Cross, Commentary on the First Geneva Convention: Convention (I) for the Amelioration of the Condition of the Wounded

Still, subsequent practice as understood under Article 31(3)(b) is not easy to establish in relation to the Geneva Conventions, as they have been universally ratified and thus require agreement between 196 States parties.

However, subsequent practice that does not meet this threshold remains relevant, according to the ILC, as a supplementary means of interpretation under Article 32.[51]

C. Relevant Rules of International Law

Finally, the Vienna Convention requires that "any relevant rules of international law applicable in the relations between the parties" be taken into account. This requirement aims to achieve coherence among different parts of international law. It envisages the systemic integration of international law and requires that different rules and treaties of international law are interpreted in a harmonious, coherent manner so that conflicts between them are avoided as much as possible.[52]

Importantly, the Vienna Convention does not refer to the law as it stood at the moment the treaty was adopted but rather to the law as it stands at the moment of interpretation.[53] This is confirmed by the drafting history of the provision, during which the ILC deleted the words "in force at the time of its conclusion" from an earlier draft.[54] It is also the approach of the ICJ, which held in the *Namibia* case that "an international instrument has to be interpreted and applied within the framework of the entire legal system prevailing *at the time of the interpretation*."[55]

This framework has developed considerably in the past seven decades. That explains why this aspect is discussed in this section on developments after the conclusion of a treaty. There can also be prior treaties that have to be taken into

AND SICK IN THE ARMED FORCES IN THE FIELD, ¶¶ 1114–19 (2016) [hereinafter "ICRC, UPDATED COMMENTARY ON GENEVA CONVENTION I"]; INTERNATIONAL COMMITTEE OF THE RED CROSS, COMMENTARY ON THE SECOND GENEVA CONVENTION: CONVENTION (II) FOR THE AMELIORATION OF THE CONDITION OF THE WOUNDED, SICK AND SHIPWRECKED MEMBERS OF ARMED FORCES AT SEA, ¶¶ 1152–57 (2017); ICRC, UPDATED COMMENTARY ON GENEVA CONVENTION III, *supra* note 3, commentary on art. 8, ¶¶ 1296–1302.

51. *See* section VI.

52. On systemic integration, *see* Panos Merkouris, *Principle of Systemic Integration*, *in* MAX PLANCK ENCYCLOPEDIA OF PUBLIC INTERNATIONAL LAW (Rüdiger Wolfrum ed., August 2020), http://opil.ouplaw.com/home/EPIL.

53. ROBERT KOLB, GOOD FAITH IN INTERNATIONAL LAW 158 (2017); GARDINER, *supra* note 18, at 467–69; ANTHONY AUST, MODERN TREATY LAW AND PRACTICE 216 (3rd ed. 2013); VILLIGER, *supra* note 18, at 433.

54. [1966] 2 YEARBOOK OF THE INTERNATIONAL LAW COMMISSION 222, ¶ 167.

55. Legal Consequences for States of the Continued Presence of South Africa in Namibia (South West Africa) notwithstanding Security Council Resolution 276 (1970), Advisory Opinion, 1971 I.C.J. Rep. 16, at 19, ¶ 53 (June 21) (emphasis added).

account in IHL, for example the 1868 St. Petersburg Declaration or the 1899 and 1907 Hague Regulations, but the bulk of the other relevant rules of international law developed after 1949.

Today, these rules include the Additional Protocols and other IHL treaties, as well as customary IHL as it has developed since 1949. It also includes other bodies of international law, such as the law of State responsibility, international criminal law, human rights law, and refugee law, which have seen tremendous developments since 1949. In the framework of the Geneva Conventions, we also find links with the law of the sea, international maritime law, international health law, international labor law, and even private international law.[56] There are examples from all these areas that show how the Geneva Conventions are interwoven with other areas of international law.

On international health law, for example, there is the famous example of access to tobacco by prisoners of war in Article 26 of the Third Geneva Convention ("The use of tobacco shall be permitted.") and how that relates to the 2003 WHO Framework Convention on Tobacco Control.[57] On private international law, there is the example of wills drawn up by prisoners of war, governed by Article 120 of the Third Geneva Convention, and how this rule relates to the 1961 Convention on the Conflicts of Laws relating to the Form of Testamentary Dispositions.[58]

So, it should be noted that the Geneva Conventions are related to a wide scope of other treaties, not just other IHL or human rights treaties. To paraphrase a famous poem, "No treaty is an island, entire of itself."[59] And the Geneva Conventions are no exception.

An important caveat is that only other treaty rules "applicable in the relations between the parties" can inform the interpretation of a given treaty. This means that the interpretation in a particular case, for example an armed conflict between States X and Y, has to look at the treaties that these States have ratified. By contrast, a general commentary such as those prepared by the ICRC or academic institutions typically looks at all treaties because it aims to provide the most complete picture of the legal landscape to cover all possible cases.

As rules of customary international law bind all States, regardless of whether or not they are party to a treaty setting out the same rule, such rules will always be "applicable in the relations between the parties." Because treaty and customary rules have equal status in international law, the later customary rule takes

56. *See* ICRC, Updated Commentary on Geneva Convention III, *supra* note 3, Introduction, ¶¶ 92–116. The drafting history of Article 31(3)(c) of the Vienna Convention confirms that the "relevant rules" are not restricted to customary rules but also include treaty rules. *See, e.g.*, Gardiner, *supra* note 18, at 301–02; Villiger, *supra* note 18, at 433.

57. ICRC, Updated Commentary on Geneva Convention III, *supra* note 3, ¶¶ 2131–33.

58. *Id.*, ¶¶ 4543–44.

59. Adapted from John Donne, *No Man Is an Island*, *in* Devotions Upon Emergent Occasions (1624).

precedence over incompatible treaty rules.[60] For example, under customary international law, the parties to the conflict must allow passage for humanitarian relief for all civilians in need.[61] This is broader than Article 23 of the Fourth Geneva Convention, which limited the items and beneficiaries.[62] So, to the extent that Article 23 of that Convention has become incompatible with the rule under customary international law, which emerged later in time, the latter prevails.[63]

VI. SUPPLEMENTARY MEANS OF INTERPRETATION

According to Article 32 of the Vienna Convention, supplementary means of interpretation may be used for two purposes: *confirming* the meaning of a term resulting from the application of Article 31 or *determining* the meaning when the application of Article 31 leaves the meaning ambiguous or obscure or leads to a manifestly absurd or unreasonable result.[64] Although Article 32 suggests that supplementary means are optional—"recourse *may* be had"—experience suggests otherwise.[65] The preparatory work, for example, is used routinely by

60. *See, e.g.*, Michael Akehurst, *The Hierarchy of the Sources of International Law*, 47 British Yearbook of International Law 273, 275 (1975); Mark E. Villiger, Customary International Law and Treaties 58–59 (2d ed. 1997); Rebecca Crootof, *Change Without Consent: How Customary International Law Modifies Treaties*, 41 Yale Journal of International Law 237, 285 (2016).

61. 1 Customary International Humanitarian Law 194 (Jean-Marie Henckaerts & Louise Doswald-Beck eds., 2005) [hereinafter "ICRC Customary IHL Study"]. This rule is also reflected in Protocol Additional to the Geneva Conventions of 12 August 1949, and Relating to the Protection of Victims of International Armed Conflicts (Protocol I), art. 70(1) and (2), June 8, 1977, 1125 U.N.T.S. 3.

62. Commentary on the Additional Protocols of 8 June 1977 to the Geneva Conventions of 12 August 1949, ¶¶ 2813–22 (Yves Sandoz, Christophe Swinarski, & Bruno Zimmermann eds., 1987).

63. Crootof, *supra* note 60, at 272–74.

64. For a view that Article 32 could also be used to "correct" the meaning of a treaty provision, *see* Stephen M. Schwebel, *May Preparatory Work Be Used to Correct Rather than Confirm the "Clear" Meaning of a Treaty Provision?*, *in* Theory of International Law at the Threshold of the 21st Century: Essays in Honour of Kzrysztof Skubiszewski 173–81 (Jerzy Makarczyk ed., 1996).

65. This was acknowledged by the principal architect of the Vienna rules, Sir Humphrey Waldock: "This formulation [the precursor to Article 32] seemed to the Commission about as near as it is possible to get to reconciling the principle of the primacy of the text . . . with frequent and quite normal recourse to travaux préparatoires without any too nice regard for the question whether the text itself is clear. Moreover, the rule . . . is inherently flexible, since the question whether the text can be said to be 'clear' is in some degree subjective." International Law Commission, *Sixth Report on the Law of Treaties*, *in* [1966] 2 Yearbook of the International Law Commission 99, para. 20, cited in Gardiner, *supra* note 18, at 347.

interpreters,[66] and not only in cases where the general rule of interpretation yields unsatisfactory results. Most treaty commentaries systematically examine the preparatory work. And that seems logical: to understand the context of the terms, one has to look at the discussions that led to the wording that was adopted.

It is important to note, however, that Article 32 is not limited to preparatory work; preparatory work is but one example of supplementary means of interpretation. It can also include subsequent practice that does not meet the requirements of Article 31, as well as judicial decisions and academic publications.

What follows is a closer look at some of the supplementary means of interpretation.

A. Preparatory Work

The first and most well known supplementary means of interpretation is the preparatory work (or *travaux préparatoires* in French). This includes successive drafts of the treaty, conference records, and explanatory statements made during the drafting.[67] In the case of the Geneva Conventions, a significant amount of documentation has been published, ranging from drafts and reports preparatory to the 1949 Diplomatic Conference to the stenographic notes (minutes) of the Conference and their official final records. These are all available on the ICRC Library's website and are very helpful in clarifying the context of all provisions and often also in confirming or clarifying the interpretation.[68]

But it is important to make a note here about the value of the preparatory work: the Vienna Convention makes clear that the preparatory work is only a supplementary means of interpretation. Thus, a treaty's interpretation is not bound by the original intent of the drafters but is left open to evolving to allow treaties to be living instruments that can keep pace with developments. In

66. Aust insists that international tribunals, and the parties arguing before them, have long had recourse to the preparatory work: Aust, *supra* note 53, at 217–18, citing Lockerbie (Libya v. UK), Preliminary Objections, 1998 I.C.J. Rep. 9, ¶¶ 4.17–4.18; [1998] ILM 587; 117 ILR 1 and 664; Lord McNair, The Law of Treaties 413, 422 (1961); and examples given in Martin Mennecke & Christian Tams, *The Right to Consular Assistance under International Law*, 42 German Yearbook of International Law 192, 223–24 (1999). *See also* Martin Ris, *Treaty Interpretation and ICJ Recourse to Travaux Préparatoires: Towards a Proposed Amendment of Articles 31 and 32 of the Vienna Convention on the Law of Treaties*, 14 Boston College International and Comparative Law Review 111, 131 (1991).

67. For more on preparatory work as a supplementary means of interpretation, *see* Aust, *supra* note 53, at 218; Gardiner, *supra* note 18, at 349–56.

68. For a full list of (and access to) the documents constituting the preparatory work of the 1949 Geneva Conventions and their 1977 Additional Protocols, *see* https://library.icrc.org/library/search/shortview?searchType=PredefinedSearch&name=1949 Geneva Conventions and https://library.icrc.org/library/search/shortview?searchType=PredefinedSearch&name=1977 Additional Protocols, respectively.

particular, the interpretation of treaties can evolve under the influence of subsequent developments in law and practice, as we have seen under Article 31.[69] An example of this can be found in the interpretation of common Article 1 today which includes, according to the ICRC, a due diligence obligation to try and stop serious violations by third parties under certain circumstances.[70]

B. Subsequent Practice in the Broad Sense

As noted, subsequent practice in the broad sense, not falling under Article 31, can be used as a supplementary means of interpretation. This is recognized by the ILC,[71] which explains that "any practice in the application of the treaty that may provide indications as to how the treaty is to be interpreted may be a relevant supplementary means of interpretation under article 32."[72] The weight of such practice may depend on its clarity and specificity and whether and how it is repeated.[73]

The ILC specifies that "an element of good faith is necessary in any 'subsequent practice in the application of the treaty.'"[74] Many examples gleaned from subsequent practice in the application of the Third Geneva Convention are instances of respect for the Convention.[75] Other references are cited as best practices, providing relevant guidance to States.[76] In this way, the updated Commentaries on the Geneva Conventions constitute a repository of practice about how the Conventions have been implemented. These examples do not thereby become "binding" on all other States but provide information that can assist practitioners in their work.

69. *See* section IV.

70. ICRC, Updated Commentary on Geneva Convention III, *supra* note 3, ¶¶ 188–89.

71. International Law Commission, *Report on the Work of its Seventieth Session*, *supra* note 45, at 17, conclusion 2.4 ("Recourse may be had to other subsequent practice in the application of the treaty as a supplementary means of interpretation under article 32.") For references to case law and doctrine supporting this, *see id.*, commentary on draft conclusion 2.4, ¶ 9, nn. 36–37 and *id.*, at 33–36, commentary on draft conclusion 4.3, ¶¶ 25–32. Practice not accompanied by an agreement of all parties is examined in International Law Commission, *Fourth Report on Subsequent Agreements and Subsequent Practice in Relation to the Interpretation of Treaties*, ¶¶ 107–09, UN Doc. A/CN.4/694 (2016).

72. International Law Commission, *Report on the Work of its Seventieth Session*, *supra* note 45, at 33, commentary on draft conclusion 4, ¶ 24.

73. *Id.* at 70, conclusion 9.

74. *Id.* at 32, commentary on draft conclusion 4.2, ¶ 19.

75. *See, e.g.*, ICRC, Updated Commentary on Geneva Convention III, *supra* note 3, commentary on art. 34 ¶ 2364 and commentary on art. 38, ¶¶ 2456, 2461, and 2463.

76. For such examples, *see id.*, ¶ 2365, n. 18 and accompanying text and commentary on art. 38, ¶¶ 2464–66.

On the other hand, a manifest misapplication of a treaty is not an "application of the treaty" in the sense of Articles 31 and 32.[77] Violations of the Conventions, therefore, do not count as practice informing their interpretation. For example, forcing prisoners of war to run laps around a camp courtyard until exhaustion is a violation of Article 38 of the Third Geneva Convention giving access to open air and sports and not a bona fide application.[78]

When discussing subsequent practice (or any other element of interpretation), one should not lose sight of the fact that each element is only one aspect of the Vienna Convention framework for interpretation. All the other elements of that framework have to be taken into account. For example, the interpretation that prisoners of war may be allowed to communicate through modern means of communication is supported by some subsequent practice in the broad sense, but it is also in line with the purpose of the provisions related to family contact. In this context, the Commentary acknowledges that the words of the Convention are "updated" in light of modern technology. For example, the function of sending letters, cards, and telegrams can now be accomplished through email, as recognized in some military manuals.[79]

C. Other Supplementary Means of Interpretation

Other supplementary means of interpretation include "judicial decisions and the teachings of the most highly qualified publicists of the various nations." These constitute "subsidiary means for the determination of rules of law" according to the ICJ Statute.[80] As such, they may also constitute relevant supplementary elements for the interpretation of treaties. The consideration of these elements is exemplified in many other commentaries.[81]

First, judicial decisions, and in particular those of international criminal courts and tribunals, have proven especially important in interpreting terms in the Geneva Conventions. For example, the definition of armed conflict—international and non-international—or of acts such as torture, cruel, or degrading treatment or hostage-taking under the Geneva Conventions is largely informed by those

77. International Law Commission, *Report on the Work of its Seventieth Session*, *supra* note 45, at 32, commentary on draft conclusion 4.2, ¶ 19.

78. ICRC, Updated Commentary on Geneva Convention III, *supra* note 3, commentary on art. 38, ¶ 2473.

79. *Id.*, Introduction, ¶ 40 and commentary on art. 71, ¶ 3186. For references to military manuals in this context, *see id.*, ¶ 3186, n. 26.

80. Statute of the International Court of Justice, art. 38(1)(d), June 26, 1946, 33 U.N.T.S. 993.

81. For a representative list, *see* ICRC, Updated Commentary on Geneva Convention III, *supra* note 3, Introduction, ¶ 119, n. 167.

developed by such courts and tribunals.[82] National courts have also applied the Geneva Conventions on numerous occasions in the past seventy years, and their pronouncements have been looked at as a supplementary means of interpretation.[83] This does not mean that the interpretation by one State's courts automatically binds other States. Rather such decisions are looked at as relevant examples of how the provisions have been interpreted. And over time, such pronouncements can become accepted by other courts and tribunals and more widely in State practice and thus become a more widely accepted interpretation.[84]

Finally, "the teachings of the most highly qualified publicists of the various nations" may be looked at as a supplementary means of interpretation. These "teachings" can be found in scholarly publications, such as books and law review articles. Such publications have been recognized as supplementary means of interpretation[85] and are often used by courts and tribunals in their interpretation of the law.[86] Scholarly publications often refer to and comment on State practice. Recently, for example, many authors have discussed the geographic scope of application of common Article 3.[87] They often do so by reviewing State practice. Hence, the updated Commentaries review this literature alongside all other elements of interpretation.

Reviewing publications on the Geneva Conventions is challenging today as these publications have proliferated in recent decades. Analyzing relevant publications requires significant time and effort to reflect the diversity of legal writing.[88] Peer

82. For the definition of international armed conflict, *see* ICRC, Updated Commentary on Geneva Convention III, *supra* note 3, commentary on art. 2, ¶¶ 243–317. For the definition of non-international armed conflict, *see id.* commentary on art. 3, ¶¶ 427–530. For the definition of torture, *see* ICRC, Updated Commentary on Geneva Convention I, *supra* note 50, commentary on art. 3, ¶¶ 626–45. Similarly, when defining "hostage-taking," the ICRC's updated Commentary on the Third Convention refers to case law from the Special Court for Sierra Leone (Prosecutor v. Sesay, Case No. SCSL-04-15-A, Appeal Judgment, ¶ 598 (Oct. 26, 2009)). ICRC, Updated Commentary on Geneva Convention III, *supra* note 3, commentary on art. 3, ¶ 648.

83. More than 120 decisions of national courts have been referenced in the updated Commentary on the Third Convention. For a complete listing, *see* ICRC, Updated Commentary on Geneva Convention III, *supra* note 3, ¶¶ 2119–36. For specific examples, *see, e.g.*, *id.*, commentary on art. 34, ¶ 2381 and commentary on art. 130, ¶¶ 5249, n. 161 and 5285, n. 233.

84. *See, e.g.*, Anthea Roberts, *Comparative International Law? The Role of National Courts in Creating and Enforcing International Law*, 60 International and Comparative Law Quarterly 57, 59 (2011).

85. Gardiner, *supra* note 18, at 401–04.

86. *See, e.g.*, Sandesh Sivakumaran, *The Influence of Teachings of Publicists on the Development of International Law*, 66 International and Comparative Law Quarterly 1, 26–29 (2017).

87. *See, e.g.*, ICRC, Updated Commentary on Geneva Convention III, *supra* note 3, commentary on art. 3, ¶ 497 and references.

88. For example, on the discussion of the geographic scope of application of IHL in non-international armed conflict, see the discussion about practice combined with references to

reviewers have proved very helpful in this regard for the ICRC's Commentaries project, signaling publications (and practice) from their regions or fields of expertise. This is particularly important as the Statute of the ICJ makes clear that the publications of the most highly qualified publicists of the "various nations" must be considered.[89] Therefore, a particular effort is made in the course of research for the updated Commentaries to include publicists from various countries and backgrounds, as well as publications in different languages.

VII. TREATIES AUTHENTICATED IN TWO OR MORE LANGUAGES

Article 33(1) of the Vienna Convention provides that "[w]hen a treaty has been authenticated in two or more languages, the text is equally authoritative in each language, unless the treaty provides or the parties agree that, in case of divergence, a particular text shall prevail." This provision is relevant for the interpretation of the Geneva Conventions, the English and French versions of which are equally authentic.[90] Neither the Geneva Conventions nor the parties thereto indicate that one language version should prevail over another in the event of a divergence.[91] Both language versions of the Conventions are therefore equally authoritative. A comparison between them can help to clarify the interpretation of the Conventions. For example, Article 19 of the Third Geneva Convention on the evacuation of prisoners of war contains three paragraphs, each using a different term in English to indicate the area from which prisoners are evacuated: paragraph 1 refers to the combat zone, paragraph 2 to the danger zone, and paragraph 3 to the fighting zone. When comparing it with the French version, however, we see that only two different terms are used:

- combat zone = zone de combat
- danger zone = zone dangereuse
- fighting zone = zone de combat

As a result, we can conclude that combat zone and fighting zone in Article 19 can be interpreted in the English version as being identical.[92] This also underlines the

legal writings in ICRC, Updated Commentary on Geneva Convention III, *supra* note 3, commentary on art. 3, sec. C.3.

89. Statute of the International Court of Justice, *supra* note 81, art. 38(1)(d).

90. *See, e.g.*, Third Geneva Convention, *supra* note 2, art. 133. The same applies to the other three Conventions.

91. For details, *see* ICRC, Updated Commentary on Geneva Convention III, *supra* note 3, commentary on art. 133, sec. B.2.

92. *See id.*, ¶ 1869.

importance for international lawyers of having at least a passive understanding of some of the main languages for treaty negotiations and drafting, in particular the official UN languages (Arabic, Chinese, English, French, Russian, and Spanish).

Furthermore, pursuant to Article 33(3) of the Vienna Convention, the terms of the English and French versions of the Conventions are to be presumed to have the same meaning. In updating the Commentaries, both language versions have been consulted to determine the meaning of the text.[93] Where the French and the English versions of a provision differ in meaning, the approach outlined in Article 33(4) of the Vienna Convention is followed.[94] First, recourse is had to Articles 31 and 32. Where this does not resolve the difference, "the meaning which best reconciles the texts, having regard to the object and purpose of the treaty," has been adopted.[95]

VIII. THE IDENTITY OF THE TREATY INTERPRETER

Even though treaty interpretation must follow a set of clearly defined rules contained in Articles 31–33 of the Vienna Convention,[96] it is not an exact science. The ILC opined in 1966 that treaty interpretation "is to some extent an art, not an exact science."[97] In this context, the question arises whether the identity of the treaty interpreter makes a difference to interpretation. Differences might exist at different levels. Here are a few examples.

First, the interpretation of IHL treaties is informed by the object and purpose of the treaties, which for IHL rely on a balance between military necessity and considerations of humanity. Balancing these elements may be subject to the perspective of each interpreter. However, the element of good faith would require any interpreter to be coherent in their interpretative methodology and to approach this balance in good faith, not overemphasizing one to the detriment of the other.

Second, the level of detail of an interpretation may differ depending on the role of the interpreter. For example, there are obvious differences between a national

93. For example, where the meaning of "fatigue" in Article 89(3) of the Third Convention was potentially unclear, the Commentary uses the French text to determine that "fatigue duties . . . do not refer to duties intended to lead to a state of fatigue." *See id.*, ¶ 3751.

94. *See, e.g., id.*, commentary on art. 3, n. 277, commentary on art. 13, ¶ 1573, commentary on art. 32, ¶ 2306, commentary on art. 56, ¶ 2806, commentary on art. 83, ¶ 3593, commentary on art. 106, ¶¶ 4147, 4154, and 4156 and commentary on art. 129, ¶ 5161.

95. *See id.*

96. *See* sections III–VII.

97. International Law Commission, *Report of the International Law Commission on the Work of its Eighteenth Session: Draft Articles on the Law of Treaties with Commentaries*, UN Doc. A/6309/Rev.1, *reproduced in* [1996] 2 Yearbook of the International Law Commission 218. Some have further asserted that "[i]nterpretation is an art, not a science" (getting rid of the qualifiers "to some extent" and "exact"). *See* Sir Michael Wood, *Preface, in* Gardiner, *supra* note 18, at xv.

military manual, a general commentary, an academic publication, or a judgment by a court in a specific case. These differences exist because of the different purposes of each type of publication. The ICRC Commentary, for instance, leaves certain points open, such as whether a cyber operation that does not physically destroy or damage infrastructure may amount to a resort to armed force under common Article 2 of the Geneva Conventions and thus trigger the application of IHL.[98] On the other hand, when a court interprets a treaty in a given case, it usually cannot leave unsettled a question that needs to be answered in order to decide that case.

Third, the authority of an interpretation also differs depending on the position of the interpreter and the intended audience. Again, there are obvious differences between a national military manual, a judgment by a court in a specific case, a general commentary, and an academic publication. A military manual typically contains interpretations that are binding for national militaries and their legal advisers. A general commentary, like the ICRC Commentaries on the Geneva Conventions, is not binding and is meant to be a tool for further guidance for a wide range of practitioners and academics. A judgment by an international (or national) court is technically only binding in the case at hand, but, as several seminal judgments have shown, they can become authoritative beyond the case at hand. Thus, for example, the 1995 decision by the International Criminal Tribunal for the former Yugoslavia in the interlocutory appeal on jurisdiction in *Tadić* put forward definitions of international and non-international armed conflict that have become the contemporary point of reference for any interpretation on this issue.[99] The effect of such a judgment and its reception in practice depend on various factors, such as the quality of the reasoning, the timing, and the need for the clarification provided.

Still, in all these cases, the interpreters remain bound to apply the list of elements in Articles 31–33 of the Vienna Convention in good faith.

IX. THE LIMITS OF TREATY INTERPRETATION

Treaty interpretation allows new developments in warfare and in technology to be taken into account. In exceptional circumstances, it can even go so far as to allow for an interpretation of the treaty at variance with the wording without constituting a formal modification or amendment, which has its own rules.[100]

98. ICRC, Updated Commentary on Geneva Convention III, *supra* note 3, ¶ 289. Another example of an interpretation left open can be found in *id.*, ¶¶ 1109–13 (on the effect of reclassification of a conflict from international to non-international).

99. Prosecutor v. Tadić, Case No. IT-94-1-AR-72, Appeals Chamber, Decision on the Defence Motion for Interlocutory Appeal on Jurisdiction (Int'l Crim. Trib. for the former Yugoslavia Oct. 2, 1995).

100. *See* Vienna Convention on the Law of Treaties, *supra* note 1, arts. 39–41.

While in its draft conclusions on subsequent agreements and subsequent practice the ILC makes clear that treaty interpretation cannot amount to the modification of a treaty (which requires a formal process regulated by distinct rules of the Vienna Convention),[101] in practice, interpretation following the Vienna Convention rules may still lead to a result approaching modification. For example, common Article 8 (Article 9 in the Fourth Convention) provides that the Convention "*shall* be applied with the co-operation and under the scrutiny of the Protecting Powers" (emphasis added). Practice of States parties since 1949, however, has led the ICRC to conclude that States came to a change of understanding of this provision, now viewing the appointment of Protecting Powers as optional rather than mandatory.[102] Similarly, Article 38(2) of the First Convention provides that the only States able to use the red crescent emblem or the red lion and sun emblem were those already doing so at the time the 1949 Geneva Conventions were adopted. But the fact that a number of States chose to use one of these two emblems upon or subsequent to their adherence to the Convention without formal objection by other parties to the Convention, led the ICRC to "conclude that a practice or custom at variance with the rule set out in Article 38 has thus been allowed to take root."[103] As mentioned, this is and should remain exceptional.

Treaty interpretation should not be stretched beyond its limits. When no developments occur in practice, or there is no clear agreement on an interpretation, new law may be necessary. For example, in the area of autonomous weapons, many States and the ICRC consider that the interpretation of existing rules of IHL is not sufficient and that new law is required.[104] This is not new, as the CCW and

101. *See* International Law Commission, *Report on the Work of its Seventieth Session*, *supra* note 45, at 51, conclusion 7.3 ("It is presumed that the parties to a treaty, by an agreement or a practice in the application of the treaty, intend to interpret the treaty, not to amend or to modify it. The possibility of amending or modifying a treaty by subsequent practice of the parties has not been generally recognized. The present draft conclusion is without prejudice to the rules on the amendment or modification of treaties under the Vienna Convention on the Law of Treaties and under customary international law.").

102. ICRC, Updated Commentary on Geneva Convention III, *supra* note 3, ¶ 1227 ("Over the decades since 1949, however, States have come to a different understanding of this provision. . . . [T]he appointment of Protecting Powers since 1949 has been the exception rather than the rule in international armed conflicts. Absent any protest, therefore, it would seem that the failure to appoint a Protecting Power is not, at least in the eyes of most States, seen as a violation of their treaty obligations. At the same time, there is no indication that the High Contracting Parties consider that Article 8 has fallen into desuetude."). For another example, *see* International Law Commission, *Report on the Work of its Seventieth Session*, *supra* note 45, at 54, commentary on draft conclusion 7, ¶ 12 (with regard to the obligation to display the distinctive emblem in Article 12 of Additional Protocol II).

103. ICRC, Updated Commentary on Geneva Convention I, *supra* note 50, ¶ 2548.

104. Droege & Giorgou, *supra* note 6, at 1809. *See also ICRC Position on Autonomous Weapon Systems*, ICRC (May 21, 2021), https://www.icrc.org/en/document/icrc-position-autonomous-weapon-systems.

its Protocols were also built on the idea that the general prohibition of weapons that are of a nature to cause unnecessary suffering or superfluous injury or have indiscriminate effects was not precise enough to restrict or prohibit per se certain weapons, such as blinding laser weapons, and that specific regulation was needed.[105]

Similar developments have occurred in other areas of international law. For example, in the area of human rights law, specific treaties on the elimination of discrimination against women and on the rights of children have been adopted, even though the general human rights conventions, notably the 1966 International Covenant on Civil and Political Rights, already contained rules on these matters.

X. CONCLUSION

In a context where the adoption in the near future of new treaties replacing or supplementing the Geneva Conventions does not seem to be a realistic prospect, the interpretation of the existing Conventions will remain crucial in making and shaping IHL. At the same time, it is important to ensure that the Conventions continue to be interpreted in a manner that is consistent with their wording and with their object and purpose.

A challenge linked to relatively older treaties such as the Geneva Conventions is that certain aspects of their language may not be adapted to today's societal, legal or technological realities. While in such cases the purpose behind the rules often remains valid and relevant, there is a need to refresh our understanding of the treaty text to take account of current law and practice. The Vienna Convention allows for, indeed mandates, such an updated reading.

The Vienna Convention offers a coherent legal framework for the interpretation of treaties, including IHL treaties. More than seventy years after the adoption of the Geneva Conventions, an up-to-date interpretation of the Conventions has to take into account developments in law and subsequent practice. However, identifying subsequent practice meeting the requirements of Article 31(3)(b) of the Vienna Convention is challenging, especially in relation to universally ratified treaties such as the Geneva Conventions. Through the ILC's work, recourse to subsequent practice under the supplementary rule of interpretation in the sense of Article 32 of the Vienna Convention has been clarified and is now understood to apply broadly.

Using the methodology set out in the Vienna Convention, the ICRC has undertaken a once-in-a-generation study to update its Commentaries on the Geneva Conventions in light of developments in law and practice since their adoption. The result of this study to date confirms that the Geneva Conventions are living instruments that continue to play an essential role in preventing and alleviating the suffering caused by contemporary armed conflicts.

105. Droege & Giorgou, *supra* note 6, at 1809.

3

Customary International Law: A Transformative Force in the Landscape of IHL

KATHARINE FORTIN*

I. INTRODUCTION

In our twenty-first-century world that offers so many varied avenues for the expression of explicit consent, it is a matter of some mystery that so many foundational areas of international law continue to be governed by custom, rather than treaty law. Indeed, despite often being seen to be a primitive method of norm-creation, it is often said that customary international law remains the "formal nest for the foundational doctrines of international law."[1] Many of the core structural rules of international law relating to key concepts such as legal personality, State responsibility, statehood, treaty interpretation, *jus cogens*, and the principle of *pacta sunt servanda* either have, or had, their source in custom.[2] Customary international law has also had, and continues to have, a profound influence in forming and shaping the substantive rules of many core areas of public international law, with international humanitarian law (IHL) being no exception.

* Katharine Fortin is Associate Professor at the Netherlands Institute of Human Rights, Utrecht University and a member of the Montaigne Centre for Rule of Law and Administration of Justice. I am grateful for the research assistance given by Yiokasti Mouratidi.

1. Jean d'Aspremont, The Discourse on Customary International Law 113 (2021). *See also* J. Kammerhofer, *Between Pragmatism and Enchantment: The Theory of Customary International Law after the ILC Project*, *in* The Theory and Practice of Customary International Law 3 (Panos Merkouris, Jörg Kammerhofer, & Noora Arajärvi eds., 2021).

2. D'Aspremont, *supra* note 1, at 114–15; James Crawford, Chance, Order, Change: The Course of International Law, at 57 (2014).

Katharine Fortin, *Customary International Law: A Transformative Force in the Landscape of IHL* In: *Making and Shaping the Law of Armed Conflict*. Edited by: Sandesh Sivakumaran and Christian R. Burne, Oxford University Press.
DOI: 10.1093/oso/9780197775134.003.0003

Indeed, while the role of customary international law in this area stretches back to as long as public international law (and warfare) began, in the last four decades a "customary revolution" has taken place in this field.[3] Customary international law has transformed understandings of what norms apply to different actors, and when and also how norms of international humanitarian law are constructed and should be interpreted.

The purpose of this chapter is to analyze the role that custom has played in the making and shaping of international humanitarian law and to comment on some of the methodological problems, controversies, and puzzles which accompany this body of law, both as a creature in a general sense and in the specific arena of international humanitarian law. The chapter starts, in section II, with a historical review that makes two broad points. First it shows that while customary international law is one of the oldest sources of international law governing armed conflict, understandings of how it is made have changed quite a lot over the years. Secondly, it briefly points out the long heritage of the entanglement between custom and treaty law in this area. The chapter then moves into the twentieth and twenty-first centuries to demonstrate the contribution that customary international law has made to the modern field of international humanitarian law, explaining why it has been so heavily relied upon and identifying some of the main contributions that it has made in normative terms (section III), despite being a source of law fraught with controversy (section IV).

The chapter then progresses by focusing on three particular issues. Section V considers the relationship between treaty norms and customary norms today, in terms of the norms themselves and the methodology used to ascertain or interpret them. Section VI analyzes customary international humanitarian law's influence on the manner in which customary international law is understood. Section VII explores the way in which customary international humanitarian law in this area might develop, considering some of the methodological challenges, puzzles, and dilemmas that it has faced over recent years. When addressing these issues, the chapter shows that the story of the role of custom in the making and shaping of international humanitarian law is interwoven with the story of the role of international humanitarian law in the making and shaping of custom. It demonstrates that as a key and core field of public international law, international humanitarian law can be seen as a microcosm, in which many of the same developments and challenges that are also seen in the wider field of public international law play out and are illustrated. These relate to the role of customary international law, its relationship with treaty law, its method of ascertainment, the role of non-State actors, and broader questions relating to the future of the field.

3. Giovanni Mantilla, Lawmaking under Pressure: International Humanitarian Law and Internal Armed Conflict 170 (2020).

II. CUSTOM AS THE FOUNDATIONAL SOURCE OF THE LAW OF WAR

When reviewing ancient legal texts demonstrating the role of customary international law in regulating warfare, it quickly becomes apparent that what constitutes custom has changed significantly over the centuries.[4] In his famous treatise on the Law of War and Peace in 1625, Hugo Grotius identified the law of nations as one of the main sources of the law of war. He stated that the "proof" of the law of nations lay in "unbroken custom and the testimony of those who are skilled in it."[5] In order to prove that something was "unbroken custom," Grotius engaged in a wide review of theological, historical, and classical sources that ranged from the Bible, the writings of Roman lawyers and historians, such as Livy, and examples of battlefield practice from ancient Greece and Roman history.[6] In the seventeenth and eighteenth centuries, custom continued to be relied upon as a source of the laws of war. In these centuries, marking a move toward positivism, authors relied less on ancient history, historical texts, and natural law as a means of establishing authority and more on practice that evidenced tacit agreement or mutual consent between States. Appreciative that customary rules could evolve over time, there was a greater focus on *recent* practice that demonstrated State consent and there was less deference to the rules of "natural reason," "natural law," and "the law of nature" as a force that could create binding obligations.[7]

It also quickly becomes apparent that the history of customary international law was already deeply entangled with treaty law in these centuries, to the extent that at some moments it is difficult to tell whether custom is catching up with treaty law or treaty law is catching up with custom. This was particularly the case in the

4. When thinking about the way that the laws of war have developed, it is important to note that several recent studies have illustrated that traditional narratives of the making and shaping of international humanitarian law centered around the United States and Europe are vastly incomplete. In particular, attention has recently been brought to the "forgotten histories" of the codification of international humanitarian law in Latin America. *See, e.g.*, Tania Ixchel Atilano, *The 1871 Mexican Criminal Code as the Missing Piece in the History of Criminalizing Violations of the Laws of War*, 104(920–21) International Review of the Red Cross 1650 (2022); and Alonso Gurmendi, *Latin Lieber: Uncovering the History of the Treaty on the Regularisation of War*, Opinio Juris (June 10, 2022), https://opiniojuris.org/2022/06/10/latin-lieber-uncovering-the-history-of-the-treaty-on-the-regularisation-of-war/. Presumably there are many more forgotten histories of customary international law to be uncovered.

5. Hugo Grotius, De Jure Belli Ac Pacis: Book I, at 32 (Stephan Neff ed., 2012).

6. *See, e.g.*, Randall Lesaffer, *Siege Warfare in the Early Modern Age: A Study on the Customary Laws of War*, *in* The Nature of Customary Law: Legal, Historical and Philosophical Perspectives 176–202 (Amanda Perreau-Saussine & James Bernard Murphy eds., 2007) (for a review of different treatises of war and how findings of custom were made by Pierino Belli (1502–1575), Albericus Gentilis (1552–1608), Balthasar de Ayala (1548–1584), and Hugo Grotius (1583–1645).

7. Lessaffer *supra* note 6, at 198–200; Crawford, *supra* note 2, at 64.

nineteenth century, when there was a general move toward the codification of international law, with the convening of many international conferences intended to produce treaties and multilateral agreements. In these years, it is sometimes hard to decipher whether particular conferences were codification or law-making initiatives. Some of the earliest attempts to codify the law of war were described as attempts to write down the laws and customs of war. For example, Francis Lieber decided to write his "little book on the Law and Usages of War. . . . which Congress might feel inclined to recommend to the Army," after giving a series of lectures on the "laws and usages of war" at Colombia University.[8] Similarly, the tsar of Russia convened the Diplomatic Conference in Brussels in 1874 with the intention to deliberate an "international agreement respecting the laws and customs of war."[9]

While many of these early treaties of international humanitarian law declare that they articulate the "laws and customs of war," it seems likely that what constituted custom at that time was controversial. For example, the drafting of the Brussels Declaration came just after the Franco-Prussian war of 1870–1871 when there had been multiple disputes regarding whether the actions of the two parties had complied with certain rules of the laws of war.[10] Changing forms of warfare and changes to State power were causing States to adopt "discordant and contradictory views on the old customs," to the extent that it had become unclear what the rules were.[11] There was particular disagreement on the question of the status of irregular forces.[12] Baron Johmini of Russia opened the debates at Brussels stating that "very contradictory ideas prevail concerning war."[13] Indeed, when one looks at accounts of these conferences' proceedings, it is clear that their purpose was probably not so much to write down the "customs and laws of war" as much to debate and clarify understandings of custom with the purpose of establishing the content of the

8. Jordan Paust, *Dr Francis Lieber and the Lieber Code*, 95 Proceedings of the Annual Meeting of the American Society of International Law 112, at 113 (2001). *See also* Richard Baxter, *The First Modern Codification of the Law of War: Francis Lieber and General Orders No* 25 (100) International Review of the Red Cross 171 (1963).

9. Although this conference was unsuccessful in the sense that it did not produce a treaty text, the outcome (the "Brussels Declaration") was very important. It provided the first draft of the text that would later become the 1899 Convention respecting the laws and customs of war and its Annex "Regulations respecting the laws and customs of war." This treaty and its attached regulations—which were revised again in 1907—contained multiple references to the "laws and customs of war."

10. Eyal Benvenisti & Doreen Lustig, *Monopolizing War: Codifying the Laws of War to Reassert Governmental Authority, 1856–1874*, at 31(1) European Journal of International Law 127, at 153 (2020).

11. Tracey Leigh Dowdeswell, *The Brussels Peace Conference of 1874 and the Modern Laws of Belligerent Qualification*, 54(3) Osgoode Hall Law Journal 805, at 812 (2017).

12. *Id.* at 812.

13. As cited by Dowdeswell, *supra* note 11, at 813.

law.[14] It is telling that although the rules in the 1907 Convention and its Annex announce themselves to be "declaratory of the laws and customs of war," the International Military Tribunal concluded many years later that at the time of their adoption, they "undoubtedly represented an advance over existing International law."[15]

III. CUSTOMARY INTERNATIONAL LAW IN THE TWENTIETH AND TWENTY-FIRST CENTURIES: SHIFTING TECTONIC PLATES

After the Second World War, customary international law continued to be a key force in shaping the legal landscape of international humanitarian law. In fact, it is no exaggeration to say that a "customary revolution" occurred in the second half of the twentieth century, when the effect of customary international law on the modern landscape of international humanitarian law was monumental and transformative.[16] The start of this customary revolution can be traced to the early decisions of the ad hoc international criminal tribunals applying customary international law. These decisions and judgments lay many of the foundation stones of modern international humanitarian law, establishing the temporal scope of its rules and the consequences of their breach. Examples of such core structural rules include the finding that breaches of international humanitarian law in non-international armed conflict (NIAC) give rise to individual criminal responsibility, the finding on the threshold test of both international and non-international armed conflicts, and the development of the overall control test to determine whether a conflict is "internationalised" due to the involvement of a third State.[17] There were also many decisions on the applicability of certain IHL norms to non-international armed conflict *as a matter of custom* and multiple clarifications of how certain substantive terms in IHL should be defined and interpreted.[18] This early case law from the ad hoc tribunals—which has sometimes been criticized

14. Benvenisti & Lustig, *supra* note 10, at 805.

15. International Military Tribunal, Judgment of 1st October 1946, at 80, https://crimeofaggression.info/documents/6/1946_Nuremberg_Judgement.pdf.

16. Mantilla, *supra* note 3, at 170.

17. Prosecutor v. Dusko Tadić, Case No. IT-94-1-AR-72, Decision on the Defence Motion for Interlocutory Appeal on Jurisdiction, ¶¶ 70 and 128–37 (Int'l Crim. Trib. for the former Yugoslavia Oct. 2, 1995); Prosecutor v. Dusko Tadić, Case No. IT-94-1-T, Opinion and Judgment, ¶ 562 (Int'l Crim. Trib. for the former Yugoslavia May 7, 1997); Prosecutor v. Dusko Tadić, Case No. IT-94-1-A, Appeals Chamber Judgment, ¶ 145 (Int'l Crim. Trib. for the former Yugoslavia July 15, 1999).

18. Shane Darcy, *The Reinvention of War Crimes by the International Criminal Tribunals*, *in* Judicial Creativity at the International Criminal Tribunals 106, 116–26 (Shane Darcy & Joe Powderly eds., 2011).

as adopting a rather "cavalier attitude to the existence of customary international law"[19]—is nevertheless widely considered to have been revolutionary, because it made significant strides in humanizing IHL, in the sense of clarifying the material, temporal, and personal scope of its treaty provisions.

Indeed, it was likely the existence of this early case law on customary international humanitarian law that gave the International Committee of the Red Cross (ICRC) the self-confidence to proceed with its monumental study on the customary rules of IHL in the 1990s.[20] In many ways, the ICRC's study deliberately set out to be transformative in the landscape of international humanitarian law. The raison d'etre of the study lay in the perceived insufficiency of the treaty law regime as it applied to both international armed conflicts (IAC) and non-international armed conflicts.[21] In the area of international armed conflicts, the problem was not a dearth of treaty rules but their formal non-application due to non-ratification of the relevant instrument. Although the treaty law that applies to international armed conflicts was detailed, several States (e.g., the United States) had not ratified Additional Protocol I, which contained inter alia a fundamentally important articulation of rules on the conduct of hostilities. In non-international armed conflict, the problems in treaty law were more severe. The treaty law provisions that applied to non-international armed conflicts were widely felt to be insufficient. This was a problem of some significance as non-international armed conflicts were proving to be the most commonly seen kind of armed conflict. The final text of Additional Protocol II, which had been hugely scaled back during the drafting process, was significantly less substantive than Additional Protocol I and contained hardly any rules on the conduct of hostilities. It was also subject to an application threshold that was generally considered to be too high for it to be applied to many armed conflicts.[22] Not only that, many of the States that faced insurgencies or restive populations had not ratified it—meaning that, in reality, common Article 3 was one of the only treaty law provisions containing

19. *Id.* at 118. For further critique of the ICTY's custom finding methodology, *see* Theodor Meron, *The Continuing Role of Custom in the Formation of International Humanitarian Law*, 80(2) American Journal of International Law 238, at 240 (1996).

20. For the word "self-confident," *see* John R. Morss & Emily Forbes, *And in the Darkness Bind Them: Hand-waving, Bootstrapping, and the Interpretation of Customary International Law After Chagos*, *in* Merkouris, Kammerhofer, & Arajärvi, *supra* note 1, at 440. Robert Cryer notes that the ICRC relied heavily on the jurisprudence of the ICTY and the International Criminal Court Statute, Robert Cryer, *Of Custom, Treaties, Scholars and the Gavel: The Influence of the International Criminal Tribunals on the ICRC Customary Law Study*, 11(2) Journal of Conflict and Security Law 239, at 240, 242 (2006).

21. *See* Jean-Marie Henckaerts, *Study on Customary International Humanitarian Law: A Contribution to the Understanding and Respect for the Rule of Law in Armed Conflict*, 87(857) International Review of the Red Cross 175, at 177–78 (2005).

22. *See* Protocol Additional to the Geneva Conventions of August 12, 1949, and Relating to the Protection of Victims of Non-international Armed Conflicts art. 1, June 8, 1977, 1125 U.N.T.S. 609.

fundamental humanitarian guarantees that applied to many of the armed conflicts that were taking place.[23]

Many of the problems of treaty law were formally bypassed by the study on customary international humanitarian law, which the ICRC was mandated to prepare in 1995.[24] When it was published in 2005, the study found that many of the rules on the conduct of hostilities in Additional Protocol I were of customary status and applied in both IAC and NIAC.[25] Moreover, of the 161 rules that the study identified, only 12 applied *solely* to IACs. As a result, the study continued the ICTY's previous work by taking huge strides in closing the gap between the protections available in IACs and NIACs, especially when it came to weapons and rules on the conduct of hostilities.[26] By extracting the core rules from many of the treaty articles and subarticles and grouping them into thematically organized sets of "rules," the customary international law study provided a version of the law of armed conflict that has proved to be temptingly citable.[27] It is no exaggeration to say that this study has had an effect of tectonic-plate shifting proportions in the landscape of international humanitarian law. It has been relied upon by domestic courts, commissions of inquiries, and the International Criminal Court and is cited in many military manuals.[28] As will be shown later, it has also informed the manner in which we think about this body of law, its scope, its making, and its name. This is quite significant when it is realized that certain aspects of its methodology and findings are quirky and certainly not preordained.

23. Article 19 of the Convention for the Protection of Cultural Property in the Event of Armed Conflict, May 14, 1954, 249 U.N.T.S. 240 also applied to non-international armed conflicts, but only related to the protection of cultural property.

24. 26th International Conference of the Red Cross and Red Crescent, Geneva, December 3–7, 1995, *Resolution 1, International humanitarian law: From law to action; Report on the follow-up to the International Conference for the Protection of War Victims*, https://www.icrc.org/en/doc/resources/documents/resolution/26-international-conference-resolution-1-1995.htm.

25. Customary International Humanitarian Law (Jean-Marie Henckaerts & Louise Doswald-Beck eds., 2005).

26. *See* Henckaerts, *supra* note 21, at 187–90, for a summary of the Study's main and most significant findings. For the ICTY's previous work in this area, *see* Meron, *supra* note 19, at 243–44.

27. Yoram Dinstein argues that the whole project is "upside down" in that he would have found it more logical for the study to systematically analyze the treaty law article by article, rather than presenting an independent set of rules. Yoram Dinstein, *The ICRC Customary International Humanitarian Law Study*, 82 International Law Studies 99, at 101 (2006).

28. *See* Jean-Marie Henckaerts & Els Debuf, *The ICRC and the Clarification of Customary International Humanitarian Law*, *in* Reexamining Customary International Law 161, at 168–79 (Brian D. Lepard ed., 2017) (for a review of the incredible impact achieved by the study). For a very detailed study of the extent to which the ICRC has been referred to, *see* Marko Milanovic & Sandesh Sivakumaran, *Assessing the Authority of the ICRC Customary IHL Study*, 104(920–21) International Review of the Red Cross 1856 (2022).

IV. CUSTOMARY INTERNATIONAL LAW: A HOUSE WITH SOLID FOUNDATIONS?

The story of the role played by custom in the making and shaping of international humanitarian law is interwoven with the story of customary international law more generally. This is evidenced by the different discussions that international humanitarian law has sparked regarding how customary international law more generally is and should be made and ascertained. Indeed, it is important to note that in the same decades that customary international law proved to be such a transformative force for international humanitarian law, it sustained a barrage of criticism as a source of law. It has been said to be riddled with indeterminacy and "ripe for manipulation, even invention—when the time came to prove a custom in a dispute."[29] The process of analysis through which its existence is assessed has "long been shrouded in confusion and scepticism."[30] It has been declared to be "unbearably light,"[31] "elastic,"[32] and vulnerable to being faked.[33] For some scholars, their cynicism has become so extreme that they have lost faith in custom as a valid source of law. Joyner writes: "[I]f CIL [customary international law] were Tinkerbell she'd be dead now. We just don't believe in her any more."[34] Generally, the reason for a loss of faith in the substantive norms of customary international law are linked to concerns about the process by which their existence is said to be ascertained. There has been endless and often unresolved academic debate on questions that were raised by the reasoning in several cases before the International Court of Justice (ICJ): Should a proper method of ascertainment be more inductive than deductive? Connectedly, should more reliance be placed on *opinio juris* than State practice in some instances? If so, what does that say about the role of State consent in the framework of customary international law? Can the same act be both State practice and *opinio juris*? The questions have been numerous.[35]

It is no surprise then that although the publication of the ICRC study was greeted with resounding admiration and appreciation, there was also a swathe

29. Emily Kadens & Ernest A. Young, *How Customary Is Customary International Law*, 54 William & Mary Law Review 885, at 897 (2013).

30. Monica Hakimi, *Making Sense of Customary International Law*, 118 (8) Michigan Law Review 1487, at 1489 (2020).

31. Hilary Charlesworth, *The Unbearable Lightness of Customary International Law*, 92 ASIL Proceedings 44 (1998).

32. Hakimi, *supra* note 30, at 1501.

33. Fernando R. Tesón, *Fake Custom*, *in* Lepard, *supra* note 28, at 86.

34. Daniel H. Joyner, *Why I Stopped Believing in Customary International Law*, 9 Asian Journal of International Law 31, at 45 (2019).

35. *See, e.g.*, Crawford, *supra* note 2, at 70; Frederic L. Kirgis, *Custom on a Sliding Scale*, 81 American Journal of International Law 146, 148–49 (1987).

of critical comments from academics picking over exactly these aspects of the study's methodology and asking many of the same questions identified above but then applied to international humanitarian law. Attention was given to inter alia the study's employment of the persistent objector rule,[36] a matter still controversial in legal doctrine, its seeming prioritization of *opinio juris* over State practice, its so-called "double counting" of acts as both State practice and *opinio juris*,[37] its perceived overfocus on written materials, its alleged overreliance on military manuals without taking due consideration that they were perhaps reflections of policy not law,[38] its exclusion of the practice and *opinio juris* of armed groups, its treatment of State silence,[39] its overly accepting reliance on the case law from the ICTY,[40] the insufficient attention given to the relationship between treaty norms and custom, and its failure to give due regard to the practice of specially affected States.[41] There were also questions asked about whether areas of law other than IHL, such as IHRL, should have been included in a study of international humanitarian law, and if so, the extent to which they should have been considered.[42] Some authors accused the study of confusing *lex lata* with *lex ferenda*.[43] One author compared the study to a "blunderbuss: indiscriminate and firing in all directions, hitting some targets but arguably damaging a great deal else besides."[44]

In many ways, these criticisms were predictable given the magnitude of the study's ambition and the amount of scholarly critique customary international law had been subject to in the same decades. In embarking on its study, its authors had had to cut through numerous Gordian knots relating to methodology before they could proceed with the task at hand. Readers accused the authors of making findings of significant legal import in a "breezy manner."[45] Yet given the

36. Malcolm MacClaren & Felix Schwendimann, *An Exercise in the Development of International Law: The New ICRC Study on Customary International Humanitarian Law*, 6(9) German Law Journal, 1217, at 1224 (2005); David Turns, *Weapons in the ICRC Study on Customary International Law*, 11(2) Journal of Conflict and Security Law 201, at 207 (2006).

37. John Bellinger III & William J. Haynes II, *A US Government Response to the International Committee of the Red Cross Study Customary International Humanitarian Law*, 89(866) International Review of the Red Cross 443, at 445 (2007).

38. Dinstein, *supra* note 27, at 103; Bellinger & Haynes, *supra* note 37, at 445.

39. Turns, *supra* note 36, at 210.

40. Cryer, *supra* note 20, at 255–56.

41. Bellinger & Haynes *supra* note 37, at 455–57.

42. François Hampson, *Other Areas of Customary Law in Relation to the Study, in* Perspectives on the ICRC Study on Customary International Humanitarian Law 50 (E. Wilmshurst ed., 2009).

43. Turns, *supra* note 36, at 208; Dinstein, *supra* note 27, at 108.

44. Turns, *supra* note 36, at 203.

45. *Id.* at 201.

enormity of some of these methodological questions, one can imagine that that the conversations behind the scenes at the ICRC were anything but breezy. The project was carried out with the assistance of research teams based in around fifty countries, international research teams, a steering committee, and an ICRC Research Team. Comments on the drafts were sought from numerous academic and governmental experts.[46] It is likely because its positions on some of these points had been well thought out beforehand that the ICRC was ready to preempt and later meet the criticisms that it received with well-reasoned explanations for its approach.[47] Its efforts to defend its methodology were also assisted by the States that welcomed the study and by the ILC project on customary international law which was finished in 2018.[48] Indeed, the draft conclusions that emerged out of the ILC project provided support for several methodological decisions that had been adopted by the ICRC, confirming, for example, that the two constituent elements of customary international law may be "intertwined," that official statements of the ICRC can contribute to the development and determination of customary international law (despite not being practice), that verbal acts may be counted as practice and that the conduct of armed groups is neither creative nor expressive of customary international law.[49]

To an observer, these enduring critiques of customary international law as a body of law might appear to delegitimize its ability to be taken seriously as a source of law. Alternatively, they might invite a conclusion that it is more or less impossible to ascertain what constitutes custom in any given situation.[50] However, it is notable that some key individuals that have been entrusted with high-profile roles relating to custom's ascertainment have shrugged off these concerns. In some ways, one could even argue that the very existence of the ICRC study is evidence that the process of finding customary international law is "workable" and the theoretical concerns regarding the finer points of its constitution are just that: "theoretical."[51] Of course, a cynic might also say that there are advantages associated with the characteristics that many scholars find to be the source of indeterminacy. As the International Military Tribunal identified long ago: "This

46. *See* Henckaerts, *supra* note 21, at 184–86, for a summary of how the study was organized in terms of consultation, collection of courses, and collaboration.

47. *See* Henckaerts, *supra* note 21; Jean-Marie Henckaerts, *International Committee of the Red Cross: Response of Jean-Marie Henckaerts to the Bellinger/Haynes Comments on the Customary International Law Study*, 46(5) International Legal Materials 959 (2007); Henckaerts & Debuf *supra* note 28.

48. For a review of positive State reactions, *see* Milanovic & Sivakumaran, *supra* note 28, at 1872–74.

49. International Law Commission, Report of the International Law Commission, Seventieth Session, April 30–June 1 and July 2–August 10, 2018, U.N. Doc. No. A/73/10, 128, 132, 133, 141.

50. Crawford, *supra* note 2, at 57.

51. Henckaerts & Debuf, *supra* note 28, at 179, writing that the Study demonstrates that the two-element approach (State practice and opinio juris) is "workable."

law [unlike treaties] is not static, but by continual adaption follows the needs of a changing world."[52] It is noteworthy that scholars—even the drafters of the ICRC's Customary International Humanitarian Law study—have commended the progressive, fluid, and changing nature of custom indicating that it facilitates a degree of flexibility and allows it to adapt to the new realities on the ground.[53] As a body of law, it opens the door for the making of authoritative statements on "what the law says," while avoiding the need for fraught treaty drafting sessions that conveners worry may do more harm than good.[54] The fact that a variety of methodologies have been employed by the ICJ in different cases and there has been a debate among scholars about which one is "right," almost inevitably provides more space for progressive interpretations to be adopted which facilitate a particular outcome or satisfy a particular interest group, whether it be humanitarian or military. The fact that custom presents an opportunity to progress the law was identified early by Antonio Cassese, who wrote that "forward looking" IHL jurists should work to strengthen the new law through "progressive interpretation."[55] Indeed, one has the impression that the ICRC and international criminal tribunals have widely and unashamedly seen customary international law as a "fixer" body of law that holds potential to solve all the perceived defects in the treaty law system.[56]

The fact that custom has played this role in the landscape of international humanitarian law shows again that there are similarities with the role that custom plays in the landscape of international law more generally. For example, the fact that custom has been used to provide a tool to fix the problems of treaty law in this area is far from unique to international humanitarian law. In many substantive areas, custom has been turned to precisely because "treaty law leaves large gaps, and often those gaps exist in those areas with the most pressing need for law."[57] Given that reality, customary law is often perceived as a convenient "stop-gap"

52. IMT Judgment, *supra* note 15, at 54.

53. Henckaerts & Debuf, *supra* note 28, at 163, stating that "the formation of customary law has allowed IHL to adapt—perhaps in a more flexible manner than treaty law is able to do—to changes in the conduct of contemporary armed conflicts."

54. Mantilla, *supra* note 3, at 172.

55. Antonio Cassese, *A Tentative Appraisal of the Old and New Humanitarian Law of Armed Conflict*, *in* The New Humanitarian Law of Armed Conflict 500–01 (Antonio Cassese ed., 1979).

56. *See* Jean-Marie Henckaerts, *Study on Customary International Humanitarian Law: A Contribution to the Understanding and Respect for the Rule of Law in Armed Conflict*, 87(857) International Review of the Red Cross 175, 177 (2005): "The purpose of the study on customary international humanitarian law was to overcome some of the problems related to the application of international humanitarian treaty law." *See also* Monica Hakimi, *Custom's Method and Process: Lessons from Humanitarian Law*, *in* Custom's Future: International Law in a Changing World 154 (Curtis A. Bradley, ed., 2016).

57. Kadens & Young, *supra* note 29, at 886.

that helps "fill possible lacunae in treaties, and assist in their interpretation."[58] Indeed, perhaps the most compelling reason why custom is attractive is that it negates any argument that there was ever a gap in the first place. To say that something is "custom" is precisely to argue that there is no gap *in law*, only a gap in treaty law. The fact that customary international law has found itself "the residual receptacle"[59] for international legal obligations that cannot be found in treaty law has several consequences for how customary international law is conceived, vis-à-vis treaty law. Perhaps most importantly, it partly explains the tendency to employ deductive methods when ascertaining custom, as a treaty provision that does not apply but already exists is held up as a norm against which an assessment of custom can be made. This method has been used time and time again by the ad hoc criminal tribunals which used the treaty text as a benchmark for the identification of the norm under consideration, and then engaged in an assessment of whether it also existed as a matter of custom. It was also to some extent used by the ICRC when assessing whether norms which applied in IAC also applied in NIAC.[60]

V. THE EVER-EVOLVING RELATIONSHIP BETWEEN CUSTOM AND TREATY LAW

The fact that customary law and treaty law are so "entangled" in this area means that the field of international humanitarian law provides a microcosm of the wider dilemmas associated with the "ever-evolving relationship between treaty and custom."[61] It has been commented already that the close connection between customary law and treaty law in this area first materialized in the early nineteenth-century efforts to codify the laws and customs of law. It was also seen in the judgment of the International Military Tribunal, which was forced to rely on custom for its consideration of "war crimes" charges, due to the argued non-application of the Hague Convention to World War II.[62] These are good examples of the tendency for the life cycles of treaty and customary law to become entangled, in the sense that (1) norms may exist in both bodies of law simultaneously, and (2) over time, a norm in one body of law may become the inspiration for a norm in the

58. Michael Wood & Omri Sender, *Custom's Bright Future: The Continuing Importance of Customary International Law*, *in* Bradley, *supra* note 56, at 341 and 365.

59. D'Aspremont, *supra* note 2, at 122.

60. It is noted however that the ICRC did not conduct an article by article review of the treaties to determine which were customary. *See* Henckaerts, *supra* note 21, 197; Dinstein, *supra* note 27. Both asked why the ICRC did not adopt this methodology more fully.

61. For the word "entangled," *see* Oscar Schachter, *Entangled Treaty and Custom*, *in* International Law in a Time of Perplexity: Essays in Honour of Shabtai Rosenne 717 (Yoram Dinstein ed., 1989).

62. IMT Judgment, *supra* note 15, at 79–80.

other body of law.[63] As a matter of methodology, the entanglement of customary international law and treaty law raises many crucial (and still largely unanswered) questions. These include how the existence of a separate norm of customary international law should best be determined when the norms are already the subject of a treaty. An old dilemma remains: How do you decide whether State practice and *opinio juris* is evidence of the constituent parts of a separate norm of customary international law or simply evidence of a State's adherence to its treaty obligations?

Indeed, as Richard Baxter pointed out long ago in an argument that has become known as the "Baxter paradox," it is particularly difficult to discern separate State practice and *opinio juris* evidencing a belief of customary (rather than treaty) obligations when the treaties under examination are, like the Geneva Conventions, universally ratified.[64] This is because there is no possibility of using the practice of non-parties as a benchmark to help differentiate from the practice of parties.[65] Of course in these circumstances, considering that the States are bound anyway by treaty law, it is a dilemma that may have little practical relevance. One potential area of relevance is at the domestic level, in States where customary international law automatically forms part of the domestic law while conventional international law does not. As a matter of outcome, the dilemma has more acute practical consequences when there are States that are not parties to the relevant treaty (i.e., the treaty is not universally ratified). In this instance, a finding that a treaty norm has become binding as a matter of custom will have more far-reaching consequences because it indicates the creation of new obligations for States that are non-parties to the treaty. However, there is also more likelihood in these situations that the content of the treaty law provision versus a customary law provision on the same issue will diverge.[66] Indeed, it is for these reasons that findings that some of the provisions in Additional Protocol I to the Geneva Conventions were of customary status were especially contentious. It is noteworthy that when reviewing rules codified in this document, the authors of the study did not limit themselves to reviewing only the practice and *opinio juris* of the thirty-odd States that had not ratified Additional Protocol I because it found that such an approach would not comply with the requirement that custom be based on widespread and representative practice.[67] Instead, it also reviewed the

63. *North Sea Continental Shelf, Judgment*, I.C.J. Rep. 1969, 3, ¶¶ 69 and 71.

64. The "paradox" that as the number of parties to a treaty increases, it becomes harder to demonstrate the state of customary international law outside the treaty was identified by Baxter, *in* Richard Baxter, *Treaties and Custom*, 129 Recueil des Cours 64 (1970). *See* Theodor Meron, *The Geneva Conventions as Customary International Law*, 81(2) American Journal of International Law 348, at 365–67 (1987). *See also North Sea Continental Shelf, Judgment*, I.C.J. Rep. 1969, 3, ¶ 76.

65. *See* Crawford, *supra* note 2, at 116–17, for a discussion of this paradox. *See* Meron, *supra* note 64. *See also North Sea Continental Shelf, Judgment*, I.C.J. Rep. 1969, 3, ¶ 76.

66. Schachter, *supra* note 61, at 728.

67. Henckaerts, *supra* note 21, at 184.

practice and *opinio juris* of the 162 States that had ratified Additional Protocol I. The United States, which is not a party to Additional Protocol I, challenged the ICRC's findings on precisely this point, stating that the supposed *opinio juris* of the States which had ratified the Geneva Conventions merely evidenced the commitment of those States to their treaty obligations.[68]

While the Untied States' criticism on this issue relies on Baxter's age-old thorny legal problem, in fact it seems hard to sustain the position that the practice of parties to a widely ratified multilateral treaty cannot be taken into account in an appraisal of custom. Indeed, it sits uncomfortably with later findings by the ICJ confirming that norms contained in widely ratified treaties—like the UN Charter—can simultaneously exist as norms of customary international law.[69] As James Crawford points out, the Court's acknowledgment that custom and treaty can exist simultaneously is evidence of the fact that "Baxter's paradox" is not actually a "genuine paradox" because it can be avoided in two ways.[70] Firstly, by understanding widespread participation in a treaty as a presumption of *opinio juris*. Secondly, by understanding that the custom-making process extends far beyond the treaty-making process, meaning that in theory even a ratifying State could consider the customary version of a particular treaty norm to be *different* from the treaty version. To its credit, the ICRC was very careful on this issue, making considerable efforts to compare the practice of non-parties with that of parties, sometimes making a finding that particular provisions of the Additional Protocol I were not of customary status on the basis of negative practice and *opinio juris* of non-contracting parties.[71] These include the prohibition of reprisal attacks against civilians, which is found in Article 51(6) of Additional Protocol I.

In recent years, the knotty entanglement between customary international law and treaty law, has entered a new life-cycle iteration in the ICRC Commentaries project. This project has seen customary international law norms feeding back into the treaty law system via the ICRC's interpretation of Article 31(3) of the Vienna Convention on the Law of Treaties.[72] Indeed, the ICRC has taken the position that the principle of systemic integration articulated in Article 31(3)(c) (referring to "any relevant rules of international law applicable in the relations between the Parties") requires it to have reference to "customary international humanitarian

68. Bellinger & Haynes, *supra* note 38, at 446.

69. *See, e.g.*, Military and Paramilitary Activities in and against Nicaragua (Nicaragua v. United States of America), Merits, Judgment. I.C.J. Rep. 1986, at 14, ¶ 188.

70. *See* Crawford, *supra* note 2, at 142–43

71. Henckaerts & Debuf, *supra* note 28, at 182.

72. This is a practice which has been seen in other areas of public international law. In its *Nuclear Weapons* Advisory Opinion, the ICJ used the customary interpretations of "necessity" and "proportionality" to interpret conventional self-defense under Article 51 of the UN Charter. *See* Crawford, *supra* note 2, note 143–44.

law" in its interpretation of treaty law.[73] This means that there are many instances where the ICRC argues that a provision of the Geneva Conventions needs to be interpreted "in the light of . . . [its broader] customary equivalent."[74] For example, although common Article 3 does not list specific judicial guarantees, the ICRC states in its commentary that the article needs to be interpreted in the light of what both Additional Protocol II and customary international law says about "judicial guarantees."[75] The Commentary takes the same approach when interpreting the term "humane," referencing the obligation in Additional Protocol II that persons deprived of their liberty are able to maintain family links, an obligation that it notes has become customary international law. A further entanglement is found in the fact that the commentaries to the treaties sometimes refer to the same State practice for the purposes of interpretation, as has already been referred to in the customary international law study.[76]

In the future, if the findings of the ICRC's customary international law study are updated at a later date, and the commentaries to the Geneva Conventions are used as a source, the feedback loop between treaty law and customary law may go full circle.[77] As fantastical as the idea that "treaty law may become custom, may become treaty law, may become custom" may seem, it is actually not that far-fetched. Indeed, the idea that customary international law can be subject to interpretation is a topic that is increasingly being explored and justified in legal scholarship.[78] Some scholars argue that the process of ascertaining the form of customary international law norms cannot help but include a process of interpretation that

73. Commentary on the First Geneva Convention, Convention (I) for the Amelioration of the Condition of the Wounded and Sick in Armed Forces in the Field 10 (2016).

74. *Id.* at 232, ¶ 684. In many ways, as long as the methodology employed for the finding of custom is sound, interpreting treaty norms through customary international law is less controversial than a finding of the existence of custom, on the basis of treaty law, because customary international law is seen to be a "general law" that is binding upon all States. As a result, there is no such thing as "non parties" of general custom, meaning that as long as a State is not claiming to be a persistent objector, a party to a treaty will not be able to argue that the rules of custom are not binding upon it. One instance where this argument could potentially hold any sway would be where customary norms that are accepted to apply in international armed conflicts are applied to help interpret treaty norms that *only* apply in non-international armed conflicts.

75. *Id.* at ¶ 684 notes that Article 6 of APII is now considered customary international law. It is noted that the commentary to Common Article 3 regularly relies on Additional Protocol II, without always providing its view that the provision in question is customary international law.

76. *Id.* at ¶¶ 593–94.

77. *See* Meron, *supra* note 19, at 247 for an early appreciation that the interpretation of the treaties may affect developing customary international law.

78. Marina Fortuna, *Different Strings of the Same Harp: Interpretation of Rules of Customary International Law, Their Identification and Treaty Interpretation, in* Merkouris, Kammerhofer, & Arajärvi, *supra* note 20, at 393–94 (concerning the newness of the enquiry).

enquires into their content.[79] John Morss and Emily Forbes have argued that "form and content are intermingled, if not circular, in the context of CIL."[80] Certainly when the act of custom interpretation is defined as "construing the relevant norm in a way that contributes to the solution of the dispute,"[81] much of the analytical discussion regarding the scope of a particular provision in the case law of the international criminal tribunals can be easily categorized as "interpretation." In some of these situations, the rules of the Vienna Convention on the Law of Treaties have even been cited by judges for the purpose of clarifying the interpretation of the equivalent customary provision.[82] In that sense, international humanitarian law will surely prove to be a prime test-site to explore the notion of how customary international law may be interpreted.

Considering the manner in which treaty law and customary international law are being used to reinforce each other in a self-reinforcing feedback loop, it can be seen that the existence of customary international law is contributing to an incremental thickening process that is taking place within the landscape of international humanitarian law. This thickening process is the product of the interaction between the two bodies of law. Commenting on this matter, Theodor Meron noted that when a norm is strengthened on two sides, by treaty on the one hand and custom on the other, "rhetorical strength" is added to the "moral claim" for their observance.[83] The notion that customary international law and treaty law will be self-reinforcing assumes of course that their content is more or less identical or substantially similar. While this will be generally the case when it comes to the norms of the Geneva Conventions due to their universal ratification, there is more scope for divergence when it comes to Additional Protocol I and II, which are not universally ratified. In instances where the content of treaty and customary norms diverge in either substance or scope, there is a danger that rather than reinforcing each other, they may have the opposite effect. In particular, extra care must be taken to ensure that any articulation of customary international norms reflecting or going beyond treaty norms that have not been universally ratified or are not thought to be declaratory of custom is well founded, so that they are not rejected out of hand.[84] Likewise, some care needs to be taken that the circularity of citation

79. Morss & Forbes, *supra* note 20, at 444.

80. *Id. See also* Fortuna, *supra* note 78, at 394 and 398.

81. *Id.* at 407.

82. *See* Prosecutor v. Galić, Case No. IT-98-29-A, Appeals Chamber Judgment, ¶ 103 (Int'l Crim. Trib. for the former Yugoslavia Nov. 30, 2006).

83. Meron, *supra* note 64, at 350.

84. For examples of specific norms in the study which have been challenged, *see* Dinstein, *supra* note 27, at 110 (he argues that the study "suffers from an unrealistic desire to show that controversial provisions of API are declaratory of customary international law (not to mention the occasional attempt to go beyond API)." As examples, he examines inter alia Rule 65 on perfidy, Rule 4 defining combatant, Rule 6 articulating civilian protection, Rule 55 on humanitarian

between the customary international law study and the commentaries project remains legitimate, so that it does not lead to what has been called "bootstrapping."[85] Equally, while State practice alone may be sufficient to prove the correct interpretation of a treaty obligation, it is not on its own enough to prove the emergence of a customary international law norm. In the words of Crawford: "Just as baking flour alone does not make a cake, relying on one element of State practice alone does not make custom."[86] This raises questions about the extent to which it would be legitimate in the future as a matter of methodology for an international criminal tribunal (or any other body) to use the outcomes of the commentaries project (which may be based solely on State practice) to interpret customary norms.

VI. CUSTOMARY INTERNATIONAL HUMANITARIAN LAW: AN INFLUENCE BEYOND IHL

When considering the role that customary international law has had in the making of international humanitarian law, it becomes clear again that the life stories of the two bodies of law are intricately intertwined. Most particularly, several developments in the field of international humanitarian law on the subject of custom have not only had an effect on the making and shaping of international humanitarian law but also on custom more generally. A first example of this phenomenon emerges from the very title "Customary International Humanitarian Law." It is actually a fact of some perplexity that customary international law—often thought of and referred to as a general law—can be conceptualized as having developed a generic specialized strand defined by subject matter.[87] Indeed, because customary international law emerges from the manner in which States approach concrete factual situations in the real world, there is no reason to imagine that the State practice and *opinio juris* defining these actions should be limited to "international humanitarian law."[88] This reality is seen in the ICRC's customary international humanitarian law study, which frequently draws upon practice linked to both international humanitarian law *and* international human rights law. Indeed, it can be assumed that especially in situations away from the battlefield, a State's practice and *opinio juris* in relation to a particular situation will be informed by

access). *See* MacLaren & Schwendimann, *supra* note 36, at 1225; Turns, *supra* note 36, at 236. *See also* Cryer, *supra* note 20, at 244 for a discussion of this point.

85. Morss & Forbes, *supra* note 20, at 435.

86. CRAWFORD, *supra* note 2, at 142.

87. For an opposite view, *see* Robert Kolb, *Selected Problems in the Theory of Customary International Law*, 50 NETHERLANDS INTERNATIONAL LAW REVIEW 119, at 128 (2003).

88. For discussion of this point, *see* Hampson, *supra* note 42, at 53–56.

multiple sources of international law in addition to international humanitarian law, for example, refugee law, human rights law, or the law on diplomatic relations.

A powerful example of this point can found in the prohibition of arbitrary detention in non-international armed conflicts identified by the study, which on close inspection is grounded almost wholly out of international human rights law norms and practice.[89] The study first notes that the prohibition of arbitrary deprivation of liberty in non-international armed conflicts is established by State practice, including military manuals, national legislation, and official statements. Commenting briefly on these sources, it then goes on to provide details of the human rights treaties enshrining the right to liberty and/or the prohibition on arbitration deprivation of liberty, including the International Covenant on Civil and Political Rights, the Convention on the Rights of the Child, and the European and American Conventions on Human Rights. One of the peculiarities of calling the resultant norm part of "Customary International Humanitarian Law" when citing practice as broad as this is that it subsumes these other bodies of law into international humanitarian law. It is not considered to be a compound norm of international law that has been created out of State practice and *opinio juris* more generally, that may in some circumstances emerge out of a variety of treaty law obligations. Another key problem in citing human rights–related State practice and *opinio juris* to support a finding that a particular norm of international humanitarian law applies to non-international armed conflicts is that it pays insufficient attention to the fact that human rights–related State practice and *opinio juris* provides objective and subjective evidence of States' view that *they* (as States) are bound by the substantive underlying norm. It is unclear how this same State practice and *opinio juris* can be understood as the basis of a resultant norm that is not only binding upon States but also upon armed groups.[90]

A second development in the field of international humanitarian law that has had an effect on the making and shaping of custom more generally is the way that international humanitarian law has impacted upon understandings that customary international law is a "general law" in a unitary system. This refers to the idea that customary international law is binding upon all States in an identical manner (persistent objectors aside).[91] Indeed, the idea that there is a category of customary international law that applies *only* to NIACs interferes with traditional understanding of customary international law, which holds that it is a general body of law that applies identically to all subjects of international law. By finding

89. *See* Rule 99, *supra* note 25, at 347.

90. Katharine Fortin, *How to Cope with Diversity While Preserving Unity in Customary International Law? Some Insights from International Humanitarian Law*, 23(3) Journal of Conflict and Security Law 337, at 353 (2018).

91. For the idea that customary international law is important to the unity of international law, *see* Mario Prost, The Concept of Unity in Public International Law 98 (2012). For a longer discussion of the concept of unity in international humanitarian law, *see* Fortin, *supra* note 90, at 337.

that the law that applies to IACs is different from the law that applies to NIACs, the ICRC customary international humanitarian law study implicitly finds that different subjects of international law are bound by different bundles of customary international norms. Whereas States are bound by the full range of CIHL norms, armed groups are bound by a different, and less extensive, category of norms and are certainly not bound by the small bundle of norms that *only* apply in international armed conflicts. While international humanitarian lawyers may have long come to accept this state of affairs as a given, it apparently remains quite a radical prospect for lawyers who are more accustomed to understand customary international law as applying generally to all subjects of international law in an identical manner.[92]

Ironically, from an international humanitarian lawyer's perspective, what is more noteworthy when considering this theme is not that the body of customary international humanitarian law applies differently to different actors, but that customary international humanitarian law only has one category of norms for non-international armed conflict instead of two, that is,Common Article 3 (CA3) and Additional Protocol II (APII). This outcome demonstrates how during the custom-making process, some of the sharper corners of treaty law relating to its temporal and material thresholds can become smoothed over or knocked off. This observation goes back to and reinforces the point made previously in relation to human rights law. It is a further demonstration of the fact that because custom emerges out of situational responses by States in the form of State practice and *opinio juris*, it has the ability to create norms where the normative or temporal boundaries that exist in treaty law are collapsed and conflated. It is likely that the ICRC ended up setting out only one "threshold" for non-international armed conflicts because despite treaty law identifying different thresholds, State practice and *opinio juris* apparently demonstrated that States do not always find the differentiation between a CA3 conflict and an APII conflict important.[93] The truth of this can be seen in the customary rule confirming that, at the end of hostilities, authorities in power must endeavor to grant the broadest possible amnesty to persons who have participated in the non-international armed conflict. Although as a rule this originates in Additional Protocol II, the practice referred to justifying the finding of the customary rule is not exclusive to States that have ratified

92. *See also* Zhuo Liang, *The Practice of Non-State Armed Groups and the Formation of Customary International Humanitarian Law: Towards Direct Relevance?*, *in* Merkouris, Kammerhofer, & Arajärvi, *supra* note 20, 298, at 313, where she notes at footnote 78 that K. Fortin "even asserted that 'different subjects of international law are bound by different forms of CIL.'" For discussion, *see* Fortin, *supra* note 90.

93. It is important to note that some States do find this distinction important in some areas. For example, the Military Manual of the UK distinguishes the rules that apply to an APII conflict. United Kingdom Ministry of Defence, The Manual of the Law of Armed Conflict ¶ 3.7 (2004).

Additional Protocol II. Likewise, much of the State practice referred to support the rule hardly ever refers to Additional Protocol II, supporting the idea that the practice and views of States regarding amnesties have not emerged solely out of Article 6(5) APII. As a result, the emergent customary rule appears to exist separately from APII's rather high threshold of application set out in its Article 1.[94]

VII. *QUO VADIS* CUSTOMARY IHL? *QUO VADIS* CUSTOM?

Considering the intimate relationship between the development of customary international law and the development of international humanitarian law, it becomes interesting to consider what insights the two bodies of law bring to how the other could develop over the next few years. When reflecting on this question, it is helpful to think back to the beginning of the chapter, which shows how significantly ways of thinking about custom have changed since the time of Grotius. While customary international law used to be thought of as a legal framework emerging out of long usage, toward the end of the nineteenth century it began to be increasingly thought of in positivist terms as a legal framework created by States, by virtue of their consent. Indeed, according to the modern theory of customary international law, it is a body of law made up of State practice and *opinio juris* which together demonstrate evidence of "obligations" between States. Of course, even in the most traditional conception of custom, it is important not to overemphasize the role played by State consent. The rule that the practice of specially affected States is given more weight in determining whether a particular rule exists implies that the practice and *opinio juris* of States does not count equally.[95] Relatedly, the ICJ has indicated that practice only needs to be "widespread and representative" rather than universal and that new States are automatically bound by norms to which they have not contributed.[96] These are all examples of the fact it would be erroneous to portray customary international law as a system based solely on State consent.

That being said, when evaluating the current state of customary international law in this field, it is helpful to remember that it has long been generally accepted that customary international law emerges out the behavior of States. Like other forms of customary law, it is understood as a "self-generative and bottom up

94. For example, amnesty agreements are referred for conflicts to which APII would not have applied because the State in question was not yet a party to the Protocol, e.g., Honduras, Nicaragua, Serbia, Philippines, and Sudan. Practice relating to Rule 159: Amnesty, ICRC Study on Customary International Humanitarian Law, https://ihl-databases.icrc.org/customary-ihl/eng/docs/v2_rul_rule159.

95. *North Sea Continental Shelf, Judgment*, I.C.J. Rep. 1969, 3, ¶ 73.

96. *Id.*

process of production normativity."[97] It is for that reason that Lon Fuller described customary law as "a language of interaction."[98] He explains:

> To interact meaningfully [individuals] require a social setting in which the moves of the participating players will generally fall into some predictable pattern. To engage in effective social behaviour [individuals] need the support of intermeshing anticipations that will let them know what their opposite numbers will do, or that will at least enable them to gauge the general scope of the repertory from which responses to their actions will be drawn.[99]

In other words, customary law is often thought to emerge out of a network of interactional and reciprocal behaviors between a certain group of actors or "from a dialogue between international actors over time."[100] This interactional and reciprocal behavior is said to be generative, because it creates a reciprocal network of obligations that are then deemed binding upon those same actors and govern their interactions.

Yet the validity of describing customary law as "a language of interaction" has been increasingly challenged in recent years in the field of international humanitarian law by a string of developments that are not necessarily related to one another but arguably end up having a cumulative effect on the legal framework. The first is the increased tendency of international courts and tribunals, particularly in the field of international humanitarian law and human rights law, to adopt a deductive method of custom ascertainment.[101] Deductive methods are characterized by a greater emphasis on *opinio juris* than State practice, a phenomenon that has been called "contra-factual custom." Instead of placing an emphasis on the behavior of States, it places an emphasis on principles such as humanity, a supreme common will, and statements of States.[102] A move toward deductive methodologies in this field is often rationalized on the basis that the practice of States is characterized by too many violations to form a reliable basis for an

97. D'Aspremont, *supra* note 1, at 6.

98. Lon Fuller, *Human Interaction and the Law*, 14(1) American Journal of Jurisprudence 1, at 2 (1969).

99. *Id.* at 2. The text in square brackets marks the insertion of gender neutral language.

100. Crawford, *supra* note 3, at 82.

101. *See, e.g.*, Military and Paramilitary Activities in and against Nicaragua (Nicaragua v. United States of America), Merits, Judgment. I.C.J. Rep. 1986, at 14. For discussion of this case, *see* Meron, *supra* note 83, at 351–70, and Kirgis, *supra* note 35.

102. For an account of the move from inductive to deductive methodology in the ascertainment of customary international law, *see* Bruno Simma & Philip Alston, *The Sources of Human Rights Law: Custom, Jus Cogens and General Principles*, Australian Yearbook of Human Rights, 88–90 (1992).

inductive process or simply unavailable or impossible to discern.[103] It has also been explained with reference to an assessment of how "destabilizing or morally distasteful the activity" underassessment is.[104]

The second development is the idea that the practice and *opinio juris* of States can produce legal obligations binding upon a different category of actors than those whose behavior is being studied, namely, non-State armed groups. While it has long been debated whether armed groups should have more of a role in the creation of custom, it remains the position of many scholars and the ICRC that this is not necessary.[105] In fact, many scholars have pointed out that the idea that armed groups' practice and *opinio juris* should be counted alongside that of States raises many questions that seemingly have no answer, the main one being how should the practice and *opinio juris* of armed groups be counted relative to that of States.[106] Yet the current belief that State practice and *opinio juris* can produce an obligation that is binding upon third parties may be seen as equally problematic, not least because it takes understandings of *what customary international law is* even further away from the idea that customary law emerges out of interactional reciprocal behavior connected to the norm. It introduces the idea that customary international law can have a unidirectional dimension, in the sense that dialogical or behavioral relations between one category of actors are capable of producing imperatives for third parties (i.e., armed groups).[107]

A third development can be found in the growing turn to understand international humanitarian law not only as a framework of horizontal obligations between the parties to the armed conflict but also as a set of vertical obligations binding upon the parties to the armed conflict and owed to rights-bearing individuals on the ground, who also have obligations.[108] These individuals may be prisoners or war, but may also be ordinary civilians who are living under the control of one of the parties. When note is taken of this element of verticality in the legal framework,

103. Kolb, *supra* note 87, at 124–26.

104. Kirgis, *supra* note 35, at 142.

105. Henckaerts & Doswald-Beck, *supra* note 25, xiii. For a review of this academic debate, *see* Fortin, note 90, 348–50. *See also* Marco Sassòli, International Humanitarian Law: Rules, Controversies, and Solutions to Problems Arising in Warfare 49–51 (2019); and Ezequiel Heffes, Detention by Non-State Armed Groups under International Law 117–18 (2022) (for more recent discussions).

106. Fortin, *supra* note 90, at 351–53.

107. For the term "projecting an imperative," *see* Fuller, *supra* note 98, at 21.

108. *See, e.g.*, Lawrence Hill-Cawthorne, *Rights under International Humanitarian Law*, 28(4) European Journal of International Law 1187 (2018); Anne Peters, *Direct Rights of Individuals in the International Law of Armed Conflict*, Max Planck Institute for Comparative Public Law & International Law (MPIL) Research Paper No. 2019-23 (Dec. 19, 2019), https://ssrn.com/abstract=3506742 or http://dx.doi.org/10.2139/ssrn.3506742. For the idea of ordinary individuals also having obligations, *see* Sassòli, *supra* note 105, 197–98.

it is seen that the interactional characteristic of customary international humanitarian law is again thrown off balance because the customary norms it contains is perceived to be binding upon yet another set of actors (i.e., individuals) whose interactional behavior is not taken into account. Indeed, it becomes notable that in the traditional custom-making process, there is no room for a consideration of practice and *opinio juris* determining the "rights" and "obligations of individuals," and there has so far been little consideration of this question in the scholarship.

When wondering what, if anything, can and should be done about these developments, it becomes important to note that the custom-making process has traditionally focused on the ascertainment of "obligations" rather than their corresponding "rights." Yet one wonders whether future iterations of customary international (humanitarian) law might be encouraged to find more space for the concept of "rights." Indeed, it is interesting to note that in the *Asylum* case, the ICJ indicated that what was required was "constant and uniform usage practiced by the States in question" and that the "usage" should be an "expression of a right appertaining to the State granting asylum and a duty incumbent on the territorial State."[109] The Court's recognition that State practice may be evidence of both rights and duties is curious and signals an area that warrants further exploration in scholarship. Notably, a connected discussion has recently taken place with regard to the doctrine of "specially affected States." It is noteworthy that some States have argued that this doctrine should be interpreted to take account of the practice of the States that bear the most pressing obligations in this area. For example, the United States and the United Kingdom have argued that "nuclear powers" and "other military powers" are the ones that are "specially affected" in the realm of IHL.[110] It is perhaps as a result of these types of interpretations that this is a doctrine that is often thought to be "easily abused by powerful States."[111] Yet it has been argued recently that there is room to question this approach.

Indeed, Kevin Jon Heller has argued that a wider interpretation of the doctrine of "specially affected States," which includes States from the Global South, holds a "transformative potential" in the realm of customary international law, which has hitherto been much underutilized and explored.[112] It is interesting to note that the ICRC has taken a wider view in its study of customary international

109. Asylum Case (Colombia v. Peru) (Judgment) [1950] I.C.J. Rep. 6, [266], [276–77].

110. *See* Legality of the Threat or Use of Nuclear Weapons, Advisory Opinion, Letter Dated 20 June 1995 from the Acting Legal Adviser to the Department of State, Together with Written Statement of the Government of the United States of America, 1995 ICJ Plead. 8–9 (June 20) ("With respect to the use of nuclear weapons, customary law could not be created over the objection of the nuclear-weapon States, which are the States whose interests are most specially affected"); *id.*, Verbatim Record, Statement of the United Kingdom, CR 95/34 (Nov. 15, 1995) at 63, as cited by Kevin Jon Heller, *Specially Affected States and the Formation of Custom*, 112(2) American Journal of International Law 191, at 204 (2018).

111. Gennady Danilenko, Law-Making in the International Community 96 (1993).

112. Heller, *supra* note 110.

humanitarian law that includes not only the State whose behavior is under scrutiny for the purposes of obligations but also the State that would suffer as a result of the obligation's violation. For example, in considering the rule preventing the export of cultural property from occupied territory, the study notes the practice of "States specially affected by occupation."[113] In a similar vein, the U.S. Department of Defense Law of War Manual indicates that both "occupying or occupied" States might qualify as "specially affected."[114] The idea that occupied States' practice can be relevant in the ascertainment process of IHL norms applying in situations of occupation is noteworthy, because arguably occupied States have no specific *obligations* under Section III of Geneva Convention IV pertaining to occupation law. Instead, the obligations are those of the Occupying Power. Understanding the "specially affected" test to provide scope for an examination of the State practice and *opinio juris* of States that are on the receiving end of particular violations and/or have a legal interest in the adherence of particular rules goes some way to showing that the customary international law ascertainment process potentially holds conceptual space to take account of practice relating not only to obligations but also rights.

A further related development that could provide room for such a conceptual shift in the future lies in the concept of *opinio juris communis*, which opens the door to considering the interests of civilians (or other individuals) in the custom-making process. As far as I can tell, this concept was first invoked by Oscar Schachter in 1989 in his chapter on "Entangled Treaty and Custom."[115] It was a concept that was not very developed in the chapter, perhaps more of an afterthought, where Schachter commented that he found it "highly unlikely" that "the exercise of military and economic power" was an effective manner to enforce rules in specific situations, particularly those of a global nature. He indicated that he thought that treaty law was a better medium to deal with such issues or "declarations of the *opinio juris communis*." Failing to define this term fully, Schachter merely stated that such declarations should "serve common interests" and be "accepted generally by the international community."[116] The concept has more recently been developed by, among others, Judge Cançado Trindade during the course of his distinguished career as a judge at the ICJ. In his Dissenting Opinion in *Marshall Islands v. Pakistan*, he accused the court of having exercised an "inter-state myopia," such that it has considered the survival of the "hypothetical State . . . rather than that of peoples and individuals, and ultimately of humankind as a

113. Customary International Humanitarian Law, *supra* note 25, Part I, xliv, 135. It is not clear whose practice was consulted here, but it seems likely occupied States.

114. Heller, *supra* note 110, at fn. 75. For the quote, *see* Office of the General Counsel, U.S. Department of Defense, Law of War Manual § 1.8.2.3 (rev. ed., Dec. 2016).

115. Schachter, *supra* note 61, at 737–38.

116. *Id.*

whole."[117] In an early lecture on the topic, he indicated that "[g]eneral or customary international law emanates not so much from the practice of States (not devoid of ambiguities and contradictions) but rather from the *opinio juris communis* of all subjects of international law (States, international organisations, human beings and humankind as a whole)."[118]

Interestingly, there is a similarity between Trindade's *opinio juris communis* and a related theoretical discussion that took place in the 1990s in human rights scholarship. In that discussion, the question arose as to how customary international law relating to human rights law could best be ascertained as a matter of methodology. Scholars were troubled by the fact that the customary norms of human rights were supposed to emerge out of State practice and *opinio juris*, whereas the performance of most human rights obligations "lacks this element of interaction proper [because] . . . it does not 'run between' States in any meaningful sense," but runs between States and individuals.[119] Some scholars engaging with this dilemma suggested that the answer lay in an acknowledgment that there are "universal norms of conduct that result from legitimate human expectations and that these expectations are as important a source of law."[120] Indeed, Philip Alston famously argued that human rights norms operate at three levels: "as the rights of individuals, as obligations assumed by States, and as legitimate expectations of the international community."[121] A reader considering these ideas may wonder how such expectations could ever be surveyed and why indeed this question even matters in the field of customary international humanitarian law. While it would be too difficult to provide an answer to the first question here, the answer to the second question is more straightforward. Giving thought to whether there could and should be a greater role for civilians (and arguably other individuals) in the making and shaping of international humanitarian law is important because (1) it would (potentially) make customary international law more interactional when conceived as a vertical (as well as horizontal) system, and (2) civilians are the true victims of every war.

117. Dissenting Judgment of Judge Antônio Augustus Cançado Trindade, Obligations Concerning Negotiations Relating to Cessation of the Nuclear Arms Race and to Nuclear Disarmament (Marshall Islands versus Pakistan), I.C.J. Rep. 2016, 552, ¶¶ 150 and 165.

118. Antônio Augustus Cançado Trindade, *Jus Cogens: The Determination and the Gradual Expansion of Its Material Content in Contemporary International Case-Law*, *in* XXXV Curso de Derecho Internacional Organizado por el Comité Jurídico Interamericano 3–29 (2008).

119. Simma & Alston, *supra* note 102, at 99.

120. Harold G. Maier, *The Role of Experts in Proving International Human Rights in Domestic Courts: A Commentary*, 25 Georgia Journal of International and Comparative Law 205 (1995/6).

121. OHCHR, "Report on the Special; Rapporteur on Extrajudicial, Summary or Arbitrary Executions, Mission to Sri Lanka" (Mar. 27, 2006) U.N. Doc. E/CN.4/2006/53/Add.5 ¶¶ 25–27.

Indeed, this thought experiment is also important because orthodox conceptions of customary international law and the methods for its proper ascertainment have undoubtedly been colored by the fact that most judgments and advisory opinions on the topic emerge from or are related to inter-State complaints or judicial institutions without an individual applicant. It is thought-provoking to wonder whether the methodology could have been radically different and more civilian-orientated, if there had ever been a court called upon to make determinations of custom where individuals were the applicant. It is also important because when it is noticed how much custom has changed over the past three centuries, it becomes obvious that it is highly likely that it will continue to evolve over the next century. Cognizant of this, it is important to engage in "design-thinking" that considers and reimagines the different ways in which this body of law *could* and *should* change in the future to take into account the interests of the panoply of actors who are affected by and involved in armed conflict. Lastly, it is important because it points out that if custom survives at all in the next century, there could be value in an ascertainment process that takes better account of it as based in interactional behaviors, and the practice not only of (powerful) States but also less powerful actors who are most at risk of being on the receiving end of military action.

VIII. CONCLUSIONS

This chapter has shown that custom has played a fundamental role in the making and shaping of international humanitarian law ever since the branch of law came into existence. It has shown that despite being a source of law that is ever plagued by scholarly debate and crises of legitimacy, it continues to be heavily relied upon. It is a source of humanitarian law that is robust and flexible enough to take account of changing needs and deficits of treaty law. Yet the chapter has also shown that there are some dangers of relying upon customary international law, especially when as a body of law it is developing in ways that seem hard to explain when considering its interactional conceptual roots. Contemporary developments that have the cumulative effect of turning customary international law into an increasingly unidirectional set of prescriptions that are divorced from the actions of its addressees—States, armed groups, and individuals—create grounds to worry about its "health and contemporary legitimacy," especially as it is increasingly being leant upon as a fixer or remedy, in a world where treaty-making initiatives show little hope of success.[122]

122. For further discussion of the "health and legitimacy" of IHL, *see* MANTILLA *supra* note 3, at 172.

4

Principles of International Humanitarian Law: A New Framework

JEROEN VAN DEN BOOGAARD*

I. INTRODUCTION

Most textbooks and State military manuals on the law of armed conflict, or international humanitarian law (IHL), contain a chapter entitled "the principles of IHL."[1] Authors and States list various principles that they see as "fundamental" for this branch of the law. Among the most cited as IHL principles are: military necessity, humanity, distinction, proportionality, and honor and good faith (or

* Jeroen van den Boogaard serves as Legal Counsel, Ministry of Foreign Affairs, The Netherlands, and lecturer in International Humanitarian Law, University of Amsterdam. This chapter is based on earlier publications by the author. Jeroen van den Boogaard, *Fighting by the Principles: Principles as a Source of International Humanitarian Law*, *in* ARMED CONFLICT AND INTERNATIONAL LAW: IN SEARCH OF THE HUMAN FACE 1–31 (M. Matthee et al. eds., 2013); Jeroen van den Boogaard, *Reimagining IHL Principles Part I: The Wrong Principles*, LIEBER INSTITUTE ARTICLES OF WAR (Dec. 8, 2020), https://lieber.westpoint.edu/reimagining-ihl-principles-part-i-wrong-principles/; Jeroen van den Boogaard, *Reimagining IHL Principles Part II: A New Framework*, LIEBER INSTITUTE ARTICLES OF WAR (Dec. 11, 2020), https://lieber.westpoint.edu/reimagining-ihl-principles-part-ii-new-framework/. *See also* JEROEN VAN DEN BOOGAARD, PROPORTIONALITY IN INTERNATIONAL HUMANITARIAN LAW: PRINCIPLE, RULE AND PRACTICE (2019).

1. *See, e.g.*, GARY SOLIS, THE LAW OF ARMED CONFLICT 268–325 (2d ed. 2016); N. MELZER, INTERNATIONAL HUMANITARIAN LAW: A COMPREHENSIVE INTRODUCTION 17–20 (ICRC 2019).

Jeroen van den Boogaard, *Principles of International Humanitarian Law: A New Framework* In: *Making and Shaping the Law of Armed Conflict*. Edited by: Sandesh Sivakumaran and Christian R. Burne, Oxford University Press.
 DOI: 10.1093/oso/9780197775134.003.0004

chivalry).[2] These five are also listed in the last update of the IHL military manual of the Royal Netherlands Army in 2005.[3] As a result, these five principles are the basis for IHL education and training within the Netherlands armed forces. Other States use similar, or even the same, principles. For example, Chapter II of the updated U.S. Department of Defense (DoD) Law of War Manual also refers to military necessity, humanity, distinction, proportionality, and honor.[4]

The problem is that these five principles are, in my view, ineffective in fulfilling their two main functions: as a tool to educate and train military forces and as guidance for military forces in planning and executing military operations in accordance with their IHL obligations. Furthermore, the majority of the five principles used currently, fail to provide sufficient specific guidance for situations where persons and objects have fallen into the hands of the enemy. They are also incomplete to be used as guidance during the conduct of hostilities because they are silent on the restrictions on the use of means and methods of warfare. In my opinion, these are grave omissions that must be corrected. As a result, I intend to open the debate on this important topic by recommending the adoption of a different set of IHL principles based on their character as a norm and their intended function.

To this end, I suggest that most of the five principles listed earlier are in fact not actually principles, but rather are norms of different characters. Military necessity, humanity, and chivalry should be recategorized as foundations, not principles, of IHL. And proportionality should be seen as a rule rather than a principle. The proposed new set of IHL principles is: distinction, precautions, superfluous injury or unnecessary suffering, protection, and humane treatment. To reach this conclusion, it is necessary to first define the term "IHL principle" by introducing a useful taxonomy of IHL norms: foundations, principles, and rules.

2. For example, SOLIS, *supra* note 1, mentions distinction, military necessity, unnecessary suffering, proportionality, and arguably humanity; MELZER, *supra* note 1, mentions military necessity, humanity, distinction, precaution, proportionality, unnecessary suffering, and humane treatment. Blank and Noone mention humanity, military necessity, humanity, distinction, and proportionality. *See* L.R. BLANK & G.P. NOONE, INTERNATIONAL LAW AND ARMED CONFLICT: FUNDAMENTAL PRINCIPLES AND CONTEMPORARY CHALLENGES IN THE LAW OF WAR 35–36 (2013). Additionally, the UN Group of Governmental Experts noted humanity, military necessity, distinction, and proportionality as the "established international legal principles." UN General Assembly, *Report of the Group of Governmental Experts on Advancing responsible State behaviour in cyberspace in the context of international security* ¶ 71(f), U.N. Doc. A/76/135 (July 14, 2021).

3. As a captain in the military lawyers' branch of the Royal Netherlands Army, the author was involved in the drafting of this Manual from 2000 to 2003.

4. OFFICE OF THE GENERAL COUNSEL, U.S. DEPARTMENT OF DEFENSE, LAW OF WAR MANUAL 50–69 (rev. ed., Dec. 2016). AJP-3.9, *Allied Joint Doctrine for Joint Targeting* ¶ 1.2.3d, NATO (Edition B, Version 1, Nov. 2021).

II. THREE TYPES OF IHL NORMS: FOUNDATIONS, PRINCIPLES, RULES

Before discussing the IHL principles in more detail, one first needs to define what we mean by "principles." Unfortunately, legal scholars, States, and judges use the term "principles" inconsistently. At times it is used to mean a basis for rules, at other times as one of the most important norms in a branch of law, and at still other times as a central concept that overrides all others in an area of law.[5] Furthermore, principles are one of the three primary sources of international law as listed in Article 38 of the International Court of Justice Statute (ICJ Statute).[6] Although equating IHL principles to those listed in the ICJ Statute is subject to debate,[7] the fact that they are identified as a source of law may be understood as an indication that IHL principles could qualify as legally binding norms of international law.

In conceptualizing IHL norms, it has been argued by myself and others that the categories of norms introduced by Ronald Dworkin in his 1977 book *Taking Rights Seriously*—policies, principles, and rules—work well as a framework.[8] Winter builds upon this structure, trading "policies" for the term "pillar," while I use the term "foundation" rather than "policy" or "pillar."[9] In my view, "foundation" best explains the function this type of norm has within a legal framework—in this case IHL.

Foundations of a legal framework are those norms that underlie principles and rules. Unlike principles and rules, foundations are not legally binding, but contain the rationale for that legal framework. As such, foundations guide the interpretation of the legally binding principles and rules of that legal framework. Foundations of IHL, I suggest, are thus the starting points of the IHL principles and rules. They are not part of the IHL "building" as such, but are necessary to avoid the building's collapse.

Principles, on the other hand, are legally binding and act as a category in between foundations and rules. They are not as specific as rules, but rather serve a broader purpose. Principles of IHL may be seen as the skeleton structure of the entire branch of IHL. They are the basis of the most specific category of norms: rules. In international law, rules are found in either treaty texts or customary law. As

5. For a more detailed discussion, *see generally* JEROEN VAN DEN BOOGAARD, PROPORTIONALITY IN INTERNATIONAL HUMANITARIAN LAW: PRINCIPLE, RULE AND PRACTICE (2019).

6. *See* IMOGEN SAUNDERS, GENERAL PRINCIPLES AS A SOURCE OF INTERNATIONAL LAW (2021).

7. *See* ANTONIO CASSESE, INTERNATIONAL LAW 103 (2d ed. 2005).

8. Jeroen van den Boogaard, *Fighting by the Principles: Principles as a Source of International Humanitarian Law*, *in* ARMED CONFLICT AND INTERNATIONAL LAW: IN SEARCH OF THE HUMAN FACE 1–31 (M. Matthee et al. eds., 2013).

9. Elliot Winter, *Pillars not Principles: The Status of Humanity and Military Necessity in the Law of Armed Conflict*, 25 JOURNAL OF CONFLICT & SECURITY LAW 1, 1–31 (2020).

such, their legally binding character is clear. IHL rules are the most specific type of norms regulating the conduct of hostilities and contain specific prohibitions and obligations. Principles are broader, yet many of them have been codified in treaty texts nonetheless.

As a result of the distinct roles of foundations, principles, and rules, it is important to look at the characteristics of IHL norms when seeking to identify IHL principles. It does not make sense to address all types of norms as "IHL principles," because each category of norm must be applied differently. To illustrate: IHL rules are legally binding and must be observed. In case they are violated, sanctions may be imposed. IHL foundations, on the other hand, are guiding norms that may help to inform the interpretation of IHL rules. There are also functional reasons for assessing which norms should be included in a list of IHL principles. *Foundations* are important for helping military forces understand the rules and principles of IHL. The *rules* are the norms that ultimately must be followed by the soldiers, because violations of the rules may lead to prosecution. But soldiers are not lawyers. They are not expected to consult their copy of the Geneva Conventions in the midst of a firefight. Therefore, *principles* play a crucial intermediate role. This role will be further discussed when I introduce a new list of IHL principles in section III.

A. IHL Foundations: Military Necessity, Humanity, and Chivalry

There is no doubt that military necessity, humanity, and chivalry play a crucial role in IHL. Military necessity and humanity have been built into the legally binding framework of IHL principles and rules. It is the careful balance between military necessity and humanitarian considerations that results in the principles and rules of IHL. And certain rules have clear roots in chivalrous traditions, such as the prohibition of perfidy.

However, it is generally agreed that these notions in and of themselves provide for no legal obligations. For example, Yoram Dinstein refers to humanity and military necessity as merely "impulses" in the first edition of his *The Conduct of Hostilities under the International Law of Armed Conflict.*[10] Indeed, an overriding character of these notions—that is, setting aside rules of IHL—must be forcefully rejected. This means that specific rules, such as the prohibition of torture, cannot be set aside in the name of military necessity, unless the rule itself has incorporated such an exception. The same is true for chivalry. Even if one considers it not chivalrous to shoot an opponent in the back or while sleeping, IHL contains no legally binding norm prohibiting such behavior. In other words, the foundations of IHL (military necessity, humanity, and chivalry) may be defined as norms that

10. Yoram Dinstein, The Conduct of Hostilities under the Law of International Armed Conflict 16 (1st ed. 2004).

underlie the legally binding IHL principles and rules, but they do not qualify as principles of IHL because they lack the required legally binding character.

Despite not qualifying as principles, let alone rules, these foundations are critical for understanding IHL as a legal framework. Other foundations with a similar role may be the notion that the parties to an armed conflict do not have an unlimited right to choose methods or means of warfare; the equality of obligation of belligerents; the sharp divide between *jus in bello* and *jus ad bellum*; and, perhaps, the Martens Clause.

Reference to the IHL foundations is often found in the nonbinding part of IHL instruments, namely, in preambles.[11] Some foundations have nonetheless been codified in treaty texts,[12] but their character as such makes it clear that they do not work as legally binding norms.

B. IHL Proportionality Is a Rule, Not a Principle

It is not always clear why a norm is generally referred to as a rule or as a principle. A good example is proportionality, which is often referred to as an IHL principle.[13] It refers to the obligation to refrain from planned attacks, or cancel ongoing ones, in which the expected incidental loss of civilian life, injury to civilians, damage to civilian objects, or a combination thereof, would be excessive in relation to the concrete and direct military advantage anticipated.

Based on the framework set out previously, my conclusion is that this norm is a rule, not a principle, because it is very specific and lacks breadth in its application. The IHL proportionality rule only applies in situations of attacks against military objectives when collateral damage is expected from that attack. That means that the rule is not relevant in military operations other than attacks, although there are a number of other rules in IHL that fulfill a similar function within IHL.[14] Nor is the IHL proportionality rule applicable to attacks when no collateral damage is

11. *E.g.*, the preamble to the 1907 Hague Convention (IV) Respecting the Laws and Customs of War on Land, citing "the interests of humanity" and the preamble to the 1868 St. Petersburg Declaration Renouncing the Use, in Time of War, of Explosive Projectiles Under 400 Grammes Weight, citing the "laws of humanity." The 1977 Additional Protocol I to the Geneva Conventions cites the foundational notion to keep *jus in bello* and *jus ad bellum* separate.

12. *E.g.*, Article 35 of Additional Protocol I (API), which contains the foundational norm that the right of the parties to the conflict to choose methods or means of warfare is not unlimited. Protocol Additional to the Geneva Conventions of 12 August 1949, and Relating to the Protection of Victims of International Armed Conflicts art. 35, June 8, 1977, 1125 U.N.T.S. 3.

13. *E.g.*, Blank & Noone, *supra* note 2, and military manuals of the Netherlands and the United States.

14. *E.g.*, the rule that a naval blockade must be proportionate, *see* San Remo Manual on the International Law Applicable to Armed Conflict at Sea ¶ 102–04 (Louise Doswald Beck ed., 1995). Another example is Article 23(g) of the 1907 Hague Regulations that prohibits "to destroy or seize enemy property unless such destruction or seizure be imperatively demanded

expected. It is in fact quite remarkable that the IHL proportionality rule is often referred to as a principle, since it was not codified until the adoption of the 1977 Additional Protocol I to the Geneva Conventions (API).[15] Although it is only one of the rules that needs to be taken into account in the planning and execution of attacks, it is generally seen as an important IHL rule. This important rule status may be the reason it is often labeled as a IHL principle. Alternatively, proportionality could owe its common understanding as a principle to the wide discretion it permits to military commanders in its application.

It may be argued that the IHL proportionality rule is only one manifestation of a broader principle that also includes precautionary measures. However, the fact that the IHL proportionality rule was drafted and incorporated in the API article as one of the precautions in attack would make the reverse more logical. I would argue that the IHL proportionality rule should be seen as part of a broader precautionary norm. In any case, given the specific nature of the norm, proportionality should not be on our list of principles of IHL.

III. A NEW FRAMEWORK FOR IHL PRINCIPLES

In section II, I argued that military necessity, humanity, chivalry, and proportionality are not IHL principles. Rather, they are either foundations (military necessity, humanity, chivalry) or rules (proportionality) of IHL. So what then are the principles of IHL? In this section, I introduce my proposed list of IHL principles: distinction, precautions, the prohibition on superfluous injury or unnecessary suffering, protection, and humane treatment.

As mentioned earlier, State views on what constitute the key principles of IHL differ. What I propose diverges from what some States, like the Netherlands, have traditionally considered to be the five main IHL principles. A comprehensive proposal is needed which is based on a review of the main functions IHL principles perform. First, to ensure that soldiers are properly prepared for their job, they must be trained in and master a limited number of IHL principles. Second, these IHL principles must also be clear and sufficiently general to find application in the bulk of situations occurring in any type of military operation. As such, the complete body of IHL rules must be covered by these principles. If these principles fail to provide sufficient guidance in a particular situation, the operator must descend to the level of the more specific rules. Therefore, in addition to guidance for the legal limits to the conduct of hostilities, the many protective rules included in the Geneva Conventions should, in my opinion, also be reflected in the list of

by the necessities of war." Convention No. IV Respecting the Laws and Customs of War on Land, Oct. 18, 1907, 36 Stat. 2227, T.S. No. 539.

15. Protocol Additional to the Geneva Conventions of 12 August 1949, and Relating to the Protection of Victims of International Armed Conflicts arts. 51(5)(b) and 57(2)(a)(ii), June 8, 1977, 1125 U.N.T.S. 3.

principles. This perspective is often lacking in sets of IHL principles currently used. Without these protective rules being represented, the principles lack relevance in guiding military forces in planning and executing all types of military operations in accordance with their IHL obligations.

A. Function of IHL Principles

To identify what norms qualify as IHL principles, I suggest we look at the function of IHL principles. There are two main functions. First, that of IHL education and training (for example, the basic IHL course for cadets at the Netherlands Defence Academy is structured in accordance with the five "principles" of military necessity, humanity, distinction, proportionality, and honor and good faith) and second, as guidance for military forces in planning and executing military operations in accordance with their IHL obligations.

1. Educational Purposes: Bring Your Phone, but Use the Principles

During armed conflict, military commanders and soldiers are bound by the rules of IHL. It is the violation of these rules for which they may be held accountable and, in some cases, criminally prosecuted. So why are IHL principles so important for the purposes of IHL education and training?

It is true that today nearly every soldier can install an app on his or her smartphone containing every applicable rule of the Geneva Conventions and other treaties (including even the ICRC collection of customary IHL rules) and bring them to the battlefield for consultation. But this is not how soldiers operate and apply IHL in the midst of combat. It is quite challenging even for IHL scholars to gain complete knowledge and understanding of all IHL rules. While there may be eminent IHL scholars, perhaps including military lawyers, who have mastered IHL, they are usually not the ones deployed in combat. We cannot expect the same level of IHL knowledge from soldiers—not even from those who have completed officers' training. Therefore, it is preferable to use a limited number of IHL principles, which can be easily remembered by any soldier. Although the number of principles may be somewhat subject to personal preferences, adding more than five principles to the list would not seem desirable for educational purposes. Of course, IHL education and training is not an end in itself, but aims to prepare soldiers to do their job on the battlefield within the limits of the law.

2. IHL Principles for Operational Guidance during Armed Conflict

Operational reasons dictate that soldiers must find guidance in IHL principles when planning and conducting their operations. Therefore, the principles must be suitable as a basis for their actions during combat. As such, the IHL principles must cover the (predominantly Hague) rules on the conduct of hostilities. In other words, the principles must provide guidance to solve the most important questions during combat—which persons or objects may be attacked, when, and where, while avoiding or at least minimizing damage and injury to the civilian population? Which methods of warfare may be used? Furthermore, guidance is needed on what protection must be provided to objects and persons if these come under the control of the forces. Thus, the principles must also cover the Geneva law.

B. The Principles

In light of the specific functions of IHL principles, I propose the following list of five principles. The first of these—distinction—is also included in the current list of IHL principles in the 2005 Army Military Manual of the Netherlands, the DoD Law of War Manual and the latest list used by the ICRC in a publication about the application of established IHL principles to cyber operations;[16] the other four differ from these lists. Due to the short nature of this chapter, I will not be able to go into detail on the arguments for each principle. I set this out as a conversation starter.

1. The Principle of Distinction

During combat, soldiers must determine their targets. The specific rule regarding the definition of a military objective is thus important, as are the rules defining combatants and the exception—members of medical personnel and chaplains. Therefore, the first principle soldiers need is the principle of distinction. The importance of this principle is without debate, and it is found in all lists of IHL principles.

2. The Principle of Precautions

While distinction is crucial, it does not paint the complete picture. Connected to distinction is the obligation to protect civilians from the effects of warfare. This requires a specific effort, and therefore, the second IHL principle soldiers need is the principle of precautions. This IHL principle determines what soldiers must do to avoid, or in any event minimize, injury and damage to protected persons and objects. This principle is the basis for active and passive precautions, warnings, and the IHL proportionality rule. As noted earlier, I argue that IHL proportionality is a rule, not a principle. Support for including the principle of precautions in the list can also be derived from a number of authors.[17]

16. Kubo Macak & Tilman Rodenhäuser, *Towards Common Understandings: The Application of Established IHL Principles to Cyber Operations*, ICRC Humanitarian Law and Policy (Mar. 7, 2023), https://blogs.icrc.org/law-and-policy/2023/03/07/towards-common-understandings-the-application-of-established-ihl-principles-to-cyber-operations/.

17. Gary S. Corn, *Precautions to Minimize Civilian Harm Are a Fundamental Principle of the Law of War*, Just Security (July 8, 2015), https://www.justsecurity.org/24493/obligation-precautions-fundamental-principle-law-war/.

3. The Principle Not to Use Means and Methods of a Nature to Cause Superfluous Injury or Unnecessary Suffering

Connected to both previous principles is the question of which means and methods soldiers may use during combat. Therefore, it would be necessary to add to the list of IHL principles one that covers the rules of weapons law and identifies permitted methods of warfare. The principle on which many of the specific rules of this are based is the prohibition on using means and methods of a nature to cause superfluous injury or unnecessary suffering, in addition to the already identified principle of distinction. This principle lies at the basis of many rules with regard to the use of means and methods of warfare, such as the prohibitions on the use of explosive and expansive bullets.[18] This principle can also be applied as guidance to the use of novel methods of warfare that soldiers my improvise on the battlefield to defeat their opponent and that are not specifically regulated.

4. The Principle of Protection

Armed conflict includes active combat, but also less eventful situations, such as that of occupation, to which IHL remains applicable. During both situations, persons and objects come under the control of foreign forces. The universally ratified Geneva Conventions provide detailed rules protecting a multitude of persons and objects. The principle of protection should therefore be added as an IHL principle. It is the basis for specific rules for the protection of wounded, shipwrecked, and sick soldiers; prisoners of war; interned civilians; children; medical installations; cultural property; the natural environment; and so on.

The essence of this principle is that the specific protection to which persons and objects are entitled must be taken into account when they come under the control of the enemy. This is a different situation to that which is already covered by the principle of distinction, which applies mainly during hostilities and often requires soldiers to take active measures. This principle would thus cover the extensive and detailed protection provided by Geneva Law, including, for example, the rules pertaining to the protection of medical installations on land and at sea, those governing the treatment of prisoners of war and detained civilians.

5. The Principle of Humane Treatment

The last IHL principle I propose adding is that of humane treatment. While this has not traditionally been included as an IHL principle, it should be. The rules for the protection of persons codified in the Geneva Conventions and the 1977 Additional Protocols are more elaborate than this principle. But especially in situations of non-international armed conflict, there are only a few specific treaty rules of IHL regulating how persons must be treated. Common Article 3 provides

18. *See* Declaration Renouncing the Use, in Time of War, of Explosive Projectiles Under 400 Grammes Weight, Nov. 29/Dec. 11, 1868, 138 Consol. T.S. 297, 18 Martens Nouveau Recueil (ser. 1) 474, http://www.icrc.org/applic/ihl/ihl.nsf/Article.xsp?action=openDocument&documentId=568842C2B90F4A29C12563CD0051547C; Declaration (IV, 3) Concerning Expanding Bullets, July 29, 1899, 187 Consol. T.S. 459, 26 Martens Nouveau Recueil.

the minimum level of protection owed to any person finding himself or herself in the hands of the adverse party. Therefore, an IHL principle of humane treatment is necessary to remind soldiers that a minimum level of protection is always required. The exact interpretation of the term "humane treatment" is difficult to assess. However, at a minimum, it includes the prohibition of torture and degrading or inhumane treatment. As the ICRC notes:

> The meaning of humane treatment is context specific and has to be considered in the concrete circumstances of each case, taking into account both objective and subjective elements, such as the environment, the physical and mental condition of the person, as well as his or her age, social, cultural, religious or political background and past experiences. In addition, there is a growing acknowledgement that women, men, girls and boys are affected by armed conflict in different ways. Sensitivity to the individual's inherent status, capacities and needs, including how these differ among men and women due to social, economic, cultural and political structures in society, contributes to the understanding of humane treatment under common Article 3.[19]

Many armed forces, including those of the United States and NATO, have proclaimed that they will apply the most important protective IHL rules and principles during all military operations.[20] This includes peace support operations, counterterrorism operations, and operations during which security forces are trained. Outside of armed conflict, the IHL principles regulating the conduct of hostilities are mostly useless. Instead, soldiers may find themselves in situations where they gain control over persons or objects. The principle of protection may thus be unsuitable for these situations. For example, since the definition of combatants is inapplicable outside international armed conflict, there are no specific, detailed protective IHL rules like those protecting prisoners of war. In such circumstances, the principle of humane treatment provides basic guidance. Additional guidance may of course also be found in other applicable legal frameworks in these situations, such as international human rights law.

19. International Committee of the Red Cross, Commentary on the First Geneva Convention: Convention (I) for the Amelioration of the Condition of the Wounded and Sick in the Armed Forces in the Field ¶ 553 (2016).

20. P.A.L. Ducheine & E.H. Pouw, ISAF Operaties in Afghanistan: Oorlogsrecht, doelbestrijding in counterinsurgency ROE, mensenrechten en ius ad bellum 41–44 (2010).

IV. CONCLUSION

In this chapter, I argued that the functions of IHL principles, and a more precise taxonomy of IHL norms into foundations, principles, and rules, would lead to a different set of IHL principles than many States use now. This is because a number of norms that are often referred to as IHL principles are not in fact principles but either a foundation or rule of IHL. Those planning, deciding on, and conducting military operations must adhere to the treaty and customary rules of IHL applicable to them. In addition, I maintain that using the five proposed IHL principles for the purpose of providing general guidance and for educational and training purposes would maximize the chance that military forces comply with the specific IHL rules during armed conflict. The proposed new set of IHL principles includes those of distinction, precautions, the prohibition of employing means and methods expected to cause superfluous injury or unnecessary suffering, the principle of protection, and that of humane treatment. Including these five IHL principles into military manuals of States is therefore encouraged with a view to increase the implementation of IHL.

5

Soft Law: What Is It Good For?

MICHAEL W. MEIER*

I. INTRODUCTION

In a 2012 speech at Georgetown University, Harold Hongju Koh, then the Legal Adviser for the U.S. Department of State, noted that twenty-first-century international legal engagement was no longer limited to those traditional methods such as treaties, executive agreements, and customary international law.[1] Koh noted that international legal engagement today is much more nuanced and it is no longer possible to categorize legal engagement into these three neat little boxes.[2] He described emerging modes of legal engagement as "nonlegal understandings," "layered cooperation," and "diplomatic law talk."[3]

A recent example of the "diplomatic law talk" or "nonlegal understandings" that Koh described occurred on June 17, 2022, when against a backdrop of the Russian invasion of Ukraine that has killed or wounded over 11,000 civilians[4] in a little more than four months, a group of States, the International Committee of the Red Cross (ICRC), and nongovernmental organizations (NGOs) concluded

* Michael Meier is the former senior civilian adviser to the Army Judge Advocate General on matters related to the law of armed conflict.

1. Harold Hongju Koh, *Address: Twenty-First-Century International Lawmaking*, 101 Georgetown Law Journal Online 1, 13 (2012).

2. *Id.*, at 2.

3. *Id.*

4. United Nations Office for the Coordination of Humanitarian Affairs, *Ukraine Situation Report* (July 8, 2022), *available at* https://reliefweb.int/attachments/2b971e48-8750-40d5-92d8-bd862226ed85/Situation Report-Ukraine-8Jul2022.pdf.

Michael W. Meier, *Soft Law: What Is It Good For?* In: *Making and Shaping the Law of Armed Conflict.*
Edited by: Sandesh Sivakumaran and Christian R. Burne, Oxford University Press. © Michael W. Meier 2024.
DOI: 10.1093/oso/9780197775134.003.0005

consultations on the final text of the *Political Declaration on Strengthening the Protection of Civilians from the Humanitarian Consequences Arising from the Use of Explosive Weapons in Populated Areas* (hereinafter the Political Declaration).[5] This Political Declaration, a result of an almost three-year diplomatic effort, seeks to address "the devastating and long-lasting humanitarian impact of the use of explosive weapons in populated areas."[6]

The Political Declaration was formally endorsed by eighty-five States in November 2022 at a conference in Dublin.[7] A review of its language makes it clear that it is not legally binding. This continues the trend over the past decade where international actors increasingly resort to nonbinding political instruments. These quasi-legal instruments, which Koh referenced, are more often referred to as "soft law."

International law has seen a growing number of quasi-legal documents, such as political declarations, guidelines, manuals, codes of conduct, and checklists. Soft law continues to gain recognition and acceptance by international law actors. So what is "soft law" good for? Why do States, international organizations, and other actors in the international community use "soft law" in place of treaties or other legally binding instruments? Importantly, how is it that these instruments, which possess no legal force and do not contain a coercive mechanism, are nevertheless followed and implemented once adopted?

This chapter will look at the role of soft law and explain why and how it has the power to impact international humanitarian law (IHL). Accordingly, this chapter will look at how soft law is used with respect to IHL (also known as the law of war, or law of armed conflict). Section II will address how soft law is defined and how it is viewed by legal scholars who work in international law. Section III will explore why States and other international law actors use soft law as opposed to legally binding instruments. Three examples will be discussed, namely, the decision by States and private industry to address private military contractors through the Montreux Document and Code of Conduct; the Tallinn Manual, which was written by a group of experts, to address cyber issues; and the Political Declaration endorsed by States to address civilian harm related to the use of explosive weapons in populated areas. Finally, Section IV will discuss how to measure the effectiveness of soft law instruments.

5. Department of Foreign Affairs, Ireland, *Political Declaration on Strengthening the Protection of Civilians from the Humanitarian Consequences Arising from the Use of Explosive Weapons in Populated Areas*, https://www.dfa.ie/media/dfa/ourrolepolicies/peaceandsecurity/ewipa/EWIPA-Political-Declaration-Final-Rev-25052022.pdf.

6. Department of Foreign Affairs, Ireland, *Protecting Civilians in Urban Warfare: A Political Declaration on Strengthening the Protection of Civilians from the Humanitarian Consequences Arising from the Use of Explosive Weapons in Populated Areas*, https://dfa.ie./our-role-policies/international-priorities/peace-and-security/ewipa-consultations/.

7. Department of Foreign Affairs, Ireland, *List of Endorsing States, as of 18 November 2022*, https://www.dfa.ie/media/dfa/ourrolepolicies/peaceandsecurity/ewipa/List-of-endorsing-states-18-November-2022.pdf.

II. WHAT IS SOFT LAW?

A. Soft Law Defined

The concept of soft law is not without controversy, and there is considerable disagreement on what it means.[8] Despite the disagreement, soft law will continue to play an important role in international humanitarian law. To understand soft law, it is important to understand what is meant both by "hard law" and "soft law."

Broadly speaking, "hard law" involves standardized governmental rulemaking procedures and outcomes. When trying to determine what constitutes international law, or "hard law," one needs to look no further than Article 38 of the Statute of the International Court of Justice.[9] The International Court of Justice (ICJ)'s function is to decide in accordance with international law such disputes as are submitted to it by member States of the United Nations and those States that have become a party to the ICJ Statute. Article 38 lists sources of international law for the ICJ to apply when deciding disputes. It provides that the ICJ shall apply:

a. international conventions, whether general or particular, establishing rules expressly recognized by the contesting states;
b. international custom, as evidence of a general practice accepted as law;
c. the general principles of law recognized by civilized nations; and
d. subject to the provisions of Article 59, judicial decisions and the teachings of the most highly qualified publicists of the various nations, as subsidiary means for the determination of rules of law.[10]

Although Article 38 is not meant to be an exhaustive list of sources, it does provide the foundation for a discussion of the sources of international law. Article 38 divides the sources of international law into those of a primary and secondary nature. The primary sources are treaties (also known as conventions), customary international law, and general principles of law recognized by civilized nations. Secondary sources are judicial decisions and the teachings of highly qualified publicists.

Treaties are the most prominent source of international law as these legally binding instruments reflect the commitments two or more States have agreed to accept. Customary international law (CIL) reflects the general practices of States, which are accepted as law. There is general agreement that "customary international law develops from a general and consistent practice of States followed by

8. Gregory C. Shaffer & Mark A. Pollack, *Hard vs. Soft Law: Alternatives, Complements and Antagonists in International Governance*, 94 Minnesota Law Review 706 (2010).

9. Statute of the International Court of Justice, art. 38, June 26, 1945, 59 Stat. 1055, 33 U.N.T.S. 993.

10. *Id.*

them out of a sense of legal obligation, or *opino juris*."[11] Whether a particular rule constitutes CIL is ultimately based on this methodology, which must necessarily relate to State practice.[12] Finally, "general principles of law recognized by civilized nations" can be a useful source for the ICJ to rely upon if there is no sufficiently articulated law available. The secondary sources, judicial opinions, and teachings of highly qualified publicists are used to determine international law when it cannot be found in one of the primary sources.

Unlike "hard law," there is no consensus over the definition of "soft law."[13] Kenneth Abbott and Duncan Snidal categorize particular instruments as hard or soft law across a spectrum involving precision, obligations, and delegation to third parties.[14] According to Abbott and Snidal, "'soft law' begins once the legal arrangements are weakened along one or more of the dimensions of obligation, precision and delegation."[15] By contrast, Gary Marchant and Brad Allenby define soft law as "a variety of nonbinding norms and techniques," which include "instruments or arrangements that create substantive expectations that are not directly enforceable, unlike 'hard law' requirements such as treaties and statutes."[16] Another scholar, Dinah Shelton, states that soft law is a "social or political norm rather than legal norm."[17] She continues: soft law "expresses a preference and not an obligation that state[s] should act, or should refrain from acting, in a specified manner."[18] Finally, one of the more recent attempts to define soft law comes from Fionnuala Ní Aoláin, the UN Special Rapporteur on the promotion and protection of human rights and fundamental freedoms while countering terrorism, who states the "most uncontroversial definition" of soft law is that it "constitutes those international norms, principles and procedures that are outside the formal sources of Article 38(1) of the Statute of the International Court of Justice and

11. Letter from John B. Bellinger, III, Legal Adviser, U.S. Dept. of State, and William J. Haynes II, General Counsel, U.S. Dept. of Defense, to Dr. Jakob Kellenberger, President, International Committee of the Red Cross, *Regarding Customary International Law Study* (Nov. 3, 2006), *reprinted in* 46 International Legal Materials 514 (2007).

12. *Id.*

13. Shaffer & Pollack, *supra* note 8, at 712.

14. Kenneth W. Abbott & Duncan Snidal, *Hard and Soft Law in International Governance*, 54 International Organization 421, 421 (2000).

15. *Id.* at 422.

16. Gary E. Marchant & Brad Allenby, *Soft Law: New Tools for Governing Emerging Technologies*, 73 Bulletin of the Atomic Scientists 108, 108 (2017).

17. Dinah L. Shelton, *Soft Law*, *in* Handbook of International Law 3 (2008), https://scholarship.law.gwu.edu/faculty_publications/1049/.

18. *Id.*

lack the requisite degree of normative content to create enforceable rights and obligations but are still able to produce certain legal effects."[19]

These definitions appear to conclude that the principal distinction between hard and soft law is whether the terms of the agreement or other document are binding or not. However, some scholars argue that weak or indeterminate provisions in a binding treaty constitute soft law.[20] These scholars argue that soft law could include the hortatory language commonly found in treaties.[21] In this author's view, this seems problematic. Though certain commitments are drafted in general terms, treaties are binding legal instruments. Almost every treaty contains this type of language, for example in the preamble, and it would be confusing to consider that portion as soft law and the remainder as "hard law."

Ryan Hagemann, Jennifer Huddleston Skees, and Adam Thierer argue that it is "tempting to conclude that the primary distinction between hard and soft law comes down to whether the governance actions in question are binding or enforceable."[22] Hard law are those agreements that, as legally binding instruments, come with the power to sanction those who violate its terms. Soft law lacks that same power.[23] However, even though soft law does not carry the same binding nature, they note that "[s]oft law rarely—if ever—operates absent support from hard law."[24] As discussed later, States have various legitimate reasons for using soft law and complying with the provisions, even though they are not legally binding. Hagemann, Skees, and Thierer argue that the reason soft law works and is followed by States is that hard law options are like "the proverbial Sword of Damocles that hangs in the room while soft law is being formulated."[25] If the goals of the State are not accomplished through soft law, then States will seek to achieve them using hard law.

It is beyond the scope of this chapter to try and resolve the definition of soft law. Therefore, for the purposes of this chapter, "soft law" constitutes those agreements, manuals, or documents that lack the normative content to create enforceable rights and obligations. It functions as a gap filler giving guidance to States and other stakeholders in the absence of legally binding norms.

19. Fionnuala Ní Aoláin (Special Rapporteur on the promotion and protection of human rights and fundamental freedoms while countering terrorism), Report, U.N. Doc. A/74/335, ¶ 8 (Aug. 29, 2019).

20. Shelton, *supra* note 17, at 3.

21. *Id.*

22. Ryan Hagemann, Jennifer Huddleston Skees, & Adam D. Thierer, *Soft Law for Hard Problems: The Governance of Emerging Technologies in an Uncertain Future*, 17 Colorado Technical Law Journal 37, at 45 (2018).

23. *Id.*

24. *Id.*

25. *Id.*

B. Types of Soft Law

There is almost an infinite variety of soft law. For example, the General Assembly of the United Nations, which lacks the authority to adopt binding measures, is a source of soft law.[26] Whereas the UN Security Council, pursuant to Article 25 of the UN Charter, has the power to pass binding commitments, the General Assembly may only initiate studies and make recommendations "promoting international co-operation in the political field and encouraging the progressive development of international law and its codification."[27] Soft law also includes political declarations or other political agreements, guidelines or codes of conduct, technical manuals, recommendations of treaty bodies that provide compliance oversight with treaty obligations, memoranda of understandings, as well as opinions from quasi-judicial bodies, such as commissions of inquiry.[28] Although soft law is often produced or driven by States through bilateral, multilateral, or institutional settings, non-State actors are increasingly contributing to the creation and implementation of soft law.[29] In certain instances, a particular text will simultaneously constitute hard law for some parties and soft law for others. For example, a decision of the European Court of Human Rights or the Inter-American Court of Human Rights will be legally binding on the States that are party to the proceedings before those courts, but for other States parties to the relevant treaty, a decision will constitute soft law.

Soft law can also be categorized as primary and secondary. Primary soft law has been described as those normative texts that are not adopted as treaties or executive agreements that describe substantive commitments that apply to the entire membership of the adopting institution or organization. These instruments may set out new norms or reaffirm existing norms previously set forth in binding or nonbinding texts. Secondary soft law can include decisions of "courts and commissions, decisions of special rapporteurs and other ad hoc bodies, and the resolutions of political organs of international organizations applying primary norms."[30] Much of this secondary soft law is generated by institutions set up under a particular treaty, whose jurisdiction is derived from that treaty and which apply norms related to the same treaty. Secondary soft law has expanded in large part as a consequence of the proliferation of treaty obligations and institutions created to supervise State compliance with them.[31]

26. Shelton, *supra* note 17, at 3; Ní Aoláin, *supra* note 19, at ¶ 13.

27. U.N. Charter art. 13; *see* Shelton, *supra* note 17.

28. *See* Rob McLaughlin & Dale Stephens, *International Humanitarian Law in the Maritime Context: Conflict Characterization in Judicial and Quasi-Judicial Contexts*, *in* APPLYING INTERNATIONAL HUMANITARIAN LAW IN JUDICIAL AND QUASI-JUDICIAL BODIES 103–32 (Derek Jinks, Jackson N. Maogoto, & Solon Solomon eds., 2014).

29. Ní Aoláin, *supra* note 19, at ¶ 13.

30. Shelton, *supra* note 17, at 5.

31. *Id.* at 5.

C. Advantages and Disadvantages of Hard and Soft Law

Soft law has its proper place in international law. States and other international law actors will seek to use all available means to ensure that their aims are achieved. States and other actors recognize that hard law and soft law have different advantages and disadvantages and the choice to use one or the other will depend on a variety of factors. In some contexts, a treaty or binding instrument will be the best solution, while in others a nonbinding agreement will be preferable. At times, a nonbinding agreement could be used as a precursor to a binding agreement.

Hard law has many advantages over soft law. First and foremost, a treaty or other legally binding instrument demonstrates a State's commitment to international law. They are more credible because the State will incur a significant cost if there is a violation of its legal commitment, whether it is through sanctions or the cost of a State's reputation in the international community.[32] Second, a legally binding agreement also creates a domestic legal obligation whether the agreement is "self-executing" or implemented through legislation. This allows a State's domestic audience to mobilize in response to a violation and creates domestic pressure to comply with its commitments. Finally, legally binding agreements normally create mechanisms for monitoring, enforcement, or elaboration of the legal commitments over time. This allows States or other actors to monitor and enforce commitments. This can be done through annual meetings of State parties to international agreements, such as is the case with the Convention on Certain Conventional Weapons (CCW).[33] With the CCW, annual meetings allow for States to address compliance with the convention, develop programs of work for the following year, and consider new issues that States may need to consider.

There are also several disadvantages with hard law. A legally binding agreement can restrict a State's behavior. For example, the Mine Ban Treaty,[34] which prohibits State parties from possessing or using antipersonnel landmines, and the Convention on Cluster Munitions,[35] which prohibits the use of certain cluster munitions, restrict the use of weapons that provide significant military utility. Accordingly, these agreements make it more difficult to adapt to changing political conditions. If a State party to one of these Conventions finds itself in a large-scale combat operation against a peer or near-peer adversary which is not a State party, it may find itself at a disadvantage in the armed conflict. As noted by

32. Shaffer & Pollack, *supra* note 8, at 717–18.

33. Convention on Prohibitions or Restrictions on the Use of Certain Conventional Weapons Which May Be Deemed to Be Excessively Injurious or to Have Indiscriminate Effects, Oct. 10, 1980, 1342 U.N.T.S. 137.

34. Convention on the Prohibition of the Use, Stockpiling, Production and Transfer of Anti-Personnel Mines and on Their Destruction, Sept. 17, 1997, 2056 U.N.T.S. 211.

35. Convention on Cluster Munitions, May 30, 2008, 2688 U.N.T.S. 39.

Gregory Shaffer and Mark Pollack, hard law "is particularly problematic . . . where it presupposes a fixed condition when situations of uncertainty demand constant experimentation and adjustment . . . ."[36]

A second disadvantage of hard law is that there are instances where it is difficult or impossible to conclude an agreement because States' views remain too divergent. This is true with the negotiations among States party to the CCW concerning an extension of the convention to address cluster munitions. From 2004 to 2006, there was a push for a negotiation on a legally binding instrument. At the CCW's Third Review Conference, twenty-six States supported the proposal, but it was rejected. On the last day of the Review Conference, Norway announced it was starting an independent process outside the CCW, which began the Oslo Process resulting in the Convention on Cluster Munitions in December 2008.[37]

Soft law offers advantages over hard law, primarily with respect to speed and flexibility. Nonbinding instruments are often easier and quicker to negotiate as there is less at stake and involves less restriction on a State's behavior as part of the negotiations. As treaties or international agreements are legally binding and require some sort of ratification process, they are much harder to adapt to changing political conditions. By contrast, soft law provides a State with flexibility to adjust to changing conditions. Nonbinding agreements also allow a State to be more ambitious as a political commitment carries less concern with enforcement. As such, there are less serious consequences relating to loss of reputation if there is a failure to comply with the commitment. Importantly, hard law is generally reserved to State actors and non-State actors normally are not parties to binding international agreements or treaties; soft law agreements allow for broader participation by international organizations, NGOs, private companies, and other business organizations.[38]

III. WHY IS SOFT LAW USED

Section II addressed the differences between soft law and hard law as well as the advantages and disadvantages of each one. The use of nonbinding instruments in international law shows no sign of dissipating, but why do States choose soft law over treaties? This section tries to answer that question.

Rarely does soft law occur on its own. As discussed previously, States and other international law actors use a wide range of instruments to achieve their aims.

36. Shaffer & Pollack, *supra* note 8, at 719.

37. Landmine and Cluster Munition Monitor, *How Is the Convention on Cluster Munitions Related to the Negotiations for a Protocol on Cluster Munitions within the Convention of Conventional Weapons?*, THEMONITOR.ORG (Sept. 2019), http://www.the-monitor.org/en-gb/the-issues/faqs/convention-on-cluster-munitions/how-is-the-ccm-related-the-negotiations-for-a-protocol-on-cluster-munitions-within-the-ccw.aspx#.

38. Shaffer & Pollack, *supra* note 8, at 719.

This means that they will look to the instrument which gives them the best advantage based on the circumstances. It often means that hard law and soft law are used together. Hard law and soft law build upon each other in two primary ways: (1) soft law can be a mechanism that leads to the adoption of hard law; and (2) hard law can be subsequently elaborated through soft law.[39]

Shelton concurs that "non-binding norms are often the precursor to treaty negotiations and often stimulate State practice leading to the formation of customary international law."[40] She provides several reasons why States use soft law, such as (1) to crystallize a trend toward a particular norm as a way to override the objections of certain States and help persuade others to develop the norm; (2) to use soft law to consolidate public opinion around the need for action on a particular problem that can lead to the formation of hard law; (3) to fill in gaps in existing treaties; (4) to form State practice that can be utilized to interpret treaties; and (5) as a substitute for hard law when it is unlikely that consensus will be reached on a new treaty.[41]

Insofar as IHL is concerned, although there are many reasons why States choose to use soft law, in this author's view they come down to three major ones. First, soft law will be used by States and other international law actors to elaborate on existing IHL. Second, States recognize that negotiating and adopting a treaty is unlikely to happen and they use soft law to push States to adopt practices and policies that will one day lead to hard law. Finally, in light of emerging technologies, soft law can be a mechanism to fill the gap in the existing law, which may in turn encourage States to explain or, where necessary, create new law with respect to those technologies.

A. Soft Law to Elaborate Existing Law

Soft law instruments are very useful tools for States and other international law actors to help elaborate on existing IHL. There are instances in armed conflict where it becomes apparent that more detailed guidance and "good practices" are needed regarding existing legal obligations. One such instrument is the *Montreux Document on Pertinent International Legal Obligations and Good Practices for States related to Operations of Private Military and Security Companies during Armed Conflict* (the Montreux Document),[42] which was endorsed by seventeen States in September 2008. The Montreux Document is intended to promote

39. *Id.* at 721.

40. Shelton, *supra* note 17, at 7.

41. *Id.* at 8.

42. International Committee of the Red Cross & Swiss Federal Department of Foreign Affairs, *The Montreux Document: On pertinent international legal obligations and good practices for States related to operations of private military and security companies during armed conflict* (2009).

respect for international humanitarian law and human rights law when private military and security companies (PMSCs) are present in armed conflict.

The Montreux Document was adopted in response to the use of PMSCs in Iraq, which is the first instance where the United States extensively used private contractors to protect persons and property.[43] PMSCs were providing security services, such as the protection of individuals, nonmilitary transport convoys, buildings, and other economic infrastructure, as well as the training of Iraqi police and military personnel. There were concerns with transparency and accountability over the use of contractors and whether the activities they were engaged in complied with IHL. By 2007, there were over 100,000 PMSCs in Iraq with almost 1,000 of them Blackwater contractor personnel.[44]

In September 2007, a convoy of Blackwater vehicles was on its way to the site of an earlier car bomb explosion. As they traveled through the neighborhood of Nisour Square, Blackwater guards attempted to stop traffic to allow the vehicles to pass. A Blackwater guard fired at a car that failed to slow down as it approached the Blackwater convoy despite signals to do so. What happened at that point remains in dispute. Some of the PMSCs maintain that they were ambushed by insurgents, who were dressed as civilians and Iraqi officers, and they returned fire in self-defense. Other eyewitness accounts, including bystanders and other Blackwater contractors, claimed that the guards fired recklessly on the crowd. The subsequent investigation revealed that seventeen individuals were killed and another twenty were injured.[45] The Montreux Document was endorsed a year and a day later.

The Montreux Document was negotiated over a three-year period from 2005 to 2008. The process giving rise to the document was initiated by the Swiss government and the ICRC.[46] In addition to the seventeen States involved,[47] there was extensive consultation with the PMSC industry and civil society. The negotiations looked at both hard law and soft law sources, domestic regulations, and industry practices.[48]

43. HEIDI M. PETERS, CONGRESSIONAL RESEARCH SERVICE, R40835 – VERSION 15, THE DEPARTMENT OF DEFENSE'S USE OF PRIVATE SECURITY CONTRACTORS IN AFGHANISTAN AND IRAQ: BACKGROUND, ANALYSIS, AND OPTIONS FOR CONGRESS 2 (May 13, 2011).

44. Dara Lind, *Why Four Blackwater Contractors Were Just Now Convicted of Killing 17 Iraqi Civilians in 2007*, VOX.COM (Oct. 23, 2014), https://www.vox.com/2014/10/23/7047519/blackwater-trial-nisour-square-massacre-2007-guilty-convicted.

45. *Id.*

46. James Cockayne, *Regulating Private Military and Security Companies: The Content, Negotiation, Weaknesses and Promise of the Montreux Document*, 13 JOURNAL OF CONFLICT & SECURITY LAW 401, 402 (2008).

47. At the time of writing, fifty-eight States supported the document. Federal Dept. of Foreign Affairs Switzerland, *Participating States of the Montreux Document* (Jan. 26, 2022), https://www.eda.admin.ch/eda/en/fdfa/foreign-policy/international-law/international-humanitarian-law/private-military-security-companies/participating-states.html.

48. Cockayne, *supra* note 46, at 402–03.

The Montreux Document contains 100 paragraphs of guidance both on "pertinent legal obligations" (Part One) and "good practices" (Part Two) for States dealing with PMSCs.[49] The Preface to the Montreux Document makes clear that it is not a "legally binding instrument" and nothing in the Document "affect[s] existing obligations of States under customary international law or treaty law, including the United Nations Charter."[50] The Preface reinforces the idea that the provisions should not be "interpreted as limiting, prejudicing, or enhancing in any manner existing obligations under international law, or as creating or developing new obligations under international law."[51] Why did the participants choose a nonbinding agreement over a legally binding agreement? The simple answer is that this is what States would accept. The participants signaled early in the process that they would not agree to a document that established binding standards or attempted to describe certain practices as "best" or even "recommended, which is why Part Two deals with "good practice."[52] James Cockayne describes the legal statements in Part One as a "conservative statement of *lex lata*."[53]

It is beyond the scope of this chapter to explore every aspect of the Montreux Document, but it will briefly examine the two parts.[54] Part One contains a statement of the pertinent law (*lex lata*) related to PMSCs during both international and non-international armed conflicts. The statements are drawn from IHL and human rights agreements, such as the Geneva Conventions, the ICRC Study on Customary International Humanitarian Law, and various statements by UN human rights bodies.[55] It sets forth the legal obligations of Contracting States, Territorial States, Home States, All Other States, and PMSCs and their personnel, as well as Superior Responsibility.[56]

Part Two reflects the "good practices" and, therefore, contains provisions that are more expansive than the narrow set of legal obligations of Part One. Instead of relying on sources of international law, the participants looked to other soft law documents, such as corporate codes of conduct, administrative decisions, political statements, as well as judicial decisions and national legislation. The Montreux Document groups statements by contractual, territorial, and home States.[57] States are encouraged to review their own legislation as well as the jurisdiction of the

49. Montreux Document, *supra* note 42, at 11–28.

50. *Id.* at ¶ 3.

51. *Id.* at ¶ 4.

52. Cockayne, *supra* note 46, at 419.

53. Montreux Document, *supra* note 42, at Part Two.

54. For a detailed discussion of the negotiations and analysis of the Montreux Document, this author recommends James Cockayne's analysis, *supra* note 46.

55. Cockayne, *supra* note 46, at 405.

56. Montreux Document, *supra* note 42, at 11.

57. Cockayne, *supra* note 46, at 412.

territory where the PMSC is going to be operating. Many of the statements focus on the authorization of PMSCs to operate in the territorial State as well as focus on accountability and monitoring compliance with each State's law and international law.[58]

Not only do soft law instruments affect the conduct of States, they also have an impact on non-State actors as they too may be able to join and participate in these instruments. The Preface of the Montreux Document states: "That while this document is addressed to States, the good practices may be of value for other entities such as international organizations, NGOs and companies that contract PMSCs, as well as for PMSCs themselves."[59]

The PMSCs that participated as advisors during the negotiation of the Montreux Document acted on this recommendation. They approached the Swiss government and developed the International Code of Conduct for Private Security Service Providers (ICoC), which enables the PMSC industry to apply the Montreux Document's good practices in their operations. The ICoC, which was originally signed by fifty-eight PMSCs in Geneva in November 2010, today includes hundreds of signatory companies that have agreed to adopt it.[60] The ICoC represents the commitment by PMSCs to abide by the obligations set forth in the Montreux Document and implement the recommended good practices of that document. It is a voluntary, industry-led initiative that supports the Montreux Document, but does not impose any obligations on States, which are not parties to the ICoC.[61]

B. Soft Law to Adopt Policies and Practice That Could Lead to Hard Law

States will often adopt soft law texts because they are easier to negotiate or may require frequent changes. However, States will also adopt soft law texts because they realize that there is no political consensus around the topic being discussed. Therefore, the choice is not between a legally binding instrument or a soft law text, but between a nonbinding instrument or no instrument at all.[62] This was the case with respect to the Political Declaration on explosive weapons in populated areas (EWIPA).

58. *Id.*

59. Montreux Document, *supra* note 42, at ¶ 8.

60. Office of the Assistant Secretary of Defense for Sustainment, U.S. Dept. of Defense, *Private Security Companies: International Efforts*, https://www.acq.osd.mil/log/LOG_CSD/psc_International_Efforts.html (last visited Feb. 27, 2023).

61. *Id.*

62. Shelton, *supra* note 17, at 15.

Over the past decade, there have been increasing calls within the international community to address the use of explosive weapons in populated areas.[63] It has been discussed at the UN Security Council, in its debates on the Protection of Civilians and Children and Armed Conflict, as well as at the UN General Assembly First Committee, the CCW, and other fora. Over 100 States, several multilateral organizations, and high-level UN officials, have called for action on EWIPA. In 2019, the ICRC and the UN Secretary-General issued a joint appeal, calling on parties to conflicts to avoid using EWIPA.[64] The ICRC also called on "states and all parties to armed conflict to avoid the use of explosive weapons with a wide impact area in populated areas, owing to the significant likelihood of indiscriminate effects."[65]

Supporters of restrictions on EWIPA recognized that there is no prohibition against attacking military objectives which are located in populated areas, but they argued that it is difficult for such attacks with wide area effects to comply with the prohibitions against indiscriminate and disproportionate attacks.[66] They sought a political commitment to take action and indicated that the best way to ensure compliance with IHL was to avoid the use of explosive weapons in populated areas.[67]

In 2015 and 2019, Austria hosted international conferences on EWIPA and protecting civilians in urban conflict. Ireland then took over the discussions and held several informal consultations in Geneva toward the development of a political declaration to address the humanitarian harm arising from the use of explosive weapons in populated areas. Although in-person consultations were postponed due to COVID-19, in June 2022, States reached consensus and concluded consultations on the final draft Political Declaration.[68]

The Declaration, as a *political* commitment by States, does not impose any new legal obligations on the part of States to do anything more or differently than they are doing right now. That said, the Declaration sets out substantive commitments regarding practical improvements that States can take to ensure

63. International Network of Explosive Weapons (INEW), *Political Response—A Commitment to Avoid the Use of Explosive Weapons with Wide Area Effects in Populated Areas Requires Political Will at the International Level*, INEW.Org, https://www.inew.org/political-response/ (last visited Feb. 26, 2023).

64. Antonio Guterres & Peter Maurer, *The Secretary-General of the United Nations, Antonio Guterres, and the President of the ICRC, Peter Maurer, Issue a Joint Appeal*, ICRC.Org (Sept. 18, 2019), https://www.icrc.org/en/document/explosive-weapons-cities-civilian-devastation-and-suffering-must-stop.

65. ICRC, *Explosive Weapons with Wide Area Effects: A Deadly Choice in Populated Areas* (Jan. 2022), at 12.

66. *Id.* at 84.

67. *Id.* at 150.

68. Political Declaration, *supra* note 5.

better implementation and compliance with their legal obligations under the law of armed conflict (LOAC).

The Political Declaration consists of two parts and four sections. Part A (Sections 1 and 2) constitute the Preamble, while Part B (Sections 3 and 4) is the Operative Section. Section 1.1 sets out the problem, namely, that armed conflicts have become "more protracted, complex, and urbanized," which has in turn increased the risk of harm to civilians. Section 1.1 notes that the risks are caused by a "range of factors, including the use of explosive weapons in populated areas . . . ." Section 1.2 notes that the risks will increase depending on the "weapon's explosive power, its level of accuracy, and the number of munitions used." Section 1.7 provides much of the basis for the operative sections that follow. It states:

> Many armed forces already implement policies and practices designed to avoid, and in any event minimise, civilian harm during hostilities. These can help armed forces to better understand the anticipated effects of explosive weapons on a military target and its surrounding areas, as well as the associated risk to civilians in populated areas. However, there is scope for practical improvements to achieve the full and universal implementation of, and compliance with, obligations under International Humanitarian Law, and the application and sharing of good policies and practices. Broadening and strengthening initiatives designed to share policies and practices on protecting civilians can support the promotion and better implementation of International Humanitarian Law.

Section 2 primarily reaffirms States' obligations under LOAC, including the obligation to hold accountable those who violate LOAC (Section 2.1). Section 2.3 recalls the requirement to comply with LOAC in all circumstances, including when conducting military operations in populated areas. It reiterates the rules and principles of distinction, the prohibitions against indiscriminate attacks and disproportionate attacks, and the obligation to take all feasible precautions by parties to the conflict. Section 2.5 recognizes that "while there is no general prohibition against the use of explosive weapons, any use of explosive weapons must comply with International Humanitarian Law."

The operative provisions of Part B begin in Section 3 with States committing to "strengthening the protections of civilians and civilian objects during and after armed conflict, addressing the humanitarian consequences arising from armed conflict involving the use of explosive weapons in populated areas, and strengthening compliance with and improving the implementation of applicable [LOAC]." The heart of Section 3 is the commitment in Section 3.3, which provides that States will:

> Ensure that our armed forces adopt and implement a range of policies and practices to help avoid civilian harm, ***including by restricting or refraining as appropriate from the use of explosive weapons in populated areas***, when

their use may be expected to cause harm to civilians or civilian objects (emphases added).

There are three important aspects to Section 3.3. First, States commit to adopt and implement a range of policies and practices to help avoid harm to civilians and civilian objects during military operations, which is broader than focusing on explosive weapons in populated areas. It extends to all manner of weapons and means and methods of warfare (e.g., strategies and tactics) that can be used in military operations. Second, this section calls for "restricting or refraining as appropriate" from the use of explosive weapons in populated areas, which is narrower than the calls for States to "avoid the use of explosive weapons with wide area effects in populated areas" from the ICRC,[69] the International Network on Explosive Weapons (INEW),[70] and the United Nations.[71] It strikes a balance between the need to successfully conduct military operations with the enhanced protections for civilians and civilian objects. It does not unnecessarily stigmatize a legitimate and necessary weapon for combat operations by calling for their "avoidance" in populated areas but relies on responsible commanders and operators to use the force needed to accomplish their mission in accordance with LOAC rules and principles. Third, these measures are not limited to situations where the expected harm to civilians may be considered excessive; rather, States commit to take such measures when the use of explosive weapons may be expected to cause incidental harm to civilians and civilian objects at all. This will likely provide more protection than what is required under LOAC principles of proportionality and precautions in attack.

Section 4 deals with how States will implement the policies and practices found in section 3. The heart of this section is Section 4.7, which provides:

> Meet on a regular basis to review in a collaborative spirit the implementation of this Declaration and identify any relevant additional measures that may need to be taken. These meetings could include the exchange and compilation of good policies and practices and an exchange of views on emerging concepts and terminology. The United Nations, the ICRC, other relevant international organisations and civil society organisations may participate in these meetings. We encourage further work, including structured intergovernmental and military-to-military exchanges, which may help to inform meetings on this Declaration.[72]

69. ICRC, *Political Declaration on Strengthening the Protection of Civilians from the Humanitarian Consequences arising from the use of Explosive Weapons in Populated Areas* (June 21, 2022), https://www.icrc.org/en/document/political-declaration-on-explosive-weapons.

70. INEW, *supra* note 63.

71. *Guterres Welcomes Consultations to Protect Civilians Caught in Urban Conflict*, UN News (Mar. 28, 2022), https://news.un.org/en/story/2022/03/1114852.

72. Political Declaration, *supra* note 5, at 4.7.

Section 4 will determine if this political declaration results in enhanced protections for civilians and civilian objects. States that join this Political Declaration are committing to meet on a regular basis and exchange and compile information and views on the protection of civilians. It also includes the participation and support from the United Nations, the ICRC, and NGOs. The outstanding question is whether and how often States will meet on a "regular" basis.

C. Soft Law as a Mechanism to Fill a Gap in the Law

As Shelton noted, soft law can be a tool used to "consolidate political opinion around the need for action on a new problem, fostering consensus that may lead to treaty negotiations or further soft law."[73] Although soft law is often produced or driven by States through bilateral, multilateral, or institutional settings, it is not the exclusive domain of States. Other international law actors, such as academics and other experts, increasingly contribute to the creation and implementation of soft law. These practitioners use soft law to point out gaps in hard law, especially with respect to emerging technologies such as cyber warfare and autonomous weapons systems. This can lead States to explain their interpretation of the law or, if necessary, create new law. One need look no further than the 2013 and 2017 Tallinn Manuals to find such an example.

The *Tallinn Manual on International Law Applicable to Cyber Warfare* (Tallinn Manual 1.0), which was published in 2013, examines the international law applicable to cyber warfare.[74] The *Tallinn Manual 2.0 on the International Law Applicable to Cyber Operations* (Tallinn Manual 2.0), which was published in 2017, expanded the scope of Tallinn Manual 1.0 and examined cyber operations both within and outside of armed conflict.[75] As noted in the introduction to Tallinn Manual 2.0, it "supersedes the first Tallinn Manual."[76]

In 2009, in response to major malicious cyber activities, including the 2007 cyber incident in Tallinn, Estonia, the NATO Cooperative Cyber Defence Centre of Excellence (NATO CCD COE), located in Tallinn, and accredited by NATO as a "Centre of Excellence," invited a group of independent experts (International Group of Experts) to produce a manual on the law applicable to cyber warfare.[77] Over the next several years, the International Group of Experts drafted Tallinn

73. Shelton, *supra* note 17, at 8.

74. Tallinn Manual on International Law Applicable to Cyber Warfare (Michael N. Schmitt ed., 2013) (hereinafter Tallinn Manual 1.0).

75. Tallinn Manual 2.0 on the International Law Applicable to Cyber Operations (Michael N. Schmitt ed., 2017).

76. *Id.* at Introduction, at 2. It includes several modifications to the original rules, a renumbering of the various rules, and inclusion of a new rule.

77. Tallinn Manual 1.0, *supra* note 74, at 1.

Manual 1.0, which analyzed how the *jus ad bellum* and *jus in bello* are applicable to cyberspace. Tallinn Manual 1.0 sets out ninety-five black-letter rules and included commentary for each rule. Part I covered rules on the *jus ad bellum* issues, including sovereignty, State responsibility, the prohibition on the use of force, and self-defense. Part II addressed rules involving *jus in bello* issues, including targeting issues, proportionality, occupation, and neutrality. The rules were adopted by consensus.[78]

In 2009, when the drafters began working on Tallinn Manual 1.0, the major challenge concerned whether international law was applicable to cyber operations and, if so, how. There were divergent views regarding the answer to this question, and States were anxious over the legal ambiguity. At that time, neither customary international law nor treaty law had sufficiently contemplated cyber technology. There are no specific treaty provisions that address "cyber warfare," and there was very little State practice or publicly available expressions of *opinio juris*, so it was extremely difficult to conclude that any cyber-specific customary international law norm existed. There was also a concern that cyber practice could quickly outpace legal understandings.[79] Tallinn Manual 1.0 was produced to help bring some clarity to these legal issues.[80]

Professor Michael Schmitt, in the Introduction to Tallinn Manual 1.0, made it clear that the Manual was not "an official document," but rather "an expression solely of the opinions of the International Group of Experts, all acting in their personal capacity."[81] Tallinn Manual 1.0 did not represent the views of NATO, NATO CCD COE, or any State.

Tallinn Manual 1.0 proved to be an invaluable resource for government practitioners and scholars. In 2013, NATO CCD COE launched the Tallinn Manual 2.0 project, which expanded the scope of the Manual to cyber operations outside of armed conflict.[82] The process for drafting Tallinn Manual 2.0 was much the same, but, unlike Tallinn Manual 1.0 where States were reluctant to participate in the process, in Tallinn Manual 2.0 they were more engaged.[83] The Netherlands hosted the "Hague Process," in which States got together to provide unofficial comments on the working drafts of Tallinn Manual 2.0.[84] The sessions included participation by over fifty States and international organizations, which provided unofficial written comments that helped refine the final text.

78. *Id.*

79. *Id.* at 3.

80. *Id.* at 3–4.

81. *Id.* at 11.

82. Tallinn Manual 2.0, *supra* note 75, at 1.

83. *See* Michael N. Schmitt, *Expert Manuals: An Insider's Account*, in this volume.

84. Tallinn Manual 2.0, *supra* note 75, at 6.

Tallinn Manual 2.0 expanded from two parts and 95 rules to 20 chapters and 154 black-letter rules. It addresses topics such as sovereignty, State responsibility, human rights, law of the sea, air law, space law, telecommunication law, conduct of hostilities, occupation, and neutrality. Each rule, which was again adopted by consensus, includes a commentary on the rule.[85]

The International Group of Experts, which did not include the same members as Tallinn Manual 1.0 since it had a broader scope, again made clear that the intent of Tallinn Manual 2.0 was not to make law or produce a manual that would have the force of law. As the introduction to Tallinn Manual 2.0 states:

> Ultimately, Tallinn Manual 2.0 must be understood only as an expression of the opinions of the two International Groups of Experts as to the state of the law . . . . This Manual is meant as a reflection of the law as it existed at the point of the Manual's adoption by the two International Groups of Experts in June 2016. It is not a "best practices guide", does not represent "progressive development of the law", and is policy and politics-neutral. In other words, Tallinn Manual 2.0 is intended as an objective restatement of *lex lata*.[86]

The International Group of Experts was clear that "international law is made and uniformly interpreted by States."[87] Tallinn Manual 2.0 represented the views of the International Group of Experts and, in terms of the "Hague Process" and the role of States, although the views of States helped refine the text, the text does not necessarily reflect the views of those States.

IV. HOW TO MEASURE IMPLEMENTATION

During the 2006 Third Review Conference of the States Parties to the Convention on Certain Conventional Weapons, States sought to conclude a legally binding protocol on anti-vehicle mines (referred to in CCW as MOTAPM—mines other than antipersonnel mines). Unfortunately, States were unable to reach consensus, so the protocol was not adopted. At the Review Conference, twenty-five States then adopted the nonbinding Declaration on Anti-Vehicle Mines,[88] a political agreement to address the use of anti-vehicle mines.

85. *Id.* at 4.

86. Eric Talbot Jensen, *The Tallinn Manual 2.0: Highlights and Insights*, 48 Georgetown Journal of International Law 736, 738 (2017).

87. Tallinn Manual 2.0, *supra* note 75, at 6.

88. Convention on Certain Conventional Weapons—Third Review Conference, *Declaration on Anti-Vehicle Mines*, CCW/CONF.III/WP.16 (Nov. 17, 2006), https://meetings.unoda.org/meeting/29465/documents.

It is unlikely that there are many who realize that this declaration exists. In fact, when MOTAPM was discussed again in 2011 at the Fourth Review Conference,[89] this author observed that many of the delegates were unaware that the Declaration on Anti-Vehicle Mines existed (let alone whether their State had joined it), even though by 2011 approximately thirty States had endorsed it.[90]

How do soft law instruments, such as the Montreux Document, the Political Declaration on EWIPA, and the Tallinn Manuals, avoid becoming like the Declaration on Anti-Vehicle Mines, which has had minimal impact on the use of anti-vehicle mines? One article has provided a suggested metric to measure whether soft law is effective. It considers three factors when trying to determine effectiveness of a particular instrument: (1) an expressed political commitment; (2) an institutional commitment (or organizational implementation); and (3) a budgetary commitment.[91] Measuring commitment can help distinguish between those soft law instruments that are merely symbolic and those that constitute effective progress.[92] This last section will assess the Montreux Document, the Political Declaration, and the Tallinn Manuals against these three criteria.

A. Expressed Political Commitment

This section will address how States have expressed their political commitment with respect to the Montreux Document, the Political Declaration on EWIPA, and the Tallinn Manuals. As each of these three soft law instruments are different, the political expression is also different. The Montreux Document was adopted by States in 2008; as such, this section will look at States' responses since its adoption. By contrast, the Political Declaration was just concluded. Many of the commitments are prospective, and this section will look at the actions that States will need to take going forward. The Tallinn Manuals have been clear that they were intended to reflect the views of an international group of experts and not the view of any particular State. Accordingly, this section will look at how State behavior has evolved due to the publication of the Tallinn Manuals.

89. Convention on Certain Conventional Weapons—Fourth Review Conference (2011), https://meetings.unoda.org/meeting/ccw-revcon-2011/.

90. Convention on Certain Conventional Weapons—Fourth Review Conference, *Mines Other Than Anti-personnel Mines (MOTAPM)*, CCW/CONF.IV/MC.I/INF.1 (Nov. 14–25, 2011), http://daccess-ods.un.org/access.nsf/Get?Open=&JN=G1164701.

91. Ashley M. Fox et al., *Measuring Political Commitment and Opportunities to Advance Food and Nutrition Security: Piloting a Rapid Assessment Tool*, 30 Health Policy and Planning 566, 569 (2015).

92. *Id.* at 569.

1. Montreux Document

Since the adoption of the Montreux Document in 2008 by seventeen States, support has continued to grow. As of the date of this chapter, participation has grown to fifty-eight States and three international organizations.[93] Although participation in the Montreux Document has tripled, there are still a significant number of States that are not part of this process. Further, many of the States that do participate in the Montreux Document are in Europe, with only small representation by African, Asian, and Latin American countries.[94] In order to be truly effective, representation will need to continue to expand, especially in these areas of the world.

2. Political Declaration on EWIPA

There were approximately sixty-five States involved in the consultations on EWIPA, including most NATO members, Australia, New Zealand, Israel, Mexico, Chile, and China.[95] States such as Russia and Syria were not part of the consultations. The first test on whether there is political commitment by States came in November 2022 when the Political Declaration was formally opened for endorsement at the signing ceremony held in Dublin, Ireland. That meeting saw eighty-three States, including the United States,[96] formally adopt the Declaration.[97]

Although it is important that the United States and the other eighty-two States endorsed the Political Declaration, other States that did not participate in the consultations, such as Russia, Syria, and Saudi Arabia among others, have not endorsed the Declaration. These States, often rightfully so, have faced heavy criticism for failing to protect civilians from the harmful effects of armed conflict.

If additional States choose not to endorse the Political Declaration, is it possible to implement true change for the protection of civilians? Without more States willing to accept the Declaration, it risks similar criticism to the Convention on Cluster Munitions (CCM). The CCM has 110 States parties, but it does not

93. Montreux Document Forum, *Participating States and International Organizations*, MONTREUXDOCUMENT.ORG, https://www.montreuxdocument.org/about/participants.html.

94. GENEVA CENTRE FOR THE DEMOCRATIC CONTROL OF ARMED FORCES, THE MONTREUX DOCUMENT: A MAPPING STUDY ON OUTREACH AND IMPLEMENTATION (2017), 4, https://www.montreuxdocument.org/resources/publications.html.

95. Reaching Critical Will, Statements from the Political Declaration Process on Explosive Weapons in Populated Areas, REACHINGCRITICALWILL.ORG, https://reachingcriticalwill.org/disarmament-fora/ewipa/political-declaration/statements#ewipa2021.

96. Charles Trumbull, Deputy Legal Adviser, U.S. Mission Geneva, Remarks at Final Consultation on the Draft Political Declaration on Strengthening the Protection of Civilians from the Humanitarian Consequences Arising from the Use of Explosive Weapons in Populated Areas (June 17, 2022), transcript available at https://geneva.usmission.gov/2022/06/21/protecting-civilians-in-urban-warfare/ ("The United States, which played an integral role in the discussions, stated it was "pleased to announce that we are prepared to endorse the [draft political Declaration]. . . . We hope and expect that this Declaration will help States improve the protection of civilians and reduce human suffering in armed conflict").

97. DFA Ireland, *supra* note 7.

include the major users or producers of cluster munitions, such as the United States, Russia, Israel, India, or China. Although this is not to suggest that the CCM has had no impact on the use of cluster munitions, especially since it has led to the destruction of more than 1.5 million cluster munitions,[98] the United States alone has more than 4.7 million cluster munitions[99] in its inventory. Therefore, in order to achieve progress in the protection of civilians, the Declaration needs to be endorsed by the widest possible number of States, especially those that cause the greatest concern about harm to civilians and civilian objects.

3. Tallinn Manuals

As noted in Professor Schmitt's Introduction to Tallinn Manual 2.0, States kept their distance from the work of the International Group of Experts during Tallinn Manual 1.0. Although there was an observer from U.S. Cyber Command during the process, there remained limited State involvement.[100] By the time Tallinn 2.0 came around, there was more State involvement. For example, the Netherlands Ministry of Foreign Affairs hosted the so-called "Hague Process," where States convened to comment on the working draft. Over the three sessions held in The Hague, more than fifty State delegations and other international organizations gathered to provide comments.[101] Certain States also provided unofficial written comments that were used to shape the text.

In addition, Professor Schmitt noted that during the Tallinn 2.0 process, there were still very few States that had made official statements regarding how international law applies in cyberspace. Since its publication, there have been many such statements with "impressive granularity," which will be used as the International Group of Experts looks to launch Tallinn Manual 3.0.[102]

Over the past decade since the release of Tallinn Manual 1.0, it has become clear that many States and practitioners have come to see the Tallinn Manuals as a valuable resource. However, as the drafters noted, States make law, and they have taken up the challenge posed by the Tallinn Manuals. Where there was once minimal evidence available of State views, there are now many official statements,

98. Mary Wareham, *Treaty Banning Cluster Munitions Turns 10, but Without the US*, Just Security (July 31, 2020), https://www.justsecurity.org/71756/treaty-banning-cluster-munitions-turns-10-but-without-the-us/.

99. United States Cluster Munition Ban Policy, Landmine & Cluster Munition Monitor, http://www.the-monitor.org/en-gb/reports/2022/united-states/cluster-munition-ban-policy.aspx (last visited Feb. 27, 2023).

100. Tallinn Manual 2.0, *supra* note 75, at 6.

101. *Id.*

102. Charlie Dunlap, *International Law and Cyber Ops: Q&A with Mike Schmitt about the Status of Tallinn 3.0*, Lawfire.com (Oct. 3, 2021), https://sites.duke.edu/lawfire/2021/10/03/international-law-and-cyber-ops-q-a-with-mike-schmitt-about-the-status-of-tallinn-3-0/.

documents, and speeches that reflect their interpretation of international law for cyberspace.[103]

B. Organizational Implementation

Once there is a commitment at the political level with respect to soft law instruments, organizational implementation focuses on the steps States take to actually implement the political commitments mentioned previously. For example, what steps have private industry taken to comply with the provisions of the Montreux Document? How will the United States implement the Declaration on EWIPA? Finally, with the Tallinn Manuals, what steps have States taken to address how international law applies in cyberspace?

1. Montreux Document

Following the adoption of the Montreux Document, States created the Montreux Document Forum (MDF), which seeks to support national implementation of the Document. The MDF is responsible for planning annual plenary meetings and working groups.[104]

The MDF also engages with States and international organizations to help implement the Montreux Document. For example, the UN Department of Safety and Security (UNDSS) has integrated the practices of the Montreux Document in its *Guidelines on the Use of Armed Private Security Companies*.[105] The Economic Community of West African States (ECOWAS) has encouraged member States to become participants to the Montreux Document in its *Policy Framework on Security Sector Reform and Governance*.[106] Further, organizations such as the Organization for Security and Co-operation in Europe (OSCE), the European Union, and NATO have adopted policy documents relating to regulation or procurement of private security services.[107]

103. *See* Michael Schmitt, *Canada Takes on International Law in Cyberspace*, EJIL: Talk (July 14, 2022), https://www.ejiltalk.org/canada-takes-on-international-law-in-cyberspace/.

104. Montreux Document Forum, *The Forum*, Montreuxdocument.org, https://www.montreuxdocument.org/about/the-forum.html.

105. United Nations Department of Safety and Security, *Guidelines on the Use of Armed Security Services from Private Security Companies* (Nov. 8, 2012), https://www.ohchr.org/Documents/Issues/Mercenaries/WG/StudyPMSC/GuidelinesOnUseOfArmedSecurityServices.pdf.

106. Economic Community of West African States, *Policy Framework on Security Sector Reform and Governance*, ¶ 36 (June 4, 2016), https://ecowas.int/wp-content/uploads/2022/08/ecowas-policy-framework-on-ssrg-english-adopted-1.pdf.

107. Montreux Document Forum, *A Mapping Study on the Montreux Document Outreach and Implementation*, 22 (2017), *citing* Emmylou Boddi, Anna Marie Burdzy, & Nelleke van Amstel, Putting Private Security Regulation into Practice: Sharing Good Practices on Procurement and Contracting 2015–2016: A Scoping Study (Geneva: DCAF, 2016);

There also was a recognition that PMSCs themselves needed to be included to effectively regulate this industry. This recognition led to the creation of the International Code of Conduct for Private Security Service Providers (ICoC).[108] The ICoC requires companies to comply with the Montreux Document principles, include them in personnel contracts, and not enter into any contracts where the terms of performance would conflict with the principles. By 2013, the number of signatory companies increased to over 700.[109] In 2013, the International Code of Conduct Association (ICOCA) was formed with representation from governments, civil society, and industry to provide a governance and oversight mechanism of the ICoC.[110] As opposed to being limited to signatory companies as there were with the ICOC, the ICOCA consists of States, industry partners including companies, and civil society. As of 2022, there are 246 members of the ICOCA.[111]

As an instrument that is focused both on States and PMSCs, the creation of the ICoC and ICoCA were important steps in ensuring the participation by private industry in supporting these principles. It is important that PMSCs' participation in the ICoCA continues to grow.

The U.S. support for the Montreux Document and the ICoC/ICOCA has remained active since its inception. The Department of Defense (DoD) continues to promote the MDF and provide an informal consultative arrangement whereby participants in the Montreux Document process can share information, review best practices, work to ensure consistency in national legislation, provide State oversight of the International Code of Conduct initiative, and review application of the goals of the Montreux Document to conditions other than armed conflict and for non-State purchasers of covered services. It has implemented various policies, directives, and instructions with respect to PMSCs to ensure compliance.[112]

for the EU, *see* Council of the European Union, *EU Concept for Contractor Support to EU-led military operations*, EEAS 00754/14, Brussels, Apr. 4, 2014; for NATO, *see* NATO, *Policy on Contractor Support to Operations C-M(2007)0004*, Jan. 12, 2007; NATO, *ACO Directive concerning the contracting with Private Security companies*, No. 060–101, May 16, 2014.

108. Nelleke Van Amstel & Tilman Rodenhauser, *The Montreux Document and the International Code of Conduct: Understanding the Relationship between International Initiatives to regulate the Global Private Security Industry*, DCAF.ORG (2016), 7, https://www.montreuxdocument.org/pdf/DCAF-PPPs-Series-Paper_The-MD-and-ICoC-Understanding-the-Relationship.pdf.

109. *Id.*

110. The International Code of Conduct Association, *About*, https://icoca.ch/about/ (last visited Feb. 27, 2023).

111. *Id.* at Members. The ICoCA includes 7 governments, 117 Private Security Companies, 50 civil society organizations, and 72 observers.

112. Office of the Assistant Secretary of Defense for Sustainment, *supra* note 60.

2. Political Declaration on EWIPA

The endorsement by States of the Political Declaration in November 2022 is merely the first step in helping further avoid civilian harm. It will be important to look to the measures that States undertake at an institutional level. This means that States must ensure that their military departments enact policies and practices that strengthen the protection of civilians in a meaningful way. For example, the United States has already begun to address civilian harm both through efforts within the DoD as well as new legislative proposals.

On January 27, 2022, Secretary of Defense Lloyd Austin directed DoD to take measures to improve its civilian harm mitigation and response. These measures included providing him with a Civilian Harm Mitigation and Response Action Plan (CHMR-AP),[113] which was released on August 25, 2022.[114] The CHMR-AP lays out a series of actions that DoD will implement to mitigate and respond to civilian harm. Importantly, it establishes a Civilian Protection Center of Excellence to institutionalize practices and tools for preventing, mitigating, and responding to civilian harm. Additionally, DoD is also finalizing its Instruction on Civilian Harm, which is expected to be released soon after the CHMR-AP is complete.[115]

Just as the United States appears to be moving forward to implement policies and procedures on civilian harm, it is important other States do the same. For example, Belgium noted the strength of the Declaration rests with the follow-up actions that States take. It committed to exchanging best practices and other actions to ensure implementation.[116] The United Kingdom noted that it would review its policies and procedures already in place and improve them where necessary to effectively implement the Declaration.[117] If other States that endorsed the Declaration take similar steps and participate in the regular meetings contemplated in Section 4.7 of the Declaration, then there can be the organizational implementation necessary to ensure true progress on avoiding civilian harm.

113. Memorandum from the Secretary of Defense to the Secretaries of the Military Departments et al. on Improving Civilian Harm Mitigation and Response (Jan. 27, 2022), https://media.defense.gov/2022/Jan/27/2002928875/-1/-1/1/DEPARTMENT%20OF%20DEFENSE%20RELEASES%20MEMORANDUM%20ON%20IMPROVING%20CIVILIAN%20HARM%20MITIGATION%20AND%20RESPONSE.PDF.

114. U.S. Department of Defense, *Civilian Harm Mitigation and Response Action Plan Fact Sheet* (Aug. 25, 2022), https://www.defense.gov/News/Releases/Release/Article/3140007/civilian-harm-mitigation-and-response-action-plan-fact-sheet/.

115. *Id.*

116. Statement by Belgium, *Statement at the Adoption of the Political Declaration on Strengthening the Protection of Civilians from the Humanitarian Consequences Arising from the Use of Explosive Weapons in Populated Areas* (Nov. 18, 2022), https://www.dfa.ie/media/dfa/ourrolepolicies/peaceandsecurity/ewipa/Belgium.pdf.

117. Statement by United Kingdom, *Dublin Conference to Adopt the Political Declaration on Explosive Weapons in Populated Area* (Nov. 18, 2002), https://www.dfa.ie/media/dfa/ourrolepolicies/peaceandsecurity/ewipa/United-Kingdom.pdf.

3. Tallinn Manuals

Over the past decade, States have begun to speak out on international law in cyberspace. The United States, beginning in 2012, offered its views on international law in speeches and statements. In 2018, the United Kingdom's Attorney General expressed its view.[118] In 2021, as part of the UN Group of Governmental Experts 2019–2021 report on State behavior in cyberspace,[119] thirteen additional States[120] joined the United States and the United Kingdom in contributing to the official compendium of voluntary national contributions.[121] There are also ongoing efforts at the United Nations and other regional fora such as the Organization of American States.[122]

Domestically, the United States has released a series of documents on cyberspace, such as the 2011 International Strategy for Cyberspace, the 2012 Presidential Policy Directive 20, the 2015 and the revised 2018 DoD Cyber Strategy, and the 2018 National Cyber Strategy.[123] Importantly, the National Cyber Strategy stressed that "international law and voluntary non-binding norms" help define acceptable State behavior and lead to predictability and stability in cyberspace.[124] It also called on other States to "publicly affirm these principles" through outreach and multilateral engagement.

118. Jeremy Wright KC MP, United Kingdom Attorney General, Speech at Chatham House Royal Institute for International Affairs: Cyber and International Law in the 21st Century (May 23, 2018), https://www.gov.uk/government/speeches/cyber-and-international-law-in-the-21st-century.

119. *Report of the Group of Governmental Experts on Advancing Responsible State Behaviour in Cyberspace in the Context of International Security* ¶ 73, U.N. Doc. A/76/135, July 14, 2021, https://undocs.org/en/A/76/135.

120. These States included Australia, Brazil, Estonia, Germany, Japan, Kazakhstan, Kenya, Netherlands, Norway, Romania, Russian Federation, Singapore, and Switzerland.

121. *Official compendium of voluntary national contributions on the subject of how international law applies to the use of information and communications technologies by States submitted by participating governmental experts in the Group of Governmental Experts on Advancing Responsible State Behaviour in Cyberspace in the Context of International Security established pursuant to General Assembly Resolution 73/266*, U.N. Doc. A/76/136, July 13, 2021, https://ccdcoe.org/uploads/2018/10/UN_-Official-compendium-of-national-contributions-on-how-international-law-applies-to-use-of-ICT-by-States_A-76-136-EN.pdf.

122. Duncan Hollis, *A Brief Primer on International Law and Cyberspace*, Carnegie Endowment for International Peace (2021), https://carnegieendowment.org/2021/06/14/brief-primer-on-international-law-and-cyberspace-pub-84763.

123. Michael N. Schmitt, *The Defense Department's Measured Take on International Law in Cyberspace*, Just Security (Mar. 11, 2020), https://www.justsecurity.org/69119/the-defense-departments-measured-take-on-international-law-in-cyberspace/.

124. *Id.*

C. Budgetary Commitment

The final critical component in ensuring whether a soft law instrument will be effective is whether States will commit financial resources against it. States must be willing to provide sufficient assets, such as personnel and funding, in order to ensure that States and other actors have the proper resources to address the issue.

1. Montreux Document

The United States is one of the seven governments that is part of the ICoCA.[125] Domestically, the United States has implemented private security company elements within U.S. law and policies. These specific elements include the determination of services, selection and vetting of PSCs, accounting for weapons and other materiel, use of force, training, and applicability of Host Nation Law. Other elements of national law and standard clauses required by the Federal Acquisition Regulations and Defense supplements apply to all contractors accompanying the force or providing operational support. These laws and implementing clauses cover elements such as anti–human trafficking, other personnel welfare provisions, measures against bribery and corruption, and contract management and oversight.[126] Accordingly, the United States continues to commit financial resources through its membership in the ICoCA and to ensure those commitments are incorporated into U.S. government contracts.

As noted previously, PMSCs that have agreed to adopt the ICoC also are required to ensure that its provisions are incorporated into contracts and to refrain from taking contracts that would not comply with these provisions.

2. Political Declaration on EWIPA

States must dedicate the necessary resources to enhance the protection of civilians in armed conflict. Sections 3 and 4 of the Political Declaration contain several provisions that require the commitment of financial resources, such as ensuring comprehensive training of States' armed forces, providing or facilitating assistance to victims and communities impacted by armed conflict, and committing resources for the regular meetings of States which have endorsed the Declaration. Failure to dedicate the necessary resources will limit the impact the Declaration will have on enhancing the protection of civilians.

With respect to the Political Declaration, the budgetary commitment relates to the "regular" meetings that are set forth in Section 4.7. What does "meet on a regular basis" mean?[127] Will it be more than once a year, an annual meeting, or something less frequent? At least initially, if the meetings occur only once a year, it will be hard to envision an effective outcome. For example, in the CCW process,

125. *See* ICoCA, *supra* note 110.

126. Office of the Assistant Secretary of Defense for Sustainment, *supra* note 60.

127. Political Declaration, *supra* note 5, at 4.7.

there are multiple meetings during the year prior to the annual meeting where decisions are often made. A similar arrangement of meetings of States which have endorsed the Declaration will be required to adequately address civilian harm. A suitable budget will therefore be necessary.

The United States, through the CHMR-AP discussed previously, appears willing to make the necessary budgetary commitment. For example, resources will be necessary to establish the Civilian Protection Center of Excellence. Staff will need to be hired to fill positions, standardized operational reporting and data management must be developed, and analysis and integration of the lessons learned from civilian casualty events and various investigations must be undertaken.[128]

3. Tallinn Manuals

With respect to the necessary budgetary commitment, the NATO CCD COE continues to support the Manuals, especially with the launch of the preparation of Tallinn Manual 3.0 in 2021. The project continues to grow larger with more participation by States and academia. Since the release of Tallinn Manual 2.0, the academic community has increased its writings on cyber issues. Accordingly, the NATO CCD COE started a second project to gather all relevant papers on the topic.[129]

States also continue to make investments in this realm through the adoption of cyber policies. Though it is unclear whether these investments are directly or indirectly a result of the Tallinn Manuals, since their publication States are increasingly focused on cyber issues. For example, the U.S. Army established Army Cyber in 2010. As the Army component for U.S. Cyber Command, its mission is to conduct cyberspace, electromagnetic warfare, and information operations to ensure freedom of action for friendly forces in the cyber domain, while denying the same to U.S. adversaries.[130] Over the past decade, the command has grown to over 16,500 uniform and civilian personnel who deliver offensive and defensive cyberspace efforts.[131] As cyberspace continues to grow in importance, States will need to continue to resource their offensive and defensive capabilities in this critical domain.

128. Department of Defense, *Civilian Harm Mitigation and Response Plan (CHMR-AP)*, 6 (Aug. 25, 2022), https://media.defense.gov/2022/Aug/25/2003064740/-1/-1/1/CIVILIAN-HARM-MITIGATION-AND-RESPONSE-ACTION-PLAN.PDF.

129. Dunlap, *supra* note 102.

130. U.S. Army Cyber Command, *History*, https://www.arcyber.army.mil/About/History/ (last visited Feb. 27, 2023).

131. *Id.*

V. CONCLUSION

This chapter began with the question of what is "soft law" good for? Why do States, international organizations, and other actors in the international community use "soft law" in place of treaties or other legally binding instruments? Although some scholars may disagree, it is clear that there is an important role for soft law. It serves as an effective tool when States and non-State actors want to elaborate on existing international law. In today's polarized environment, it is hard to gain consensus that would lead to a treaty. Therefore, States must choose between taking no action or adopting practices and policies that may one day lead to hard law. Finally, as the Tallinn Manuals have demonstrated, soft law can be a mechanism to fill a gap in the law and encourage States to explain their views on the law or, if necessary, create new law with respect to emerging technologies.

In creating soft law, there needs to be a way to measure its effectiveness. One such method is to look at the political, institutional, and budgetary commitments States are willing to make with respect to the agreements. If those are made, the query of "what is it good for?" can be answered positively. This is true with the Montreux Document and the Tallinn Manuals. It remains to be seen with the Political Declaration on EWIPA. Ambassador Michael Gaffey of Ireland did a tremendous job leading the discussions on the Declaration that eighty-five States have now endorsed. It remains to be seen whether additional States will endorse the Declaration, particularly those States that did not engage in the consultations. Moving forward, we will be able to better measure whether this Declaration will enhance the protection of civilians in armed conflict based on whether those endorsing States make the political, institutional, and budgetary commitments necessary to implement it. If they do, then we may see true progress for mitigating civilian harm. If they do not, then this Declaration will be like other soft law instruments that are soon forgotten in history.

PART THREE

Actors and Influences

6

Expert Manuals: An Insider's Account

MICHAEL N. SCHMITT*

I. INTRODUCTION

Expert manuals are in vogue. The modern "round" of manual projects commenced with the 1995 publication of the International Institute of Humanitarian Law's *San Remo Manual on Armed Conflicts at Sea*.[1] In 2006, the Institute also published the *Manual on the Law of Non-International Armed Conflict* (*NIAC Manual*).[2]

Since then, other significant manual projects include: Harvard's 2010 *Manual on the International Law Applicable to Air and Missile Warfare* (*AMW Manual*);[3] the NATO Cooperative Cyber Defence Centre of Excellence sponsored 2013 *Tallinn Manual on the International Law Applicable to Cyber Warfare* (*Tallinn Manual 1.0*)[4] and 2017 *Tallinn Manual 2.0 on the International Law Applicable to*

* Michael N. Schmitt is the G. Norman Lieber Distinguished Scholar at West Point's Lieber Institute; Professor of Public International Law at the University of Reading (UK); and Professor Emeritus and Charles H. Stockton Distinguished Scholar-in-Residence at the United States Naval War College.

1. San Remo Manual on International Law Applicable to Armed Conflicts at Sea (Louise Doswald Beck ed., 1995).

2. Michael N. Schmitt, Charles H.B. Garraway, & Yoram Dinstein, The Manual on the Law of Non-International Armed Conflict with Commentary (2006).

3. Program on Humanitarian Policy and Conflict Research at Harvard University, Commentary on the HPCR Manual on International Law Applicable to Air and Missile Warfare (2010).

4. Tallinn Manual on the International Law Applicable to Cyber Warfare (Michael N. Schmitt gen. ed., 2013) [hereinafter Tallinn Manual 1.0].

Michael N. Schmitt, *Expert Manuals: An Insider's Account* In: *Making and Shaping the Law of Armed Conflict*.
Edited by: Sandesh Sivakumaran and Christian R. Burne, Oxford University Press. © Michael N. Schmitt 2024.
DOI: 10.1093/oso/9780197775134.003.0006

Cyber Operations;[5] the International Society for Military Law and the Law of War's 2017 *Leuven Manual on the International Law Applicable to Peace Operations*;[6] and the Norwegian Ministry of Defense supported 2020 *Oslo Manual on Select Topics of the Law of Armed Conflict*.[7] Additional projects are underway, including two space law manuals (*Manual on International Law Applicable to Military Uses of Outerspace*[8] and *Woomera Manual on the International Law Applicable to Space Operations*[9]), the *Newport Manual on the Law of Naval Warfare* sponsored by the Naval War College's Stockton Center,[10] and *Tallinn Manual 3.0*.[11]

These efforts involve ad hoc expert groups of varying sizes comprised of academics and former or present practitioners. Government legal advisers participate in most of them, although typically in their personal capacity. Such projects usually produce consensus "rules," which are meant to restate existing treaty and, more often, customary law. Commentary explaining the source of each rule accompanies them. That commentary constitutes the normative heart of the publications, for it is there that interpretive nuance is addressed and unsettled issues are identified.

Expert manuals are not an entirely modern phenomenon. In 1874, fifteen European States gathered to consider a draft treaty on the law of war prepared by the government of Russian Tsar Alexander II. The resulting Brussels Declaration[12] was not ratified but did motivate the Institut de Droit International to establish a committee to study the Declaration. Its work led in 1880 to the Institute's adoption at Oxford of the *Manual of the Laws and Customs of War*.[13]

5. Tallinn Manual 2.0 on the International Law Applicable to Cyber Operations (Michael N. Schmitt gen. ed., 2017).

6. Leuven Manual on the International Law Applicable to Peace Operations (Terry Gill, Dieter Fleck, & William H. Boothby eds., 2017).

7. Oslo Manual on Select Topics of the Law of Armed Conflict (Yoram Dinstein & Arne Dahl eds., 2020)

8. *See* description at *Manual on International Law Applicable to Military Uses of Outer Space*, McGill University, https://www.mcgill.ca/milamos/about#:~:text=The%20McGill%20Manual%20on%20International,of%20force%20in%20outer%20space.

9. *See* description at *The Woomera Manual*, Adelaide Law School, https://law.adelaide.edu.au/woomera/.

10. Newport Manual on the Law of Naval Warfare (James Kraska, gen. ed., 2023).

11. Tallinn Manual 3.0 on the International Law Applicable to Cyber Operations (Michael Schmitt, Liis Vihul, & Marko Milanovic eds., forthcoming 2026).

12. Project of an International Declaration concerning the Laws and Customs of War, Brussels, Aug. 27, 1874, *reprinted in*The Laws of Armed Conflicts 23 (Dietrich Schindler & Jiri Toman eds., 4th ed. 2004).

13. Institute of International Law, The Laws of War on Land (1880) (Oxford Manual), reprinted in The Laws of Armed Conflicts 29 (Dietrich Schindler & Jiri Toman eds., 4th ed. 2004).

Demonstrating the normative influence a manual can wield, the Oxford Manual, together with the Brussels Declaration, served as the basis for the 1899 Hague Convention II[14] and 1907 Hague Convention IV[15] on the laws and customs of land warfare and their annexed Regulations. The International Court of Justice (ICJ) acknowledged the customary law status of the Regulations in its 1996 *Nuclear Weapons* Advisory Opinion,[16] as the Nuremberg Tribunal had for the 1907 Hague IV Regulations.[17] The ICJ characterized them as "fundamental rules" that reflect "intransgressible principles of international customary law."[18]

Manual writing continued in the early years of the twentieth century. The 1907 Peace Conference that had produced Hague Convention IV agreed "that the preparation of regulations relative to the laws and customs of naval war should figure in the programme of the next Conference."[19] In response, the Institut de Droit International appointed a committee to consider scholarly work in the field and organize discussions on the subject. These led to the preparation of the 1913 *Oxford Manual of the Laws of Naval Warfare*,[20] similar to its 1880 counterpart on land warfare. Although it did not form the basis for subsequent treaty law, the manual's influence on the law of naval operations proved significant, as would that of the *San Remo Manual* as the century was coming to a close.

In this chapter, I offer my reflections as a participant in four manual projects: the *NIAC Manual*, *AMW Manual*, and both *Tallinn Manuals*. I served on the drafting team of the first two and as director of the *Tallinn Manuals* effort. Of them, *Tallinn Manual 2.0* has proven to be the most influential for reasons I suggest later.

The chapter begins with a discussion of the de jure status of expert manuals under international law. As will be explained, the work of scholars and other international law experts exerts particular influence on the interpretation of international law rules. I then examine how manuals can influence international law in practice, drawing in particular on how the *Tallinn Manuals* (especially 2.0) have affected discourse among States regarding the application of international

14. Convention No. II with Respect to the Laws and Customs of War on Land, July 29, 1899, 32 Stat. 1803, T.S. No. 403.

15. Convention No. IV Respecting the Laws and Customs of War on Land, Oct. 18, 1907, 36 Stat. 2227, T.S. No. 539.

16. Legality of the Threat or Use of Nuclear Weapons, Advisory Opinion, 1996 I.C.J. 226, ¶ 80 (July 8).

17. Trial of the Major War Criminals, 14 November 1945–1 October 1946, Nuremberg, 1947, Vol. 1, at. 254.

18. Nuclear Weapons, *supra* note 16, ¶ 79.

19. *Manual of the Laws of Naval War (Background)*, ICRC Database, https://ihl-databases.icrc.org/ihl/INTRO/265?OpenDocument.

20. Institute of International Law, The Law of Naval Warfare Governing the Relations between Belligerents (1913) (Oxford Manual of Naval Warfare), *reprinted in* THE LAWS OF ARMED CONFLICTS 1123 (Dietrich Schindler & Jiri Toman eds., 4th ed. 2004).

law to cyber operations. The chapter concludes with my thoughts on why *Tallinn Manual 2.0* has proven more influential than the others.

By "influence," I mean an effect on State understandings of international law. I focus on that form of influence because nongovernmental organizations, entities, and individuals lack the *authority* States enjoy in making, identifying, and interpreting international law. In my estimation, a manual's impact on international law depends chiefly on the reception it receives among States.

Such influence may exert itself in three ways. First, it may bear on the existence of a rule of law altogether. In the international humanitarian law (IHL) space, this dynamic usually occurs in the guise of debates over whether a rule found in treaty law also exists as a rule of customary law. Examples include whether the environment enjoys special protection under IHL[21] and whether a presumption of civilian status applies in cases of doubt during targeting.[22] The conclusions of the various groups of experts has exerted significant influence on these and similar debates.

Second, and much more frequently, the influence of expert manuals lies in the interpretation of extant rules. For example, the definition of a military objective found in Article 52(2) is universally considered to reflect customary law.[23] However, the extension of the concept to "war-sustaining" objects by the United States is controversial.[24] When expert manuals that address military objectives take a position on the matter (usually rejection), they influence that controversy.

Third, expert manuals themselves sometimes identify an interpretive issue. For example, the *Tallinn Manual 1.0* group of experts drew attention to the novel issue of the meaning of the IHL term "attack" in the cyber context, specifically, whether a non-injurious and non-destructive cyber operation ever qualifies as an attack subject to the prohibitions and obligations attendant to attacks.[25] Its experts also questioned whether data qualifies as an object such that the alteration or erasure

21. *See generally* Michael N. Schmitt, *Green War: An Assessment of the Environmental Law of International Armed Conflict*, 22 Yale Journal of International Law 1–109 (1997).

22. *See generally* Michael N. Schmitt & Michael Schauss, *Uncertainty in the Law of Targeting: Towards a Cognitive Framework*, 10 Harvard National Security Journal 148–94 (2019).

23. Protocol Additional to the Geneva Conventions of 12 August 1949, and Relating to the Protection of Victims of International Armed Conflicts art. 52(2), June 8, 1977, 1125 U.N.T.S. 3; 1 Customary International Humanitarian Law r. 8 (Jean-Marie Henckaerts & Louise Doswald-Beck eds., 2005). The United States is not a party to the instrument but nevertheless applies the same rule as a matter of customary law. Office of the General Counsel, U.S. Department of Defense, Law of War Manual § 5.6.3. (rev. ed. Dec. 2016).

24. DoD Law of War Manual, *supra* note 23, § 5.6.6. For competing views, *see* Ryan Goodman, *The Obama Administration and Targeting "War-Sustaining" Objects in Noninternational Armed Conflict*, 110 American Journal of International Law 663 (2016); Yoram Dinstein, The Conduct of Hostilities under the Law of International Armed Conflict 126-27 (4th ed. 2022).

25. Tallinn Manual 1.0, *supra* note 4, ¶¶ 10–12 of commentary to r. 30.

of civilian data is subject to the prohibition on attacking a civilian object.[26] The *Tallinn Manuals*' analysis of these two key IHL questions remains at the heart of their analysis by States.[27]

I caution readers that the mere fact of influence on the vector and shape of the law is neither necessarily a positive nor negative phenomenon. Expert groups are at greater liberty than States to examine the law objectively, free from national interests and policy constraints. They also often bring legal insight to the table that many States may lack. They are, after all, *expert* groups.

At the same time, their work can exert a negative influence on the law. The liberty to examine the law freed from such constraints does not mean the experts are free from bias. Indeed, the two groups studying military operations under space law began as a single group but split when some members saw others as insufficiently objective. And, of course, the quality of manuals can only be as good as the expertise of the experts drafting them. The composition of expert groups is the product of many factors; they are seldom pure meritocracies. Because of these realities, I deal only with the fact, not the quality, of expert manuals' influence on the law.

Finally, I limit discussion to manuals crafted by groups of experts, not organizations or States. For example, I do not examine the ICRC's 2009 *Interpretive Guidance on the Notion of Direct Participation in Hostilities*.[28] Although the project involved a large group of experts (including myself), the final product solely represented the organization's views. Similarly, input from distinguished academics and other nongovernmental experts directly informed the 2004 U.K. *Manual on the Law of Armed Conflict*.[29] But the product was promulgated as an official Ministry of Defence Joint Service Publication (JSP 383). This chapter considers only manuals drafted beyond direct institutional influence or approval.

26. *Id.*, ¶ 5 of commentary to r. 38.

27. Tallinn Manual 2.0, *supra* note 5, dealt with then again in the commentary to rules 92 and 100. On the debates among States, *see* Michael N. Schmitt, *Wired Warfare 3.0: Protecting the Civilian Population During Cyber Operations*, 101 International Review of the Red Cross 333 (2019). The debate continues. For instance, in 2022, Israel publicly opined that only cyber operations causing damage or injury qualified as an attack and that data is not an object. Roy Schöndorf, *Israel's Perspective on Key Legal and Practical Issues Concerning the Application of International Law to Cyber Operations*, 97 International Law Studies 395 (2021).

28. International Committee of the Red Cross, Interpretive Guidance on the Notion of Direct Participation in Hostilities under International Humanitarian Law (2009).

29. United Kingdom Ministry of Defence, The Manual of the Law of Armed Conflict (2004).

II. DE JURE STATUS: TEACHINGS OF PUBLICISTS

As the co-editor of this volume, Sandesh Sivakumaran, noted in his insightful work on publicists: "Once upon a time, the teachings of publicists were considered hugely significant. . . . But by the late twentieth century, the common view, including among publicists themselves, was that the teaching of publicists had become far less influential."[30] He is right. The decline in influence can be traced to many factors, including the proliferation of treaties, the cacophony of commentary that has resulted from modern publication opportunities, and the growing size of the international law scholarly community that makes it challenging to separate analytical wheat from the chaff.

Yet despite the perceived decline, scholarship enjoys normative valence as a *matter of law*. According to Article 38(1) of the Statute of the International Court of Justice, which is accepted as accurately reflecting customary law, international law consists of (a) "international conventions, whether general or particular"; (b) "international custom, as evidence of a general practice accepted as law"; and (c) "the general principles of law recognized by civilized nations."[31] By Article 38(1)(d), judicial decisions and the "teachings of the most highly qualified publicists of the various nations" are "subsidiary means for the determination of rules of law."[32]

Subsidiary means are used as evidence of the existence of a rule in one of the three binding sources of law; they do not set forth international law rights and obligations in themselves, except, of course, for the parties in the case of judicial decision. As Shabtai Rosenne observed in his classic *Law and Practice of the International Court*, subsidiary means are the "store-house from which the rules of heads (a), (b), and (c) can be extracted."[33]

"Teachings" denote scholarship, while "publicists" refers to scholars and others who opine with a high degree of authority on the law, like Professor Yoram Dinstein on IHL matters. It can also refer to the work of organizations that consist of experts, such as the International Law Commission and the International Committee of the Red Cross. "Publicist" further includes groups of experts that produce manuals of law, whether they be standing bodies like the Institut de Droit International or established on an ad hoc basis to consider select topics, as in those that have produced the manuals considered here. But as the International Law Association has noted, "The reference to 'the most highly qualified' publicists emphasizes that attention ought to be paid to the writings of those who are

30. Sandesh Sivakumaran, *The Influence of Teachings of Publicists on the Development of International Law*, 66 International and Comparative Law Quarterly 1, 1–2 (2017).

31. Statute of the International Court of Justice, June 26, 1945, 59 Stat. 1055.

32. ICJ Statute, *supra* note 31, art. 38(1)(d).

33. Shabtai Rosenne, III The Law and Practice of the International Court 1920–2005, at 51 (2006).

eminent in the field. In the final analysis, however, it is the quality of the particular writing that matters rather than the reputation of the author."[34]

Acceptance of the teachings of publicists as a means of elaborating international law has long characterized modern international law. In the 1900 *Paquete Habana Case*, for example, the U.S. Supreme Court famously explained:

> International law is part of our law, and must be ascertained and administered by the courts of justice of appropriate jurisdiction as often as questions of right depending upon it are duly presented for their determination. For this purpose, where there is no treaty and no controlling executive or legislative act or judicial decision, resort must be had to the customs and usages of civilized nations, and, as evidence of these, to the works of jurists and commentators who by years of labor, research and experience have made themselves peculiarly well acquainted with the subjects of which they treat. Such works are resorted to by judicial tribunals, not for the speculations of their authors concerning what the law ought to be, but for trustworthy evidence of what the law really is.[35]

This acceptance motivated Elihu Root and Lord Phillimore, the American and British representatives on the Committee of Jurists tasked with drafting the 1920 Statute of the Permanent Court of International Justice (PCIJ), to provide for consideration of scholarship.[36] In 1945, the PCIJ Statute's text was adopted verbatim into the ICJ Statute's Article 38.

Accordingly, it is incontestable that international courts may look to the writings of publicists in rendering their judgments. For instance, the Permanent Court of Justice did so in its 1927 *S.S. Lotus* judgment to confirm exclusive flag State jurisdiction on the high seas, although it did not address the "question as to what their value may be from the point of view of establishing the existence of a rule of customary law."[37] Although infrequently, its successor has done so as well, for example, by looking to the works of successive editors of Oppenheim's

34. U.N. International Law Commission, Report of the International Law Commission (May 2–June 10 and July 4–August 12, 2016), Text of the Draft Conclusions on Identification of Customary International Law, ¶ 4 of commentary to draft conclusion 14, U.N. Doc. A/71/10 (2016).

35. The Paquete Habana, 175 U.S. 677 at 700 (1900).

36. Statute of the Permanent Court of International Justice art. 38(4).

37. S.S. Lotus (Fr. v. Turk.), Judgment, 1927 P.C.I.J. (ser. A) No. 10 at ¶ 68 (Sept. 7 ("In the first place, as regards teachings of publicists, and apart from the question as to what their value may be from the point of view of establishing the existence of a rule of customary law, it is no doubt true that all or nearly all writers teach that ships on the high seas are subject exclusively to the jurisdiction of the State whose flag they fly."). *See also* Certain German Interests, Preliminary Objections, P.CI.J., Series A, No. 6, at 4, 20; Customs Régime between Germany and Austria, Advisory Opinion, P.C.I.J, Series A/B, No. 41, at 37, 45.

International Law and Gidel's *Le Droit international Public de la Mer* on the issue of historic bays in its 1992 *Land, Island and Maritime Frontier Dispute* judgment.[38] And other international courts, like the European Court of Human Rights[39] and the International Criminal Tribunal for the former Yugoslavia,[40] also occasionally take the writings of publicists into account. Such reliance appears with even greater frequency in national cases that deal with international law. To illustrate, Israel's Supreme Court relied heavily on scholarship in its 2005 *Public Committee against Torture* (Targeting Killings) judgment.[41] Of note, it cited the *NIAC Manual*.[42]

In the field of IHL, scholarship sometimes, but not always, plays a visible and prominent role in State military manuals that set forth and explain national legal positions on IHL. For example, the U.S. Department of Defense's *Law of War Manual* has extensive citations to scholarly works to justify the positions it takes, the U.K. *Manual on the Law of Armed Conflict* and Canada's 2001 *Law of Armed Conflict* manual acknowledge relying heavily on the *San Remo Manual* in preparing the chapters on naval operations,[43] and the 2016 Danish *Military Manual on the Law Relevant to Danish Armed Forces in International Operations*[44] repeatedly cites *Tallinn Manual 2.0*, the *AMW Manual*, the *NIAC Manual*, and the *San Remo Manual*. Reference to scholarship in this manner is consistent with the de jure role of the teachings of publicists as a supplementary means for determining the law.

38. Land, Island and Maritime Frontier Dispute, 1992 I.C.J. 351, ¶ 394. *See also* Nottebohm, Second Phase, Judgment, 1955 I.C.J. at 4, 23; North Sea Continental Shelf cases, Judgment, 1969 I.C.J. 3, 35. References to scholarship are more common in separate and dissenting opinions, as illustrated in the Joint Separate Opinions of Judges Higgins, Kooijmans, and Buergenthal in the Arrest Warrant Case (DRC v. Bel.), 2002 I.C.J. 75, at ¶ 44). *See also* Michael Peil, *Scholarly Writings as a Source of Law: A Survey of the Use of Doctrine by the International Court of Justice*, 1 Cambridge Journal of International and Comparative Law 136 (2012).

39. *See, e.g.*, Hanan v. Germany, Grand Chamber Judgment, European Court of Human Rights, Application No. 4871/16, ¶¶ 129–30, Feb. 16, 2021; Banković v. Belgium, 2001-XII Eur. Ct. H.R. 333.

40. *See, e.g.*, Prosecutor v. Nikolic, ICTY, Decision on Defence Motion to Challenge the Exercise of Jurisdiction by the Tribunal, Case IT-94-2-PT (2002). *See also* Michael Bohlander, *The Influence of Academic Research on the Jurisprudence of the International Criminal Tribunal for the Former Yugoslavia—A First Overview*, The Global Community: Yearbook of International Law and Jurisprudence 195 (2003).

41. The Public Committee against Torture in Israel et al. v. Israel et al., Supreme Court of Israel, HCJ 769/02 14, December 2005, https://ihl-databases.icrc.org/applic/ihl/ihl-nat.nsf/0/D14F3F94989B702FC12572D80043927B.

42. *Id.*, ¶ 21.

43. U.K. Manual, *supra* note 29, editorial notes in preface; Chief of the General Staff (Canada), B-GJ-005-104/FP-021, Law of Armed Conflict at the Operational and Tactical Levels § 801 (2001).

44. Ministry of Defence, Denmark, Military Manual on the Law Relevant to Danish Armed Forces in International Operations 2016, updated 2020).

These examples raise the issue of whether expert manuals should enjoy particular weight in the Article 38(1)(d) sense. In fact, the Chairman of the Committee of Jurists, Baron Deschamps of Belgium, suggested during the proceedings that the opinions to which the Root-Phillimore proposal referred should be in agreement.[45] Although that proposal was not adopted, Sir Michael Wood has suggested in his commentary on the article that "it is surely the case that more authority attaches to the coincident views of writers than to controversial or speculative positions."[46]

Indisputably, he is correct with respect to manual projects for at least three reasons. First, the more experts concur on a position, the more persuasive that view as a matter of simple logic. Of course, expertise matters more than numbers, but numbers do matter. Second, properly run expert meetings subject interpretive positions to give and take discussions that point out weaknesses and highlight strengths. Such discussions may not always refine the views in a positive direction, as in the case of a dominant personality misguiding the group. But generally, the group dynamic that leads to consensus is a positive one. Third, expert manuals are usually produced over a period measured in years. For instance, the *AMW Manual* project ran for five years, and each *Tallinn Manual* group of experts worked together for over three years. The length of the proceedings allowed the experts' assessments to benefit from reflection over time.

And most expert groups gather participants from multiple nations, thereby satisfying the reference to "of the various nations" in Article 38(1)(d), especially when its members represent different legal systems. Assuming the quality of the participants, then, expert manuals should wield significant weight as "teachings."

However, textually, only the work of "the most highly qualified publicists" enjoys the legal character recognized in Article 38(1)(d). This being so, expert group products must be cautiously accorded this status, for there are so-called expert groups and actual expert groups. For example, an expert group pursuing *lex ferenda* does not qualify for the status because teachings are a subsidiary means for identifying the *lex lata*. Moreover, for many reasons, almost all expert groups include individuals who fairly do not qualify as "most highly qualified." This might be so because the desire for geographical and other forms of diversity sometimes results in pro forma inclusion of individuals who would not be invited based on merit. In other cases, projects intentionally include junior individuals to help develop their expertise and give promising scholars and practitioners visibility. Albeit a laudable practice, such participants would usually not qualify as highly qualified, at least not yet. Whatever the reason, the authority of the group's

45. Michael Wood, *Teachings of the Most Highly Qualified Publicists (Art. 38(1) ICJ Statute)*, Encyclopedia of Public International Law, https://opil.ouplaw.com/view/10.1093/law:epil/9780199231690/law-9780199231690-e1480?rskey=ky7VOJ&result=1&prd=MPIL (last updated Mar. 2017).

46. *Id.*

product as a composite teaching of highly qualified publicists depends on its members' legal wherewithal or lack thereof.

To summarize, as a matter of law, expert manuals are highly likely to qualify as the teachings of highly qualified publicists. If so, using them to identify and understand treaty and customary law is appropriate. Yet despite their legal status, the question remains whether they influence the shape of the law in fact. As noted, "teachings" generally do not loom large in judicial proceedings, and their influence on military manuals is mixed. This begs the question of their de facto influence on State legal views.

III. DE FACTO INFLUENCE

Expert manuals can exert varying degrees of influence, either directly or indirectly. The fact that the *Danish Military Manual* relied on numerous manuals and that the *San Remo Manual* served as the basis of the chapters on the law of naval operations in both the U.K. and Canadian military manuals illustrate direct impact. The *AMW Manual* has affected State practice more indirectly. It is occasionally cited, as in the *Danish Military Manual*, but its more influential impact came through the so-called AMPLE courses that were based on it.[47] Sponsored by Switzerland, they were offered in various formats by project participants and by the Geneva Centre for Security Policy. This approach allowed direct access to military legal advisers and operators, which undoubtedly influenced their understanding of the law of air warfare.

The *Tallinn Manuals*, however, have had the most significant influence on States. Initially, the first manual, published in 2013, was met with skepticism. During the drafting, several States informally approached leaders of the group to offer input, but generally, States kept the project at arm's length. There was a feeling among State legal advisers that the law governing cyber operations was very unsettled, and they did not want to add credibility to the work of independent scholars and practitioners lest the manual take positions with which they disagreed. Moreover, some non-NATO States wrongly characterized *Tallinn Manual 1.0* as a NATO product, criticizing the work on that basis. In fact, NATO did not influence the product at all. Opposition to the manual was perhaps best illustrated by public criticism at a conference from the Staff Judge Advocate of a U.S. Combatant Command . . . who clearly had not read it.

But that hostility faded quickly, with the NATO Cooperative Cyber Defence Centre of Excellence (CCD COE) asking for an expansion of the project from coverage of the law governing the *jus ad bellum* and IHL into peacetime law that ranged from sovereignty to space law. The Center's Steering Committee, comprised of representatives from its member nations, had to approve the request, which it

47. *See, e.g.*, Geneva Centre for Security Policy, Advanced AMPLE, https://www.gcsp.ch/courses/air-and-missile-warfare-navigating-legal-dimension-advanced-ample-2019.

promptly did. This confirmed the view of States that the project was making a valuable contribution to understanding a very unsettled aspect of international law. In 2017, a new group of experts published *Tallinn Manual 2.0*.

This time, there was significant support from States throughout the process. In a 2016 speech at Berkeley Law School, the State Department's Legal Adviser Brian Egan noted, "I commend the Tallinn Manual project team on what has clearly been a tremendous and thoughtful effort. The United States has unequivocally been in accord with the premise of this project, which is that existing international law applies to State behavior in cyberspace. In this respect, the *Tallinn Manuals* will make a valuable contribution to underscoring and demonstrating this point across a number of bodies of international law."[48]

In perhaps the most significant indicator of State acknowledgment of *Tallinn Manual 2.0*'s potential for influencing the application of the international law to cyberspace, the Netherlands Ministry of Foreign Affairs hosted three meetings (the "Hague Process) to discuss the draft text. Fifty States (including all P5 members) and international organizations sent delegations to them. Additionally, States separately submitted many hundreds of individual comments on the text directly to the team.

The result? Speaking at the launch of *Tallinn Manual 2.0*, the Dutch Minister of Foreign Affairs emphasized that "the *Tallinn Manual* reduces ambiguity and uncertainty. It reduces malicious actors' room for manoeuvre. The manual shows that cyberspace is not simply a jungle, where the strong do what they want and the weak suffer what they must."[49] A year later, at an anniversary event hosted by the Netherlands, the new Dutch Foreign Minister and the Minister of Defense gave speeches praising the manual,[50] while in 2019, the President of Estonia noted that it "contributed an important first step towards the analysis" of international law's applicability in cyberspace.[51] And on two separate occasions, I was asked to address NATO's North Atlantic Council on issues raised in the *Tallinn Manuals*.

An additional form of the *Tallinn Manuals*' influence, modeled on the AMPLE program, is capacity-building. Before the publication of *Tallinn Manual 2.0*, the NATO CCD COE launched week-long capacity-building courses for NATO and partner nations. Following publication, the Netherlands initiated a global program

48. Brian Egan, State Department Legal Adviser, Remarks on International Law and Stability in Cyberspace, Berkeley Law School, Nov. 10, 2016, https://2009-2017.state.gov/s/l/releases/remarks/264303.htm.

49. Bert Koenders, Foreign Minister, Netherlands, Remarks on Launch of Tallinn Manual 2.0, Feb. 13, 2017, The Hague (on file with author).

50. Stef Blok, Minister of Foreign Affairs, Netherlands, Speech on First Anniversary of the Tallinn Manual 2.0, The Hague, June 20, 2018 (on file with author); Ank Bijleveld, Minister of Defence, Netherlands, Speech on First Anniversary of the Tallinn Manual 2.0, The Hague, June 20, 2018 (on file with author).

51. Kersti Kaljulaid, President, Estonia, Opening address at the 11th International Conference on Cyber Conflict (CyCon), Tallinn, May 29, 2019.

of capacity-building courses for State officials that draws on the work of the manual and is taught by members of its expert group. Today, Australia, Singapore, and Canada also support these programs for individual States and regions, sometimes in collaboration with international organizations like the Organization for Security and Cooperation in Europe and the Organization of American States. Its graduates have been deeply involved in the UN Groups of Governmental Experts, Open-Ended Working Groups, and national efforts to craft cyber strategy and policy. In addition, *Tallinn Manual* experts have run many other educational sessions based on the manual. These range from multiple sessions for NATO general and flag officers to global virtual sessions for "Women in Cyber."

The numerous supportive references to the *Tallinn Manuals* in official documents demonstrate its reception among States. Australia's 2017 *International Cyber Engagement Strategy*, for instance, labels them "an important academic contribution to international legal dialogue in this area,"[52] and the 2017 Dutch cyber strategy, "Building Digital Bridges," notes that "by means of the Hague Process and on the basis of the Tallinn Manual 2.0 . . . , the Netherlands supports a more inclusive and detailed debate on the application of international law to cyber operations."[53] At the regional level, the European Parliament passed a Resolution noting "the relevance of the *Tallinn Manual 2.0* as a basis for a debate and as an analysis of how existing international law can be applied in cyber space" and "called" on the Member States to "start analysing and applying what the experts have stated in the Tallinn Manual, and to agree on further voluntary norms of international behaviour."[54] And in the United Nations, for example, Colombia cited the manual in its 2019 response to General Assembly Resolutions 73/27 and 73/266 on advancing responsible State behavior in cyberspace.[55]

Importantly, *Tallinn Manual 2.0* is also having a direct impact on operational cyber practices. To illustrate, the Danish Ministry of Defence's *Military Manual* relies on the *Tallinn Manual 2.0* for its guidance on military cyber operations.[56] Germany's *Law of Armed Conflict Manual* also cited it.[57]

But the most visible indicator of influence is the citation to a "teaching" in statements by States setting forth their views on international law, for it evidences its use by State legal advisers to develop specific positions taken by the State served. Early examples of reference to the *Tallinn Manuals* include the robust 2019 French

52. Australia's International Cyber Engagement Strategy 48 (2017).

53. Netherlands, Building Digital Bridges: Integrated Cyber Strategy, AVT17/BZ122203, § 4.5.2.

54. European Parliament Resolution of 13 June 2018 on Cyber Defence (2018/2004(INI)), ¶ 47.

55. Report of the Secretary-General, Developments in the Field of Information and Telecommunications in the Context of International Security, U.N. Doc. A/74/120, June 24, 2019, at 7.

56. Denmark, Military Manual, *supra* note 44, § 1.4.1

57. Ministry of Defense, Germany, Law of Armed Conflict Manual, ZDv 15/2, ¶¶ 131, 488 (May 2013).

Ministry of the Armies' *International Law Applied to Cyberspace*,[58] which repeatedly references the manual noting points of agreement and disagreement, and the 2019 Netherlands MFA statement on Dutch legal policy in cyberspace, which took numerous positions tracking those in the manual, and that indicated that nation's support for "a more inclusive and detailed debate on the application of international law using *Tallinn Manual 2.0*."[59]

Reference to the *Tallinn Manuals* has appeared in many subsequent statements States have issued on the topic. In its 2021 statement on how international law governs cyber operations, Japan noted that it had looked to *Tallinn Manual 1.0* and *2.0* in preparing its positions. For instance, it adopted the "loss of functionality" approach the *Tallinn Manual* experts had developed when addressing violations of the obligation to respect the sovereignty of other States and the prohibition on intervention into their internal affairs.[60] Similarly, in the Compendium on State international law views annexed to the 2019–2021 Group of Governmental Experts report, Brazil labeled the manual "important reference material,"[61] while Germany repeatedly cited it when setting forth its positions.[62] And at the time this chapter is being written, Canada has issued the most recent statement.[63] It cited the manual to support its positions on sovereignty, cyber espionage, non-intervention, and proxy actors. This was especially significant because it adopted a position on sovereignty contrary to that taken by its "five eyes" partner, the United Kingdom.[64]

In fact, most debates over the interpretation of international law in cyberspace among States today were first presaged in a developed form in one of the *Tallinn Manuals*. These include the thresholds for violation of the rule of sovereignty, use of force, and armed attack in the cyber contexts; whether there is a notification

58. France, Ministry of the Armies, International Law Applied to Cyberspace (English Version) (2019).

59. Netherlands, Ministry of Foreign Affairs, Letter to Parliament, Appendix: International Law in Cyberspace 3 (2019).

60. Japan, Ministry of Foreign Affairs, Basic Position of the Government of Japan on International Law Applicable to Cyber Operations 3, 7, May 28, 2021.

61. Official Compendium of Voluntary National Contributions on the Subject of How International Law Applies to the Use of Information and Communications Technologies by States Submitted by Participating Governmental Experts in the Group of Governmental Experts on Advancing Responsible State Behaviour in Cyberspace in the Context of International Security Established Pursuant to General Assembly Resolution 73/266, Brazil, at 18, U.N. Doc. A/76/136, July 13, 2021.

62. *Id.*, Germany, at 31–43.

63. Canada, International Law Applicable in Cyberspace, June 9, 2022.

64. *Id.*, ¶¶ 10–21. The term "five eyes" refers to Australia, Canada, New Zealand, United Kingdom, and United States. New Zealand took a similar position. New Zealand, Foreign Affairs and Trade, The Application of International Law to State Activity in Cyberspace, ¶ 11, Dec. 1, 2020, which cited the work of "experts, including the Tallinn Manual process" (¶ 2).

requirement for countermeasures and whether collective cyber countermeasures are permissible; whether a rule of due diligence exists and, if so, its scope; whether cyber operations standing alone can trigger a non-international or international armed conflict; whether data is an object in international humanitarian law terms such that altering or destroying civilian data amounts to an unlawful attack on a civilian object; and the meaning of the word "attack" in the IHL rules imposing prohibitions, limitations, and obligations on attacks.

Indeed, there were only two significant debates the experts did not anticipate fully. The first was whether sovereignty is a rule of law. The experts unanimously agreed it had that status, but in 2018 the United Kingdom curiously rejected that conclusion.[65] No other State has endorsed the U.K. position publicly, while many, including five-eyes States Canada and New Zealand, have adopted the opposite view in their national statements,[66] as did NATO (except the United Kingdom) in its Cyber Doctrine.[67] The other unanticipated debate was whether due diligence is a rule of law in the cyber context. The *Tallinn Manuals* experts agreed it was but noted the question was difficult. Pushback on the position was greater than the experts anticipated. For instance, all "five-eyes" countries doubt that rule status had yet been achieved at the time this chapter is being written.

At times, the group developed concepts that States subsequently adopted. Although there are numerous examples, three, drawn from both the IHL and the *jus ad bellum*, stand out. First, the experts were the first to suggest that the notion of damage in international law rules like sovereignty, use of force, and IHL "attacks" could extend in the cyber context to "loss of functionality." It was initially conceived of in the context of IHL attacks, before being used for other purposes.[68] Numerous States, such as Canada, are beginning to embrace the approach.[69]

Second, the *Tallinn Manuals* identified the fraught issue of whether data qualified as an "object," such that destroying or altering civilian data constituted an "attack" on a civilian object. It offered two competing approaches, one citing the intangible nature of data (not an object), the other taking an object and purpose approach to the issue and, therefore, finding data was an object in order to extend protection to civilian data.[70] The issue has not been resolved, but the dialogue on the matter among States was sparked by the *Tallinn Manuals*, and States are almost exclusively analyzing the issue from one of the two perspectives the *Manuals* identified.

65. Jeremy Wright, Attorney General, Cyber and International Law in the 21st Century, Speech at Chatham House (May, 23, 2018).

66. New Zealand, *supra* note 64, ¶ 11; Canada, *supra* note 63, ¶¶ 10–21.

67. NATO, Allied Joint Doctrine for Cyberspace Operations, AJP 3.20, at 20, Jan. 2020.

68. Tallinn Manual 1.0, *supra* note 4, ¶¶ 10–11 of Commentary to r. 30.

69. Canada, *supra* note 63, ¶ 16.

70. Tallinn Manual 1.0, *supra* note 4, ¶¶ 6–7 of Commentary to r. 100.

Third, in the *ad bellum* context, but illustrative of the point being made, the experts developed criteria with which to assess how States are likely to characterize cyber operations conducted by or against them, such as severity, directness, immediacy, and military character vis-à-vis the prohibition on the use of force.[71] States are increasingly adopting the same criteria-based approach. Indeed, although developed to assess the use of force, member States of NATO, inter alia, use a variant to determine whether a cyber operation amounts to an armed attack in the law of self-defense.[72]

IV. POSSIBLE REASONS FOR INFLUENCE

Sandesh Sivakumaran has observed that "[t]here does not seem to be an appreciable reason as to why the work of some groups has profoundly influenced the law while the work of other groups, equally distinguished has not."[73] Yet the global influence of the *Tallinn Manuals* has exceeded that achieved by other expert manuals, including even the highly influential *San Remo Manual*. It is fair to say that the *Tallinn Manuals*, in significant part, set the agenda for States concerning both consensus among them and points of possible disagreement regarding the role of international law in cyberspace. Thus, perhaps the differences between the *Tallinn Manuals* and the others can shed some light on factors that generate influence. Being familiar with all of the manuals mentioned at the outset of this chapter, including serving as a drafter of some of them, allow me to offer some reflections on which differences mattered most in terms of influence.

To begin with, in the land of the blind, the one-eyed man is king. The *Tallinn Manual 1.0* project was launched in 2009 when global attention had been drawn to the subject by the cyber operations directed against Estonia and the employment of cyber operations during the 2008 international armed conflict between Russia and Georgia.[74] Those events raised significant *jus ad bellum* and IHL questions that no State or scholar had seriously considered in depth. *Tallinn Manual 1.0* took on both areas of concern and, at the time of its publication, represented the only relatively comprehensive work on them. Accordingly, it quickly became the go-to source for State legal advisers who were hungry for answers to the questions they were being asked by their principals, if only because there was nothing much else available to them at the time of the manual's publication in 2013.

71. *Id.*, ¶¶ 8–10 of Commentary to r. 11; Tallinn Manual 2.0, *supra* note 5, ¶¶ 8–10 of Commentary to r. 69.

72. NATO Cyber Doctrine, *supra* note 67, ¶ 3.7.

73. Sivakumaran, *supra* note 30, at 9.

74. For a discussion of the incidents, *see* Eneken Tikk, Kadfri Kaska, & Liis Vihul, International Cyber Incidents: Legal Considerations (2010), https://ccdcoe.org/uploads/2018/10/legalconsiderations_0.pdf.

The same is true with *Tallinn Manual 2.0*, which expanded coverage to cyberspace's peacetime legal regime. Although the first manual dealt with the most severe forms of cyber operations, its successor addressed the most common—the deluge of hostile cyber operations into States from abroad. Again, the new expert group that worked on the manual between 2013 and 2016 moved much more quickly than academia or States in providing a comprehensive survey that considered the legal issues and their interrelationship. Thus, for instance, if State legal advisers were trying to assess, for example, how the rule of non-intervention applied to cyber interference with elections or whether remotely conducted operations violated the sovereignty of the State into which they were conducted, there was little else to which they could look. In the case of both manuals, reliance on them quickly became a habit, if only because there were few alternatives. By contrast, significant scholarship and a great deal of State practice predated the other expert manuals.

So my first observation is that timing matters. The *Tallinn Manuals* were written at a time when there was little existing scholarship, very few individuals were taking a deep dive into the subject, almost no State practice to challenge the conclusions being drawn existed, and State legal advisers were desperate for answers. As Sir Michael Wood has observed, "it is undoubtedly the case that the less certain the law, the more primitive the legal system, the more influential writers are likely to be."[75]

My second observation is that if States are to be influenced by an expert manual, they must buy into it. This can occur based on State support and involvement on the one hand, and the attractiveness of the product itself, on the other. The *Tallinn Manual* actively engaged States on different levels. As with other expert manuals, this is done in part by having State legal advisers on the project, even if only in their personal capacity. Their presence lends authority to the final product as being realistic from the perspective of States. The *Tallinn Manuals* project included State legal advisers, past and present, as both experts and observers (e.g., from NATO), as did most other expert projects.

But what distinguished *Tallinn Manual 2.0* was the Hague Process mentioned earlier, by which the Netherlands Ministry of Foreign Affairs (MFA) invited States to send representatives to meetings to discuss the draft text of the manual with leaders of the expert group. This idea was drawn from the *AMW Manual*'s practice of regional meetings with States. As noted, approximately fifty States and intergovernmental organizations, including all P5 members, sent delegations, while States provided extensive written comments following the meetings. The *Tallinn Manual 2.0* editors spent months reviewing them and adjusting the manual accordingly. This process led States to believe, accurately so, that they had a voice in the manual's content, thereby lending credibility to the final product.

And more generally, the direct support of the Netherlands, as was the case with Switzerland and the *AMW Manual*, was seen by other States as a vote of

75. Wood, *supra* note 45.

confidence by a State that wielded a great deal of credibility in the field of international law. The same was true when the Netherlands, Australia, Canada, and Singapore supported robust capacity-building efforts based on the work of the manual.

This involvement by key States relates to the attraction of the *Tallinn Manuals* to State legal advisers. Early in the process, the *Tallinn Manual 1.0* experts agreed that it should reflect all reasonable views, for they often addressed subjects that had not been considered. The team understood that the manual's primary audience consisted of State legal advisers. Many of the experts had acted, or were still serving, as State legal advisers. As such, they understood that what those advisers needed in light of the fact that the topic was so new was a menu of reasonable interpretive options from which they could choose based on their national interests. *Tallinn Manual 1.0* needed to be crafted in a way that would enable it to be a tool in the work of the legal advisers.

This led to the "all-majority-minority-few-acknowledge" approach, which was maintained in *Tallinn Manual 2.0*. The *rules* required unanimity, which meant that they were drafted very broadly. *Commentary*, therefore, was the essence of the manual; it was there that the group dealt with controversies and interpretive differences. On nearly every issue, the manuals indicated whether there was unanimity. If not, they generally identified the majority and minority views among the experts. "Few" denoted a position taken by one to three participants (there were twenty), whereas "acknowledge" signified views that no member of the group held but that the group believed were not unreasonable. For example, none of the experts believed that sovereignty could be violated by non-State actors whose conduct was not attributable to a State. Still, one State, which has engaged in armed conflict with the groups it faces, expressed that view during the Hague Process. The view was acknowledged in *Tallinn Manual 2.0* without citing the State concerned.[76]

In my estimation, this was the critical factor in State acceptance. The decision to set forth all reasonable views created the impression, an accurate one in my opinion, that the expert group was working hard to be as objective as possible. And by this approach, many legal advisers saw the manuals as tools for identifying issues they needed to deal with and setting forth the full range of interpretive options for doing so. The experts did not avoid expressing their views, but the approach allowed State legal advisers to consider a range of positions and assess them in light of their own national interests.

My third observation is that participant diversity is crucial to credibility. I was skeptical about the role of diversity during the *Tallinn Manual 1.0* phase of the project. For that phase, we gathered world-class use of force and IHL experts, albeit primarily from NATO countries. In part, this was because the NATO CCD COE was sponsoring the project. Although they produced what I believe was a high-quality product, when the manual was published, it was, as noted, criticized

76. Tallinn Manual 2.0, *supra* note 5, ¶ 3 of Commentary to r. 4.

outside the NATO space as a NATO-centric document.[77] At least in the months following publication, this negatively impacted the product's credibility. But because it was the most comprehensive treatment of the topic, it quickly became widely used by State legal advisers worldwide.

For *Tallinn Manual 2.0*, the NATO CCD COE wisely insisted on greater geographical diversity. The inclusion of individuals from a variety of nations, especially beyond Europe and North America, including China and Belorussia, added to the sense of States that the process was objective. In fact, geographical origin seldom drove the legal positions taken; but there is no question that it enhanced the credibility of the final product, especially among non-European States. For instance, the manual was very well received in Japan, which can in part be attributed to the participation of a senior, well-respected Japanese scholar.

The *Tallinn Manual 2.0* experience thus confirmed Sivakumaran's observation that "[w]here the composition of the group takes into account geographical distribution, it is likely to be considered more representative and thus potentially more influential than a group that is solely from the global north or global south."[78] Other expert manual projects also emphasized diversity, contributing to their credibility and influence. But in *Tallinn Manual 2.0*, diversity was a *sine qua non* requirement of sponsors.

The editors therefore expended enormous effort to ensure that the group was diverse, but not at the expense of expertise. Because of my (misguided) skepticism about diversity and the limit to twenty experts, no expert was invited to participate unless they were a first-rate scholar or practitioner (sometimes both). Thus, the key is diversity combined with expertise. Both those factors drive influence.

My fourth observation is related to the third. A robust peer review process involving sixty experts from around the world provided further refinements to the additional product. Notably, the group included not only distinguished scholars but also government legal practitioners who dealt with the issues daily. The *Tallinn Manuals* team relied on these external experts to guard against groupthink and to identify issues they might have missed.

Moreover, technical peer reviewers examined the legal conclusion in light of technical factors (as with the attachment of a non-lawyer fighter-pilot to the *AMW* group). Indeed, throughout the process, including deliberations and drafting, a representative of the NATO CCD COE technical branch was always present to ensure the legal experts realistically addressed real issues. The result was a product that most State legal advisers and their clients find fair and practically helpful.

Although these four factors significantly enhanced the *Tallinn Manuals*' unique influence on inter- and intra-State dialogue, the factors that contributed to the influence of the other manuals equally played a role. Most significantly, the *Tallinn*

77. *See, e.g.*, Rain Liivoja & Timothy McCormack, *Law in the Virtual Battlespace: The Tallinn Manual and the Jus in Bello*, 15 Yearbook of International Humanitarian Law 45, 57 (2012).

78. Sivakumaran, *supra* note 30, at 9.

Manuals project participants were generally recognized as serious scholars or experienced practitioners, or both. Expertise at a very high level is ultimately the most important factor. An expert manual with distinguished scholars and solid legal analysis may not prove influential for various reasons, such as timing or competing scholarship. But one that lacks recognized expertise or contains spurious conclusions has little chance of ever proving influential.

V. CONCLUDING THOUGHTS

It may surprise readers, but I find the proliferation of expert manuals suboptimal for international law, especially when dealing with armed conflict. Only States may authoritatively interpret international law, and it is only when their interpretations achieve a critical mass that legal clarity is achieved. Of course, the teachings of publicists have a formal role in the process, as noted in Article 38(1)(d) of the Statute of the International Court of Justice. But at the end of the day, State positions matter more than scholarly opinions. This is especially so in light of war's complexity, which is sometimes difficult to grasp without operational understanding.

However, States are seldom agile enough to respond to new phenomena. This means that in the default of State *opinio juris*, scholarship inevitably will act to fill the interpretive void. This, of course, can be counterproductive. For instance, I am concerned about the direction scholarly discourse of IHL's role regarding autonomy and artificial intelligence is taking; it undervalues IHL and tends to depart from operational reality. However, scholarship can play a positive role, as in pushing back against the nonsensical notion popular several decades ago that cyberspace was a normative Wild West, in particular that IHL might not govern cyber operations during armed conflict. But for scholarship, this flawed position might still have advocates among States.

And in my estimation, the work of expert groups is particularly import in this respect, for it is generally more legally reliable than individual work due to the give-and-take dynamic that infuses it. Accordingly, much as I wish States were more aggressive in dealing with international law interpretation, I believe the work of expert groups and the influence of their products on States plays a vital role in the development and application of international law.

7

The Development of International Humanitarian Law by the International Committee of the Red Cross

SANDESH SIVAKUMARAN*

I. INTRODUCTION

The International Committee of the Red Cross (ICRC) is inextricably linked with international humanitarian law (IHL). Founded in 1863, the Comité genevois de secours pour les militaires blessés, which would later become the ICRC,[1] was pivotal in the drafting of the 1864 Convention for the Amelioration of the Condition of the Wounded in Armies in the Field. Ever since that time, the ICRC has been heavily involved in the drafting of other major IHL treaties, such as the 1949 Geneva Conventions and the 1977 Protocols additional thereto.

The ICRC's contribution to the development of IHL is by no means limited to the drafting of treaties. Cognizant of the limitations of conventional law, with its need for State ratification of treaties and the sometimes limited substantive

* Sandesh Sivakumaran is Professor of International Law, University of Cambridge; Director of the Lauterpacht Centre for International Law; and Fellow of St Edmund's College, Cambridge; and was the 2022 Lieber Scholar at the Lieber Institute for Law and Warfare, United States Military Academy.

1. Various names were used: the Comité international de secours pour les militaires blessés; Comité international de secours aux militaires blesses, Geneva Committee, Geneva International Committee, Committee of Five. *See* François Bugnion, The International Committee of the Red Cross and the Protection of War Victims 9, n.11 (2003).

Sandesh Sivakumaran, *The Development of International Humanitarian Law by the International Committee of the Red Cross* In: *Making and Shaping the Law of Armed Conflict*. Edited by: Sandesh Sivakumaran and Christian R. Burne, Oxford University Press. DOI: 10.1093/oso/9780197775134.003.0007

content of certain instruments, the International Conference of the Red Cross and the Red Crescent tasked the ICRC in 1995 with preparing a report on customary international humanitarian law. The report in question—the Customary International Humanitarian Law Study—has proven hugely influential ever since its publication. States as well as courts and tribunals have relied on it heavily for the identification of rules of customary IHL.

The ICRC has also contributed to the development of IHL in a myriad of other ways, such as through publication of its commentaries on the Geneva Conventions and Additional Protocols, convening expert meetings, and publishing the resulting reports in order to try and shape debate, and by catalyzing States' views on the law.[2] Indeed, the Statutes of the International Red Cross and Red Crescent Movement task the ICRC inter alia "to work for the understanding and dissemination of knowledge of international humanitarian law applicable in armed conflicts and to prepare any development thereof."[3] And it has been suggested that "no other non-State actor has had such a distinguished impact on the (historic) development of a specific area of international law."[4]

This chapter considers the ICRC's various contributions to the development of IHL. Section II considers the ICRC's role in the making of the Geneva Conventions. Section III explores the ICRC's contribution to the interpretation of treaty law, notably through its commentaries to the Geneva Conventions and Additional Protocols, and to the clarification of the law, through other ICRC projects. Section IV analyzes the ICRC's role in the identification of customary IHL. Section V illustrates how the ICRC has acted as a catalyst for the formation and publication of States' views on various legal issues. The chapter ends with a discussion of some of the themes that run through these different types of contributions to the development of IHL.

2. *See generally* François Bugnion, *The International Committee of the Red Cross and the Development of International Humanitarian Law*, 5 Chicago Journal of International Law 191 (2004); Humanizing the Laws of War: The Red Cross and the Development of International Humanitarian Law (Robin Geiß, Andreas Zimmermann, & Stefanie Haumer eds., 2017); Knut Dörmann, *The Role of Nonstate Entities in Developing and Promoting International Humanitarian Law*, 51 Vanderbilt Journal of Transnational Law 713 (2018).

3. Statutes of the International Red Cross and Red Crescent Movement, art. 5(2)(g), (adopted by the 25th International Conference of the Red Cross at Geneva in 1986, amended in 1995 and 2006), https://www.icrc.org/en/doc/assets/files/other/statutes-en-a5.pdf.

4. Stefanie Haumer, Robin Geiß, & Andreas Zimmermann, *Introduction*, *in* Humanizing the Laws of War, *supra* note 2, at 1.

II. THE MAKING OF THE CONVENTIONAL LAW

A. The Drafting of the 1949 Geneva Conventions

Ever since its establishment, the ICRC has sought to develop the law applicable to armed conflicts. At the conventional level, early efforts included the development of the 1864 Geneva Convention,[5] the Additional Articles of 1868 (which did not enter into force),[6] the 1906 Geneva Convention,[7] and the 1929 Geneva Conventions on the Wounded and Sick and on Prisoners of War.[8] Various draft conventions were also prepared, including, most importantly, the 1934 Draft International Convention on the Condition and Protection of Civilians of enemy nationality who are on territory belonging to or occupied by a belligerent.[9]

This process of development and refinement of the law applicable to armed conflict was ongoing when the Second World War broke out and interrupted this process. The Draft Convention on the Condition and Protection of Civilians had been discussed at the XVth International Conference of the Red Cross in Tokyo in 1934 and was awaiting consideration at a diplomatic conference which had been convened by the government of Switzerland to take place in 1940. The outbreak of the Second World War prevented that conference from going ahead.

Thus, although the 1949 Geneva Conventions are often said to be a response to the Second World War, the process of developing and improving the law was ongoing before the war, and the war interrupted this process. The 1949 Geneva Conventions should accordingly be seen both as a continuation of this ongoing process as well as a reaction to the Second World War.

Following the conclusion of the Second World War and based on its earlier work as well as the practice of the Second World War, the ICRC prepared draft conventions. These were put before various meetings of experts—in particular, representatives of National Red Cross Societies in 1946[10] and government experts

5. Convention for the Amelioration of the Condition of the Wounded in Armies in the Field, Aug. 22, 1864, 22 Stat. 940, 129 Consol. T.S. 361.

6. Additional Articles relating to the Condition of the Wounded in War, October 20, 1868.

7. Convention for the Amelioration of the Condition of the Wounded and Sick in Armies in the Field, July 6, 1906, 35 Stat. 1885, 202 Consol. T.S. 144.

8. Convention for the Amelioration of the Condition of the Wounded and Sick in Armies in the Field, July 27, 1929, 47 Stat. 2074, 118 L.N.T.S. 303; Convention Relative to the Treatment of Prisoners of War, July 27, 1929, 47 Stat. 2021, 118 L.N.T.S. 343.

9. *Available at* https://ihl-databases.icrc.org/en/ihl-treaties/tokyo-draft-conv-1934?activeTab=historical.

10. ICRC, Report on the Work of the Preliminary Conference of National Red Cross Societies for the Study of the Conventions and of Various Problems Relative to the Red Cross (Geneva, July 26–August 3, 1946) (1947).

in 1947[11]—and changes to the draft conventions were made following each meeting. The drafts were then put before the XVIIth International Conference of the Red Cross in Stockholm in 1948, where they were approved with a few amendments.[12] New drafts were then put before the Diplomatic Conference of 1949 where they were considered by States.[13] During the Diplomatic Conference itself, ICRC officials acted as experts.[14]

The process of drafting the 1949 Geneva Conventions is informative for a number of reasons. First, it reveals that it was the ICRC which prepared the drafts of the Conventions that were put before States at the Diplomatic Conference. The earlier the involvement in the drafting process, the greater the likelihood of making a substantial contribution. By the time a full draft is discussed, the general approach and direction of the text has often been decided. Discussion then revolves around the particular wording used and whether to retain a particular provision rather than deciding on the general approach to be taken. This is not always the case, as is evident by the inclusion of wars of national liberation in the First Additional Protocol to the Geneva Conventions,[15] and drafts can still be rejected in their entirety. Nonetheless, it is generally the case that early involvement in a drafting process leads to a greater likelihood of making a substantial contribution.

Second, the first three Geneva Conventions of 1949 build on preexisting conventions, conventions which were also prepared by the ICRC. This again confirms the important contribution of the ICRC to the creation of the 1949 Geneva Conventions. The First Convention built on the 1929 Convention on the Wounded and Sick, which in turn built on the 1906 Convention and the 1864 Convention before that. The Third Convention was largely a development of the 1929 Convention on Prisoners of War. The ICRC was heavily involved in the preparation of each of these Conventions. The Second Convention was somewhat different, updating as it did the Xth Hague Convention of 1907, which in turn updated the 1899 Hague Convention III. Here, too, the ICRC had an indirect, but

11. ICRC, Report on the Work of the Conference of Government Experts for the Study of the Conventions for the Protection of War Victims (Geneva, April 14–26, 1947) (1947).

12. ICRC, Draft Revised or New Conventions for the Protection of War Victims (1948); ICRC, Revised and New Draft Conventions for the Protection of War Victims (1948).

13. The texts are contained in I Final Record of the Diplomatic Conference of Geneva of 1949, 45–143 (undated).

14. *Id.*, 171.

15. *Compare* Protocol Additional to the Geneva Conventions of 12 August 1949, and Relating to the Protection of Victims of International Armed Conflicts art. 1(4), June 8, 1977, 1125 U.N.T.S. 3, *with* Article 1 of the text that was put before the Diplomatic Conference, in I Official Records of the Diplomatic Conference on the Reaffirmation and Development

influential, role. The full title of the Xth Hague Convention is the Convention for the Adaptation to Maritime Warfare of the Principles of the Geneva Convention; and the full title of the 1899 Hague Convention III is the Convention for the Adaptation to Maritime Warfare of the Principles of the Geneva Convention of 22 August 1864. Thus, the Xth Hague Convention of 1907 and the 1899 Hague Convention III were both adaptations of the rules of land warfare to maritime warfare.

Third, the ICRC worked with other actors in preparing the draft Conventions and involved key constituencies throughout the drafting process. This can be seen through the meetings with government experts and National Red Cross Societies in particular, both of which influenced the content of the Conventions. It can also be seen through the meetings with other actors, such as neutral members of Mixed Medical Commissions, for the development of the provisions on Mixed Medical Commissions;[16] welfare institutions, for the development of the provisions concerning spiritual and intellectual relief for prisoners of war and civilian internees;[17] and independent experts, for the development of the provisions on grave breaches.[18] In preparing the initial drafts of the Conventions, the ICRC did not act in isolation.

Fourth, the ICRC had an important role to play also during the diplomatic conference itself. ICRC delegates at the Diplomatic Conference were designated "Experts."[19] It was said that "[t]he Heads of Delegations are unanimously of the opinion that our work will be greatly facilitated if the International Committee takes part in it in the capacity of expert."[20] And this turned out to be correct. ICRC experts were frequently called upon to introduce an article, offer insight into the language of a provision, and respond to queries from States.[21]

Fifth, the role of the ICRC did not end with the adoption of the Conventions. Just one year after their adoption, the ICRC published for the benefit of National

of International Humanitarian Law applicable in Armed Conflicts, Geneva (1974–1977), Part 3, at 3 (1978).

16. ICRC, Report on the Meeting of Neutral Members of the Mixed Medical Commissions (Geneva, September 27–28, 1945) (1945).

17. ICRC, Proceedings of the Meeting for the Study of Treaty Stipulations Relative to the Spiritual and Intellectual Needs of Prisoners of War and Civilian Internees (Geneva, March 3 and 4, 1947) (1947).

18. Comité d'experts pour l'examen de la sanction pénale à insérer dans les projets de Conventions révisées ou nouvelles établis par le CICR, Genève, 21–23 décembre 1948, ACICR, B CR 238-7. I am grateful to the ICRC Library for assistance in locating this document.

19. *See* I Final Record, *supra* note 13, at 171.

20. IIA Final Record of the Diplomatic Conference of Geneva of 1949, 15 (undated).

21. *See generally* IIA and IIB Final Record of the Diplomatic Conference of Geneva of 1949 (undated).

Red Cross Societies a two-volume analysis of the Geneva Conventions.[22] This was followed by the publication of the ICRC Commentaries, which, as will be discussed in section III, have proven invaluable in the understanding of the provisions. In this way, even following the adoption of the Conventions, the ICRC has continued to play a role in shaping the interpretation of their substantive content.

B. The Substantive Content of the 1949 Geneva Conventions

It is impossible in this chapter to do justice to the ICRC's contribution to the development of the substance of the 1949 Geneva Conventions. I will instead discuss three major substantive contributions: common Article 3; the grave breaches provisions; and the Fourth Geneva Convention. Many other contributions could be discussed, such as common Article 2.

As is well known, common Article 3 represents the first conventional regulation of non-international armed conflicts under international law. National Red Cross Societies played an important role in the ICRC becoming involved in non-international armed conflicts.[23] In its 1937 study on the revision of the 1929 Conventions, the ICRC decided that extension of the scope of application of the Conventions to civil wars was "desirable" but not possible as there are not two States parties to the Convention but two factions of the same country.[24] By contrast, experts of National Red Cross Societies took the view that "the humanitarian principles" of the Convention "must be respected under all circumstances," even when the Convention was not "juridically applicable."[25]

By the time of the Conference of National Red Cross Societies in 1946, the Commission for the Study of the Conventions was in favor of inviting the adversaries in a civil war to "declare their readiness to apply the principles of the Convention, subject to reciprocity being observed."[26] The experts of National Red Cross Societies went further, recommending that the Conventions themselves be applicable unless one of the parties to the conflict "announces expressly its intention to the contrary."[27] The matter was considered by the 1947

22. ICRC, The Geneva Conventions of August 12, 1949: Analysis for the Use of National Red Cross Societies (1950).

23. *See* Sandesh Sivakumaran, The Law of Non-International Armed Conflict 34–36 (2012).

24. ICRC, Report on the Interpretation, Revision and Extension of the Geneva Convention of July 27, 1929, at 7–8 (1938).

25. *Id.*

26. Report on the Work of the Preliminary Conference of National Red Cross Societies, *supra* note 10, at 15.

27. *Id.*

Conference of Government Experts, which proved to be more reluctant, preferring the application of "the principles of the Convention" rather than the Conventions themselves and "subject to the adverse Party also conforming thereto."[28] On the basis of these discussions, the ICRC drew up texts and submitted them to the XVIIth International Conference of the Red Cross in Stockholm in 1948. The ICRC adopted the "provisions" approach and deleted reference to the notion of reciprocity, remarking that "the condition of reciprocity . . . might . . . render this . . . valueless, as one Party could always allege that its adversary disregarded some specific clause of the Convention."[29] The Stockholm Conference largely accepted the drafts, but reintroduced the notion of reciprocity into the Third and Fourth Conventions.[30] Following the Stockholm Conference, draft conventions were circulated to States in anticipation of the Diplomatic Conference. Also circulated to States were comments and proposals of the ICRC on the drafts, one of which again suggested deletion of the reference to reciprocity.[31] At the Diplomatic Conference, after considerable discussion, common Article 3 was adopted. That provision sets out certain rules which are applicable to non-international armed conflicts and the provision is applicable without any reference to reciprocity. Thus, even though the ICRC's desire was not fully realized, the contribution of the ICRC, as well as those of National Red Cross Societies and government experts, was crucial.

Another important ICRC contribution is that of the grave breaches regime. Grave breaches of the Geneva Conventions are certain acts which are listed as such in each of the four Conventions. For example, Article 50 of the First Geneva Convention provides:

> Grave breaches . . . shall be those involving any of the following acts, if committed against persons or property protected by the Convention: wilful killing, torture or inhuman treatment, including biological experiments, wilfully causing great suffering or serious injury to body or health, and extensive destruction and appropriation of property, not justified by military necessity and carried out unlawfully and wantonly.

States parties to the Geneva Conventions are required to criminalize grave breaches of the Conventions, search for persons alleged to have committed grave breaches, and try such persons or extradite them to another State party for prosecution.[32]

28. Report on the Work of the Conference of Government Experts, *supra* note 11, at 8.

29. Draft Revised or New Conventions, *supra* note 12, at 6.

30. Revised and New Draft Conventions, *supra* note 12, at 10, 32, 51–52, and 114.

31. Remarks and Proposals Submitted by the International Commission of the Red Cross: Documents for the Consideration of Governments invited by the Swiss Federal Council to Attend the Diplomatic Conference at Geneva (April 21, 1949), 38 (1949).

32. Common Article 49/50/129/146.

Following discussion of the issue of war crimes at the 1947 Conference of Government Experts, the draft conventions submitted by the ICRC to the International Conference of the Red Cross in 1948 contained provisions on the repression of abuses and infractions.[33] The International Conference included provisions on repression in the texts it adopted, while recommending that the ICRC "continue its work" on the subject and "submit proposals to a later Conference."[34] Taking the reference to a later conference to mean the Diplomatic Conference of 1949, and not a later International Conference of the Red Cross,[35] the ICRC convened a meeting of experts to examine the issue. The experts, consisting of Jean Graven, Hersch Lauterpacht, Captain Martinus Mouton, and Colonel Henry Philimore, met with ICRC officials, including Claude Pilloud, Jean Pictet, and Pierre Bossier, under the chairmanship of Max Huber, in Geneva in December 1948. Four draft articles were produced.[36] These were on "Legislative measures," "Grave violations," "Superior orders," and "Safeguard."[37] After some maneuvering,[38] the Diplomatic Conference considered the four draft articles, and, although watered down, the four draft articles ended up significantly influencing the drafting of the grave breaches provisions as adopted.[39]

The final ICRC contribution to the 1949 Geneva Conventions which will be discussed in this chapter is that of the Fourth Geneva Convention. The Fourth Convention is particularly important, as, unlike the First, Second, and Third Conventions, it was largely new in 1949. The ICRC was the driving force behind the Convention, as it had recognized the lack of protections afforded to civilians, particularly in situations other than occupation. During the First World War, the ICRC encountered difficulties in assisting individuals who had been interned,[40]

33. Draft Revised or New Conventions, *supra* note 12, at 28, 49, and 238.

34. Resolution XXIII, *in* Seventeenth International Red Cross Conference, Stockholm, August 1948 (undated).

35. Boyd van Dijk, Preparing for War 278 (2022).

36. *See* Report Comité d'experts, *supra* note 18.

37. *See* Remarks and Proposals, *supra* note 31, at 5 and 18–23.

38. *See* Robert Heinsch, *The International Committee of the Red Cross and the Geneva Conventions of 1949*, *in* Humanizing the Laws of War, *supra* note 2, at 50–51; International Committee of the Red Cross, Commentary on the First Geneva Convention: Convention (I) for the Amelioration of the Condition of the Wounded and Sick in the Armed Forces in the Field, ¶¶ 2834–37 (2016).

39. The Delegate of the Netherlands, Captain Mouton, introducing a joint amendment of the Netherlands, Australia, Belgium, Brazil, the United States, France, Italy, Norway, the United Kingdom, and Switzerland, stated that "[t]he proposals made by the International Committee of the Red Cross were gratefully used" and also indicated that "this text which was evolved with much pain and labor is an advance and improvement on the past and goes as far as is possible at this moment." IIB Final Record of the Diplomatic Conference of Geneva of 1949 115 (undated).

40. Commentary to Geneva Convention IV Relative to the Protection of Civilian Persons in Time of War 3 (Jean S. Pictet ed., 1958).

and, following that War, it prepared a draft Convention on the protection of civilians for consideration at the International Conference of the Red Cross in 1923. However, owing to State resistance at the Conference, as well as variable interest within the ICRC itself, the draft was not taken further.[41] The 1929 Diplomatic Conference focused instead on prisoners of war and the wounded and sick. The Conference did, however, express the wish that in-depth studies be undertaken with a view to concluding a convention concerning the condition and protection of civilians of enemy nationality who are on territory belonging to or occupied by a belligerent.[42] This led to the ICRC preparing new drafts on the subject, one of which was put before, and adopted by, the International Conference of the Red Cross in Tokyo in 1934.[43] The Tokyo Draft Convention was scheduled for consideration at the Diplomatic Conference intended to be held in 1940, but, owing to the outbreak of the Second World War, the Conference did not take place.

Following the Second World War and the evident lack of protection for civilians, the ICRC made a renewed push for the protection of civilians, although it was uncertain at the time whether this would take the form of a new convention.[44] At the 1946 Conference of National Red Cross Societies, the Belgian Red Cross presented a revised version of the Tokyo Draft Convention,[45] and, following the Conference, the ICRC itself updated the Tokyo Draft Convention. The ICRC presented a draft Convention for the Protection of Civilian Persons in Time of War to the International Conference of the Red Cross at Stockholm in 1948,

41. van Dijk, *supra* note 35, at 62. A slightly different explanation is given by Pictet, Commentary on the Fourth Geneva Convention, *supra* note 40, at 4.

42. Actes de la conférence diplomatique convoquée par le conseil fédéral suisse pour la révision de la Convention du 6 juillet 1906 pour l'amélioration du sort des blessés et malades dans les armées en campagne et pour l'élaboration d'une convention relative au traitement des prisonniers de guerre et réunie à Genève du 1er au 27 juillet 1929, at 732 (1930) ("La Conférence, faisant siennes les résolutions unanimes de ses deux Commissions, exprime le vœu que des études approfondies soient entreprises en vue de la conclusion d'une Convention internationale concernant la condition et la protection des civils de nationalité ennemie qui se trouvent sur le territoire d'un belligérant ou sur un territoire occupé par lui.").

43. *Available at* https://ihl-databases.icrc.org/en/ihl-treaties/tokyo-draft-conv-1934?activeTab=historical.

44. *See* van Dijk, *supra* note 35, at 68, noting that "[t]he Legal Division considered a whole range of different alternatives, from amalgamating the POW and Civilian Conventions to creating a 'Charter,' or 'Civil réduit,' with a set of basic rights for every detainee against inhumane treatment."

45. Convention internationale relative au traitement des internes civils et de detenus, Etude de la Croix Rouge de Belgique, *available at* https://library.icrc.org/library/docs/CD/CSN_1946_DOCSN_02.pdf.

which was accepted with minor modifications.[46] At the Diplomatic Conference of 1949, States generally recognized the need to regulate the treatment of civilians "in the hands of a Party to the conflict or Occupying Power of which they are not nationals."[47] And the Fourth Convention, as adopted, closely resembles in many respects the substance of the Stockholm draft that was put before the Diplomatic Conference, while also differing from it in certain respects, such as in relation to its (personal) scope of application.

The ICRC has thus made an important contribution to the *making* of treaty law.[48] This was done alongside the contribution of other actors such as National Red Cross Societies, government experts, and independent experts, and with States as the ultimate drafters and adopters of treaty law.

III. THE INTERPRETATION OF THE CONVENTIONAL LAW: COMMENTARIES AND CLARIFICATIONS

A. Commentaries

Following the adoption of each of the Geneva Conventions, ICRC officials published article-by-article commentaries on the Conventions. Moynier's *Étude sur la Convention de Genève pour l'amélioration du sort des militaires blessés dans les armées en campagne: 1864 et 1868*, "part legal treatise, part article-by-article commentary,"[49] was published in 1870.[50] This was followed by Louis Renault's commentary on the 1906 Convention;[51] Paul des Gouttes' commentary on the 1929 Wounded and Sick Convention;[52] Georges Werner's commentary on the

46. DRAFT REVISED OR NEW CONVENTIONS, *supra* note 12, at 51; REVISED AND NEW DRAFT CONVENTIONS, *supra* note 12, at 113.

47. Fourth Geneva Convention, art. 4.

48. The ICRC played a similarly influential role in the development of the Additional Protocols of 1977 and also contributed to the development of other IHL treaties. On the former, *see* Michael Bothe, *The International Committee of the Red Cross and the Additional Protocols of 1977*, *in* HUMANIZING THE LAWS OF WAR, *supra* note 2, at 57. On the latter, *see* Knut Dörmann & Louis Maresca, *The International Committee of the Red Cross and Its Contribution to the Development of International Humanitarian Law in Specialized Instruments*, 5 CHICAGO JOURNAL OF INTERNATIONAL LAW 217 (2004).

49. Charlotte Mohr & Ellen Policinski, *From the Gilded Age to the Digital Age: The Evolution of ICRC Legal Commentaries*, 104 INTERNATIONAL REVIEW OF THE RED CROSS 1898, 1901 (2022).

50. GUSTAVE MOYNIER, ÉTUDE SUR LA CONVENTION DE GENÈVE POUR L'AMÉLIORATION DU SORT DES MILITAIRES BLESSÉS DANSLES ARMÉES EN CAMPAGNE: 1864 ET 1868 (1870).

51. *La conference de revision de la Convention de Genève*, 37(148) BULLETIN INTERNATIONAL DES SOCIÉTÉS DE LA CROIX-ROUGE, 229 (1906).

52. PAUL DES GOUTTES, LA CONVENTION DE GENÈVE DU 27 JUILLET 1929: COMMENTAIRE (1930).

1929 Prisoners of War Convention;[53] the commentaries on the 1949 Geneva Conventions under the general editorship of Jean Pictet;[54] the commentary on Additional Protocols I and II under the editorship of Sandoz, Swinarski, and Zimmermann;[55] and Jean-François Quéguiner's commentary on Additional Protocol III.[56] Almost all those involved in drafting the commentaries had been involved in the drafting of the treaties themselves.[57]

As of the writing of this chapter, the ICRC, under the direction of Jean-Marie Henckaerts, is in the process of updating its commentaries on the 1949 Geneva Conventions and Additional Protocols I and II. The commentaries on the first three Geneva Conventions have been published,[58] and the commentary on the Fourth Geneva Convention is in preparation. According to lawyers in the Commentaries Update Unit of the ICRC Legal Division, the commentaries were updated pursuant to the ICRC's statutory mandate "'to work for the understanding and dissemination of knowledge of international humanitarian law' (IHL) and for its faithful application."[59] Commentaries on the individual articles were written by ICRC legal advisers, as well as by individuals from outside

53. Georges Werner, *Un commentaire du Code des prisonniers de guerre*, 14(159) Revue Internationale de la Croix- Rouge, 199 (1932).

54. Commentary to Geneva Convention I for the Amelioration of the Condition of the Wounded and Sick in the Armed Forces in the Field (Jean Pictet ed., 1952); Commentary to Geneva Convention II for the Amelioration of the Condition of the Wounded, Sick, and Shipwrecked Members of Armed Forces at Sea (Jean Pictet ed., 1960); Commentary to Geneva Convention III Relative to the Treatment of Prisoners of War (Jean Pictet ed., 1960); Commentary to Geneva Convention IV Relative to the Protection of Civilian Persons in Time of War (Jean Pictet ed., 1958).

55. Commentary on the Additional Protocols of 8 June 1977 to the Geneva Conventions of 12 August 1949 (Yves Sandoz, Christophe Swinarski, & Bruno Zimmermann eds., 1987).

56. Jean-François Quéguiner, *Commentary on the Protocol Additional to the Geneva Conventions of 12 August 1949, and relating to the Adoption of an Additional Distinctive Emblem (Protocol III)*, 89(865) International Review of the Red Cross 175 (2005).

57. *See* Mohr & Policinski, *supra* note 49, at 1903–06.

58. International Committee of the Red Cross, Commentary on the First Geneva Convention: Convention (I) for the Amelioration of the Condition of the Wounded and Sick in the Armed Forces in the Field (2016); International Committee of the Red Cross, Commentary on the Second Geneva Convention: Convention (II) for the Amelioration of the Condition of the Wounded, Sick and Shipwrecked Members of Armed Forces at Sea (2017); International Committee of the Red Cross, Commentary on the Third Geneva Convention: Convention (III) relative to the Treatment of Prisoners of War (2021).

59. Lindsey Cameron et al., *The Updated Commentary on the First Geneva Convention—A New Tool for Generating Respect for International Humanitarian Law*, 97(900) International Review of the Red Cross 1209, 1210 (2015).

the ICRC.[60] Authors of individual commentaries also reviewed drafts of other commentaries. An editorial committee, consisting of senior ICRC and non-ICRC lawyers also reviewed the draft commentary.[61] For the commentary on the First Geneva Convention, more than sixty academics and practitioners acted as peer reviewers;[62] for the commentary on the Second Geneva Convention, there were over forty peer reviewers.[63]

Each of the commentaries mentioned are article-by-article commentaries; however, each is of a slightly different sort. Moynier's 1870 Commentary was also designed to "raise support for the Convention, provide guidance on its application on the battlefield and convince States of its applicability," partly in light of the criticism the 1864 Convention had received.[64] Given their date of publication, the Pictet Commentaries rely heavily on the drafting histories of the 1949 Conventions and make frequent mention of the experiences of the Second World War.[65] They also make not infrequent appeal to considerations of humanity.[66] By contrast, the updated commentaries come across as more positivist in nature. The updated commentaries apply the Vienna Convention on the Law of Treaties rule on treaty interpretation, thus considering the ordinary meaning of the terms of the treaty, their context, the object and purpose of the treaty, as well as subsequent practice in the application of the treaty, any relevant rules of international law, and the drafting history.[67] In light of the decades that have passed since the adoption of the 1949 Conventions, the updated commentaries utilize the significant State practice in the interpretation and application of the conventions. The updated commentaries also benefit from materials contained in ICRC archives and the numerous judicial decisions that have interpreted the relevant provisions.[68]

60. The present author has written some of the commentaries on individual articles.

61. Cameron et al., *supra* note 59, at 1210.

62. *Id.*, 1212.

63. Bruno Demeyere et al., *The Updated ICRC Commentary on the Second Geneva Convention: Demystifying the Law of Armed Conflict at Sea*, 98 International Review of the Red Cross 401, 403 (2016).

64. Mohr & Policinski, *supra* note 49, 1902.

65. This was deliberate. *See id.* at 1910.

66. *E.g.*, Commentary on the First Geneva Convention, *supra* note 54, at 16, 48, 60, 157, 349 (Pictet ed.).

67. Vienna Convention on the Law of Treaties arts. 31 and 32, May 23, 1969, 1155 U.N.T.S. 331.

68. *See generally* Jean-Marie Henckaerts, *Bringing the Commentaries on the Geneva Conventions and Their Additional Protocols into the Twenty-first Century*, 94(888) International Review of the Red Cross 1551 (2012); Cameron et al., *supra* note 59, at 1211–14.

The formal status of the ICRC Commentaries is that of teachings of publicists.[69] However, in practice, the ICRC Commentaries are afforded an outsized role. They are one of the most influential of all teachings and are regularly described as "authoritative"[70] and "valuable."[71] They are relied upon frequently and significantly by courts and tribunals in such a way as to go beyond their formal legal status. For example, the Pictet Commentaries definition of an international armed conflict, as "[a]ny difference arising between two States and leading to the intervention of the armed forces,"[72] has been particularly influential.[73]

In certain cases, the Commentaries have been treated as determinative. According to the Trial Chamber of the International Criminal Tribunal for the former Yugoslavia (ICTY) in *Martić*, on one particular issue, the Appeals Chamber in *Blaškić* "based its holding on the ICRC Commentary."[74] Likewise, in the *Stakić* Appeal Judgment, the Appeals Chamber noted that ICTY trial judgments on a particular issue "rely for their authority on a statement in the ICRC Commentary."[75] Such an approach is not limited to the ICTY. In the *Duch* case, the Extraordinary Chambers in the Courts of Cambodia (ECCC) quote a passage from the ICRC Commentary and states that "[t]he Chamber adopts this early analysis."[76] For its part, the Eritrea-Ethiopia Claims Commission used the ICRC Commentary to rebut an argument of Ethiopia.[77] The U.S. Supreme Court in *Hamdan v. Rumsfeld* has also referred several times to the Pictet Commentary on the Third Convention.[78] And this citation led to other U.S. courts also referencing

69. Statute of the International Court of Justice art. 38(1)(d), June 26, 1945, 59 Stat. 1055, 33 U.N.T.S. 993.

70. Prosecutor v. Tadić, Case No. IT-94-1, Judgment, ¶ 93 (July 15, 1999).

71. Serdar Mohammed and Others v. Secretary of State for Defence, [2015] EWCA Civ. 843, ¶ 171. *See also* Haidar Ali Hussein v. Secretary of State for Defence, [2013] EWHC 95, ¶ 33 ("long been regarded as a valuable source of determining the correct construction of the various Conventions").

72. Commentary on the First Geneva Convention, *supra* note 54, at 32 (Pictet ed.).

73. *E.g.*, Prosecutor v. Dyilo, Case No. ICC-01/04-01/06, Judgment pursuant to Article 74 of the Statute, ¶ 541 (Mar. 14, 2012); Prosecutor v. KAING Guek Eav alias Duch, Case File/Dossier No. 001/18-07-2007/ECCC/TC, Judgment, ¶ 414 (July 26, 2020).

74. Prosecutor v. Martić, Case No. IT-95-11-T, Judgment, fn. 137 (June 12, 2007).

75. Prosecutor v. Stakić, Case No. IT-97-24-A, Judgment, ¶ 305 (Mar. 22, 2006).

76. Prosecutor v. KAING Guek Eav alias Duch, *supra* note 73, at ¶ 452.

77. Partial Award, Prisoners of War, Eritrea's Claim 17, ¶ 68 (July 1, 2003) (Eritrea Ethiopia Claims Commission).

78. Hamdan v. Rumsfeld, 548 U.S. 557 (2006).

the Commentary.[79] The updated commentaries have also started to be cited by courts and tribunals.[80]

The ICRC Commentaries have also proven instructive for military lawyers. For example, Hays Parks, the then Chief of International Law at the Office of the Judge Advocate General of the (U.S.) Army, observed that "[i]n the development of any legal advice regarding the *1949 Geneva Conventions*, they [the Pictet Commentaries] are the first reference to which one resorts; and more than one meeting or discussion has been shortened by the question, 'What does Pictet say about this?'"[81] And John Reid, the Head of the Office of International Law at the Australian Commonwealth Attorney-General's Department, has indicated that "Government legal advisers frequently avail themselves of the Commentaries in advising their governments on IHL. In that sense, this Updated Commentary [on the First Geneva Convention] forms an essential and welcome addition to the legal advisers' toolkit. The frequency with which States refer to the Commentaries in interpreting their obligations demonstrates not only the practical utility of this work, but also the special legitimacy that States, including Australia, accord to the ICRC."[82]

Through its commentaries, the ICRC has contributed to the *interpretation* of the treaty law.

B. Clarifications of the Law

Not every ICRC output has been as influential as its Commentaries on the Geneva Conventions and Additional Protocols. Other projects have had different, lesser impacts. For example, the ICRC's SIrUS (Superfluous Injury or Unnecessary Suffering) project,[83] which sought to "elaborate criteria that could be applied to any weapon to make an evidence-based determination of whether or not its use

79. *E.g.*, United States v. Hamidullin, 888 F.3d 62 (4th Cir. 2018) ("The Pictet Commentary, which the Supreme Court has found instructive in interpreting the Third Geneva Convention in *Hamdan*, 548 U.S. at 619–20, supports the conclusion that . . .").

80. *E.g.*, Prosecutor v. Ntaganda, Case No. ICC-01/04-02/06, Second Decision on the Defence's Challenge to the Jurisdiction of the Court in Respect of Counts 6 and 9, ¶ 50 (Jan. 17, 2017); Public Prosecutor v. Sakhanh, No B 3787-16, Judgment, ¶ 30 (Feb. 16, 2017) (Stockholm District Court).

81. W. Hays Parks, *Pictet's Commentaries*, *in* Studies and Essays on International Humanitarian Law and Red Cross Principles in Honour of Jean Pictet 495, 496 (Christophe Swinarski ed., 1984).

82. John Reid, *Ensuring Respect: The Role of State Practice in Interpreting the Geneva Conventions*, ILA Reporter (Nov. 9, 2016), https://ilareporter.org.au/2016/11/ensuring-respect-the-role-of-state-practice-in-interpreting-the-geneva-conventions-john-reid/.

83. The SIrUS Project: Towards a Determination of which Weapons Cause "Superfluous Injury or Unnecessary Suffering" (Robin M. Coupland ed., 1997).

was lawful under the superfluous injury rule,"[84] has had limited impact and been described as "not very successful."[85]

Another output, which has had a different level of influence, is the ICRC's Interpretive Guidance on Direct Participation in Hostilities.[86] That Guidance sought "to provide recommendations" concerning the interpretation of the notion of direct participation in hostilities under international humanitarian law.[87] Publication of the guidance was met with unusually significant criticism by influential academics and military lawyers, including by some of those who were involved in the expert process related to the preparation of the guidance.[88] The criticism notwithstanding, the Interpretative Guidance has had some influence, being described as "useful guidance" by one court,[89] and cited in judgments of other international and domestic courts and tribunals.[90] It is also referenced in

84. Annyssa Bellal & Stuart Casey-Maslen, The Additional Protocols to the Geneva Conventions in Context 190 (2022).

85. Marie Jacobsson, *Modern Weaponry and Warfare: The Application of Article 36 of Additional Protocol I by Governments*, 82 International Law Studies 183, 185 (2006). Boothby has suggested that "the SIrUS Project was seeking to shed light on what really amounted to only a part of the underlying problem and was therefore seen by a number of States as analysing the problem on a partial basis." William H. Boothby, Weapons and the Law of Armed Conflict 56–57 (2016).

86. International Committee of the Red Cross, Interpretive Guidance on the Notion of Direct Participation in Hostilities under International Humanitarian Law (2009).

87. *Id.* at 9.

88. *See* Bill Boothby, *"And for Such Time As": The Time Dimension to Direct Participation in Hostilities*, 42 New York University Journal of International Law & Politics 741 (2010); W. Hays Parks, *Part IX of the ICRC Direct Participation in Hostilities Study: No Mandate, No Expertise, and Legally Incorrect*, 42 New York University Journal of International Law & Politics 769 (2010); Michael Schmitt, *Deconstructing Direct Participation in Hostilities: The Constitutive Elements*, 42 New York University Journal of International Law & Politics 697 (2010); Kenneth Watkin, *Opportunity Lost: Organized Armed Groups and the ICRC "Direct Participation in Hostilities" Interpretive Guidance*, 42 New York University Journal of International Law & Politics 641 (2010). *But see* Nils Melzer, *Keeping the Balance between Military Necessity and Humanity: A Response to Four Critiques of the ICRC's Interpretive Guidance on the Notion of Direct Participation in Hostilities*, 42 New York University Journal of International Law & Politics 831 (2010).

89. Prosecutor v. Mbarushimana, Case No. ICC-01/04-01/10, Decision on Confirmation of Charges, ¶ 148 (Dec. 16, 2011).

90. *E.g.*, Prosecutor v. Katanga, Case No. ICC-01/04-01/07, Judgment pursuant to Article 74 of the Statute (Mar. 7, 2014); Prosecutor v Đorđević, Case No. IT-05-87/1-T, Public Judgment, ¶ 2066 (Feb. 23, 2011); Yesh Din—Volunteers for Human Rights v. Chief of General Staff, Israel Defense Forces, HCJ 3003/18; Aerial Drone Deployment on 4 October 2010 in Mir Ali/Pakistan, Case No. 3 BJs 7/12-4, Decision to Terminate Proceedings (July 23, 2013) (Germany (Federal Prosecutor General)) 157 ILR 722, 747–49.

State military manuals,[91] with the Danish military manual indicating that, "[w]ith this document, the ICRC assists in interpreting the existing rules in the area. The document makes a significant contribution towards clarifying the conditions for the loss of protection for civilians."[92] Furthermore, as the official position of the ICRC, "it is the basis upon which the ICRC will make representations to States and (perhaps) make critiques of the State's conduct."[93] Notably, the Interpretive Guidance tends to be a point of reference even for those who disagree with it. Different understandings of the law are contrasted against the Guidance, thus implicitly confirming it as a point of reference.

IV. THE IDENTIFICATION OF CUSTOMARY INTERNATIONAL HUMANITARIAN LAW

The ICRC has also made an important contribution to the identification of customary IHL.

In 1993, the International Conference for the Protection of War Victims "reaffirm[ed] the necessity to make the implementation of humanitarian law more effective" and "call[ed] upon the Swiss government to convene an open-ended intergovernmental group of experts to study practical means of promoting full respect for and compliance with that law, and to prepare a report for submission to the States and to the next session of the International Conference of the Red Cross and Red Crescent."[94]

The Intergovernmental Group of Experts for the Protection of War Victims, which consisted of "experts, representing 107 States and 28 governmental and non-governmental organizations," subsequently prepared a series of recommendations on enhancing respect for the law.[95] One such recommendation was:

> [T]he ICRC be invited to prepare, with the assistance of experts on IHL representing various geographical regions and different legal systems, and in consultation with experts from governments and international organisations, a report on customary rules of IHL applicable in international

91. *E.g.*, Comando General de las Fuerzas Militares, Manual de Derecho Operacional: Manual FF.MM 3-41 Público 95 (2009).

92. Danish Ministry of Defence, Military Manual on International Law Relevant to Danish Armed Forces in International Operations 121 (2016).

93. Robert Cryer, *The International Committee of the Red Cross' "Interpretive Guidance on the Notion of Direct Participation in Hostilities": See a Little Light*, *in* Humanizing the Laws of War, *supra* note 2, at 116 and 118.

94. *International Conference for the Protection of War Victims, Geneva, 30 August–1 September 1993, Final Declaration*, 296 International Review of the Red Cross 381 (1993).

95. *Meeting of Intergovernmental Group of Experts for the Protection of War Victims (Geneva, 23–27 January 1995)*, 304 International Review of the Red Cross 4, 5 (1995).

and non-international armed conflicts, and to circulate the report to States and competent international bodies.[96]

Later that year, the Twenty-sixth International Conference of the Red Cross and Red Crescent adopted a resolution which endorsed the recommendations of the Intergovernmental Group of Experts and mandated the ICRC to prepare a report on customary IHL.[97] The Customary International Humanitarian Law Study "is the outcome of the research carried out pursuant to this mandate."[98]

Following the resolution of the International Conference, the ICRC established a Steering Committee for the preparation of the Study.[99] The Steering Committee adopted a plan of action and research commenced in October 1996. Research was undertaken in national sources of practice, with the cooperation of national researchers; international sources of practice; and the ICRC archives. For the national sources of practice, "50 countries were selected (9 in Africa, 15 in Asia, 11 in Europe, 11 in the Americas and 1 in Australasia)."[100] The countries were selected "on the basis of geographic representation, as well as recent experience of different kinds of armed conflicts in which a variety of methods of warfare had been used. . . . Significant practice of other countries was identified through research into international sources and ICRC archives."[101] The ICRC carried out research in its archives relating to "nearly 40 recent armed conflicts, some 20 of which occurred in Africa, 8 in Asia, 8 in Europe and 2 in the Americas."[102] The conflicts "were selected so that countries and conflicts not yet dealt with by a report on State practice would also be covered."[103] Various iterations of the Study were reviewed by academic and governmental experts, as well as members of the ICRC legal division.[104] All told, more than 150 experts were involved.[105]

96. *Id.*

97. International Conference of the Red Cross and Red Crescent, Resolutions of the 26th International Conference of the Red Cross and Red Crescent, Resolution 1 (Dec. 7, 1995), https://www.icrc.org/eng/resources/documents/resolution/26-international-conference-resolution-1-1995.htm.

98. 1 Customary International Humanitarian Law, at xxxiii (Jean-Marie Henckaerts & Louise Doswald-Beck eds., 2005).

99. "The Steering Committee consisted of Professors Georges Abi-Saab, Salah El-Din Amer, Ove Bring, Eric David, John Dugard, Florentino Feliciano, Horst Fischer, Françoise Hampson, Theodor Meron, Djamchid Momtaz, Milan Sahović and Raúl Emilio Vinuesa." *See id.* at li.

100. *Id.*

101. *Id.*

102. *Id.* at liii.

103. *Id.* at liii.

104. *Id.* at liv.

105. Jean-Marie Henckaerts, *Customary International Humanitarian Law: A Response to US Comments*, 89 International Review of the Red Cross 473, 474 (2007). The experts are listed at 1 Customary International Humanitarian Law, *supra* note 98, at lvi–lvii.

After nearly ten years of research and writing, in 2005, the Study was published. The Study identified 161 rules of customary IHL applicable in international armed conflicts, of which the vast majority are applicable also in non-international armed conflicts.[106] Customary IHL is particularly important given that not all States are parties to key IHL treaties such as Additional Protocol I and Additional Protocol II to the Geneva Conventions, as well as the limited number of treaty rules that are applicable in non-international armed conflicts.

The Study itself does not have the status of customary international law. Rather, it is the ICRC's view of the state of customary IHL at a particular moment in time. This was aptly described by the then president of the ICRC in his foreword to the Study as a "'photograph' of customary international humanitarian law as it stands" at the time of publication.[107]

In the period since the publication of the Study, the ICRC has engaged in a continuous process of updating the State practice that feeds into the Study,[108] but, at the time of writing, had not gone through a similar process of updating the rules part of the Study. Ironically, given the considerable influence of the Study (on which see immediately following), this could mean that the Study has the effect of freezing custom to how it existed in 2005. If the Customary IHL Study does not indicate the existence of a particular customary rule, actors who rely on the Study might consider there to be no such rule.

The Study has been enormously influential.[109] Although two States—the United States[110] and Israel[111]—remain skeptical of at least parts of the Study, other States

106. A small number of rules are described as being "arguably" applicable to non-international armed conflicts "because practice generally pointed in that direction but was less extensive." *See* Jean-Marie Henckaerts, *Study on Customary International Humanitarian Law: A Contribution to the Understanding and Respect for the Rule of Law in Armed Conflict*, 87 International Review of the Red Cross 175, 198 (2005).

107. Jakob Kellenberger, *Foreword*, *in* 1 Customary International Humanitarian Law, *supra* note 98, at xvii.

108. *See* https://ihl-databases.icrc.org/en/customary-ihl/practice.

109. *See* Jean-Marie Henckaerts, *The International Committee of the Red Cross and Customary International Humanitarian Law*, *in* Humanizing the Laws of War, *supra* note 2, at 96–102; Marko Milanovic & Sandesh Sivakumaran, *Assessing the Authority of the ICRC Customary IHL Study*, 104(920–21) International Review of the Red Cross 1856 (2022).

110. International Law Commission, Protection of the Environment in Relation to Armed Conflicts: Comments and Observations Received from Governments, International Organizations and Others, U.N. Doc. A/CN.4/749, at 29 and 79 (Jan. 17, 2022); International Law Commission, Subsequent Agreements and Subsequent Practice in Relation to the Interpretation of Treaties: Comments and Observations Received from Governments, U.N. Doc. A/CN.4/712, at 17 (Feb. 21, 2018); International Law Commission, Identification of Customary International Law: Comments and Observations Received from Governments, U.N. Doc. A/CN.4/716, at 22, 29, and 42–43 (Feb. 14, 2018).

111. International Law Commission, Protection of the Environment in Relation to Armed Conflicts, Comments and Observations Received from Governments, International Organizations and Others, U.N. Doc. A/CN.4/749, at 102 (Jan. 17, 2022).

are far more favorable. Many States refer to the Study in their manuals and statements, sometimes on numerous occasions and in very positive language. For example, Azerbaijan has described the Study as "authoritative";[112] Malaysia has treated the rules of the Study as akin to a treaty;[113] and Colombia, Denmark, and New Zealand cite the Study *extensively* in their manuals.[114] Despite its skepticism, Israel has also referenced various rules contained in the Study.[115] Courts and tribunals—including the International Criminal Court, ICTY, International Criminal Tribunal for Rwanda, Mechanism for International Criminal Tribunals, Special Court for Sierra Leone, ECCC, European Court of Human Rights, Inter-American Court of Human Rights, and domestic courts—have cited the Study multiple times and in the vast majority of cases in favorable terms.[116] The Study is frequently cited as authority for the existence of a customary rule, oftentimes as the sole or principal authority, and sometimes treated as if it were a binding text.[117] For example, the *Popović* appeal judgment reads:

> The Appeals Chamber observes that according to customary international law applicable both in international and non-international armed conflicts "[t]he parties to the conflict must allow and facilitate rapid and unimpeded passage of humanitarian relief for civilians in need, which is impartial in character and conducted without any adverse distinction, subject to their right of control.[1746]
>
> Fn 1746 Henckaerts and Doswald-Beck, Customary International Humanitarian Law, Vol. I, Rule 55, pp. 193–200. See also Article 23 of Geneva Convention IV; Article 70 of Additional Protocol I; Article 18 of Additional Protocol II.[118]

112. *Letter dated 10 April 2017 from the Permanent Representative of Azerbaijan to the United Nations Addressed to the Secretary-General*, U.N. Doc. A/71/880–S/2017/316, ¶ 128 (Apr. 26, 2017).

113. *See Letter dated 1 June 2015 from the Permanent Representative of Malaysia to the United Nations Addressed to the Secretary-General*, U.N. Doc. S/2015/402 (June 2, 2015).

114. New Zealand Defence Force (NZDF), Manual of Armed Forces Law, Vol. 4: Law of Armed Conflict (2017); Manual de Derecho Operacional, *supra* note 91; Military Manual on International Law relevant to Danish Armed Forces in International Operations, *supra* note 92.

115. The State of Israel, The Operation in Gaza, 27 December 2008–18 January 2009: Factual and Legal Aspects (July 2009).

116. *See generally* Milanovic & Sivakumaran, *supra* note 109, at 1876 (identifying 162 citations in 69 decisions).

117. *Id.*

118. Prosecutor v. Popović et al., Case No. IT-05-88-A, Judgment, ¶ 615 (Jan. 30, 2015). *See also* Milanovic & Sivakumaran, *supra* note 109, at 1880–84.

Thus, even though the ICRC's own practice and *opinio juris* does not contribute to the *formation* of customary IHL, it has made a major contribution to the *identification* of customary IHL. The Customary International Humanitarian Law Study has become a hugely influential document on which many States and other actors have relied.

V. CATALYZING THE VIEWS OF STATES

ICRC outputs (commentaries, guidance, etc.) do not themselves contribute to the formation of customary IHL. The same is true of ICRC practice. However, ICRC practice has led States to modify their own practice, and ICRC outputs have led States to set out in public their own views on various legal issues. For example, "[i]n 1991, in response to an ICRC memorandum on the applicability of IHL in the Gulf region, the U.S. Department of the Army pointed out that 'the obligation of distinguishing combatants and military objectives from civilians and civilian objects is a shared responsibility of the attacker, defender, and the civilian population as such.'"[119] Likewise in 1991, "in response to an ICRC memorandum on the applicability of IHL in the Gulf region, the United States commented that its practice was consistent with the prohibition on ordering that there shall be no survivors."[120] This State practice does contribute to the formation of customary international law. Thus, the ICRC has played an *indirect* role in the formation of custom, acting as a catalyst to States forming and publishing their own views on IHL matters. The International Law Commission has put it thus:

> Official statements of the International Committee of the Red Cross (ICRC), such as appeals for and memorandums on respect for international humanitarian law, may likewise play an important role in shaping the practice of States reacting to such statements; and publications of the ICRC may assist in identifying relevant practice. Such activities may thus contribute to the development and determination of customary international law, but they are not practice as such.[121]

A similar approach applies at the level of the *identification* of customary international law. As noted above, the Customary International Humanitarian Law Study does not itself have the status of customary international law. However, following the publication of the Study, a number of States expressly accepted or rejected particular rules which were identified in the Study. The United States published a response to the Study, inter alia taking issue

119. 2 Customary International Humanitarian Law, *supra* note 98, at 9.

120. *Id.* at 926.

121. International Law Commission, Conclusions on identification of customary international law, with commentaries, Commentary on Conclusion 4, ¶ 9.

with specific rules which were identified in the Study as having customary status.[122] In a submission to the Baha Mousa Inquiry, the U.K. government, while expressing reservations about the Study, noted its acceptance of certain rules identified in the Study.[123] Other States have accepted particular rules indirectly, through citation of those rules in their military manuals.[124] These examples indicate the relevant States' position on the existence or otherwise of particular customary rules, positions which were catalyzed by the publication of the Study.

A similar dynamic exists with respect to treaty interpretation. One of the elements of treaty interpretation is that "[t]here shall be taken into account, together with the context . . . any subsequent practice in the application of the treaty which establishes the agreement of the parties regarding its interpretation."[125] Subsequent practice which does not meet these criteria can also be taken into account, but as a supplementary means of interpretation.[126] In both respects, the subsequent practice in question is that of States. The International Law Commission, in its Conclusions on subsequent agreements and subsequent practice in relation to the interpretation of treaties, has indicated:

> 1. Subsequent practice under articles 31 and 32 [VCLT] may consist of any conduct of a party in the application of a treaty, whether in the exercise of its executive, legislative, judicial or other functions.
> 2. Other conduct, including by non-State actors, does not constitute subsequent practice under articles 31 and 32. Such conduct may, however, be relevant when assessing the subsequent practice of parties to a treaty.[127]

ICRC practice does not count as subsequent practice as such. However, ICRC practice can catalyze State practice.[128] A good example relates to the interpretation

122. Letter from John Bellinger III, Legal Adviser, U.S. Dept. of State, and William J. Haynes, General Counsel, U.S. Dept. of Defense, to Dr. Jakob Kellenberger, President, International Committee of the Red Cross, Regarding Customary International Law Study (Nov. 3, 2006), *reprinted in* 46 International Legal Materials 514 (2007).

123. Ministry of Defence, Closing Submissions to the Baha Mousa Public Inquiry on Modules 1–3, 25 June 2010, at 28–33, archived online at https://web.archive.org/web/20120215220215/http://www.bahamousainquiry.org/linkedfiles/baha_mousa/hearings/oral_submission/sub000947.pdf.

124. *Supra* note 114.

125. VCLT, art. 31(3)(b).

126. *See, e.g.*, Kasikili/Sedudu Island (Botswana/Namibia), 1999 I.C.J. 1045, ¶¶ 79–80.

127. International Law Commission, Conclusions on subsequent agreements and subsequent practice in relation to the interpretation of treaties, Conclusion 5.

128. The International Law Commission Commentary to Conclusion 5, ¶ 17, notes that "non-State actors can provide valuable information about subsequent practice of parties, contribute to assessing this information and even solicit its coming into being." Report of the International Law Commission, seventieth session (April 30–June 1 and July 2–August 10, 2018), A/73/10, 42 (2018).

of common Article 1 of the 1949 Geneva Conventions. In its updated commentary to the First Geneva Convention, the ICRC inter alia set out an interpretation of the "ensure respect" dimension of common Article 1. The Commentary provides that High Contracting Parties "must do everything reasonably in their power to ensure respect for the Conventions by others that are Party to a conflict."[129] This includes a negative obligation not to encourage, aid, or assist in violations, as well as a positive obligation to "do everything reasonably in their power to prevent and bring such violations to an end."[130]

Some States expressed their disagreement with this interpretation. John Reid, the Head of the Office of International Law at the Australian Commonwealth Attorney-General's Department, noted that "[t]here will always be disagreements about the content of the law, amongst States, and between States and organisations such as the ICRC. Common Article 1 is one such obligation where different views persist."[131] He took issue with two of the examples of measures that were said in the updated commentary to be within the scope of a State's power and indicated that those examples "go beyond what is reasonably within a State's power, and do not find support in State practice."[132] Brian Egan, the then Legal Adviser of the U.S. Department of State, has also indicated that "[s]ome have argued that the obligation in Common Article 1 of the Geneva Conventions to 'ensure respect' for the Conventions legally requires us to undertake [certain specified] steps and more vis-à-vis not only our partners, but all States and non-State actors engaged in armed conflict. Although we do not share this expansive interpretation of Common Article 1, as a matter of policy, we always seek to promote adherence to the law of armed conflict generally and encourage other States to do the same."[133]

While the ICRC interpretation of common Article 1 does not constitute subsequent practice for the purposes of Articles 31 and 32 VCLT, the practice of the United States and Australia to which it gave rise does constitute subsequent practice.[134] In this way, the ICRC has acted as a catalyst for the formation of the subsequent practice of States.

129. ICRC, Updated Commentary on the First Geneva Convention, *supra* note 58, at ¶ 153.

130. *Id.*, ¶ 154.

131. Reid, *supra* note 82.

132. *Id.*

133. Brian Egan, *Keynote Address: International Law, Legal Diplomacy, and the Counter-ISIL Campaign: Some Observations*, 92 international law studies 235, 245 (2016).

134. Practice can include "statements." *See* International Law Commission, Commentary to Conclusion 6, *supra* note 128, ¶ 22.

VI. CONCLUSION

The ICRC has made a major contribution to the development of IHL. It has produced initial drafts of treaties, contributed to the interpretation of treaty provisions, and proved hugely influential in the identification of customary international humanitarian law.

Three points cut across these contributions. First, the ICRC has a mandate to produce various outputs. One of the ICRC's mandates comes from the Statutes of the International Red Cross and Red Crescent Movement, which were adopted by the Twenty-fifth International Conference of the Red Cross in 1986. The Statutes provide that the role of ICRC is inter alia "to work for the understanding and dissemination of knowledge of international humanitarian law applicable in armed conflicts and to prepare any development thereof."[135] Outputs such as the updated commentaries on the Geneva Conventions and Additional Protocols are linked to this statutory mandate. The ICRC has also been mandated to undertake specific projects, such as to prepare a report on customary rules of IHL, at the request of the International Conference of the Red Cross and Red Crescent.[136] This, in turn, is linked to the ICRC's statutory mandate, which also provides that the ICRC is to "carry out mandates entrusted to it by the International Conference."[137] As the Statutes were adopted by the International Conference, the mandate of the ICRC comes in part from the High Contracting Parties to the Geneva Conventions, that is, States.

Second, substance is linked to process and the process indicates that the ICRC does not work in isolation. On the contrary, the ICRC works with other actors. For example, in the drafting of the Geneva Conventions, the ICRC consulted with, among others, experts and National Red Cross and Red Crescent Societies, prior to putting the draft texts before the International Conference of the Red Cross and then before the Diplomatic Conference. The various reports and records suggest that the process involved sharing and receiving ideas, benefiting from experiences, and reacting to suggestions. It was something of a dialogue, albeit one that was clearly led and closely managed by the ICRC. In the preparation of the Customary International Humanitarian Law Study, the ICRC convened a Steering Committee, involved external researchers in the research of State practice, and benefited from expert input. The contribution of the ICRC to the development of IHL took place alongside other actors.

135. Statutes of the International Red Cross and Red Crescent Movement, *supra* note 3, art. 5(2)(g).

136. RESOLUTIONS OF THE 26TH INTERNATIONAL CONFERENCE OF THE RED CROSS AND RED CRESCENT, *supra* note 97, Resolution 1.

137. Statutes of the International Red Cross and Red Crescent Movement, *supra* note 3, art. 5(2)(h).

Third and finally, the reaction to an ICRC output is crucial for whether that output has an impact on the development of the law. If an output is met with near-universal rejection or even total silence, it would not amount to a contribution to the development of the law (although it might catalyze States' views). By contrast, if the output is received positively—if it is repeated in statements of States and followed in their practice—the output will make far more of a contribution to the development of the law. Reception of the output can be almost as important as the output itself, but that is often beyond the control of the ICRC.

8

Applying the Law of Armed Conflict in Domestic Courts: The Fusion of Domestic and International Law and the Question of IHL Expertise

YAHLI SHERESHEVSKY*

I. INTRODUCTION

When considering the role of domestic courts in the development of international law, a good starting point would be to note that domestic courts are not merely agents of compliance with international law.[1] They play a significant role in the interpretation and development of international law in general[2] and specifically the law of armed conflict (international humanitarian law, or IHL).[3] The role of

* Yahli Shereshevsky is a Senior Lecturer at the Faculty of Law, University of Haifa.

1. Karen Knop, *Here and There: International Law and Domestic Courts*, 32 New York University Journal of International Law and Policy 501, 503 (2000).

2. *See, e.g.*, Roger O'Keefe, *Domestic Courts as Agents of Development of the International Law of Jurisdiction*, 26 Leiden Journal of International Law 541 (2013); Antonios Tzanakopoulos & Christian J. Tams, *Introduction: Domestic Courts as Agents of Development of International Law*, 26 Leiden Journal of International Law 531 (2013); André Nollkaemper, National Courts and the International Rule of Law (2011).

3. Lawrence Hill-Cawthorne, *Detention in the Context of Counterterrorism and Armed Conflict: Continuities and New Challenges*, 103 International Review of the Red Cross 555,

Yahli Shereshevsky, *Applying the Law of Armed Conflict in Domestic Courts: The Fusion of Domestic and International Law and the Question of IHL Expertise* In: *Making and Shaping the Law of Armed Conflict.* Edited by: Sandesh Sivakumaran and Christian R. Burņe, Oxford University Press. © Yahli Shereshevsky 2024. DOI: 10.1093/oso/9780197775134.003.0008 domestic courts in the development of international law is twofold due to the two hats that the courts wear.[4] On the one hand, domestic courts are State organs and their decisions represent State practice and *opinio juris* for the identification of customary international law.[5] On the other hand, the interpretations of the law by domestic courts may have a broader influence on the development of international law. Regardless of the debate over their formal role as a subsidiary source of international law, in practice, domestic cases can serve as a focal point of reference for the interpretation of international law.[6] This latter role explains the significance of seminal domestic law cases, such as *Quebec Succession*,[7] *Filartiga*,[8] or *Pinochet*,[9] that influence the development of international law far beyond a mere expression of the practice and *opinio juris* of one State.

The role of domestic courts in the development of IHL has been widely recognized in the literature, although attitudes toward the substance of domestic cases vary from highly critical accounts of the case law to commendations of the courts' role in developing IHL.[10] Most of the contemporary literature focuses on States involved in transnational armed conflicts with non-State armed groups—the United States, the United Kingdom, and Israel.[11] However, the application of

559–68 (2021); SHARON WEILL, THE ROLE OF NATIONAL COURTS IN APPLYING INTERNATIONAL HUMANITARIAN LAW (2014); APPLYING INTERNATIONAL HUMANITARIAN LAW IN JUDICIAL AND QUASI-JUDICIAL BODIES: INTERNATIONAL AND DOMESTIC ASPECTS (Derek Jinks, Jackson N. Maogoto, & Solon Solomon eds., 2014).

4. Anthea Roberts, *Comparative International Law? The Role of National Courts in Creating and Enforcing International Law*, 60 INTERNATIONAL & COMPARATIVE LAW QUARTERLY 57 (2011).

5. Antonios Tzanakopoulos, *Domestic Judicial Lawmaking*, *in* RESEARCH HANDBOOK ON INTERNATIONAL LAWMAKING 222, 230 (Catherine Brölmann & Yannick Radi eds., 2016); Ingrid Wuerth, *International Law in Domestic Courts and the Jurisdictional Immunities of the State Case*, 13 MELBOURNE JOURNAL OF INTERNATIONAL LAW 1, 3 (2013).

6. There is disagreement about whether domestic courts' decisions should be regarded as "judicial decisions" under Article 38(1)(d) of the ICJ Statute. *See* Cedric Ryngaert, *Book Review: Odile Ammann, Domestic Courts and the Interpretation of International Law. Methods and Reasoning Based on the Swiss Example*, 34 LEIDEN JOURNAL OF INTERNATIONAL LAW 279, 281 (2021); *but see* O'Keefe, *supra* note 2, at 542. In practice, the difference between the competing views is questionable due to the interpretive effect of the decisions regardless of their formal definition.

7. Reference re Secession of Quebec, [1998] 2 S.C.R. 217 (Can.).

8. Filartiga v. Pena-Irala 630 F.2d 876 (2d Cir. 1980).

9. Regina v. Bartle and the Commissioner of Police for the Metropolis and others Ex Parte Pinochet, 38 I.L.M. 581 (H.L. 1999) (UK).

10. *See, e.g.*, WEILL, *supra* note 3; Amichai Cohen & Stuart A. Cohen, *Israel and International Humanitarian Law: Between the Neo-Realism of State Security and the "Soft Power" of Legal Acceptability*, 16 ISRAEL STUDIES 1 (2011).

11. Lord Lloyd-Jones, *International Law Before United Kingdom Courts: A Quiet Revolution*, 71 International & Comparative Law Quarterly 503 (2022); Andrew Sanger, *Review of Executive Action Abroad: The UK Supreme Court in the International Legal Order*, 68 International & Comparative Law Quarterly 35 (2019); WEILL, *supra* note 3; Hill-Cawthorne, *supra* note 3; David

IHL by domestic courts is also discussed in relation to other domestic courts.[12] The focus of the literature on domestic courts is often on the ability of these courts to fill gaps or inform interpretive debates over the regulation of contemporary IHL questions.[13]

Relying as it does on documents that are available in English and Hebrew, this chapter also focuses on the domestic courts of three States (the United States, the United Kingdom, and Israel), although it also considers cases involving "foreign fighters" in Belgian courts. This chapter addresses two issues that have been largely left outside the conversation about the interaction between domestic courts and IHL, namely, the fusion of domestic and international law, and the role of (or lack of) expertise vis-à-vis the application of IHL by domestic courts. As to the fusion of domestic law and international law, the chapter identifies three main types of domestic court decisions on IHL that fuse international and domestic law. The first is the general discussion of the application of international law by domestic courts as part of domestic law. The second is the direct application of domestic law doctrines when deciding questions of international law. A key example of such a case is the *Targeted Killings* case of the Israeli Supreme Court sitting as a High Court of Justice (HCJ) in which the court applied the domestic public law doctrine of proportionality in its decision on the legality of targeted killings under international law.[14] The third is when the legality under international law is dependent on the existence of adequate regulation under domestic law. A seminal example is the *Serdar Mohammed* case in which the High Court of England and Wales determined that under the law of non-international armed conflict (NIAC), lawful detention is dependent upon the authority to detain under domestic law.[15]

Weissbrodt & Nathaniel Nesbitt, *The Role of the United States Supreme Court in Interpreting and Developing Humanitarian Law*, 95 Minnesota Law Review 1339 (2011).

12. *See, e.g.*, Marcela Giraldo Muñoz & Jose Serralvo, *International Humanitarian Law in Colombia: Going a Step Beyond*, 101 International Review of the REd Cross 1117 (2019); Hanne Cuyckens & Christophe Paulussen, *The Prosecution of Foreign Fighters in Western Europe: The Difficult Relationship Between Counter-Terrorism and International Humanitarian Law*, 24 Journal of Conflict & Security Law 537 (2019); Chintan Chandrachud, *International Humanitarian Law in Indian Courts: Application, Misapplication and Non-Application*, *in* Applying International Humanitarian Law in Judicial and Quasi-Judicial Bodies: International and Domestic Aspects 389 (Derek Jinks, Jackson N. Maogoto, & Solon Solomon eds., 2014); Ekaterina Ortiz Linares & Marisela Silva Chau, *Reflections in the Colombian Case Law on the Protection of Medical Personnel against Punishment*, 95 International Review of the Red Cross 251 (2013).

13. *See, e.g.*, Ashley Deeks, *Domestic Humanitarian Law: Developing the Law of War in Domestic Courts*, *in* Applying International Humanitarian Law in Judicial and Quasi-Judicial Bodies: International and Domestic Aspects (D. Jinks, J. Maogoto, & S. Solomon eds., 2014).

14. *See infra* section II.B.

15. *See infra* section II.C.

As to expertise, the chapter suggests that a key explanation for the direct application of domestic law is insufficient IHL expertise. While domestic courts are often comprised of prominent legal experts, their expertise often lies in domestic rather than international law. The combination of domestic legal expertise and judicial intuition regarding the desired outcome of the relevant cases can lead to the fusion of domestic and international law. This is especially the case when similar terms with different meanings exist under domestic and international law, the above-mentioned *Targeted Killings* case serving as a good example. The term "proportionality" exists under both IHL and domestic public law but has a different meaning in each. In that case, the Court applied the domestic version of proportionality to reach a desirable outcome. The chapter then provides a thorough examination of domestic courts' expertise. It starts with IHL expertise in domestic courts, providing several examples of misapplication of the law. Then it examines the role of general legal expertise in domestic courts and its potential to mitigate insufficient IHL expertise. Finally, the chapter addresses the implications of the fusion of international and domestic law and concludes that domestic courts' insufficient IHL expertise raises significant concerns regarding their role in developing IHL.

II. THE FUSION OF DOMESTIC AND INTERNATIONAL LAW

There are three main types of interaction between domestic and international law in IHL cases—discussion of IHL as part of domestic law, direct application of domestic law doctrines to IHL questions, and reliance on domestic law for legality under IHL.

A. IHL as Part of Domestic Law

The first and most common form of interaction between domestic and international law in domestic courts is when courts apply international law as part of domestic law or use IHL to inform their interpretation of domestic law. Under this type of interaction, legality under domestic law is often dependent on the legality of the relevant conduct under international law. The vast majority of the scholarly discussion about the role of domestic courts in the interpretation and development of international law focuses on these types of interactions between domestic courts and international law. For example, David Weissbrodt and Nathaniel Nesbitt focus most of their discussion regarding the interpretation and development of IHL in the U.S. Supreme Court on this type of application, examining, inter alia, how the U.S. Supreme Court uses IHL as a tool of constitutional interpretation.[16]

16. Weissbrodt & Nesbitt, *supra* note 11.

It should be noted that such interaction between domestic and international law does not necessarily exist in all domestic cases in which international law is relevant. In some cases, domestic law is used as the main avenue, even in cases that seem to be primarily about international law issues. In this context, Tamar Hostovesky Brandes recently suggested that domestic law can be used by domestic courts as an alternative legal framework to international law. Hostovsky Brandes argued that a recent case of the Israeli Supreme Court, *Silwad Municipality v. The Knesset*,[17] which determined that the Settlement Regularization Law is unconstitutional, represents a potential shift from international to constitutional law as the main legal paradigm for discussing the occupation.[18]

The direction of the interaction between international and domestic law in these cases is from the international to the domestic. This touches on the broader subject of the relationship between international law and domestic law and is mostly beyond the scope of this chapter. In contrast, the next two types of interaction focus on the less common direction of influence—cases in which domestic law influences international law.

B. Direct Application of Domestic Law Doctrines to IHL Questions

The *Targeted Killings* case,[19] which is one of the paradigmatic examples of the application of IHL by domestic courts, has been discussed in numerous scholarly works. The international law community's reactions to the judgment were mixed. Some authors criticized the case and its aftermath as an example of deference to State authorities, while emphasizing the legitimizing aspects of the decision.[20] Others emphasized the limiting role of the decision on State conduct.[21]

From the perspective of IHL's development, the case included several important positions. These include the classification of the conflict between Israel and Palestinian armed groups as an international armed conflict, a reliance on the notion of direct participation in hostilities to determine the legality of targeted

17. HCJ 1308/17 Silwad Municipality v. the Knesset (2020) (Isr.), https://supremedecisions.court.gov.il/Home/Download?path=HebrewVerdicts/17/080/013/v48&fileName=17013080.V48&type=4.

18. Tamar Hostovskt Brandes, *Constitutional Adjudication of International Law Violations*, Verfassungsblog (June 14, 2020), https://verfassungsblog.de/constitutional-adjudication-of-international-law-violations/.

19. HCJ 769/02 Pub. Comm. Against Torture in Israel v. Gov't of Israel (*Targeted Killings* case) PD 62(1) 507 (2006) (Isr.).

20. Weill, *supra* note 3, at 142–44.

21. Amichai Cohen & Yuval Shany, *A Development of Modest Proportions: The Application of the Principle of Proportionality in the Targeted Killings Case*, 5 Journal of International Criminal Justice 310 (2007).

killings, the introduction of the least harmful means requirement, as well as an obligation to undertake post hoc investigation of civilian deaths.

The focus of this section is on one particular element of the contribution of the *Targeted Killings* case to the debate over the targeting of non-State armed group members, namely, the least harmful means requirement. The court determined that a person can be targeted only where it is not possible "to act against him by means of a less harmful measure."[22] The court explicitly recognized the domestic law origin of this requirement, stating that "[i]n our internal law this rule is derived from the principle of proportionality. Indeed, of the possible military measures, one should choose the measure whose violation of the victim's human rights is the least."[23]

The position of the court has been discussed by various authors. For example, Marko Milanovic discussed it as part of the integration of IHL and international human rights law. He suggested that both the requirement for the least harmful means and the requirement for an effective investigation stem from human rights law.[24] Amichai Cohen and Yuval Shany briefly address the merger of the proportionality test under domestic law and IHL, criticizing the use of the least harmful means requirement as contradictory to IHL proportionality.[25]

For the purposes of this chapter, I focus on the domestic law aspect of the least harmful means requirement. The requirement demonstrates the strongest way in which domestic courts use domestic law as part of an international law discussion—a direct application of domestic law doctrine to an international law question. Under Israeli public law, the principle of proportionality is comprised of a three-part test: (1) a rational link between the measure that is taken and the desired objective; (2) implementing the least harmful measure; and (3) proportionality in the strict sense, namely, measuring the benefit of the policy against the harm to human rights. The least harmful means requirement in the *Targeted Killings* case is a direct application of the domestic law understanding of proportionality to IHL proportionality. The court did not address the serious doctrinal challenges of such an application, which was contradictory to the *lex lata* at the time of the decision.[26]

The uniqueness of such a direct application calls for further reflection on the reasons for such an application. It seems that the direct application of domestic law was not made on the basis of a comprehensive theory regarding the merger

22. *Targeted Killings* case, *supra* note 19, at ¶ 40.

23. *Id.*

24. Marko Milanovic, *Lessons for Human Rights and Humanitarian Law in the War on Terror: Comparing Hamdan and the Israeli Targeted Killing Case*, 89 International Review of the Red Cross 373, 290 (2007).

25. Cohen & Shany, *supra* note 21, at 312–15.

26. *Id.*; Roy S. Schondorf, *The Targeted Killings Judgment: A Preliminary Assessment*, 5 Journal of International Criminal Justice 301 (2007).

of domestic and international law. Instead, as this chapter discusses in depth in section III, it seems that it might be the result of a broader phenomenon, namely, insufficient IHL expertise.

C. Domestic Law as an Integral Part of Legality under IHL

The third type of relationship between international and domestic law is when domestic law constitutes an integral part of the legality of conduct under IHL. The main example of this approach is the *Serdar Mohammed* case.[27] In *Serdar Mohammed*, the High Court of England and Wales had to decide, inter alia, whether the law of NIAC contains an independent authority to detain. The issue was subject to debate among international lawyers.[28] While under the law of international armed conflict (IAC), the authority of the parties to the conflict to detain combatants and civilians is explicitly mentioned in the relevant conventions, no similar provisions exist in the context of NIAC. The judgment by Justice Leggatt of the High Court of England and Wales determined that the law of NIAC does not contain an independent right to detain. As such, for detention in NIAC to be lawful, it must be based on an external authority to detain (i.e., outside the law of NIAC). In most cases, this will be under domestic law. Without such authority, the detention will be unlawful under Article 5 of the European Convention on Human Rights (ECHR), and probably also under Article 9 of the International Covenant on Civil and Political Rights (ICCPR).[29] The judgment of Justice Leggatt included a detailed discussion of international humanitarian law, international human rights law, and the relationship between these two regimes that was

27. Al-Waheed v. Ministry of Defence [2017] UKSC 2; Serdar Mohammed v. Ministry of Defence [2014] EWHC 1369 (QB) (Leggatt J); Serdar Mohammed v. Ministry of Defence [2015] EWCA Civ. 843 (CA(Civ.)) (CA).

28. *See, e.g.*, Darragh Murray, *Non-State Armed Groups, Detention Authority in Non-International Armed Conflict, and the Coherence of International Law: Searching for a Way Forward*, 30 Leiden Journal of International Law 435 (2017); Sean Aughey & Aurel Sari, *Targeting and Detention in Non-International Armed Conflict: Serdar Mohammed and the Limits of Human Rights Convergence*, 91 International Law Studies 60 (2015); Lawrence Hill-Cawthorne & Dapo Akande, *Does IHL Provide a Legal Basis for Detention in Non-International Armed Conflicts?*, EJIL Talk! (May 7, 2014), https://www.ejiltalk.org/does-ihl-provide-a-legal-basis-for-detention-in-non-international-armed-conflicts/; Sandesh Sivakumaran, The Law of Non-International Armed Conflict 71 (2012); Jelena Pejic, *Procedural Principles and Safeguards for Internment/Administrative Detention in Armed Conflict and Other Situations of Violence*, 87 International Review of the Red Cross 375 (2005).

29. The relevant legal framework in the case is the ECHR, but similar reasoning could have been used under the ICCPR.

described as a "heroic effort" to address a complex set of international law issues.[30] The decision regarding the lack of authority to detain under the law of NIAC was later approved by the Court of Appeal and the Supreme Court, although the latter determined that the UN Security Council (UNSC) provided authority to detain in the circumstances of the case.[31]

The result of the *Serdar Mohammed* case is that the legality of detention in NIACs is dependent on its legality under domestic law or an international law authorization outside IHL. This is the mirror image of the first type of interaction between domestic and international law, according to which legality under domestic law is dependent on the legality of the relevant conduct under international law.

While areas in which legality under international law is dependent on legality under domestic law is not uncommon under human rights law, it is unique in the context of IHL. This complex relationship between domestic law, IHL, and IHRL is further developed in the next section.

D. Human Rights, Domestic Law, and the Limits of Convergence

Modern international law is built to a large extent on universal norms.[32] This is especially the case in the context of international humanitarian law. In the context of armed conflict, it is widely believed that IHL must establish clear and universally applicable rules in order to improve compliance. There is concern that taking into account unique contextual factors of the parties involved could undermine this goal.[33] Similarly, when considering the use of domestic law to inform IHL, the variation in domestic laws between States raises concerns about consistency and effectiveness in promoting compliance with IHL.

The common thread between the *Targeted Killings* case and the *Serdar Mohammed* case, as well as between the two latter types of convergence between

30. Marko Milanovic, *High Court Rules that the UK Lacks Detention Authority in Afghanistan*, EJIL Talk! (May 3, 2014), https://www.ejiltalk.org/high-court-rules-that-the-uk-lacks-ihl-detention-authority-in-afghanistan/.

31. *Al-Waheed*, *supra* note 27, at ¶¶ 59–63.

32. *See, e.g.*, John Tasioulas, *International Law and the Limits of Fairness*, 13 European Journal of International Law 993 (2002); Jonathan I. Charney, *Universal International Law*, 87 American Journal of International Law 529 (1993).

33. *See, e.g.*, Yahli Shereshevsky, *Are All Soldiers Created Equal?—On the Equal Application of the Law to Enhanced Soldiers*, 61 Virginia Journal of International Law 271, 284–88 (2021); Amichai Cohen & Yuval Shany, *Contextualizing Proportionality Analysis? A Response to Schmitt and Merriam on Israel's Targeting Practices*, Just Security (May 7, 2015), https://www.justsecurity.org/22786/contextualizing-proportionality-analysis-response-schmitt-merriam/; Michael Schmitt, *The Relationship Between Context and Proportionality: A Reply to Cohen and Shany*, Just Security (May 11, 2015), https://www.justsecurity.org/22948/response-cohen-shany/.

domestic law and international law, is human rights. In the *Targeted Killings* case, the court applied the proportionality doctrine that is applied in the domestic context to examine the legality of infringement upon human rights. In the *Serdar Mohammed* case, the court required domestic (or UNSC) authority for detention as required under human rights law. It seems that the application of domestic law in these contexts is less concerning in relation to the previous discussion regarding consistency and universal norms, since there is much correlation between domestic human rights and international human rights. Nonetheless, the application of human rights law in the context of armed conflicts is not without concerns and is the subject of regular debate.[34] Due to the complicated nature of the issue, it seems highly important for a court that actively participates in the debate, and perhaps even intentionally promotes a specific position on the relationship between IHL and IHRL, to have a reasoned and well-grounded position on the subject. On this issue, there is a significant difference between the *Serdar Mohammed* case and the *Targeted Killings* case. While the former included an in-depth discussion of the issue, the latter did not address the convergence of IHL and IHRL, nor the application of domestic law doctrines to international law issues. The lack of discussion is particularly problematic since the HCJ addresses one of the stark differences between IHL and IHRL—a status-based distinction that does not take into account the lives of combatants in the proportionality equation.

It is important to note that it is not necessarily the case that IHRL will always be part of such a fusion between international and domestic law. Take, for example, the recent proposal for the definition of the crime of ecocide. The proposal states that ecocide is "unlawful or wanton acts committed with knowledge that there is a substantial likelihood of severe and either widespread or long-term damage to the environment being caused by those acts."[35] The commentary to the proposed definition provides that "unlawful" includes international and domestic law, suggesting that "there is no reason that national illegality—in particular as a matter of domestic criminal law—should not be part of an international law definition."[36] Such reliance on domestic law raises significant concerns in the context of global regulation. To give just one example, consider a situation where two

34. *See, e.g.*, Yuval Shany, *Co-Application and Harmonization of IHL and IHRL: Are Rumours about the Death of Lex Specialis Premature?*, *in* Research Handbook on Human Rights and Humanitarian Law 9 (Robert Kolb et. al. eds., 2022); Marko Milanovic, *The Lost Origins of Lex Specialis: Rethinking the Relationship Between Human Rights and International Humanitarian Law*, *in* Theoretical Boundaries of Armed Conflict and Human Rights 78 (Jens D. Ohlin ed., 2016); Cordula Droege, *The Interplay between International Humanitarian Law and International Human Rights Law in Situations of Armed Conflict*, 40 Israel Law Review 310 (2007).

35. *Independent Expert Panel for the Legal Definition of Ecocide, Commentary and Core Text* (June, 2021), https://static1.squarespace.com/static/5ca2608ab914493c64ef1f6d/t/60d7479cf8e7e5461534dd07/1624721314430/SE+Foundation+Commentary+and+core+text+revised+%281%29.pdf.

36. *Id.*

persons perform a similar act in two different States. In one of those States, the conduct violates domestic law, whereas in the other it does not. Is it just or desirable to treat only one of these persons as guilty of ecocide under international criminal law?

Among the three types of relationship between international and domestic law, it seems that the most far-reaching example of the use of domestic law, the *Targeted Killings* case, was to a large extent a result of insufficient expertise rather than part of a comprehensive theoretical framework for the fusion of international and domestic law. The next section further develops the discussion of expertise in the context of the development of IHL by domestic courts.

III. DOMESTIC COURTS AND IHL EXPERTISE

Insufficient expertise has been one of the main concerns discussed in the literature on international law in domestic courts.[37] For example, Roger O'Keefe noted that "when it comes to international law, domestic courts not infrequently get it wrong, especially when assisted less than ably by the parties' counsel."[38] When describing the traditional view of international lawyers, Karen Knop noted that they believe that "there is work to be done before domestic judges will be equal to their part in international law."[39] Nonetheless, beyond acknowledging the issue, lack of expertise does not play a significant part in the systemic general discussion of domestic courts' decisions, and moreover, it is rarely discussed in the context of IHL in domestic courts.[40] Take, for example, the *Targeted Killings* case: the vast

37. *See, e.g.*, ODILE AMMANN, DOMESTIC COURTS AND THE INTERPRETATION OF INTERNATIONAL LAW—METHODS AND REASONING BASED OF THE SWISS EXAMPLE 41 (2019); Cedric M.J. Ryngaert & Duco W. Hora Siccama, *Ascertaining Customary International Law: An Inquiry into the Methods Used by Domestic Courts*, 65 NETHERLANDS INTERNATIONAL LAW REVIEW 1, 20–21 (2018); ANDRE NOLLKAEMPER, NATIONAL COURTS AND THE INTERNATIONAL RULE OF LAW 278 (2011).

38. Roger O'Keefe, *Domestic Courts as Agents of Development of the International Law of Jurisdiction*, 26 LEIDEN JOURNAL OF INTERNATIONAL LAW 541, 549 (2013).

39. Knop, *supra* note 1, at 502.

40. Two notable exceptions in this regard are Naz K. Modirzadeh, *Folk International Law: 9/11 Lawyering and the Transformation of the Law of Armed Conflict to Human Rights Policy and Human Rights Law to War Governance*, 5 HARVARD NATIONAL SECURITY JOURNAL 225, 257–58 (2014) (stating that in the U.S context "most judges deciding these cases did not have a background or training in the complex arguments and style of IHL and would have been unlikely to develop it while presiding over a case, particularly given the other complex and critical issues of law at stake"); Lawrence Hill-Cawthorne, *Joint Blog Series: Application of International Humanitarian Law by Domestic Courts*, EJIL: TALK! (Sept. 15, 2015), https://www.ejiltalk.org/application-of-international-humanitarian-law-by-domestic-courts/.

majority of the relevant literature does not discuss the issue of expertise.[41] Instead, courts are more often presented as strategic or political actors when addressing nondoctrinal explanations for domestic courts' decisions.[42] Ideology, politics, and strategic behavior play a significant role in domestic (and international) courts' decisions.[43] Nonetheless, insufficient expertise is an additional factor that should be taken into account as an alternative or complementary explanation for some of the decisions.

In what follows, I will distinguish between two types of expertise. One is IHL, or more generally, international law expertise; the other is general legal expertise and expertise in judicial decision-making. While domestic courts lack the former type of expertise in IHL cases, they still maintain the latter type of experience. This can, at least partially, explain the reasoning and outcome of the *Targeted Killings* case and inform the analysis of the application of IHL by other domestic courts. The section begins with several examples of the limited IHL expertise of domestic courts. It then discusses three ways in which domestic courts can, and often do, try to mitigate their limited IHL expertise: (1) reliance on domestic law, (2) reliance (or overreliance) on the submissions to the court, and (3) reliance on general judicial expertise.

A. Insufficient Expertise in the *Targeted Killings* Case and Beyond

The use of the least harmful means requirement by the Israeli HCJ in the *Targeted Killings* case serves in this chapter as a key example of the direct application of domestic law doctrines to international law. However, it seems that it was not derived from a comprehensive and well-grounded approach to the relationship between international and domestic law, but was rather a result of the insufficient IHL and international law expertise of the Court. While the legal framework that

41. For example, while Cohen and Shany criticize the application of IHL by the HCJ, they do not attribute it to a lack of expertise. Cohen & Shany, *supra* note 21.

42. This is not to say that such explanations do not explain much of the external factors that influence domestic (and international) courts, and I, too, used strategic explanations in my analysis of the effect of the ICC on domestic courts. *See, e.g.*, Yahli Shereshevsky, *The Unintended Negative Effect of Complementarity*, 18 Journal of International Criminal Justice 1017 (2020).

43. *See* Sharon Weil, *Building Respect for IHL Through National Courts*, 96 International Review of the Red Cross 859, 865–68 (2014); Eyal Benvenisti & George Downs, *Democratizing Courts: How National and International Courts Promote Democracy in an Era of Global Governance*, 46 New York University Journal of International Law & Politics 741 (2013); Eyal Benvenisti, *Reclaiming Democracy: The Strategic Uses of Foreign and International Law by National Courts*, 102 American Journal of International Law 241 (2008); Eyal Benvenisti, *Judicial Misgivings Regarding the Application of International Law: An Analysis of Attitudes of National Courts*, 4 European Journal of International Law 159 (1993).

the Court applied to the case was IHL, the Court's examination of the issue lacks any significant discussion of the existence of the least harmful means requirement under IHL,[44] or a comprehensive discussion about the relationship between IHL and IHRL. It seems that when faced with a challenging question and without sufficient international law expertise, the Court resorted to the safe harbor of domestic law doctrines that it frequently applies. This is the first mitigating technique that courts can use, namely, reliance on seemingly similar domestic law doctrines.

Another example of insufficient IHL expertise in the *Targeted Killings* case is the classification of the conflict between Israel and Palestinian armed groups as an international armed conflict. The HCJ determined that an international armed conflict is any conflict that "crosses the borders of the state."[45] This position, which is based on a textual interpretation of the term "international armed conflict," faces significant challenges in light of the text of Common Article 2 (CA2) of the Geneva Conventions, which states that international armed conflict is a conflict between "two or more of the High Contracting Parties," parties which are exclusively States.[46] That the classification of transnational armed conflicts as international armed conflicts is an overwhelming minority position[47] is not the main, or only, reason for the suggestion that it reveals insufficient expertise. Indeed, it is possible to defend such a minority position on classification with a sophisticated analysis of international law.[48] Rather, it is the lack of any acknowledgment by the Court of CA2 and the challenges that that article poses to the classification of the conflict as an international armed conflict that suggests a lack of sufficient knowledge of IHL.

Classification of transnational armed conflicts between States and non-State armed groups has received much attention in the international law literature. The position of the HCJ has been discussed and criticized.[49] For example, Roy

44. For an in-depth discussion of the issue under IHL, *see* Ryan Goodman, *The Power to Kill or Capture Enemy Combatants*, 24 European Journal of International Law 819 (2013); Michael N. Schmitt, *Wound, Capture or Kill: A Reply to Ryan Goodman's "The Power to Capture or Kill Enemy Combatants,"* 24 European Journal of International Law 855 (2013).

45. *Targeted Killings* case, *supra* note 19, at ¶ 18.

46. *See, e.g.*, Convention (I) for the Amelioration of the Condition of the Wounded and Sick in Armed Forces in the Field, art. 2, Aug. 12, 1949, 6 U.S.T. 3114, 75 U.N.T.S. 31 [hereinafter GC I].

47. For a discussion of the classification debate, *see* Yahli Shereshevsky, *Politics by Other Means: The Battle over the Classification of Asymmetrical Conflicts*, 49 Vanderbilt Journal of Transnational Law 455 (2015).

48. *See* Dapo Akande, *Classification of Armed Conflicts: Relevant Legal Concepts*, *in* International Law and the Classification of Conflicts 32, 57–67 (Elizabeth Wilmshurst ed., 2012).

49. *See, e.g.*, Douglas Guilfoyle, *The Mavi Marmara Incident and Blockade in Armed Conflict*, 81 British Yearbook of International Law, 171, 185–86 (2011); Roy Schöndorf, *The Targeted Killings Judgment: A Preliminary Assessment*, 5 Journal of International Criminal Justice 301 (2007).

Schöndorf observed that the decision was not grounded in primary sources and called for future justification of the decision.[50] Marko Milanovic tried to mitigate the consequences of the decision by suggesting that the Court only classified conflicts in occupied territories as international armed conflicts.[51] However, the Court explicitly stated in the decision that its approach applies to any cross-border conflict "whether the place where the armed conflict is occurring is subject to a belligerent occupation or not."[52]

To the best of my knowledge, none of the discussions on the puzzling classification of the Court suggests that it was a result of insufficient knowledge of IHL. The application of domestic law doctrines revealed one type of solution that domestic courts use to mitigate their insufficient expertise. The following paragraphs suggest that the decision on classification is a result of the other two, much more common mitigation techniques: reliance on submissions to the court and common-sense interpretation.

During the proceedings in the *Targeted Killings* case, the HCJ received various submissions from the petitioners and the government. Interestingly, none of these documents refer to the CA2 definition of international armed conflict or the challenge of classifying a conflict that involves non-State actors as an international armed conflict. In fact, the petition did not address the classification of the conflict at all. In a later submission to the Court in response to the government's position, the petitioners argued that if a conflict exists, it should be classified as an international armed conflict, but that the law enforcement paradigm governs much of the situation.[53] The government, on the other side, mostly discussed IHL in general without making a distinction between the two types of conflicts.[54] The main discussion that did take place was whether the events in question amounted to an armed conflict, rather than a situation that is governed by the law enforcement paradigm alone.[55] This left the Court to decide the classification of the conflict mostly on its own. Without reference to CA2 and due to its lack of IHL expertise, it was challenging for the Court to understand that the common understanding of "international armed conflict" is a conflict between two or more States. As a result, it is not surprising that the Court decided to rely on another reasonable textual interpretation of the term "international armed conflict."

What is also interesting in this regard is the aftermath of the decision. It demonstrates the precedential nature of domestic courts' positions, even when they lack a strong doctrinal basis and face significant domestic and international

50. *Id.* at 304.

51. Milanovic, *supra* note 24, at 383–84.

52. *Targeted Killings* case, *supra* note 19, at ¶ 18.

53. *Targeted Killings* case, *supra* note 19, Petitioners Response to the Government's Ccomplementary Submission, at ¶ 77.

54. *Id.* at Government's Complementary Submission.

55. *Id.* at ¶¶ 13–22.

criticism. Not only did the classification of the conflict by the Court receive considerable scholarly criticism, it was also the subject of subtle domestic criticism from the government itself. In the 2014 Gaza Conflict Report, the Israeli government addressed the issue of classification. After referring to the classification of the HCJ in the *Targeted Killings* case, the government acknowledged the majority positions regarding the classification of the conflict as a NIAC. It added that the Court itself seemed to recognize the challenges to its position, referring to the decision in the *Physicians for Human Rights* case concerning the 2009 Gaza Conflict (Cast Lead operation).[56] The government then stated that, "[u]nder these circumstances, Israel conducted its military operations during the 2014 Gaza Conflict in accordance with the rules of the Law of Armed Conflict governing both international and NIACs, including the rules relating to distinction, precautions and proportionality."[57]

Nonetheless, subsequent HCJ cases followed the *Targeted Killings* approach to classification. Indeed, in the *Physicians for Human Rights* case, the HCJ acknowledged, without in-depth elaboration, that "the classification of the armed conflict between the state of Israel and the Hamas organization as an international conflict raises several difficulties,"[58] but it then repeated the position of the *Targeted Killings* case on classification. Moreover, in the *Yesh Din* decision, Chief Justice Chayut laconically classified the conflict in Gaza as an international armed conflict, citing the *Targeting Killings* case, while failing to address any of the doctrinal challenges or the critical accounts in the literature.[59]

A related statement of Chief Justice Chayut in the *Yesh Din* decision is another indication of insufficient expertise. When introducing the factual background of the events, Chief Justice Chayut casually stated that Israel and Hamas have been engaged in an armed conflict for more than thirty years.[60] It is quite clear that Chief Justice Chayut had no intention to determine that IHL's conduct of hostilities norms have applied to the situation for such a long period, but rather used the ordinary, laypersons' meaning of the term "armed conflict" (in Hebrew) to describe the general context. It is reasonable to assume that the poor choice of words is a result of insufficient IHL expertise that does not fully realize the potential implications of such a statement.

56. State of Israel, The 2014 Gaza Conflict: Factual and Legal Aspects ¶ 233 (2015); HCJ 201/09 Physicians for Human Rights v. Prime Minister PD 63(1) 521 (2009) (Isr.).

57. The 2014 Gaza Conflict, *supra* note 56, at ¶ 233. I suspect that the politics of classification from the government side here is related to international criminal law and the fact that there are fewer war crimes in NIACs under the Rome Statute, but developing this point is beyond the scope of this chapter.

58. *Physicians for Human Rights*, *supra* note 56, at ¶ 14.

59. HCJ 3003/18 Yesh Din—Volunteers for Human Rights v. Chief of General Staff, IDF (2018) (Isr.), Chief Justice Chayut's opinion, ¶ 2, https://www.adalah.org/uploads/uploads/18030030_K08.doc.pdf.

60. *Id.* at ¶ 1.

Interestingly, a similar discussion regarding conflict classification took place around the same time in the U.S. Supreme Court in the context of the *Hamdan* case.[61] The case addressed the conflict between the United States and Al Qaida, and specifically the (un)lawfulness of the military commissions that were established by the George W. Bush administration. The Court had to classify the conflict in order to address the IHL aspects of the case. The case is to some extent a positive story about the defeat of the infamous "legal black hole" approach of the early Bush administration,[62] but also a story about insufficient IHL expertise of domestic courts and the concerns that arise from decisions made by such courts.[63] The *Hamdan* case is a unique instance in which insufficient expertise and reliance on submissions to the court were specifically discussed by various authors. Naz Modirzadeh described this insufficient knowledge, stating:

> Whatever one thinks of the outcome of the cases or their jurisprudence, it is clear that neither a majority of lawyers litigating the cases nor the judges deciding them had a great deal of familiarity with IHL and its inner workings. IHL rules and concepts were often watered down in order to fit within the methodology, form, and language of U.S. courts. In some cases they were simply presented incorrectly or out of context.[64]

She discussed *Hamdan* specifically, suggesting that the decision was probably highly influenced by numerous amici briefs that were submitted to the court by IHL and international human rights law experts.[65] The Court adopted the approach in the briefs according to which the protections of Common Article 3 of the Geneva Conventions (CA3) apply to transnational armed conflicts between States and non-State actors. It stated that conflicts with non-State armed groups cannot be regarded as international armed conflicts since they only involve conflicts between States, and interpreted CA3 as extending the notion of NIAC beyond internal armed conflicts such as civil wars.[66] The reliance on the amici briefs by the Court is not limited to the legal argument itself. As was demonstrated by Marko Milanovic, both one of the amici briefs and the Court cited to the wrong page of

61. Hamdan v. Rumsfeld, 548 U.S. 557 (2006).

62. *See, e.g.*, Modirzadeh, *supra* note 40, at 254–55; Miles P. Fischer, *Applicability of the Geneva Conventions to "Armed Conflict" in the War on Terror*, 30 Fordham International Law Journal 509, 509 (2007).

63. *See, e.g.*, Milanovic, *supra* note 24.

64. Modirzadeh, *supra* note 40, at 257.

65. *Id.* at 258.

66. It should be noted that some suggested that it is unclear to what extent the brief and the court made the argument that the conflict is a global NIAC, due to conflicting statements in the decision. I think that the most reasonable reading of the decision suggests that it classified it as a NIAC.

a similar partial quote of the International Committee of the Red Cross (ICRC) Commentary to the Second Additional Protocol to the Geneva Conventions.[67] This quote and the other sources that the Court used were criticized for not giving proper weight to the traditional understanding of CA3 as applying exclusively to internal armed conflicts.[68] In addition, the insufficient expertise of the Court was revealed in other aspects of the decision, such as its reference to prisoner of war status, which is relevant only to international armed conflicts.[69] Finally, the decision was also substantially criticized as opening the door for the legitimizing aspects of IHL in a global NIAC.[70]

The previous paragraphs demonstrate how two supreme courts, almost at the same time, discussed the classification of similar conflicts and reached opposing conclusions, to a large extent due to their reliance on submissions to the court. In *Hamdan*, there was a more serious discussion of the relevant rules compared to the *Targeted Killings* case, as the submissions addressed the issue in more depth. Nonetheless, as Milanovic showed, the discussion was still very much limited to the scope of the arguments in the submissions to the court.[71]

Another prominent example of insufficient expertise and overreliance on submissions to the court is the HCJ's *Yesh Din* decision.[72] The decision addressed the legality of the Israeli Defense Forces' (IDF's) rules of engagement in the context of the mass demonstrations near the Gaza border. Here, similar to the *Hamdan* case, the overreliance on the submissions went beyond the legal argument to overreliance on the text of the submissions itself. For example, Deputy Chief Justice Melcer significantly relied on the government response for the contextual background and the reasoning of the decision. Thus, paragraph five of Deputy Chief Justice Melcer's opinion repeats almost word for word paragraph nine of the government response that describes the factual background of the

67. *See* Milanovic *supra* note 24, at 380; Marko Milanovic, *Footnote Filching and Other Unsavory Practices in the U.S. Supreme Court, Part I*, Opinio Juris (Apr. 30, 2007), http://opiniojuris.org/2007/04/30/footnote-filchingand-other-unsavory-practices-in-the-us-supreme-court-part-i/.

68. Marko Milanovic, *Footnote Filching and Other Unsavory Practices in the U.S. Supreme Court, Part III*, Opinio Juris (May 2, 2007), http://opiniojuris.org/2007/05/02/footnote-filching-and-other-unsavory-practices-in-the-us-supreme-court-part-iii/.

69. Milanovic, *supra* note 24, at 379.

70. Shane R. Reeves, Winston Williams, & Amy H. McCarthy, *How Do You Like Me Now? Hamdan v. Rumsfeld and the Legal Justification for Global Targeting*, 41 University of Pennsylvania Journal of International Law 329 (2019).

71. Milanovic, *Footnote Filching*, *supra* note 67.

72. I have discussed the case elsewhere. *See* Yahli Shereshevsky, *International Decision: HCJ 3003/18 Yesh Din—Volunteers for Human Rights v. Chief of General Staff, Israel Defense Forces (IDF)*, 113 American Journal of International 361 (2019).

events.[73] Similarly, paragraph forty of his decision, which provides supporting sources for the existence of a law enforcement paradigm under IHL repeats almost word for word paragraph thirty-three of the government response.[74] Another example of such reliance, this time on the petitioner's submission, is the court discussion of the notion of direct participation in hostilities (DPH). The only source that was mentioned by the court is the ICRC Interpretive Guidance on the Notion of Direct Participation in Hostilities.[75] This is highly surprising since the notion of DPH was discussed in depth by the HCJ itself in the *Targeted Killings* case, and there are significant differences between the positions of the two sources.[76] The most reasonable explanation for the lack of reference to the *Targeted Killings* case in this context seems to be an overreliance on the submissions to the court. The petitioners referred only to the Interpretive Guidance in their discussion of DPH, while the government criticized the petitioners' position but also did not address the *Targeted Killings* case.

There are two significant concerns that result from insufficient expertise and overreliance on the submissions to the court.[77] First, it can incentivize far-reaching and unsubstantiated legal claims by the parties to the case in the hope that at least some of the claims will be adopted by the court. Second, it can lead to ambiguous discussions that do not offer concrete solutions to the problems at hand. This can be seen, for example, in the conflation between substantial and imminent threats in the *Yesh Din* case that ignores one of the strongest controversies between the petitioners and the government regarding when it is permissible to use force. While the petitioners suggested that force can be used only if the threat is imminent, the government argued that force can be used if the threat is substantial, even if the threat is not immediate. However, the Court did not explicitly discuss this controversy and even referred to the government position as requiring an immediate threat.

Not every mistake in domestic court decisions is necessarily a result of insufficient expertise. The following discussion of Belgian cases involving "foreign fighters" sheds light on the challenge of ascertaining whether domestic court decisions reflect insufficient IHL expertise, or whether there are alternative explanations, such as political or ideological motivation. While it is possible that

73. *Yesh Din*, *supra* note 59, Deputy-Chief Justice Melcer Opinion, ¶ 5; Response of the Government, HCJ 3003/18 Yesh Din—Volunteers for Human Rights v. Chief of General Staff, IDF, ¶ 9 (Apr. 29, 2018) (Isr.).

74. *Yesh Din*, *supra* note 59, Deputy-Chief Justice Melcer Opinion, ¶ 40; Response of the Government, HCJ 3003/18 Yesh Din—Volunteers for Human Rights v. Chief of General Staff, IDF, ¶ 40 (Apr. 29, 2018) (Isr.).

75. *Yesh Din*, *supra* note 59, Deputy-Chief Justice Melcer Opinion, ¶ 45.

76. *Cf.* *Targeted Killings* case, *supra* note 19, at ¶ 35; International Committee of the Red Cross, Interpretive Guidance on the notion of Direct Participation in Hostilities under International Humanitarian Law 34–35, 56 (2009).

77. Shereshevsky, *supra* note 72, at 367–68.

insufficient expertise affected the decisions, I cannot exclude the possibility that other factors are the main explanation.

The issue of foreign fighters and IHL was discussed in several domestic cases following the return of foreign fighters to their home countries.[78] One of the main issues that such cases discussed was the exclusion clauses in domestic counter-terrorism legislation according to which foreign fighters will not be charged with terrorist offenses if their conduct was governed by IHL. In Belgium, the clause in question is the national implementation of EU Directive 2017/541 on combating terrorism, which states, "This Directive does not govern the activities of armed forces during periods of armed conflict, which are governed by international humanitarian law within the meaning of those terms under that law."[79] The Belgian criminal code adopted a similar provision, and there is wide agreement that it covers all types of conflicts and that the term "armed forces" includes non-State armed groups.[80] As a result, in criminal cases of foreign fighters, the Belgian courts had to decide whether the conduct of the foreign fighters took place by armed forces in the context of an armed conflict. In the *Sharia4Belgium* case, the Court decided that the individuals who joined the Jabhat Al-Nusra and Majlis Shura Al-Mujahideen groups in Syria did not fall within the exclusion clause because these groups do not qualify as armed forces.[81] The Court determined that the groups were not sufficiently organized and did not comply with IHL and therefore could not be regarded as armed forces under IHL. There seems to be a consensus in the literature that the reasoning of the court is a clear misapplication of IHL both doctrinally and in relation to the specific groups it addressed.[82] However, there is insufficient evidence to determine whether this is a result of limited IHL expertise, and some commentators have suggested that it represents an ideological

78. *See* Thomas Van Poecke, Frank Verbruggen, & Ward Yperman, *Terrorist Offenses and International Humanitarian Law: The Armed Conflict Exclusion Clause*, 103 International Review of the Red Cross 295 (2021).

79. European Commission, Report from the Commission to the European Parliament and the Council Based on Article 29(1) of Directive (EU) 2017/51 of the European Parliament and of the Council of 15 March 2017 on Combating Terrorism and Replacing Council Framework Decision 2002/75/JHA and Amending Council Decision 2005/671/JHA, COM(2020) 619 final, Brussels, Sept. 30, 2020, ¶ 37.

80. Belgian Criminal Code, 8 June 1867 (as of Feb. 24, 2021), art. 141bis, *available at* https://www.ejustice.just.fgov.be/cgi_loi/change_lg.pl?language=nl&la=N&cn=1867.

81. Rechtbank van eerste aanleg (Antwerpen), Vonnis, Feb. 11, 2015, at 33 [Sharia4Belgium case]; Hof van Beroep (Brussel); Hof van Beroep Antwerpen, Appeal Judgment of Jan. 26, 2016, 2015/FP/1-7, FD35.98.47-12; Hof van Cassatie van België, Judgment of May 24, 2016, P.16.0244.N.

82. Cuyckens & Paulussen, *supra* note 12, at 555–56; Van Poecke, Verbruggen, & Yperman, *supra* note 78, at 312.

decision in favor of prosecuting individuals who have joined jihadist armed groups.[83]

It should be noted that insufficient expertise is not necessarily an inherent problem in all of the discussions of IHL by domestic courts. The *Serdar Mohammed* case, for example, included an in-depth discussion of the relevant legal questions. However, insufficient expertise should be considered a potential explanation for puzzling discussions of international law by domestic courts. That said, even when domestic courts suffer from insufficient IHL expertise, they still have general legal expertise. The next section suggests that general legal expertise can mitigate, at least partially, the lack of IHL expertise.

B. General Judicial Expertise

The second type of expertise is general judicial expertise. It is beyond the scope of this chapter to fully address the complicated question of judicial expertise. It has been discussed in the literature in the context of judicial specialization, as well as in relation to potential differences between judges and laypersons.[84] Here, I want to focus on the notion that judges are experts in dispute resolution, that they have or develop expertise in legal interpretation and in solving legal questions reasonably. Lawrence Solum described this type of judicial virtue as "a practical ability to choose wisely in particular circumstances."[85]

In the introduction to section III, I mentioned three types of responses to the insufficient IHL expertise of domestic courts, namely, resorting to domestic law, reliance on the submissions to the court, and using the judicial expertise of the court for the interpretation of relevant rules. The first and last types of response rely on the expertise of the court, while the second type defers much of the fact-finding and reasoning to other actors. In the next paragraphs, I will further explore the responses that rely on the general expertise of the court.

In the *Targeted Killings* case, while basing its decisions on poor IHL reasoning, the approach of the decision to targeting proved to be in line with one of the two main IHL approaches to the targeting of members of non-State armed

83. Cuyckens & Paulussen, *supra* note 12, at 557; Van Poecke, Verbruggen, & Yperman, *supra* note 78, at 313.

84. *See, e.g.*, Eyal Zamir & Doron Teichman, Behavioral Law and Economics 561–63 (2018); Frederick Schauer, *Is There a Psychology of Judging?*, *in* The Psychology of Judicial Decision-Making 103 (David Klein & Gregory Mitchell eds., 2010); Lawrence Baum, *Probing the Effects of Judicial Specialization*, 58 Duke Law Journal 1667 (2009); Chris Guthrie, Jeffrey J. Rachlinski, & Andrew J. Wistrich, *Blinking on the Bench: How Judges Decide Cases*, 93 Cornell Law Review 1 (2007); Lawrence B. Solum, *The Virtues and Vices of a Judge: An Aristotelian Guide to Judicial Selection*, 61 Southern California Law Review 1735 (1988); Owen M. Fiss, *Forward: The Forms of Justice*, 93 Harvard Law Review 1, 34 (1979).

85. Solum, *supra* note 84, at 1738.

groups—the functional approach of the ICRC Interpretive Guidance on Direct Participation in Hostilities.[86]

The Interpretive Guidance is much more grounded in IHL compared to the *Targeted Killings* case, although it offers an unorthodox approach to some of the issues. The main innovation of the Interpretive Guidance is its reliance on the principles of military necessity and humanity to endorse a least harmful means requirement under IHL.[87] Although it has been subject to criticism,[88] it has had a prominent role and significant influence on the debate over the targeting of members of organized armed groups.[89] Interestingly, despite the significant differences in its reasoning, the bottom line of the Interpretive Guidance is rather similar to the approach the HCJ took in the *Targeted Killings* case.[90] First, both take a functional approach to targeting, according to which those who continuously participate in hostilities are targetable. Second, both accept that these persons are targetable at all times, not only when they directly participate in hostilities. Finally, both support the obligation to use the least harmful means when targeting members of non-State armed groups. The similarity in the outcome of both, in addition to the significant support for the functional approach in the international law community, might suggest that although the HCJ demonstrated insufficient IHL expertise, its general judicial expertise resulted in a reasonable substantive outcome in the case. This was the result of the direct application of the domestic law doctrine of proportionality combined with judicial intuition regarding the legal solution to the problem at hand.

It is possible to suggest that the approach of the Court to classification is similarly informed by judicial intuition, when it had insufficient expertise and no guidance from the submissions of the parties to the case. As Marko Milanovic has suggested, "it is, of course, from a purely humanitarian standpoint desirable for the law of international conflicts to apply, since it provides significantly more protections than the law of internal armed conflicts."[91] Nonetheless, in contrast to the question of when members of non-State armed groups can be targeted,

86. Interpretive Guidance, *supra* note 76.

87. *Id.* at 77–82.

88. *See, e.g.*, Michael Schmitt, *Deconstructing Direct Participation in Hostilities: The Constitutive Elements*, 42 New York University Journal of International Law & Politics 697 (2010); Bill Boothby, *And for Such Time As: The Time Dimension to Direct Participation in Hostilities*, 42 New York University Journal of International Law & Politics 741 (2010); Hays W. Parks, *Part IX of the ICRC "Direct Participation in Hostilities" Study: No Mandate, No Expertise, and Legally Incorrect*, 42 New York University Journal of International Law & Politics 769 (2010).

89. Ka Lok Yip, *Participation in Hostilities: Sociological and Democratic Legitimacy in Domestic Legal Orders*, 2 Transnational Legal Theory 224 (2017).

90. Yahli Shereshevsky, *Targeting the Targeted Killings Case—International Lawmaking in Domestic Contexts*, 39 Michigan Journal of International Law 241, 251–53 (2018).

91. Milanovic, *supra* note 24, at 385.

and despite some opportunities to offer a justification for its classification of the conflict as an international armed conflict, the classification of the Court remains an overwhelming minority position. This is perhaps because of growing support for the convergence between IHL and human rights that has much more room in NIAC.[92]

One final example of reliance on general judicial expertise is the *Al-Bassiouni* case.[93] In this case, the Court had to decide whether it was lawful to limit or completely stop the supply of electricity and fuel to Gaza following the Israeli disengagement from Gaza. While there is a straightforward moral answer to the question, the legal analysis is more complicated. One potential source of a legal obligation is to rely on the law of occupation that contains an obligation to supply the needs of the population. This is the path that many international lawyers adopted, since a prominent view is that even after the disengagement from Gaza, it remains occupied territory.[94] However, if one accepts the Israeli position that Gaza is not occupied, as the Court did, the legal basis for such an obligation is more complicated. The HCJ offered a very thin international law analysis for an obligation to provide basic needs for the population, stating:

> [I]n the prevailing circumstances, the main duties of the State of Israel relating to the residents of the Gaza Strip derive from the state of armed conflict that exists between it and the Hamas organization that controls the Gaza Strip; these duties also derive from the degree of control exercised by the State of Israel over the border crossings between it and the Gaza Strip, as well as from the relationship that was created between Israel and the territory of the Gaza Strip after the years of Israeli military rule in the territory, as a result of which the Gaza Strip is currently almost completely dependent upon the supply of electricity from Israel.[95]

Such a thin discussion demonstrates the insufficient IHL and more broadly international law expertise of the Court. On the other hand, it is also an expression of a strong judicial intuition regarding an obligation to provide basic needs to the population. Similar to the other cases, a more grounded legal justification for the Court's position has been suggested in the literature. Yuval Shany proposed that the laconic justification of the Court should be read to suggest that there are three

92. Shereshevsky, *supra* note 47.

93. HCJ 9132/07 Gaber Al-Bassiouni v. The Prime Minister (2008) (Isr.), https://versa.cardozo.yu.edu/sites/default/files/upload/opinions/Ahmed%20v.%20Prime%20Minister.pdf.

94. *See, e.g.*, Shane Darcy & John Reynolds, *An Enduring Occupation: The Status of the Gaza Strip from the Perspective of International Humanitarian Law*, 15 Journal of Conflict and Security Law 211 (2010).

95. *Al-Bassiouni*, *supra* note 93, at ¶ 12.

sources for the obligation to provide basic needs; IHL, and, more importantly, IHRL and *jus post bellum*.[96]

It should be noted that the decision of the Court was subject to criticism for failing to establish a higher threshold that prohibits any type of intervention in the supply of electricity and fuel.[97] Such criticism is not unique to this case, and when it comes to its IHL cases, there is significant debate on where the HCJ is positioned in the constant tension between the limiting and legitimizing aspects of IHL.[98] This demonstrates the interplay between politics, strategic behavior, and expertise, which will be addressed in the conclusion.

IV. CONCLUSION

When I began the process of writing this chapter, I intended to focus on the fusion of domestic and international law and offer an analysis of how domestic law can shape international law through the decisions of domestic courts. However, I found myself focusing instead on the notion of international law expertise when I realized that the most prominent example of direct application of domestic law doctrine by a domestic court is to a large extent a story about compensation for insufficient international law expertise.

The chapter does not suggest that insufficient international law expertise is *the* prominent factor in explaining domestic court decisions on IHL. In fact, the other main example in this chapter, that of the *Serdar Mohammed* case, does not demonstrate a similar lack of subject matter expertise. Moreover, there are other important external factors that affect the decisions of domestic courts. It is widely acknowledged that national courts often tend to decide in favor of the government. This is a key factor in explaining some of the problematic tendencies of the Israeli and U.S. Supreme Courts.[99] There is also wide recognition that domestic courts can act as strategic actors that promote ideological and institutional interests.[100]

However, this chapter does call for more serious attention to be paid to the question of expertise as a significant factor in domestic court decisions. While

96. Yuval Shany, *The Law Applicable to Non-Occupied Gaza: A Comment on Bassiouni v. Prime Minister of Israel*, 42 Israel. Law Review. 101 (2009).

97. *See, e.g.*, Aeyal Gross & Tamar Feldman, *We Didn't Want to Hear the Word Calories: Rethinking Food Security, Food Power, and Food Sovereignty—Lessons from the Gaza Closure*, 33 Berkeley Journal of International Law 379, 387–89 (2015).

98. Nimer Sultany, *Activism and Legitimation in Israel's Jurisprudence of Occupation*, 23 Social & Legal Studies 315 (2014); Cohen & Cohen, *supra* note 10.

99. *See, e.g.*, Weissbrodt & Nesbitt, *supra* note 11, at 1423 ("from Yamashita to Hamdan, the Court's use of humanitarian law often seems result-driven, calculated to achieve a politically palatable outcome").

100. *Supra* note 43.

expertise is recognized as a limiting factor of domestic courts, it does not receive a sufficient role in the analysis of domestic court decisions; the focus is instead on the more attractive scholarly arguments regarding the politics and strategic behavior of courts. Insufficient expertise should be considered a simple, nonsophisticated complementary or alternative explanation to IHL decisions of domestic courts.

What does the combination of insufficient IHL expertise and general legal expertise tell us about the role of domestic courts in the interpretation and development of IHL? First, it calls for more caution in relation to the role of domestic courts in developing IHL. This is especially the case in relation to the legal analysis of domestic courts and in instances where the courts mitigate their insufficient IHL expertise through overreliance on submissions to the court. Second, it suggests that based on their general judicial expertise, domestic courts can offer valuable insights about the desired outcomes of cases, even without sufficient IHL expertise. While these cases can offer useful guidance toward a desirable substantive outcome, it is often up to IHL experts to provide a more robust grounding of such an outcome in IHL. By building on these cases, it is possible to develop future interpretations of the law that not only align with the desired outcome but also adequately apply IHL doctrine.[101]

101. This, of course, is less relevant in areas in which ideology and politics influence the decisions of the courts so strongly that it renders these decisions almost useless, as is often the case in HCJ cases that discuss the law of occupation, in contrast to the conduct of hostilities issues. For a comprehensive account of the HCJ cases on occupation, *see* David Kretzmer & Yael Ronen, The Occupation of Justice (2021).

9

The Development of the Law of Armed Conflict by International Criminal Tribunals

MARTHA M. BRADLEY*

I. INTRODUCTION

This chapter offers an evaluation of how judicial decisions of international criminal tribunals[1] have influenced the development of international humanitarian law (IHL). These tribunals have contributed to that development in a variety of ways, for example, by clarifying and giving definition to key terms such as "armed

* Martha Bradley is Associate Professor in the Department of Public Law, Faculty of Law, University of Johannesburg.

1. For the purposes of this chapter, the term "international criminal tribunal" includes the contributions made by temporary and ad hoc international criminal tribunals as well as the permanent International Criminal Court.

Martha M. Bradley, *The Development of the Law of Armed Conflict by International Criminal Tribunals* In: *Making and Shaping the Law of Armed Conflict*. Edited by: Sandesh Sivakumaran and Christian R. Burne, Oxford University Press.
 DOI: 10.1093/oso/9780197775134.003.0009

conflict"[2] and "rape"[3] and by identifying rules of customary international humanitarian law.[4]

As per Article 38(1)(d) of the International Court of Justice (ICJ) Statute, judicial decisions are a subsidiary means of determining the rules of law.[5] Determination of the rules comprises a verification of the existence and state of rules of law and, further, serves to confirm their proper interpretation.[6] Thus, in general, judicial decisions in public international law serve as "law-determining agencies."[7]

War crimes are essentially criminalized versions of the primary rules of IHL. As such, in adjudicating war crimes, judicial decisions of international criminal tribunals necessarily interpret primary rules of IHL. War crimes adjudication has contributed to a better understanding of the underlying prohibitions established under IHL, such as the prohibition on the crime of rape. Indeed, the "discovery" and "identification of IHL" is a process that is facilitated by interpretations captured in judicial decisions.[8] Examples include the contribution of international criminal tribunals to the definition of "armed conflict" and, more specifically, "non-international armed conflict," as well as the law of conflict classification. However, not all contributions of international criminal tribunals have been positive. In some of their decisions, international criminal tribunals have appeared

2. In *Tadić*, the ICTY formulated a definition of "armed conflict," a term not defined in the Geneva Conventions (Prosecutor v. Tadić, Case No. IT-94-1-AR-72, Decision on the Defence Motion for Interlocutory Appeal on Jurisdiction, ¶ 70 (Int'l Crim. Trib. for the former Yugoslavia Oct. 2, 1995).

3. Prosecutor v. Akayesu, Case No. ICTR-96-4-T, Judgment, ¶ 688 (Sept. 2, 1998); Prosecutor v. Gacumbitsi, Case No. ICTR-2001-64-A, Judgment, ¶ 155 (July 7, 2006); Prosecutor v. Ntaganda, Case No. ICC-01/04-02/06, Judgment, ¶ 935 (July 8, 2019); Prosecutor v. Kamara and Another, Case No. SCSL-2004-16-PT, Prosecution's Pre-Trial Brief Pursuant to Order for Filing Pre-Trial Briefs, ¶ 145 (Mar. 5, 2004); Prosecutor v. Furundžija, Case No. IT-95-17/1, Judgment, ¶ 174 (Int'l Crim. Trib. for the former Yugoslavia Dec. 10, 1998); *see* Valerie Oosterveld, *The Legacy of the ICTY and ICTR on Sexual and Gender-Based Violence, in* The Legacy of Ad Hoc Tribunals in International Criminal Law: Assessing the ICTY's and the ICTR's Most Significant Legal Accomplishments 197, 197–220 (Milena Sterio & Michael Scharf eds., 2019).

4. *Tadić*, Decision on the Defence Motion for Interlocutory Appeal on Jurisdiction, *supra* note 2, ¶¶ 94 and 126.

5. Statute of the International Court of Justice, art. 38, June 26, 1945, 59 Stat. 1055, 33 U.N.T.S. 993 [hereinafter ICJ Statute].

6. Aldo Zammit Borda, *A Formal Approach to Article 38(1)(d) of the ICJ Statute from the Perspective of the International Criminal Courts and Tribunals*, 24 European Journal of International Law 650 (2013).

7. *Id.*

8. Jean-Marie Henckaerts, *History and Sources, in* The Oxford Guide to International Humanitarian Law 1, 17 (Ben Saul & Dapo Akande eds., 2020). For an in-depth understanding

to misunderstand aspects of IHL and have introduced errors, for example, in the interpretation of "attack" in the *Ntaganda* decision.[9]

Section II of this chapter is focused on the positive contributions of international criminal tribunals, specifically to the definitions of non-international armed conflict (NIAC) and rape. Sections III and IV indicate how a judicial decision, that of *Ntaganda*, created confusion in the understanding of IHL by employing an international criminal law (ICL)-centric lens in its interpretation of those persons entitled to protection under Common Article 3 of the Geneva Conventions,[10] as well as of the meaning of the term "attack."[11] Section V reflects critically on the decisions highlighted in sections II to IV and explores how the positive contributions, as well as the errors, impact on the "delicate relationship" between IHL and ICL.

II. PIVOTAL CONTRIBUTIONS: DEFINING NON-INTERNATIONAL ARMED CONFLICT AND RAPE

A. Defining Non-international Armed Conflict: The *Tadić* Formulation

A unique characteristic of IHL is that it is not applicable to "all people in all places and at all times."[12] Furthermore, different legal frameworks apply to international

of the development of IHL through custom, *see* Cordula Droege & Erini Giorgou, *How International Humanitarian Law Develops*, 104 International Review of the Red Cross 1810–15 (2022).

9. Prosecutor v. Ntaganda, Case No. ICC-01/04-02/06 A A2, Appeals Chamber Judgment, ¶ 1170 (Mar. 30, 2021).

10. Prosecutor v. Ntaganda, Case No. ICC-01/04-02/06-1962 OAS, Judgment on the appeal of Mr. Ntaganda against the "Second decision on the Defence's challenge to the jurisdiction of the Court in respect of Counts 6 and 9" (June 15, 2017). Common Article 3 provides minimum standards of protection during non-international armed conflicts; *see* Convention (I) for the Amelioration of the Condition of the Wounded and Sick in the Armed Forces in the Field, Aug. 12, 1949, 6 U.S.T. 3114, 75 U.N.T.S. 31 [hereinafter First Geneva Convention]; Convention (II) for the Amelioration of the Condition of the Wounded, Sick, and Shipwrecked Members of Armed Forces at Sea, Aug. 12, 1949, 6 U.S.T. 3217, 75 U.N.T.S. 85 [hereinafter Second Geneva Convention]; Convention (III) Relative to the Treatment of Prisoners of War, Aug. 12, 1949, 6 U.S.T. 3316, 75 U.N.T.S. 135 [hereinafter Third Geneva Convention]; Convention (IV) Relative to the Protection of Civilian Persons in Time of War, Aug. 12, 1949, 6 U.S.T. 3516, 75 U.N.T.S. 287 [hereinafter Fourth Geneva Convention]).

11. *Ntaganda*, Appeals Chamber Judgment, *supra* note 9, ¶ 1170.

12. Marco Sassòli, International Humanitarian Law: Rules, Controversies, and Solutions to Problems Arising in Warfare 168, ¶ 6.01 (2019).

armed conflicts[13] and non-international armed conflicts.[14] Conflict classification is the preliminary stage in the application of IHL. Equally, as war crimes are committed only during an armed conflict, conflict classification is a preliminary issue to be settled before the adjudication of war crimes by international criminal tribunals. In the context of the International Criminal Court (ICC), the type of armed conflict further determines the category of war crimes under which an accused is charged.[15]

The Geneva Conventions do not define the general term "armed conflict" or the specific terms "international armed conflict" and "non-international armed conflict." In *Prosecutor v. Dusko Tadić*, the first case before the International Criminal Tribunal for the former Yugoslavia (ICTY), the Appeals Chamber grappled with the lack of definition of the term "armed conflict" in the Geneva Conventions as a prerequisite to the prosecution of war crimes.[16] The Appeals Chamber defined the characteristics of the two categories of armed conflict as follows: "An armed conflict exists whenever there is a resort to armed force between States or protracted armed violence between governmental authorities and organized armed groups or between such groups within a State."[17]

This *Tadić* formulation is accepted to reflect customary international law. Subsequent international criminal tribunals, including the International Criminal Tribunal for Rwanda (ICTR), the Special Court for Sierra Leone, and the International Criminal Court all employ the *Tadić* formulation to determine the existence of an armed conflict.[18] The inclusion of the *Tadić* definition in the war crimes provisions of the Rome Statute[19] also supports this conclusion as the drafters of the Rome Statute codified existing custom only.

13. Common Article 2 of the Geneva Conventions promotes a better understanding of the notion "international armed conflict." *See* Geneva Conventions, *supra* note 10.

14. The legal framework applicable to non-international armed conflicts meeting the *Tadić* threshold includes Common Article 3 and customary law of non-international armed conflict.

15. Article 8(2) of the Rome Statute classifies the types of conflict as "international" (arts. 8(2)(a) and (b)), "armed conflicts not of an international character" (arts. 8(2)(c) and (d)) and/or "protracted armed conflict" (arts. 8(2)(e) and (f)). Rome Statute of the International Criminal Court, July 17, 1998, 2187 U.N.T.S. 90. For an overview of the classification of armed conflict in the Rome Statute, *see* CARSTEN STAHN, THE LAW ND PRACTICE OF THE INTERNATIONAL CRIMINAL COURT 764–74 (2015).

16. *See Tadić*, Decision on the Defence Motion for Interlocutory Appeal on Jurisdiction, *supra* note 2, ¶ 70.

17. *Id.*

18. *See, e.g.*, Prosecutor v. Delalić et al., Case No. IT-96-21-T, Judgment, ¶¶ 183–92 (Int'l Crim. Trib. for the former Yugoslavia Nov. 16, 1998); *Akayesu*, *supra* note 3, ¶ 627; Prosecutor v. Thomas Lubanga Dyilo, Case No. ICC-01/04-01/06, Judgment Pursuant to Article 74 of the Statute, ¶ 538 (Mar. 14, 2012); Prosecutor v. Moinina Fofana, Allieu Kondewa, Case No. SCSL-04-14-T, Judgment, ¶ 124 (Aug. 2, 2007).

19. Rome Statute, *supra* note 15, art. 8(2)(f).

The *Tadić* formulation confirms that an international armed conflict refers to inter-State armed conflict. It further delineates the two elements that are required for a non-international armed conflict to exist. First, the severity of fighting must satisfy the notion of intensity and equate to protracted armed violence and, second, the non-State armed group must meet a minimum threshold of organization.[20] The *Tadić* Trial Chamber refined the Appeals Chamber's formulation as follows:

> The test applied by the Appeals Chamber to the existence of an armed conflict for the purposes of the rules contained in Common Article 3 focuses on *two aspects* of a conflict, the *intensity of the conflict* and the *organization of the parties to the conflict*. In an armed conflict of an internal or mixed character, these closely-related criteria are used solely for the purpose, as a minimum, of distinguishing an armed conflict from banditry, unorganized and short-lived insurrections, or terrorist activities, which are not subject to international humanitarian law.[21]

The Trial Chamber thus promotes a functional approach towards assessing the existence of a NIAC. It makes it clear that the purpose of these two aspects of a conflict is to differentiate between situations that sink below the threshold of NIAC, such as riots, isolated and sporadic attacks, terrorism, and so forth, that should be regulated through a law-enforcement paradigm, and NIACs that call for the application of the law of non-international armed conflict.[22]

The jurisprudence of the international criminal tribunals has also contributed to clarifying the two elements of the *Tadić* formulation, namely, intensity of violence and organization of the non-State armed group.

1. The Intensity of Violence

Turning to the concept of "protracted armed violence," a minimum level of fighting must be present in order to satisfy the threshold of violence required of a non-international armed conflict.[23] In *Tadić*, the Appeals Chamber understood "intensity" as necessitating that the level of violence resulting from the fighting between the parties to the conflict matches the estimation of "protracted armed violence."[24] In *Kordić* and *Čerkez*, the ICTY echoed the *Tadić* formula's purposive approach, highlighting that the significance of the term "protracted" in its relation

20. International Committee of the Red Cross, *How Is the Term "Armed Conflict" Defined in International Humanitarian Law?*, INT'L COMM. OF THE RED CROSS OPINION PAPER (2008).

21. Prosecutor v. Tadić, Case No. IT-94-1-T, Opinion and Judgment, ¶ 561 (Int'l Crim. Trib. for the former Yugoslavia May 7, 1997).

22. *Id.*, ¶ 561.

23. *Tadić*, Decision on the Defence Motion for Interlocutory Appeal on Jurisdiction, *supra* note 2, ¶ 70.

24. *Id.*

to the term "violence" stems from an aim to exclude cases of mere civil unrest or single acts of terrorism from the assessment of cases of armed conflict not of an international character.[25] Protracted armed violence is widely accepted as descriptive of the minimum threshold of intensity.[26] However, *Tadić* did not elaborate on the minimum level of fighting that equates to protracted armed violence.[27]

In the *Haradinaj* case,[28] the Trial Chamber considered how the criterion of "protracted violence" had been understood in previous cases. The Trial Chamber determined that the following indicative factors determine whether the nature of the violence is protracted:

> [T]he number, duration and intensity of individual confrontations; the type of weapons and other military equipment used; the number and calibre of munitions fired; the number of persons and type of forces partaking in the fighting; the number of casualties; the extent of material destruction; and the number of civilians fleeing combat zones. The involvement of the UN Security Council may also be a reflection of the intensity of a conflict.[29]

Other international tribunals, such as the ICC, have confirmed the indicative factors developed by the ICTY in relation to the definition of "protracted armed violence."[30]

2. The Organization of a Non-State Armed Group

In *Tadić*, the Appeals Chamber referred to the non-State party to the conflict as an "organized armed group."[31] The Trial Chamber clarified that the concept of "organization" in the construct "organized armed group" serves to differentiate between mere criminals, bandits, protestors, or terrorists, whose conduct is regulated by domestic law and human rights law, from organized armed groups that are bound by the law of non-international armed conflict.[32] However, the

25. Prosecutor v. Kordić and Čerkez, Case No. IT-95-14/2-A, Appeals Chamber Judgment, ¶ 341 (Int'l Crim. Trib. for the former Yugoslavia Dec. 17, 2004).

26. *Tadić*, Opinion and Judgment, *supra* note 21, ¶ 561.

27. *See* both *Tadić*, Decision on the Defence Motion for Interlocutory Appeal on Jurisdiction, *supra* note 2, ¶ 70, and *Tadić*, Opinion and Judgment, *supra* note 21, ¶ 561.

28. Prosecutor v. Haradinaj, Case No. IT-04-84-T, Judgment, ¶ 49 (Int'l Crim. Trib. for the former Yugoslavia Apr. 3, 2008).

29. *Id.*

30. *See, e.g.*, *Lubanga*, *supra* note 18, ¶ 538.

31. *See Tadić*, Decision on the Defence Motion for Interlocutory Appeal on Jurisdiction, *supra* note 2, ¶ 70.

32. *Tadić*, Opinion and Judgment, *supra* note 21, ¶ 561

Trial Chamber neglected to provide insight into the degree of organization that is needed to qualify a group as being sufficiently organized to be a party to a NIAC.[33]

In the *Boškoski* case, the Trial Chamber laid down criteria in this regard.[34] The factors indicated in the *Boškoski* case may be grouped as follows: possession of a command structure; the existence of an internal disciplinary system and the possession of the ability to implement the laws of armed conflict; engaging in military tactics and achieving military objectives by carrying out military operations in an organized manner; the logistical capacity of the armed group; and the ability of the armed group to speak with one voice.[35] These factors have been employed to classify conflicts in subsequent cases before the ICTY[36] and the ICC.[37] The International Committee of the Red Cross (ICRC) Commentaries on the Geneva Conventions confirm that the indicators of organization, as identified in the case law of the ICTY, remain the essential tools for an assessment of the degree of organization of an armed group.[38]

In *Boškoski*, the Trial Chamber stressed that the factors identified are not an exhaustive list and that each armed group should be evaluated on a case-by-case basis.[39] Furthermore, it must be underlined that these factors are merely indicative, as the Tribunal has not explained to what extent they must be fulfilled.[40] This

33. *Id.*

34. Prosecutor v. Boškoski and Tarčulovski, Case No. IT-04-82-T, Judgment, ¶¶ 199–203 (Int'l Crim. Trib. for the former Yugoslavia July 10, 2008). *See* SANDESH SIVAKUMARAN, THE LAW OF NON-INTERNATIONAL ARMED CONFLICT 171–74 (2012) (for an analysis of the organizational criteria). For an in-depth discussion, *see* Martha M. Bradley, *Revisiting the Notion of "Organised Armed Group" in Accordance with Common Article 3: Exploring the Minimum Threshold Requirements* 1 AFRICAN YEARBOOK OF INTERNATIONAL HUMANITARIAN LAW 67–77 (2018).

35. *Boškoski*, *supra* note 34, ¶¶ 199–203. *See also* Prosecutor v. Vlastimir Dordevic, Case No. IT-05-87/1-T, Public Judgment with Confidential Annex Vol. II, ¶¶ 1525–26, 1537–78 (Int'l Crim. Trib. for the former Yugoslavia Feb. 23, 2011); *Boškoski*, *supra* note 34, ¶¶ 23–24.

36. *Akayesu*, *supra* note 3, ¶¶ 620–21; Prosecutor v. Musema, Case No. ICTR-96-13-A, Judgment and Sentence, ¶¶ 248–51 (Jan. 27, 2000); Prosecutor v. Limaj, Case No. IT-03-66-T, Judgment, ¶¶ 90, 94–134 (Int'l Crim. Trib. for the former Yugoslavia Nov. 30, 2005); Prosecutor v. Milošević, Case No. IT-02-54-T, Decision on Motion for Judgment of Acquittal (Int'l Crim. Trib. for the former Yugoslavia June 16, 2004); *Boškoski*, *supra* note 34, ¶ 194–206, 250–91; *Haradinaj*, *supra* note 28, ¶¶ 50–60; *Lubanga*, *supra* note 18, ¶ 537.

37. *See, e.g.*, *Ntaganda*, *supra* note 9, ¶¶ 704–10, 713–14; Prosecutor v. Katanga, Case No. ICC-01/04-01/07, Judgment, ¶¶ 671–81, 1186, 1207–11 (Mar. 7, 2014); *Lubanga*, *supra* note 18, ¶¶ 537, 546.

38. COMMENTARY ON THE FIRST GENEVA CONVENTION: CONVENTION (I) FOR THE AMELIORATION OF THE CONDITIONS OF THE WOUNDED AND SICK IN ARMED FORCES IN THE FIELD 156, ¶ 156 (Knut Dörmann et al. eds., 2016). For insight into the value of the ICRC's commentaries as a source of teachings, *see* Sandesh Sivakumaran, *The Influence of Teachings of Publicists on the Development of International Law*, 66 INTERNATIONAL AND COMPARATIVE LAW QUARTERLY 15 (2017).

39. *Boškoski*, *supra* note 34, ¶ 204.

40. In its 2016 Commentaries on Common Article 3, the ICRC emphasized that by itself none of these indicative factors is essential. *See* Dörmann et al., *supra* note 38, at 156, ¶ 430.

fudging of the issue allows for flexibility as not all organized armed groups are similar in structure.

A valuable contribution by the ICC in terms of elucidation of the notion "organized armed group" is the *Katanga* case.[41] In practice, a sophisticated organized armed group with a vertical structure and territorial control is unproblematic to identify as qualifying as an organized armed group for the purposes of the definition of a NIAC. The difficulty lies in the categorization of an armed group with only a basic organization. In the *Katanga* case, the ICC Trial Chamber clarified that the minimum threshold of organization inherent in the notion "organized armed group" is fulfilled to the extent that there is a leader and there are followers even if the hierarchical structure of an organized armed group lacks sophistication.[42] In this case, the Trial Chamber found that a relatively low threshold of organization nevertheless qualified the *Walendu-Bindi Collectivité* as an organized armed group.[43] The ICC described this group as "form[ing] a somewhat rag-tag collection."[44] The description of "a somewhat rag-tag collection" is instructive as, even though the *Walendu-Bindi Collectivité* lacked a command structure with more than two levels of hierarchy akin to more sophisticated organized armed groups previously classified by international criminal tribunals as organized armed groups,[45] the group was found to meet the minimum threshold of organization.[46]

The analysis of the organizational structure of the *Walendu-Bindi Collectivité* by the *Katanga* Trial Chamber shows that, at a minimum, a non-State fighting unit needs to be able to organize itself to the extent that it can execute a military attack.[47] The ICC allowed for a flexible interpretation of a command structure and of communication and did not emphasize the need for the clear existence of a headquarters.[48] An efficient ability to conduct a military operation as a collective in this case may be construed as the minimum requirement.[49] The contribution of *Katanga* is important as it clearly indicates that a sophisticated command

41. *Katanga, supra* note 37.

42. *Id.*, ¶ 681.

43. *Id.*, ¶¶ 671–84. In *Katanga*, the Court mimicked the approach of the Inter-American Commission on Human Rights in the *La Tablada* case. Abella v. Argentina, Case 11.137, Inter-Amer. Comm'n. H.R., Report No. 55/97, OEA/Ser.L/V/II.95, Doc. 7 rev., ¶ 157 (1997) [hereinafter *La Tablada*].

44. *Katanga, supra* note 37, ¶ 681 (emphasis added).

45. The Kosovo Liberation Army (KLA) is an example of an organized armed group with a sophisticated command structure. *See* Prosecutor v. Vlastimir Dordevic, Case No. IT-05-87/1-T, ¶ 1541 (Feb. 23, 2011).

46. *Katanga, supra* note 37, ¶ 681.

47. *Id.*

48. *Id.*

49. *Id.*

structure is not required for an armed group to meet the minimum threshold of organization.

The approach followed in *Katanga* is practical from an operational perspective. In the IHL paradigm, those responsible for conflict classification, especially as the situation on the ground is constantly evolving, do not have the benefit of hindsight; that privilege is the preserve of after-the-fact classification by war crimes tribunals. The *Katanga* approach enables assessment in real time of when a non-State entity evolves to be sufficiently organized to transform into an organized armed group able to launch military attacks sufficiently severe that the fighting between the parties equates to protracted armed violence. This approach is cognizant of the fact that organized armed groups often operate in secret and intelligence often is delayed or limited. Furthermore, the *Katanga* approach correctly identifies that the two notions established in *Tadić*, of intensity of violence and organization of the armed group, are not mutually exclusive but interlinked. Without the necessary degree of organization it would not be possible to engage in fighting of a military nature that meets the threshold of protracted armed violence. Similarly, the existence of fighting that is protracted in nature confirms that the non-State party is sufficiently organized.

As these cases reveal, the contribution made by international criminal tribunals in defining NIAC cannot be overstated. It is crucial to know when IHL applies to a situation and that, in turn, depends on whether the situation is one of armed conflict. Today, a majority of armed conflicts are non-international in nature, and territorial States are often eager to downplay as sporadic acts of violence, situations that in reality should be classified as non-international armed conflicts. This misclassification would be at the expense of those who need protection under the law of non-international armed conflict.

B. Defining Rape

International criminal tribunals have helped to clarify aspects of international humanitarian law concerned with the prohibition of sexual and gender-based violence (SGBV).[50] Sexual and gender-based crimes were not prosecuted at the Nuremberg International Military Tribunal.[51] Despite the neglect by the drafters of the Charter of the International Military Tribunal for the Far East (Tokyo Tribunal) specifically to include the term "rape," Japanese defendants were charged with rape as an underlying offense of command responsibility for brutalities committed in Nanking.[52] Yet it took until the 1990s for international

50. Miranda Das & Sukhdev Singh, *Crimes of Sexual Violence Within International Criminal Law: A Historical Outline*, 14 Journal of Politics and Law 3 (2021).

51. Shane Darcy, Judges, Law and War: The Judicial Development of International Humanitarian Law 176–77 (2016).

52. Das & Singh, *supra* note 50, at 4.

criminal tribunals to prosecute those responsible for the commission of rape as a war crime.[53] It was the jurisprudence of the ICTY and the ICTR that developed IHL by inter alia clarifying the understanding of rape as a violation of the law of international and non-international armed conflict.[54]

There is a specific treaty prohibition on rape in the law of international armed conflict.[55] Article 27 of the Fourth Geneva Convention guarantees special protection of women against SGBV, including rape.[56] By contrast, there is no specific mention of the prohibition of rape or SGBV in Common Article 3 of the Geneva Conventions. ICTY and ICTR jurisprudence is pivotal in demonstrating that a prohibition of SGBV is implicit in Common Article 3 and thus in the law of non-international armed conflict. In *Akayesu*, the ICTR Trial Chamber held that rape was akin to torture in that it is a violation of personal dignity.[57] The Trial Chamber further stated that rape constituted a form of torture.[58] In *Bagosora*, the ICTR also found outrages upon personal dignity to include the prohibition on rape.[59] As Common Article 3 expressly prohibits torture as well as outrages upon personal dignity, the ICTY and ICTR's holdings confirm that rape is also prohibited in common Article 3.

Although Article 27 of the Fourth Geneva Convention prohibits rape, it does not provide a definition of rape. The international criminal tribunals' definitions of rape are thus groundbreaking for the development of IHL. The *Akayesu* Trial Chamber was the first international criminal tribunal to define rape.[60] *Akayesu* defines rape in a nonmechanical manner as

53. *Delalić et al.*, *supra* note 18, ¶ 173; *Akayesu*, *supra* note 3; *Furundžija*, *supra* note 3, ¶¶ 166–69.

54. For an overview of the major contributions made by both the ICTY and ICTR with respect to SGBV, *see* Oosterveld, *supra* note 3, at 197–220; for a judicial confirmation of "forced marriages" amounting to a form of SGBV during conflict, *see* Prosecutor v. Dominic Ongwen, Case No. ICC-02/04-01/15, Decision on confirmation of charges, ¶¶ 87, 89, 91 (Mar. 23, 2016),; for an in-depth discussion of Ongwen's contribution to divorcing "sexual slavery" and "forced marriage," *see* Annie Bunting & Izevbuwa Kehinde Ikhimiukor, *The Expressive Nature of War: What We Learn from Conjugal Slavery to Forced Marriage in International Criminal Law*, 19 International Criminal Law Review 331 (2018); *see also* Tanja Altunjan for an overview of Ongwen's contribution to "forced marriages" as a war crime in Tanja Altunjan, *The International Criminal Court and Sexual Violence: Between Aspirations and Reality*, 22 German Law Journal 878, 889–91 (2021).

55. Fourth Geneva Convention, *supra* note 10, art. 27.

56. *Id.* "Women shall be especially protected against any attack on their honour, in particular against rape, enforced prostitution, or any other form of indecent assault." "Honour" has been interpreted to refer to a woman's sexuality.

57. *Akayesu*, *supra* note 3, ¶ 687.

58. *Id.*

59. Prosecutor v. Bagosora, Case No. ICTR-98-41-T, Judgment and Sentence, ¶ 2250 (Dec. 18, 2008).

60. *Akayesu*, *supra* note 3.

> [a] physical invasion of a sexual nature committed on a person under circumstances which are coercive. The Tribunal considers sexual violence, which includes rape, as any act of a sexual nature which is committed on a person under circumstances which are coercive. Sexual violence is not limited to physical invasion of the human body and may include acts which do not involve penetration or even physical contact.[61]

The *Furundžija* case followed shortly after *Akayesu.*[62] In *Furundžija*, the ICTY Trial Chamber took a different, mechanical approach, defining rape to include the penetration not only of the vagina but also of the anus or mouth. It furthermore held that the object of penetration was not restricted to the penis but included any other object.[63] Penetration, however shallow, of the vulva, anus, or oral cavity is sufficient for it to qualify as rape if accompanied by coercion or force or the threat of force against the victim.[64]

Particular attention has been paid to the role of consent in the definition of rape as a war crime. In *Kunarac*, the Trial Chamber surveyed domestic statutes and judicial decisions that define the crime of rape and, consequently, identified three broad categories of factors which classify sexual acts as rape: First, the sexual activity is accompanied by force or a threat of force against the victim or a third party; second, the sexual activity is accompanied by force or a variety of other specified circumstances that make the victim particularly vulnerable or negate an ability to state an informed refusal; and, third, the sexual activity takes place without the consent of the victim.[65] Niamh Hayes observes that in its definition of rape the Trial Chamber places consent at the core of the physical and mental elements.[66] Hayes also observes that *Kunarac* differs from *Furundžija* in that it considers the violation of sexual autonomy rather than force or coercion as the basic principle underlying rape in national jurisdictions.[67]

61. *Id.*, ¶ 688.

62. *Furundžija*, *supra* note 3, ¶¶ 174, 185.

63. *Id.*, ¶ 174 reads: ". . . [T]he penetration of the vagina, the anus or mouth by the penis, or of the vagina or anus by other object . . ." In *Bemba* and *Ntaganda*, the ICC expressly confirmed that "rape" is gender neutral. *See Ntaganda*, *supra* note 9, ¶¶ 933, 940–42; Prosecutor v. Bemba Combo, Case No. ICC-01/05-01/08, Judgment ¶¶ 100, 494, 633–34 (Mar. 21, 2016). For a discussion on the ICC's contribution to promoting gender neutrality with regard to SGBV, *see* Altunjan, *supra* note 54, at 888–89.

64. *Furundžija*, *supra* note 3, ¶¶ 174, 185.

65. Prosecutor v. Kunarac, Case No. IT-96-23 & IT-96-23/1-A, Judgment, ¶ 442 (Int'l Crim. Trib. for the former Yugoslavia June 12, 2022).

66. *See* Niamh Hayes, *Creating a Definition of Rape in International Law: The Contribution of the International Criminal Tribunals*, *in* JUDICIAL CREATIVITY AT THE INTERNATIONAL CRIMINAL TRIBUNALS 129, 142 (Shane Darcy & Joseph Powderly eds., 2010). .

67. *Furundžija*, *supra* note 3, ¶ 440; Hayes, *supra* note 66, at 142.

The Appeals Chamber in *Kunarac* explained that the consent of the victim must be provided voluntarily and that consent as a manifestation of the victim's free will must be assessed in the context of the circumstances at the time of the commission of the act.[68] The Appeals Chamber highlighted that the "surrounding circumstances" in wartime "will be almost universally coercive" and thus "true" consent simply is impossible.[69] The ICTR Appeals Chamber in *Gacumbitsi* confirmed the *Kunarac* Appeals Chamber's finding that nonconsent is an element of the crime of rape (in the context of crimes against humanity) and also explained that "[t]he Prosecution can prove non-consent beyond reasonable doubt by proving the existence of coercive circumstances under which meaningful consent is not possible."[70]

The ICTY and ICTR thus have contributed to the development of international humanitarian law concerned with the prohibition of rape and other forms of SGBV through confirmation that rape can amount to torture, that the prohibition applies also in non-international armed conflicts, and through their definitions of rape.

III. A POSSIBLE CASE OF JUDICIAL ACTIVISM: *NTAGANDA* OWN FORCE VIOLATIONS

Not all of the contributions of the international criminal tribunals to the development of international humanitarian law have been positive. The *Ntaganda* case is an example of the risks that arise from employing a victim-centric lens in the interpretation of war crimes provisions and from divorcing war crimes law from the ambit of IHL.

Among other charges, Mr. Bosco Ntaganda was charged under Article 8(2)(e)(vi) of the Rome Statute with the alleged rape and sexual slavery of Union of Congolese Patriots/The Patriotic Forces for the Liberation of the Congo (UPC/FPLC) child soldiers under fifteen years of age in the context of a NIAC in the Democratic Republic of the Congo (DRC).[71] Ntaganda was a member of the organized armed group, the UPC/FPLC, and the victims were child soldiers of that same group.[72] In the *Ntaganda* case, the Appeals Chamber of the ICC was tasked with considering whether own-force violations are an essential jurisdictional

68. *Kunarac*, *supra* note 65, ¶¶ 129–30.

69. *Id.*, ¶ 130.

70. *Gacumbitsi*, *supra* note 3, ¶ 155. *See* Hayes, *supra* note 66, at 146–47.

71. Prosecutor v. Ntaganda, Case No. ICC-01/04-02/06, Decision Pursuant to Article 61(7)(a) and (b) of the Rome Statute on the Charges of the Prosecutor Against Bosco Ntaganda, ¶ 76 (June 9, 2014).

72. *Id.*, ¶¶ 76–77.

issue pertaining to the war crimes of rape and sexual slavery.[73] The practical benefit to victims of the interpretation that own-force violations are included in the protective scope of the war crimes provisions of the Rome Statute is that it fills a legal vacuum under IHL, which does not include violations committed by certain persons (i.e., intra-party protection). This application might be applauded for closing an accountability gap in international criminal law,[74] but, as will be illustrated, it is also a cause of confusion as a departure from the position under international humanitarian law.

In *Ntaganda*, the Appeals Chamber had to determine whether the war crimes of rape and sexual slavery included acts committed by a member of an armed group against other members of the same armed group.[75] In deciding the issue, the Appeals Chamber first turned to the ordinary meaning, context, and drafting history of Article 8(2)(e)(vi) of the Rome Statute.[76] The Appeals Chamber implicitly employed Articles 31 and 32 of the Vienna Convention on the Law of Treaties (VCLT) in its analysis.[77] The Appeals Chamber emphasized the fact that Article 8(2)(e)(vi) of the Rome Statute did not expressly include the language "protected persons" or "persons taking no active part in hostilities."[78] Noting that the drafting history of Article 8(2)(e) is silent on the issue, the Appeals Chamber considered the lack of reference to "protected persons" and "persons taking no active part in hostilities" in the article to mean that the victims of the war crimes of rape and sexual slavery were not limited to such persons.[79]

The Appeals Chamber erred in its methodology when it employed Articles 31 and 32 of the VCLT in interpreting Article 8(2)(e)(vi) of the Rome Statute.[80] Article 21 of the Rome Statute sets out the applicable law and provides that the Court shall apply, as a first resort, the Statute, Elements of Crimes and Rules of Procedure and Evidence;[81] and as the second resort, the appropriate treaties,

73. *Ntaganda*, Judgment on the appeal of Mr. Ntaganda against the "Second decision," *supra* note 10, ¶¶ 8, 9.

74. For a discussion on how own force protection could benefit SGBV victims who suffer at the hand of their own forces, *see* Coman Kenny & Yvonne McDermott, *The Expanding Protection of Members of a Party's Own Armed Forces under International Criminal Law*, 68 International and Comparative Law Quarterly 943 (2019).

75. *Ntaganda*, Judgment on the appeal of Mr. Ntaganda against the "Second decision," *supra* note 10, ¶ 8.

76. *Id.*, ¶¶ 46–51.

77. Vienna Convention on the Law of Treaties, May 23, 1969, 1155 U.N.T.S. 331 [hereinafter VCLT].

78. *Ntaganda*, Judgment on the appeal of Mr. Ntaganda against the "Second decision," *supra* note 10, ¶ 46.

79. *Id.*, ¶¶ 50, 51.

80. *Id.*, ¶¶ 46–51.

81. Rome Statute, *supra* note 15, art. 21(1)(a).

principles, and rules of international law and, specifically, IHL.[82] The Appeals Chamber should have relied on the VCLT to interpret Common Article 3, which contains the prohibition corresponding to the war crime codified in Article 8(2)(e)(vi).

Ntaganda argued that the "established framework of international law" introduces a status requirement.[83] The Appeals Chamber asserted that for the argument to hold, it had to be established that IHL limits the protection provided under Common Article 3 to persons not actively taking part in hostilities.[84] Instead of interrogating Common Article 3 and determining whether it relates to protected persons only, the Appeals Chamber evaluated whether the Geneva Conventions imposed a status requirement as a general rule of IHL.[85] In finding that they do not and, consequently, that Common Article 3 provides for "unqualified protection against inhumane treatment,"[86] Common Article 3 was left unexamined.

An interrogation of Common Article 3 from an IHL perspective does not support the finding of intra-party protection. The war crime of rape of which Mr. Ntaganda was found guilty is codified in Article 8(2)(e)(vi) of the Rome Statute. This provision is a criminalization of Common Article 3(1)(c). Common Article 3(1) categorizes those who benefit from its protection as "persons taking no active part in the hostilities, including members of armed forces who have laid down their arms and those placed *hors de combat* by sickness, wounds, detention or any other cause."

An ordinary reading of the protected categories of persons clearly indicates that they do not include members of an armed group or the armed forces who have not laid down their arms or who are not *hors de combat*.[87] "Taking no active part in hostilities" is a qualification that does not extend to the fighting forces of the organized armed group but is limited only to civilians and persons *hors de combat*.[88]

82. *Id.*, art. 21(1)(b).

83. *Ntaganda*, Judgment on the appeal of Mr. Ntaganda against the "Second decision," *supra* note 10. ¶¶ 56–69.

84. *Id.*, ¶ 56.

85. *Id.*, ¶¶ 58–60.

86. *Id.*, ¶ 60.

87. Indeed, Kleffner observes that the assessment of whether an individual enjoys protection under Common Article 3 is a "conduct-based" test, which means that protection under Common Article 3 attaches to the actual activities of the person. *See* Jann K. Kleffner, *The Beneficiaries of Rights Stemming from Common Article 3*, *in* THE 1949 GENEVA CONVENTIONS: A COMMENTARY 433, 435–36 (Andrew Clapham, Paola Gaeta, & Marco Sassòli eds., 2014).

88. *See* INTERNATIONAL COMMITTEE OF THE RED CROSS, INTERPRETIVE GUIDANCE ON THE NOTION OF DIRECT PARTICIPATION IN HOSTILITIES UNDER INTERNATIONAL HUMANITARIAN LAW (2009), which explains that "civilian" in the context of non-international armed conflict means "for the purposes of the principle of distinction in non-international armed conflict, all persons who are not members of State armed forces or organized armed groups of a party to

Child soldiers are a part of the fighting forces of an organized armed group and are not civilians and, therefore, cannot be treated as persons taking no active part in hostilities.[89] They only enjoy protection when placed *hors de combat*.[90] The protections offered under Common Article 3 clearly relate to members of enemy armed groups or enemy armed forces that are *hors de combat*, and not own forces. In this sense, "enemy" means the opposing party to the NIAC.[91] The rape by one member of an armed force against another member, regardless of the age of the victim, is not regulated by Common Article 3. The correct legal framework for the prosecution of the crime is domestic criminal law or domestic military law.[92]

The *Ntaganda* decision thus departs from IHL. The legal consequence of *Ntaganda* is summarized as follows by Kevin Jon Heller:

> In each and every case, war crimes are limited to violations of IHL. No more. The Appeals Chamber (AC) at the ICC has just unanimously held in *Ntaganda* that a perpetrator can be convicted of a war crime even if his act does not violate IHL. That decision is not simply "unprecedented," as the AC openly acknowledges. It is simply incorrect.[93]

Scholars who support this example of judicial activism by the ICC in *Ntaganda* argue that it fills a *lacuna* by offering protection to the victims of SGBV in the context of acts committed by their own forces.[94] This author shares the argument

the conflict are civilians and, therefore, entitled to protection against direct attack unless and for such time as they take a direct part in hostilities. In non-international armed conflict, organized armed groups constitute the armed forces of a non-State party to the conflict and consist only of individuals whose continuous function it is to take a direct part in hostilities ('continuous combat function')."

89. *See* Fernanda García Pinto, *The International Committee of the Red Cross and the International Criminal Court: Turning International Humanitarian Law into a Two-Headed Snake?*, 102 International Review of the Red Cross 757 (2020).

90. *See also* Kevin Jon Heller, *ICC Appeals Chamber Says a War Crime Does Not Have to Violate IHL*, Opinio Juris (June 15, 2017), https://opiniojuris.org/2017/06/15/icc-appeals-chamber-holds-a-war-crime-does-not-have-to-violate-ihl/, where he explains: "To begin with, there is a *specific* rule excluding active combatants form the war crimes of rape and sexual slavery in member-against-member situations: namely, the rule that says violence in member-against-member situations violates IHL only when the victim is *hors de combat*."

91. *Id.* Heller critiques the Appeals Chamber's interpretation of the ICRC's 2020 Commentary's understanding of the protective scope under Common Article 3: "[T]hat statement is incomplete and misleading, because the ICRC makes unequivocally clear that CA3's prohibitions apply only to individuals who are *hors de combat*."

92. *See* Kenny & McDermott, *supra* note 74, at 944; Antonio Cassese, International Criminal Law 82 (2d ed. 2008).

93. Heller, *supra* note 90.

94. *See* Joanna Frivet, *Expanding IHL through ICL: How Prosecutorial Opportunism and Judicial Activism Redefined Intra-Party SGBV Crimes at the ICC*, 1 Humanitäres Völkerrecht 64–66

in response of Marco Sassòli, concerning the relationship between IHL and ICL, who cautions that "[i]t would be wrong and dangerous, however, to view IHL solely from the perspective of criminal law."[95] Sassòli emphasizes the fact that IHL is not an auxiliary arm of ICL, but a discipline on its own.[96] ICL relates to IHL in that it enforces its rules or serves to clarify them.[97] The relationship between IHL and ICL can be viewed as one in which IHL constitutes a set of substantive prohibitions that are criminalized under the ICL paradigm as war crimes.[98] In *Ntaganda*, in order to afford protection under ICL, the various Chambers misinterpreted IHL. Consequently, *Ntaganda* is a departure from a basic assumption in IHL, that "not all violations of IHL are war crimes; but all war crimes are violations of IHL."[99] Heller cautions against a separation of IHL from ICL as was performed by the ICC in *Ntaganda*:

> Ultimately, the decision of the Appeals Chamber in *Ntaganda* is little more than the latest iteration of the Court's willingness to rely on teleological reasoning when the Rome Statute does not protect victims as much as the judges think it should. No one is in favor of raping and sexually enslaving child soldiers. However, the solution is not to detach the law of war crimes from its moorings in IHL by holding—if only implicitly—that an act can be a war crime even if it does not violate IHL. To do so is not only legally indefensible, but risks delegitimizing both the Court and the law of war crimes itself.[100]

Ntaganda serves as a cautionary tale against a failure to respect the fragile relationship between IHL and ICL and a warning to uphold the principle that first and foremost the categorization of a war crime rests on a prohibition under IHL.

IV. CREATING CONFUSION: *NTAGANDA* AND THE MEANING OF "ATTACK"

Another example of an international criminal tribunal, perhaps lacking in its understanding of IHL, approaching war crimes adjudication from an exclusively ICL perspective in disregard of the source that underpins the war crime, is the

(2019), illustrating how judicial activism has been employed to offer "blanket protection" for victims of SGBV.

95. Sassòli, *supra* note 12, at 447, ¶ 9.65.

96. *Id.*, at 444, ¶ 9.57.

97. *Id.*, at 444, ¶ 9.55.

98. 2 Introduction to International Criminal Law and Procedure 267, 271 (Robert Cryer et al. eds., 2010).

99. *Id.* 272.

100. Heller, *supra* note 90.

Ntaganda Appeals Chamber decision relating to the definition of "attack" as employed in Article 8(2)(e)(iv) of the Rome Statute.[101] The *Ntaganda* decision has led to confusion concerning the meaning of a term that was settled and uncontested in IHL.[102] As with the decision on intra-party violence, perhaps it acts on a consideration that judicial activism will offer better protection for victims.

In the *Ntaganda* case, Ntaganda was charged inter alia with the war crime of attacking protected objects as provided for in Article 8(2)(e)(iv) of the Rome Statute.[103] The Trial Chamber had to establish whether two *ratissage* operations[104] constituted "attacks."[105] The first operation was the looting of and damage to a hospital.[106] The second operation concerned soldiers repurposing a church as a military base.[107] These operations occurred only after the initial military attack on Sayo, a town in the DRC, which enabled the UPC/FPLC to execute its *ratissage* operations.[108] The Trial Chamber defined the term "attack" in Article 8(2)(e)(iv) to mean an "act of violence against the adversary, whether in offence or defense."[109] The Trial Chamber explained that the crime of attacking protected objects (in the present case, a church and a hospital) had to be committed during the actual conduct of hostilities.[110] The Trial Chamber also clarified that under Article 8(2)(e)

101. *Ntaganda*, Appeals Chamber Judgment, *supra* note 9, ¶¶ 1163–68.

102. *See* the scholarly debate concerning the meaning of "attack" generated by the prosecutor's appeal in *Ntaganda* as discussed in West Point's Lieber Institute for Law and Warfare's Articles of War blog, including Ronald Alcala & Sasha Radin, *Symposium Intro: The ICC Considers the Definition of Attack*, ARTICLES OF WAR (Oct. 27, 2020), https://lieber.westpoint.edu/symposium-intro-icc-definition-attack/; Shane Reeves & Sean Watts, *Military Considerations and the Ntaganda "Attack" Question*, ARTICLES OF WAR (Nov. 24, 2020), https://lieber.westpoint.edu/military-considerations-ntaganda-attack/; Eian Katz, Milena Sterio, & Jonathan Worboys, *"Attacks" Against Hospitals and Cultural Property: Broad in Time, Broad in Substance*, ARTICLES OF WAR (Nov. 17, 2020), https://lieber.westpoint.edu/attacks-against-hospitals-cultural-property-broad/; Ori Pomson, *Ntaganda Appeals Chamber Judgment Divided on Meaning of "Attack,"* ARTICLES OF WAR (May 12, 2021), https://lieber.westpoint.edu/ntaganda-appeals-chamber-judgment-divided-meaning-attack/.

103. Prosecutor v. Ntaganda, Case No. ICC-01/04-02/06, Judgment, ¶ 935 (July 8, 2019), ¶ 1134. Article 8(2)(e)(iv) refers to the war crime of "[i]ntentionally directing attacks against buildings dedicated to religion, education, art, science or charitable purposes, historic monuments, hospitals and places where the sick and wounded are collected, provided they are not military objectives."

104. The term "ratissage" operation in this context refers to a search and sweep operation conducted in the aftermath of the initial attack.

105. *Ntaganda*, Judgment, *supra* note 103, ¶ 1134.

106. *Id.*, ¶ 1138.

107. *Id.*

108. *Id.* ¶¶ 1134–38.

109. *Id.*, ¶ 1136.

110. *Id.*

(iv), the perpetrator must have launched an attack against the protected object, but actual damage or destruction need not be established.[111]

The Trial Chamber found that the shelling of the healthcare center qualified as an attack,[112] but that the pillaging of protected objects did not constitute an attack for the purposes of Article 8(2)(e)(iv) of the Rome Statute.[113] The Court correctly reasoned that pillage was not an act of violence against the adversary[114] and, consequently, that the act of pillaging protected objects did not qualify as an attack for the purposes of Article 8(2)(e)(iv).[115] This matter clearly is a case of pillage and should have been charged under Article 8(2)(e)(v) under the terms "pillaging a town or place even when taken by assault."

The Prosecutor appealed the decision on two grounds: first, that the term "attack" has a special meaning in relation to protected objects and, second, that "attack" under Article 8(2)(e)(iv) "is not limited to the conduct of hostilities."[116] If the Appeals Chamber were to uphold the argument, there would be significant negative consequences for IHL and ICL as the Prosecutor was arguing for a broadening of the meaning of "attack" under ICL. "Attack" would mean different things under different war crime provisions, and "attack" would have different meanings under IHL and ICL. This outcome would produce a position diametrically opposed to the proper relationship between IHL and war crimes by which each war crime is a criminalization of a rule of IHL. The Prosecutor's appeal was perceived as being "likely remembered as the focus for a confused and chaotic debate on the meaning of 'attack' within IHL and ICL."[117]

Following the Prosecutor's appeal, the Appeals Chamber invited amici curiae to respond on the merits of the legal questions. A variety of different interpretations and conclusions were offered. More surprising was the way in which the judges of the Appeals Chamber (mis)understood the meaning of "attack."[118] While the Appeals Chamber ultimately dismissed the Prosecutor's appeal to broaden the scope of "attack,"[119] a confusing range of opinions and definitions were generated.

111. *Id.*

112. *Id.*, ¶ 1140.

113. *Id.*, ¶ 1141.

114. *Id.*

115. *Id.*, ¶ 1142.

116. *Ntaganda*, Appeals Chamber Judgment, *supra* note 9, ¶ 1145.

117. Pearce Clancy, *Ntaganda and the "Conduct of Hostilities Crimes,"* EJIL: TALK! (Aug. 20, 2021), https://www.ejiltalk.org/ntaganda-and-the-conduct-of-hostilities-crimes/.

118. *Ntaganda*, Appeals Chamber Judgment, *supra* note 9, ¶¶ 1163–68. *See also* Abhimanyu George Jain, *The Ntaganda Appeal Judgment and the Meaning of "Attack" in Conduct of Hostilities War Crimes*, EJIL: TALK! (Apr. 2, 2021), https://www.ejiltalk.org/the-ntaganda-appeal-judgment-and-the-meaning-of-attack-in-conduct-of-hostilities-war-crimes/; Clancy, *supra* note 117.

119. *Ntaganda*, Appeals Chamber Judgment, *supra* note 9, ¶ 1169.

The issue should have been straightforward. As war crimes are serious violations of IHL, any plausible interpretation of the meaning of "attack" in Article 8(2)(e)(iv) of the Rome Statute should begin with the definition of attack codified in Article 49(1) of Additional Protocol I.[120]

The chapeau of Article 8(2)(e) reads: "Other serious violations of the *laws and customs applicable in armed conflicts not of an international character, within the established framework of international law* . . ."[121] The established legal framework is IHL and, therefore, to be able to determine the meaning of "attack" in Article 8(2)(e)(iv), the interpreter necessarily has to rely on IHL. IHL, indeed, offers a definition of the term "attack" in Article 49(1) of Additional Protocol I. Article 49(1) defines "attacks" to mean "acts of violence against the adversary, whether in offence or in defence."[122] This definition applies to international and to non-international armed conflicts alike.[123]

If Article 21(1) of the Rome Statute is consulted as the point of departure, the result would be the same. Article 21(1) provides that "[t]he Court shall apply: (a) In the first place, this Statute, Elements of Crimes and its Rules of Procedure and Evidence; (b) In the second place, where appropriate, applicable treaties and the principles and rules of international law, including the established principles of the international law of armed conflict." The Elements of Crimes do not offer a definition of "attack."[124] As such, the interpreter must turn to Article 21(1)(b) and the applicable rules of international law, specifically, the international law of armed conflict. This leads back to Article 49(1) of Additional Protocol I.

As already indicated, Additional Protocol I defines the term "attacks" as "acts of violence against the adversary, whether in offense or defence."[125] Using the rules of treaty interpretation codified in the Vienna Convention on the Law of Treaties,[126] the ordinary meaning of "adversary" in the context of the object and purpose of Additional Protocol I is "enemy."[127] The ordinary meaning of "offense" is "the act of attacking" or "assault"[128] which, read in context, refers

120. Protocol Additional to the Geneva Conventions of 12 August 1949, and Relating to the Protection of Victims of International Armed Conflicts, June 8, 1977, 1125 U.N.T.S. 3 [hereinafter Additional Protocol I].

121. Emphasis added.

122. Art. 49(1) of Additional Protocol I, *supra* note 120.

123. International Committee of the Red Cross, Commentary on the Additional Protocols 1452 (1987).

124. International Criminal Court, Elements of Crimes art. 8(2)(e)(iv) (2011).

125. Art. 49(1) of Additional Protocol I, *supra* note 120.

126. VCLT, *supra* note 77.

127. Merriam-Webster's Dictionary and Thesaurus 14 (2020).

128. *Id.* 575.

to a military assault on the enemy. The term "defence" is defined as "the act of defending: resistance against 'attack,'"[129] which in context refers to a counter-attack. The inclusion of counterattacks is a broadening of the understanding in military manuals that attacks are offensive and are aimed at "destroying enemy forces and gaining ground."[130] The 1987 ICRC Commentary to Additional Protocol I reveals that the term "attack" and counterattack mean "combat action."[131] Under IHL, "pillaging and looting" is a construct separate from "attack."[132]

The judges of the Appeals Chamber did not follow this logic or draw the same conclusion.[133] In her separate opinion, Judge Bossa disagreed with the Trial Chamber's narrow construction of the term "attack" on the ground that it erroneously divorced the *ratissage* operations from the "attack."[134] In her view, the *ratissage* operations "were part and parcel" of the attack.[135] Judge Carronza similarly reasoned that "attack" is to be interpreted broadly to include the preparation and the carrying out of combat actions, as well as actions taken in the immediate aftermath of the combat action, including the *ratissage* operation.[136] Both Judges Bossa and Carronza blurred the distinction between IHL and ICL and employed an ICL lens to broaden the meaning of "attack." The closest to an IHL-aligned interpretation is the reasoning of Judges Morrison and Hofmánski in their separate opinion on the Prosecutor's appeal.[137] Judges Morrison and Hofmánski consider the definition of "attacks" in Article 8(2)(e)(iv) as being ambiguous,[138] an interpretation with which this author disagrees, but

129. *Id.* 207.

130. *See* ¶¶ 1879–80 of the 1987 Commentaries to Protocol Additional to the Geneva Conventions of August 12, 1949, and relating to the Protection of Victims of International Armed Conflicts (Protocol I), June 8, 1977, ICRC, https://ihl-databases.icrc.org/en/ihl-treaties/api-1977/article-49/commentary/1987?activeTab=undefined.

131. *Id.*

132. Prosecutor v. Ntaganda, Case No. ICC ICC-01/04-02/06 A2, Observations by Professor Roger O'Keefe, pursuant to rule 103 of the Rules of Procedure and Evidence, on the merits of the legal questions presented in "Order inviting expressions of interest as amici curiae in judicial proceedings (pursuant to rule 103 of the Rules of Procedure and Evidence)" of July 24, 2020 (ICC-01/04-02/06-2554), ¶ 2 (Sept. 17, 2020) [hereinafter O'Keefe Amicus Curia Brief].

133. *Ntaganda*, Appeals Chamber Judgment, *supra* note 9, ¶¶ 1163–68.

134. Annex 4, Separate Opinion of Judge Solomy Balungi Bossa on the Prosecutor's Appeal, *Ntaganda*, Appeals Chamber Judgment, *supra* note 9, ¶ 18.

135. *Id.*, ¶ 18.

136. *Ntaganda*, Appeals Chamber Judgment, *supra* note 9, ¶¶ 1167–68.

137. Annex 1, Judgment Separate Opinion of Judge Howard Morrison and Judge Piotr Hofmánski on the Prosecutor's Appeal, *Ntaganda*, Appeals Chamber Judgment, *supra* note 9.

138. *Id.*, ¶ 46.

they arrive at the conclusion that the notion of "attack" should be interpreted narrowly as defined in Article 49(1) of Additional Protocol I.[139]

The views of the amici curiae were similarly split. Some of the amicus curiae observations did not consider Article 49 of Additional Protocol I[140] and thus failed to observe the delicate relationship between IHL and ICL and the rules of interpretation in Article 21 of the Rome Statue. By contrast, Professor Roger O'Keefe provided clear guidance as to the interpretation of the meaning of "attack" by referring to Article 49(1) of Additional Protocol I.[141] Similarly, Geoffrey S. Corn et al. carefully explained key concepts of IHL and also referred to Article 49(1) of Additional Protocol I.[142] These amici curiae have supplied much needed clarification.[143]

The Appeals Chamber judgment, dissenting opinion, separate opinions, and amicus curiae briefs qualify as subsidiary means of determining rules of international law. These varying and, in some instances, incorrect opinions are now included in the literature and provide a fractured and confusing kaleidoscope of interpretations of the term "attack"—a term that is fundamental to IHL. The practical consequences of a broadened interpretation of the term "attack" for members of the armed forces serve as a cautionary tale, as the following quotation illustrates:

> [H]ow does one explain to that same average soldier that international conduct which up to today has been practiced by militaries worldwide and been considered lawful and indispensable conduct in armed conflict—such as breaching of walls, fortification, and clearing fields of fire—is now deemed unlawful? How does one explain that the same conduct would now constitute

139. *Id.*, ¶ 43.

140. *See, e.g.*, Prosecutor v. Ntaganda, Case No. ICC-01/04-02/06 A2, Amicus Curiae Observations Pursuant to Rule 103 of the Rules of Procedure and Evidence on the Merits of the Legal Questions Presented in the Appeal of the Prosecutor against the Judgment of Trial Chamber VI of July 8, 2019 (ICC-01/04- 02/06-2359), by Prof. Dra Yolanda Gamarra (Sept. 17, 2020); Prosecutor v. Ntaganda, Case No. ICC ICC-01/04-02/06, Amicus Curiae Observations Pursuant to Rule 103 of the Rules of Procedure and Evidence on Behalf of Professor Christof Heyns, Professor Stuart Casey-Maslen, Dr. Thomas Probert, & Mr. Fikire Tinsae Birhane (Centre for Human Rights, University of Pretoria) (Oct. 6, 2020); Prosecutor v. Ntaganda, Case No. ICC-01/04-02/06, Amicus Curiae Submission Pursuant to Rule 103 of the Rules of Procedure and Evidence, by Mr. Pearce Clancy & Dr. Michael Kearney, Al-Haq (Sept. 18, 2020).

141. O'Keefe Amicus Curia Brief, *supra* note 132.

142. Prosecutor v. Ntaganda, Case No. ICC-01/04-02/06 A2, Submission of Observations to the Appeals Chamber Pursuant to Rule 103 (Sept. 18, 2020).

143. *See also* valuable contribution made by Professor Newton in Prosecutor v. Ntaganda, Case No. ICC-01/04-02/06 A2, Observations of Professor Michael A. Newton on the merits of the legal questions presented by the Appeals Chamber in the Case of The Prosecutor v. Bosco Ntaganda, Observations by Professor Geoffrey S. Corn et al. Ntaganda Submission of Observations to the Appeals Chamber Pursuant to Rule 103 (Sept. 17, 2020).

a violation of distinction rules—and even a crime—because the term "attack" must now have a meaning divorced from that traditionally accepted?[144]

V. CONCLUSION: REVISITING THE RELATIONSHIP BETWEEN INTERNATIONAL HUMANITARIAN LAW AND INTERNATIONAL CRIMINAL LAW

IHL and ICL are separate but related fields of public international law. The close relationship between the two bodies can be seen in the arena of war crimes—a war crime being essentially a serious violation of IHL that triggers individual criminal responsibility under ICL.[145] In *Tadić*, the Appeals Chamber of the ICTY set out the elements of a war crime as follows:[146] First, the violation must constitute an infraction of a rule of IHL; second, a rule of IHL must derive from either customary IHL or an IHL treaty; third, the violation must be of a serious nature breaching a rule that serves to protect important values and a breach that inflicts grave consequences on the victim; and, lastly, the violation must entail individual criminal responsibility.[147]

García Pinto suggests navigating the complicated relationship between IHL and ICL, from an IHL perspective, as follows:

> A good starting point for examining this relationship could be considering ICL as an IHL enforcement mechanism, though this is quite constraining from an ICL perspective. A second level would be that of development—i.e., ICL treaties as a means of IHL codification, and thus an IHL source. And finally, ICL may offer clarification by law-making or application as many judges provide helpful interpretation of substantive IHL norms or even concepts.[148]

From the ICL perspective, IHL serves as a point of reference for the understanding and interpretation of the corresponding war crime provision.[149] However, an ICL-centric lens, by which IHL is considered merely a source of ICL, carries a risk. An illustration of this danger was presented in sections III and IV of this chapter, which discussed the erroneous interpretation in the *Ntaganda* decision

144. Pomson, *supra* note 102.

145. *Id.*, at 267.

146. *Tadić*, Decision on the Defence Motion for Interlocutory Appeal on Jurisdiction, *supra* note 2, ¶ 94.

147. *Id.*

148. Pinto, *supra* note 89, at 749.

149. Cryer et al., *supra* note 98, at 15.

of own-forces violations and of "attack." The *Ntaganda* case serves as an example where the separation of IHL from ICL, or even the slightest disregard for the delicate relationship between IHL and ICL, generates conflicting, confusing, and even erroneous judicial decisions that stimulate even greater contradictions in the scholarly interpretation of these decisions. The consequences for the regulation of military operations in real time are even greater. To safeguard against contradictory interpretations in ICL and IHL, it is important that the judiciary is cognizant, as Sassóli reminds us, of the fact that IHL is not "an auxiliary science" of ICL (as is sometimes considered to be the case from an ICL point of view).[150] Rather, IHL relates to ICL in that ICL either enforces IHL or ICL clarifies rules or concepts in IHL.[151]

The ICTY and ICTR contributed significantly to the development of IHL through the interpretation of IHL concepts when their decisions demonstrated an understanding of the interplay between IHL and ICL. These contributions include identification of customary international law rules that form part of the law of non-international armed conflict;[152] establishing that serious violations of IHL constitute war crimes in NIAC;[153] and, as discussed in section II, clarifying key notions such as "non-international armed conflict" and "rape." These examples illustrate a process of judicial interpretation and not rulemaking in pursuit of activism. To keep this "arranged marriage"[154] happy and prevent it from turning into a "two-headed snake"[155] in the interpretation of war crimes law, the international criminal tribunals must demonstrate a cognizance of the underpinning principle that all war crimes vest in IHL; their task is to interpret the rules of IHL and not to create new law under ICL.

This chapter has critically reflected on how, as subsidiary sources of international law, the judicial decisions of international criminal tribunals have contributed to the development of IHL as well as the consequences of these judicial decisions. In drawing attention to these consequences, the intention is to prompt international criminal tribunals to keep in mind the purpose of IHL and that judicial decision-making aims not to make law or to fill a gap but to interpret and to clarify. War-crimes law is embedded in IHL, and to overlook this principle is to overthrow the relationship between IHL and ICL. The positive contribution made by international criminal tribunals is welcomed, but in their actions they need to be mindful of the impact caused by their rulings extending to the practical operation of IHL. The goal is more of *Tadić* and *Akayesu*, but fewer of *Ntaganda*-like rulings and less of the confusion to which they contribute.

150. SASSÒLI, *supra* note 12, at 444, ¶ 9.57.

151. *Id.*

152. Droege & Giorgou, *supra* note 8, at 1813.

153. *Id.*

154. Pinto, *supra* note 89, at 746.

155. *Id.*, at 761.

10

The Role of Human Rights Mechanisms in Shaping International Humanitarian Law

ALESSANDRA SPADARO*

I. INTRODUCTION

Permanent and temporary judicial and nonjudicial human rights mechanisms that are broadly tasked with protecting and promoting human rights exist at both the regional and the international level. Because of the weaknesses of mechanisms specifically dedicated to the enforcement of international humanitarian law, both regional and international human rights bodies have had to examine situations of armed conflict and consider international humanitarian law (IHL) in their work.[1]

The way in which various human rights mechanisms have dealt with armed conflicts and approached IHL varies greatly from one mechanism to another. International human rights law (IHRL) has had a significant influence on the law of armed conflict, prompting what Theodor Meron has deemed its "humanization."[2] While this process has been spearheaded by several actors, human rights

* Alessandra Spadaro is Assistant Professor of Public International Law at Utrecht University, where she is also a member of the Montaigne Centre for Rule of Law and Administration of Justice.

1. Christine Byron, *A Blurring of the Boundaries: The Application of International Humanitarian Law by Human Rights Bodies*, 47 VIRGINIA JOURNAL OF INTERNATIONAL LAW 839, 847 (2007); THEODOR MERON, THE HUMANIZATION OF INTERNATIONAL LAW 51 (2006).

2. MERON, *supra* note 1, at 1.

Alessandra Spadaro, *The Role of Human Rights Mechanisms in Shaping International Humanitarian Law* In: *Making and Shaping the Law of Armed Conflict*. Edited by: Sandesh Sivakumaran and Christian R. Burne, Oxford University Press.
 DOI: 10.1093/oso/9780197775134.003.0010

bodies have also directly contributed to giving IHL an "even more pro-human rights orientation."[3]

However, when assessing whether and in which ways human rights mechanisms have affected the development of IHL, scholars have often concluded that their role in doing so has not been substantial. In the words of Gerd Oberleitner, "human rights bodies have not made significant contributions to IHL. This is also because they for the most part only deal with IHL incidentally and have been wary to apply IHL."[4] Other authors argue that the approach of different human rights bodies to IHL in some circumstances has remained "unclear or even contradictory," but they note a general move "towards a stronger convergence of IHL and IHRL" in the approach of UN and regional human rights bodies.[5]

In contrast, this chapter argues that human rights mechanisms have played a role in shaping IHL. The different meanings of the term "shaping" used in this chapter are explained in section II. That section then goes on to explain, in relation to a few specific examples, in which ways we can say that human rights mechanisms have already shaped IHL. Section III, focusing on the role of the Human Rights Council in shaping the obligations of armed groups parties to non-international armed conflicts (NIAC), then turns to new developments that have the potential to shape IHL in the future.

II. SHAPING INTERNATIONAL HUMANITARIAN LAW

A. Shaping as a Process and as Its Outcome

IHL enforcement is characterized by the absence—or silence—of IHL-specific mechanisms. Even though the Geneva Conventions and their First Additional Protocol do foresee the existence of an enquiry procedure[6] and of an

3. *Id.* at 8.

4. Gerd Oberleitner, *The Development of IHL by Human Rights Bodies*, *in* INTERNATIONAL HUMANITARIAN LAW AND NON-STATE ACTORS 297, 314 (Ezequiel Heffes, Marcos D. Kotlik, & Manuel J. Ventura eds., 2020).

5. Walter Kälin & Jörg Künzli, *Human Rights Bodies: A Comparative Approach*, *in* RESEARCH HANDBOOK ON HUMAN RIGHTS AND HUMANITARIAN LAW: FURTHER REFLECTIONS AND PERSPECTIVES 188, 208 (Robert Kolb, Gloria Gaggioli, & Pavle Kilibarda eds., 2022).

6. Convention (I) for the Amelioration of the Condition of the Wounded and Sick in the Armed Forces in the Field art. 52, Aug. 12, 1949, 6 U.S.T. 3114, 75 U.N.T.S. 31; Convention (II) for the Amelioration of the Condition of the Wounded, Sick, and Shipwrecked Members of Armed Forces at Sea art. 53, Aug. 12, 1949, 6 U.S.T. 3217, 75 U.N.T.S. 85; Convention (III) Relative to the Treatment of Prisoners of War art. 132, Aug. 12, 1949, 6 U.S.T. 3316, 75 U.N.T.S. 135; Convention (IV) Relative to the Protection of Civilian Persons in Time of War art. 149, Aug. 12, 1949, 6 U.S.T. 3516, 75 U.N.T.S. 287.

International Humanitarian Fact-Finding Commission (IHFFC),[7] respectively, these mechanisms have never been used. The IHFFC has offered its services to the parties of various armed conflicts, including, recently, to Yemen,[8] Russia and Ukraine,[9] Ethiopia, Azerbaijan, and Armenia,[10] but was never invited to conduct any enquiries into these or other conflicts, remaining to this day a "sleeping beauty."[11] Instead, allegations of violations of IHL have been assessed in the context of international dispute settlement,[12] in international criminal trials,[13] and by human rights mechanisms. The latter's part in enforcing IHL has sparked some discontent. As discussed later in more detail in section II.C, States and scholars on occasion have argued that IHL fell beyond the mandate of certain human rights mechanisms. Various actors have also criticized the alleged political nature of some human rights bodies, particularly the Human Rights Council and its mechanisms. In its report marking the twenty-fifth anniversary of its establishment, the IHFFC bitterly noted that "States Parties and international organizations have established numerous ad hoc commissions of inquiry regarding violations of international humanitarian law, which often blur the lines between international humanitarian law and international human rights law, instead of mandating the Commission, which is the only permanent intergovernmental supervisory body on international humanitarian law."[14] This reaction, which is a fair portrayal of the way in which human rights mechanisms tend to approach IHL and IHRL, is hardly surprising. As explained by Martti Koskenniemi, institutional proliferation and substantive fragmentation result in the pitting of different legal regimes against one another, given that each regime "points to a different

7. Protocol Additional to the Geneva Conventions of 12 August 1949, and Relating to the Protection of Victims of International Armed Conflicts art. 90, June 8, 1977, 1125 U.N.T.S. 3 [hereinafter API].

8. Presidential Report on Activities of the Commission 2021, at 4 (2022), https://www.ihffc.org/Images/am-2022-05-en-presidential-report-2.pdf.

9. IHFFC has proposed its services (Mar. 10, 2022), https://www.ihffc.org/index.asp?Language=EN&page=news.

10. Presidential Report on Activities of the Commission 2020, at 3 (2021), https://www.ihffc.org/Images/presidential-report-2020-en.pdf.

11. Frits Kalshoven, *The International Humanitarian Fact-Finding Commission: A Sleeping Beauty?*, *in* Reflections on the Law of War 835 (2007).

12. *E.g.*, Armed Activities on the Territory of the Congo (Democratic Republic of the Congo v. Uganda), Judgment, 2005 I.C.J. Rep. 168; Partial Award—Civilian Claims: Ethiopia's Claim 5 (2004).

13. The role of international criminal tribunals and courts in shaping IHL is addressed in a different chapter in this volume and as such will not be analyzed here.

14. The IHFFC at 25: Reflecting on Our History and Moving Forward, 3 (2016), https://www.ihffc.org/Files/en/pdf/ihffc-presidential-report-2015-en.pdf.

authority that will decide [the issue], with preferences and practices deviating from those of competing bodies."[15]

The various non-IHL entities and enforcement mechanisms that have made pronouncements on IHL have not all affected IHL in the same way. For instance, the International Criminal Tribunal for the former Yugoslavia (ICTY) is considered to have had a tremendous impact on IHL. Today, we refer to the case law of the ICTY for the criteria concerning the existence of a non-international armed conflict and for an armed group to be considered a party to such type of conflict,[16] as well as the requirements for the existence of an international armed conflict by proxy.[17] ICTY case law has also importantly prompted the convergence of the customary IHL rules that regulate international and non-international armed conflicts.[18]

In order to assess the role of human rights mechanisms in shaping IHL, in this chapter, I take shaping to indicate two interrelated aspects: first, the process of shaping, and second, its outcome on the law in substantive terms.

First, shaping can refer to a process of causing changes over time, including in terms of sensitivity and discourse, by putting issues on the table and on the agenda for States to react to them. In this sense, the Teheran Conference of 1968 was a pivotal moment for shaping IHL and the relationship between IHL and IHRL,[19] even though no hard law was created. From a critical international law scholarship perspective, legal interpretation consists in the exercise of power.[20] Not all interpretations are successful; only those that are recognized as expressions of trustworthy expertise by institutions that have authority enjoy success.[21] In this vein, Ingo Venzke theorized the concept of "semantic authority" as referring to "an actor's capacity to find acceptance for its interpretive claims or to establish its

15. Martti Koskenniemi, *International Law and Hegemony: A Reconfiguration*, 17 Cambridge Review of International Affairs 197, 205–06 (2004).

16. Prosecutor v. Tadić, Case No. IT-94-1-AR72, Decision on Defence Motion for Interlocutory Appeal on Jurisdiction, 70 (Oct. 2, 1995); Prosecutor v. Haradinaj et al., Case No. IT-04-84-T, Judgment, 60 (Apr. 3, 2008); Prosecutor v. Boškoski and Tarčulovski, Case No. IT-04-82-T, Judgment, 195 (July 10, 2008). *See* the chapter by Martha Bradley in this volume.

17. Prosecutor v. Tadić, Case No. IT-94-1-A, Appeals Chamber Judgment, 62 (July 15, 1999); Application of the Convention on the Prevention and Punishment of the Crime of Genocide (Bosnia and Herzegovina v. Serbia and Montenegro), Judgment, 2007 I.C.J. Rep. 43, ¶¶ 404–06.

18. Prosecutor v. Dusko Tadić, Decision on the Defence Motion on Jurisdiction, *supra* note 16, 98, 126; *see generally* 1 Customary International Humanitarian Law (Jean-Marie Henckaerts & Louise Doswald-Beck eds., 2005).

19. Meron, *supra* note 1, at 9.

20. *See, e.g.*, Koskenniemi, *supra* note 15, at 199; Ingo Venzke, *Legal Contestation about "Enemy Combatants." On the Exercise of Power in Legal Interpretation*, 5 Journal of International Law and International Relations 155, 162 (2009).

21. Michael Zürn, Martin Binder, & Matthias Ecker-Ehrhardt, *International Authority and Its Politicization*, 4 International Theory 69, 85–86 (2012).

own statements about the law as content-laden reference points for legal discourse that others can hardly escape."[22] According to Sandesh Sivakumaran:

> The precise lawmaking and law-shaping role of state-empowered entities varies and includes, inter alia, creating, developing, interpreting, applying, and proposing changes to the law. State-empowered entities shape hard law, through actions like the development and interpretation of treaties or the identification of custom, and also shape soft law, through actions like the creation of principles or guidelines.[23]

A variety of factors can be said to affect whether State-empowered entities,[24] such as human rights mechanisms, play a role in shaping international law. Sivakumaran mentions among them the authority of the entity that issued the output, the features of the output, and the reactions of the international community, primarily States and other interested actors.[25]

Second, and relatedly, in terms of substance, shaping can also be taken to indicate the effects of the process on the law, and particularly how the latter is interpreted and applied.[26] Indeed, as I elaborate on later, different entities and actors have varying preferences that guide the way in which they interpret the scope of application of IHL and of specific rules, the relationship of IHL with other branches of international law (including IHRL and international criminal law), and therefore the role that IHL occupies in the regulation of specific cases and phenomena in armed conflict.

In light of this dual understanding of shaping, the role of human rights mechanisms in the shaping of IHL will be examined.

B. Human Rights Mechanisms Shaping IHL

Human rights mechanisms have repeatedly affirmed the applicability of IHRL in armed conflict. For example, the Human Rights Committee, which monitors the implementation of the International Covenant on Civil and Political

22. Ingo Venzke, *Semantic Authority*, *in* CONCEPTS FOR INTERNATIONAL LAW: CONTRIBUTIONS TO DISCIPLINARY THOUGHT 815, 815 (Jean d'Aspremont & Sahib Singh eds., 2019).

23. Sandesh Sivakumaran, *Beyond States and Non-State Actors: The Role of State-Empowered Entities in the Making and Shaping of International Law*, 55 COLUMBIA JOURNAL OF TRANSNATIONAL LAW 343, 358 (2017).

24. *Id.* at 352 defines state-empowered entity as "an entity that States have empowered to carry out particular functions."

25. *Id.* at 366.

26. Generally on how the interpretation of international law differs depending on who interprets it, *see* Michael Waibel, *Interpretive Communities in International Law*, *in* INTERPRETATION IN INTERNATIONAL LAW 147 (Andrea Bianchi, Daniel Peat, & Matthew Windsor eds., 2015).

Rights (ICCPR), has affirmed that the ICCPR continues to apply in situations of armed conflict, and that the ICCPR and IHL are "complementary, not mutually exclusive."[27] Several other human rights mechanisms have affirmed the continued applicability of IHRL in armed conflict,[28] including in occupied territory.[29] While the exact contours of the relationship between IHL and IHRL in armed conflict, including the requirements for the extraterritorial applicability of IHRL, are subject to scholarly debates and inconsistent approaches by human rights mechanisms,[30] interested actors nowadays widely accept that IHRL does apply alongside IHL in armed conflict.[31] Among others, the International Court of Justice confirmed the applicability of IHRL in armed conflict in different circumstances,[32] including by making specific reference to the findings of human rights mechanisms in this respect.[33] States almost universally acknowledge the applicability of IHRL in armed conflict,[34] with rare

27. U.N. Human Rights Comm., *General Comment No. 31: The Nature of the General Legal Obligation Imposed on States Parties to the Covenant*, ¶ 11, U.N. Doc. CCPR/C/21/Rev.1/Add. 13 (May 26, 2004); U.N. Human Rights Comm., *General Comment No. 36. Article 6: Right to Life*, ¶ 64, U.N. Doc. CCPR/C/GC/36 (Sept. 3, 2019).

28. *E.g.*, Committee Against Torture, *Convention against torture and other cruel, inhuman or degrading treatment or punishment, General Comment No. 2: Implementation of article 2 by States parties*, ¶ 5, U.N. Doc. CAT/C/GC/2 (Jan. 24, 2008); Hassan v. United Kingdom, App. No. 29750/09, ¶ 104 (2014) (ECtHR), https://hudoc.echr.coe.int/fre?i=001-146501; Coard et al. v. United States, Case 10.951, Inter-Amer. Comm'n H.R., Report No. 109/99, ¶¶ 38–44 (1999); Committee on the Elimination of Discrimination against Women, *General recommendation no. 30 on women in conflict prevention, conflict and post-conflict situations*, ¶¶ 4, 19–20, U.N. Doc. CEDAW/C/GC/30 (Nov. 1, 2013).

29. U.N. Human Rights Committee, *Concluding observations, Israel*, ¶ 11, U.N. Doc. CCPR/CO/78/ISR (Aug. 21, 2003); U.N. Committee on Economic, Social and Cultural Rights, *Concluding observations, Israel*, ¶¶ 15, 31, U.N. Doc. E/C.12/1/Add.90 (June 26, 2003).

30. *See, e.g.*, Noam Lubell, *Challenges in Applying Human Rights Law to Armed Conflict*, 87 International Review of the Red Cross 737 (2005); Katharine Fortin, *The Relationship between International Human Rights Law and International Humanitarian Law: Taking Stock at the End of 2022?*, 40 Netherlands Quarterly of Human Rights 343 (2022).

31. *See* Christopher Greenwood, *Scope of Application of Humanitarian Law*, *in* The Handbook of Humanitarian Law in Armed Conflict 74 (D. Fleck ed., 2d ed. 2007).

32. Legality of the Threat or Use of Nuclear Weapons, Advisory Opinion, 1996 I.C.J. Rep. 226, ¶ 25; Legal Consequences of the Construction of a Wall in the Occupied Palestinian Territory, Advisory Opinion, 2004 I.C.J. Rep. 136, ¶¶ 105–06; Armed Activities on the Territory of the Congo, *supra* note 12, at 178–80.

33. Legal Consequences of the Construction of a Wall in the Occupied Palestinian Territory, *supra* note 32, at 109–12.

34. *See, e.g.*, Sarah Cleveland, *The United States and the Torture Convention, Part II: Armed Conflict*, Just Security (Nov. 19, 2014), https://www.justsecurity.org/17581/united-states-torture-convention-armed-conflict/ (explaining the changed U.S. position on the applicability of the Convention Against Torture in armed conflict and its relationship with IHL).

exceptions.[35]

The applicability of IHRL in armed conflict opens the possibility for human rights mechanisms mandated with monitoring the implementation of a specific human rights treaty, such as the Human Rights Committee and the European Court of Human Rights (ECtHR), to hear complaints stemming from situations of armed conflicts in which the relevant treaty applies. Even though their mandate concerns the application of and compliance with a specific human rights treaty, these mechanisms have often acknowledged the applicability and relevance of IHL and, consequently, have taken IHL into account in their output and for the interpretation of their respective treaties.

In view of their co-application, IHL and IHRL end up having a mutual influence on, or mutually shape, one another. The issue of internment in armed conflict provides a good illustration of this. IHL treaties do not contain a provision explicitly prohibiting arbitrary deprivation of liberty—although such a prohibition arguably exists as a matter of customary IHL in both international and non-international armed conflicts.[36] On the other hand, under IHRL, not only is arbitrary detention prohibited, but internment is hardly tolerated as it is considered to present a high risk of arbitrariness.[37] The Human Rights Committee considers that in situations of armed conflict the prohibition of arbitrary detention enshrined in Article 9 ICCPR remains applicable. However, it maintains that, in IAC, internment "authorized and regulated by and complying with international humanitarian law in principle is not arbitrary."[38] Similarly, the ECtHR held that, whereas the European Convention on Human Rights (ECHR) does not cease to apply in armed conflict, its Article 5 should be interpreted to accommodate the internment of civilians who pose a security threat and of prisoners of war in IAC.[39] These findings have important practical repercussions on the application of IHL in specific cases. In fact, States parties to the ICCPR and the ECHR can intern individuals in IAC on the basis of the rules contained in the Third and Fourth Geneva Conventions. Nevertheless, they will also have to consider the IHRL framework in which they act, as a violation of the relevant IHL rules

35. *See, e.g.*, the Israeli state's position reported in U.N. Human Rights Committee, *Concluding observations*, *supra* note 29, ¶ 11.

36. Henckaerts & Doswald-Beck, *supra* note 18, Rule 99.

37. U.N. Human Rights Comm., *General Comment No. 35: Article 9 (Liberty and Security of Person)*, ¶15, U.N. Doc. CCPR/C/GC/35 (Dec. 16, 2014).

38. *Id.*, ¶ 64.

39. Hassan v. United Kingdom, *supra* note 28, ¶¶ 100–05; *but see* Marko Milanovic, *Norm Conflicts, International Humanitarian Law, and Human Rights Law*, *in* International Humanitarian Law and International Human Rights Law 95, 475 (Orna Ben-Naftali ed., 2011) (warning that interpreting Article 5 ECHR as if it included an arbitrariness standard akin to Article 9 ICCPR so as to avoid a conflict with IHL would amount to "judicial vandalism" of the treaty).

would also entail a violation of the IHRL guarantees against arbitrary detention and open to the scrutiny of their operations by human rights bodies.

Further examples show how the concurrent application of IHL and IHRL in armed conflict in turn affects the way in which IHL is interpreted and applied, thus shaping it. For one, IHRL notably reinforces the obligations of the detaining power concerning the treatment of individuals captured and detained in the context of an armed conflict, for instance, in relation to the respect for the religious practices of detainees.[40] Another is the applicability of the International Covenant on Economic, Social and Cultural Rights (ICESCR) in situations of occupation, which has been reiterated on various occasions by the Committee which monitors the interpretation of this treaty.[41] The applicability of the ICESCR is considered to affect the scope of the obligations of the occupying power towards the population of the occupied territory, including in relation to matters such as education, work, and the occupier's legislative powers.[42] States have been variously receptive of these interpretations. For example, the Danish Military Manual interprets Article 64 of the Fourth Geneva Convention as allowing the occupying power "to pass legislation to bring the laws applicable in the occupied territory in line" with the occupier's human rights obligations.[43]

C. Criticism and Limitations

When human rights mechanisms dealing with cases arising out of armed conflicts have applied IHRL alone instead of applying it alongside IHL, this approach has not been met with widespread approval. Indeed, scholars criticized the initial reluctance of the ECtHR to apply IHL in cases arises from situations of armed

40. *See, e.g.*, Leila Zerrougui (Chairperson-Rapporteur of the Working Group on Arbitrary Detention), Leandro Despouy (Special Rapporteur on the independence of judges and lawyers), Manfred Nowak (Special Rapporteur on torture and other cruel, inhuman or degrading treatment or punishment), Asma Jahangir (Special Rapporteur on freedom of religion or belief), Paul Hunt (Special Rapporteur on the right of everyone to the enjoyment of the highest attainable standard of physical and mental health), *Situation of detainees at Guantanamo Bay*, ¶¶ 57–59, U.N. Doc. E/CN.4/2006/120 (Feb. 27, 2006).

41. Human Rights Committee, *Concluding observations, Israel*, *supra* note 29; *see also* Committee on Economic, Social and Cultural Rights, *Concluding observations, Israel*, U.N. Doc. E/C.12/ISR/CO/3 (Dec. 16, 2011); Committee on Economic, Social and Cultural Rights, *Concluding observations on the fourth periodic report of Israel*, U.N. Doc. E/C.12/ISR/CO/4 (Nov. 12, 2019).

42. Gilles Giacca, *Economic, Social, and Cultural Rights in Occupied Territories*, *in* THE 1949 GENEVA CONVENTIONS: A COMMENTARY 1485, 1503–08 (Andrew Clapham, Paola Gaeta, & Marco Sassòli eds., 2015).

43. DANISH MINISTRY OF DEFENCE, DEFENCE COMMAND DENMARK, MILITARY MANUAL ON INTERNATIONAL LAW RELEVANT TO DANISH ARMED FORCES IN INTERNATIONAL OPERATIONS 437 (2016).

conflict, such as in *Loizidou v. Turkey*, which concerned occupied Northern Cyprus.[44] Although the direct application by the ECtHR of IHRL standards in lieu of IHL rules on the conduct of hostilities in a few cases arising from the Chechen conflict sparked some scholarly interest,[45] this approach has not successfully influenced the way that the interplay of IHL and IHRL in the conduct of hostilities is usually understood.[46]

At the same time, the engagement of human rights mechanisms with situations of armed conflict and their application of IHL has also attracted criticism. The Human Rights Council has been both one of the most active human rights mechanisms in recent years to deal with situations of armed conflicts and IHL and one of the most criticized. IHL is not specifically mentioned in the UN General Assembly resolution creating the Human Rights Council,[47] nor was IHL explicitly included in the mandate of its predecessor.[48] However, a "process of expanding the reach of bodies dealing with human rights norms to include also norms of international humanitarian law" has been "gradual but inexorable,"[49] and the Human Rights Council and its Special Procedures (e.g., Special Rapporteurs, Independent Experts, Working Groups, etc.) and Independent Investigations (e.g., Commission of Inquiry, Fact-Finding Commissions, Group of Experts, etc.) have been "generally comfortable in expanding their mandates to include IHL."[50]

The Human Rights Council has often been criticized for being politically biased[51] and both the mandate and expertise of the Human Rights Council, and some of

44. *E.g.*, Hans-Joachim Heintze, *The European Court of Human Rights and the Implementation of Human Rights Standards during Armed Conflicts Focus Section: The Non-International Armed Conflict*, 45 German Yearbook of International Law 60, 75–78 (2002).

45. William Abresch, *A Human Rights Law of Internal Armed Conflict: The European Court of Human Rights in Chechnya*, 16 European Journal of International Law 741 (2005).

46. Charles Garraway, *The Law Applies, But Which Law?: A Consumer Guide to the Laws of War*, *in* The American Way of Bombing: Changing Ethical and Legal Norms, from B-17s to Drones 87, 100 (Matthew Evangelista & Henry Shue eds., 2014).

47. G.A. Res. 60/251, Human Rights Council (Apr. 3, 2006).

48. IHL is mentioned only in relation to the Universal Periodic Review in Human Rights Council, *Resolution 5/1. Institution-building of the United Nations Human Rights Council*, U.N. Doc. A/HRC/RES/5/1, Annex, ¶ 2 (June 18, 2007).

49. Philip Alston, Jason Morgan-Foster, & William Abresch, *The Competence of the UN Human Rights Council and Its Special Procedures in Relation to Armed Conflicts: Extrajudicial Executions in the "War on Terror,"* 19 European Journal of International Law 183, 202 (2008); *see also* Meron, *supra* note 1, at 51.

50. Catherine Harwood, The Roles and Functions of Atrocity-related United Nations Commissions of Inquiry in the International Legal Order: Navigating between Principle and Pragmatism 173 (2020).

51. 31st International Conference of the Red Cross and Red Crescent. Strengthening Legal Protection for Victims of Armed Conflicts, Draft Resolution & Report, Document Prepared by the International Committee of the Red Cross, 14 (2011),

its mechanisms (specifically Special Rapporteurs and Independent Investigations) to deal with IHL have been questioned.[52] Daphné Richemond-Barak argued that "[t]he objections of various states to the treatment of IHL by human rights bodies reveal a level of support for the view that human rights bodies lack competence to apply international humanitarian law."[53] However, the only examples that she offered in support of this conclusion concerned States that objected to having their own actions scrutinized by human rights bodies.[54] The United States notoriously claimed that its actions in Guantanamo were regulated by IHL and as such fell beyond the jurisdiction of the Inter-American Court of Human Rights and of the Inter-American Commission on Human Rights, as well as beyond the mandate of the Commission on Human Rights and of the Special Rapporteur on extrajudicial, summary, or arbitrary executions.[55] Yet as recently as March 2022, the United States voted in favor of a Human Rights Council resolution establishing a commission of inquiry to investigate violations of IHL and human rights committed by the Russian Federation in Ukraine.[56] It seems therefore that the United States does not have a problem with exploiting the political bias of the Human Rights Council nor with the Human Rights Council concerning itself with armed conflicts and IHL generally.[57]

Criticism has also related to the lack of necessary expertise of members of human rights mechanisms that find themselves making pronouncements on IHL. Christine Chinkin, who was a member of the high-level fact-finding mission to Beit

https://www.icrc.org/en/doc/assets/files/red-cross-crescent-movement/31st-international-conference/31-int-conference-strengthening-legal-protection-11-5-1-1-en.pdf.

52. Daphné Richemond-Barak, *The Human Rights Council and the Convergence of Humanitarian Law and Human Rights Law*, *in* COUNTERINSURGENCY LAW: NEW DIRECTIONS IN ASYMMETRIC WARFARE 3, 12–19 (William Banks ed., 2013).

53. *Id.* at 14.

54. *Id.* at 13–14.

55. *Id.* at 13–14; Alston, Morgan-Foster, and Abresch, *supra* note 49; *see also* Theodor Meron, *The Humanization of Humanitarian Law*, 94 AMERICAN JOURNAL OF INTERNATIONAL LAW 239, 270 (2000) (recounting that Turkey questioned the authority of the Special Rapporteur on extrajudicial, summary, or arbitrary executions to address its conflict with the Kurdistan Workers' Party claiming human rights mechanisms were not to "encroach upon the field of international humanitarian law").

56. Human Rights Council, *Resolution 49/1. Situation of human rights in Ukraine stemming from the Russian aggression*, U.N. Doc. A/HRC/RES/49/1, ¶ 11(a) (Mar. 7, 2022).

57. A recent development is also worth noting. The United States agreed to have the UN Special Rapporteur on the promotion and protection of human rights and fundamental freedoms while countering terrorism, Fionnuala Ní Aoláin, undertake a technical visit of the detention facility at the U.S. Naval Station Guantánamo Bay in February 2023. At the time of writing, no report or statements about the visit are available. *See UN Counterterrorism Expert to Visit the United States and Guantanamo Detention Facility*, OHCHR (Feb. 1, 2023), https://www.ohchr.org/en/press-releases/2023/02/un-counterterrorism-expert-visit-united-states-and-guantanamo-detention.

Hanoun established by the Human Rights Council in 2006,[58] indicated that mission members "should be unbiased and seen to be so, serve in their personal capacity, and have the requisite competence, expertise and experience," which may include technical or military expertise.[59] This problem should not be overstated. It is true that a solution to this issue would simply be for States to appoint individuals that do have the necessary expertise, and this does happen. For example, Charles Garraway, a renowned expert on IHL, was a member of the Group of Eminent Experts on Yemen. Andrew Clapham, former member of the South Sudan Commission, and Nils Melzer, former Special Rapporteur on torture, both have extensive IHRL and IHL expertise. At the same time, because of the nature of the work they undertake, it is virtually impossible to find, for each mandate, individuals who are experts on all the relevant branches of international law, as well as on investigation, fact-finding, technical, and evidentiary matters, or on the regional or country-specific context. While single individuals will hardly if ever be able to meet all these requirements, they are aided by UN support staff that can supply the necessary expertise in different areas, although this is not always the case.[60]

It is also true that while many Independent Investigations of the Human Rights Council are created on an *ad hoc* basis to investigate certain situations of armed conflict, treaty bodies and human rights courts only exceptionally find themselves dealing with cases concerning armed conflict. Their members therefore do not necessarily have an IHL background, nor do they generally need it. Their perspective as human rights experts will necessarily affect how they approach cases of armed conflict, when such situations do come before them. The premises of IHRL—and thus of the approach of human rights mechanisms to armed conflict situations—fundamentally differ from those of IHL, particularly in relation to the conduct of hostilities. Indeed, from the perspective of IHL, while the commander must avoid and minimize "incidental loss of civilian life, injury to civilians, damage to civilian objects,"[61] harm to civilians and civilian objects are nevertheless considered acceptable in some circumstances. What is more, the standard of lawfulness under IHL is assessed "primarily through the eyes of the attacker, and he or she will be judged not by an absolute standard but based on the information that was reasonably available to him or her at the time."[62] By contrast, IHRL "looks at the situation through the eyes of the victim . . . The onus is on the attacker and

58. Fact-Finding Mission, *Human rights situation in Palestine and other occupied Arab territories, Report of the high-level fact-finding mission to Beit Hanoun established under Council Resolution S-3/1*, U.N. Doc. A/HRC/9/26, ¶ 1 (Sept. 1, 2008).

59. Christine Chinkin, *U.N. Human Rights Fact-Finding Missions: Lessons from Gaza*, *in* LOOKING TO THE FUTURE: ESSAYS ON INTERNATIONAL LAW IN HONOR OF W. MICHAEL REISMAN 475, 489–90 (Mahnoush H. Arsanjani et al. eds., 2011).

60. *See* the chapter by Yousuf Syed Khan in this volume.

61. API, art. 57(2)(a)(ii).

62. Garraway, *supra* note 46, at 101.

the loss of life itself creates a prima facie case."[63] It should nonetheless be noticed that human rights mechanisms have occasionally shown a remarkable understanding of both the requirements of IHL and the realities of armed conflict.[64]

One might also consider that a further limitation of human rights mechanisms dealing with armed conflicts and IHL is that they can only shape the obligations of States. This is because the mandate or jurisdiction of some mechanisms is restricted to State parties to specific human rights treaties. However, the applicability of IHRL to armed groups, albeit still subject to some contestation, is increasingly accepted.[65] Additionally, some human rights mechanisms are not shying away from also considering the obligations of armed groups which are parties to NIACs. This relatively new trend and its potential to shape IHL in relation to armed groups parties to NIACs is the subject of the next section.

III. NEW AVENUES FOR SHAPING IHL? THE HUMAN RIGHTS COUNCIL AND THE OBLIGATIONS OF ARMED GROUPS

The obligations of armed groups parties to NIACs is an area of IHL in need of clarification and in relation to which there is a lack of binding legal pronouncements. While international criminal tribunals and courts have tried and convicted members of armed groups for violations of IHL amounting to war crimes and for massive human rights violations characterized as crimes against humanity or genocide, these pronouncements have concerned the criminal responsibility of individuals, and not the obligations of armed groups as collective entities.

IHL treaty rules applicable in NIAC are few, while customary rules have developed largely by analogy with the law of international armed conflict. With the mushrooming of NIACs and of violations committed by armed groups, the limitations of existing norms regulating the conduct of armed groups and the weakness and paucity of existing mechanisms to hold them accountable have become evident. Nevertheless, the Human Rights Council has held extraordinary sessions and adopted resolutions addressing specific armed groups, such as the Islamic State[66] or Boko Haram.[67] Its Special Rapporteurs and Independent Investigations

63. *Id.*

64. *See supra* text accompanying notes 37–39.

65. For an overview of different positions, *see* Andrew Clapham, *Human Rights Obligations of Non-State Actors: Where Are We Now?*, *in* Doing Peace the Rights Way: Essays in International Law and Relations in Honour of Louise Arbour 11 (Fannie Lafontaine & François Larocque eds., 2019).

66. Human Rights Council, *Resolution S-22/1. The human rights situation in Iraq in the light of abuses committed by the so-called Islamic State in Iraq and the Levant and associated groups*, U.N. Doc. A/HRC/RES/S-22/1 (Sept. 3, 2014).

67. Human Rights Council, *Resolution S-23/1. Atrocities committed by the terrorist group Boko Haram and its effects on human rights in the affected States*, U.N. Doc. A/HRC/RES/S-23/1 (May 21, 2015).

have often considered the actions of armed groups, analyzed them in light of international law, and made recommendations in this respect. Some of the most recent developments in this respect are analyzed in this section, which concludes with an appraisal of these mechanisms' role in shaping the law in relation to the obligations of armed groups.

A. Special Procedures and Armed Groups

Special Procedures have often dealt with armed groups when carrying out their tasks. The mandate of the Special Rapporteur on extrajudicial, summary, or arbitrary executions is exemplary in this respect. The first holder of this post, Amos Wako, occasionally considered extrajudicial executions carried out by paramilitary groups.[68] He was asked to include information on these executions in his reports by the Commission on Human Rights,[69] and on a few occasions received information by the government of the State in which this type of execution was alleged to have occurred or be imminent.[70] However, Amos Wako questioned the Special Rapporteur's, and more broadly the UN system's, ability to address entities with no "standing in international law."[71] Subsequent holders of this mandate nevertheless addressed a range of non-State actors.[72] Philip Alston, in particular, considered that addressing complaints to armed groups and calling on them to respect relevant norms was "both appropriate and feasible where the group exercises significant control over territory and population and has an identifiable political structure."[73] One of Alston's successors, Agnès Callamard, following in

68. *See, e.g.*, S. Amos Wako (Special Rapporteur on Arbitrary Executions), *Summary or arbitrary executions. Report by the Special Rapporteur, Mr. S. Amos Wako, appointed pursuant to resolution 1982/35 of 7 May 1982 of the Economic and Social Council*, U.N. Doc. E/CN.4/1983/16, ¶¶ 111, 186 (Jan. 31, 1983).

69. S. Amos Wako (Special Rapporteur on Arbitrary Executions), *Question of the violation of human rights and fundamental freedoms in any part of the world, with particular reference to colonial and other dependent countries and territories. Summary or arbitrary executions. Report by the Special Rapporteur, Mr. S. Amos Wako, pursuant to Commission on Human Rights resolution 1991/71*, U.N. Doc. E/CN.4/1992/30, ¶ 614 (Jan. 31, 1992).

70. *Id.* at 627.

71. *Id.*

72. Philip Alston (Special Rapporteur on extrajudicial, summary or arbitrary executions), *Report*, U.N. Doc. A/62/265, ¶ 42 (Aug. 16, 2007).

73. Philip Alston (Special Rapporteur on Extrajudicial, Summary or Arbitrary Executions), *Civil and Political Rights, Including the Questions of Disappearances and Summary Executions*, U.N. Doc. E/CN.4/2005/7, ¶ 76 (Dec. 22, 2004).

his footsteps, dedicated an entire report to armed groups and the right to life.[74] In her concluding recommendations, Callamard urged armed groups, among others, to "adopt and implement policies, practices and codes of conduct to protect human rights" and to "draft or contribute to the drafting of commitments."[75] Similar recommendations were included in a joint statement "on human rights responsibilities of armed non-State actors" issued by over forty independent UN human rights experts in February 2021.[76] The experts called on armed groups to "expressly commit and signify their willingness to respect, protect and fulfil human rights," to "implement their human rights responsibilities in their codes of conduct or other internal documents" and to "ensure proper and genuine accountability within their ranks and organizations for abuses of human rights."[77]

The efforts of Special Procedures in relation to shaping the content and scope of the obligations of armed groups in NIAC have included also forms of more direct engagement with the concerned entities. In recent years, Special Procedures have addressed joint communications to armed groups. At times, these communications have concerned allegations of IHL and IHRL violations committed against specific individuals, with a view to setting out the armed group's obligations, obtaining information about their activities, and bringing their activities in line with the law. For instance, in 2018, three Special Procedures transmitted a letter about the detention of a woman and her three children in the Roj camp in North East Syria to the Syrian Democratic Council.[78] In 2019, the Working Groups on Arbitrary Detention and on Enforced Disappearances and the Special Rapporteurs on freedom of opinion and on torture sent a letter to the "De facto authorities of Sana'a, Yemen" concerning the alleged abduction of two Yemeni journalists.[79]

74. Agnès Callamard (Special Rapporteur on extrajudicial, summary or arbitrary executions), *Report on armed non-State actors: the protection of the right to life*, U.N. Doc. A/HRC/38/44 (Dec. 7, 2020).

75. *Id.*, ¶ 99(c) and (d).

76. *Joint Statement by independent United Nations human rights experts on human rights responsibilities of armed non-State actors* (Feb. 25, 2021), https://www.ohchr.org/EN/NewsEvents/Pages/DisplayNews.aspx?NewsID=26797&LangID=E.

77. *Id.*

78. Letter by the Mandates of the Working Group on Arbitrary Detention; the Special Rapporteur on torture and other cruel, inhumane, or degrading treatment or punishment and the Working Group on the issue of discrimination against women in law and in practice, OL OTH 44/2018 (July 27, 2018).

79. Letter by the Mandates of the Working Group on Enforced or Involuntary Disappearances; the Working Group on Arbitrary Detention; the Special Rapporteur on the promotion and protection of the right to freedom of opinion and expression and the Special Rapporteur on torture and other cruel, inhuman or degrading treatment or punishment, AL OTH 55/2019 (Dec. 3, 2019).

In another instance, a group of four Special Procedures sent a communication to the Autonomous Administration of North East Syria (AANES) relating to alleged violations of the right to life, the prohibition of enforced disappearance, and the prohibition of arbitrary detention, asking for information in this regard and reminding AANES of their obligations under IHL and IHRL.[80] This communication lamented "the lack of progress in uncovering the fate and whereabouts of individuals disappeared by ISIL in territories now controlled by AANES, the lack of identification of remains excavated from mass graves and failure to investigate and preserve former ISIL detention sites" and "the alleged failure of local counter-terrorism courts to comply with international due process standards, the alleged failure to consistently question and prosecute former ISIL members in relation to crimes such as enforced disappearance and extra-judicial execution and the application of amnesties or similar measures leading to impunity."[81]

B. Independent Investigations and Armed Groups

Independent Investigations are frequently established in relation to NIACs, where at least one of the parties is an organized armed group. When this is the case, the "mandate is clearly designed so that the international community will hear reports about all actors and not only about the state."[82] Concerned States even complain that not enough attention is paid to violations of IHL and IHRL committed by armed groups.[83] Although we can safely assume that when States allege the underreporting of violations by armed groups and the overreporting of their own violations they do so to deflect attention from themselves, this does not detract from either the importance of holding armed groups accountable for their violations or the continued relevance of violations committed by States.[84]

80. Letter by the Mandates of the Special Rapporteur on extrajudicial, summary or arbitrary executions; the Working Group on Arbitrary Detention; the Working Group on Enforced or Involuntary Disappearances and the Special Rapporteur on the promotion of truth, justice, reparation and guarantees of non-recurrence, AL OTH 28/2022 (May 12, 2022).

81. *Id.* at 4.

82. Andrew Clapham, *Challenging the Myths which Suggest that Human Rights Bodies Cannot Address Armed Non-State Actors in Situations of Armed Conflict: With Special Emphasis on the Case of Agnes Taylor*, *in* The Role of Human Rights Mechanisms in Implementing International Humanitarian Law 11 (Gloria Gaggioli ed., forthcoming), https://dx.doi.org/10.2139/ssrn.3728049.

83. *See* examples *infra* in section III.C.

84. Andrew Clapham, Human Rights Obligations of Non-State Actors 42–43 (2006).

Having human rights mechanisms whose mandate encompasses violations of international law committed by armed groups in armed conflict has great practical relevance. To put this phenomenon into perspective, it is worth recalling that, in 2022, the International Committee of the Red Cross (ICRC) identified 524 "armed groups of humanitarian concern to the organization globally" and estimated that at least 175 million people live in areas fully or partially controlled by armed groups.[85]

In addition to reaching findings concerning violations of IHL and IHRL by armed groups, Independent Investigations have often formulated recommendations addressed to all parties to a NIAC generally or to armed groups specifically. Often, these recommendations have been quite detailed and far-reaching, substantially shaping the obligations of armed groups in NIAC. Both when formulating recommendations that are equally addressed to all parties to the conflict, regardless of whether they are a State or an armed group, and when addressing some recommendations specifically to armed groups, the reports do not distinguish between obligations that stem from IHL and those that stem from IHRL or ICL. Notably, some of the obligations identified are generally believed to only be binding upon States. For example, in addition to States being still considered by some as the only duty-bearers under IHRL, the obligation to make reparation for violations of IHL that have caused injury or loss[86] and the obligation to prosecute war crimes[87] are traditionally considered to pertain only to States. Yet recommendations addressed by various Independent Investigations to all parties to a NIAC, thus including armed groups, have included calls to respect IHL,[88] or both IHL and IHRL,[89]

85. Matthew Bamber-Zryd, *ICRC Engagement with Armed Groups in 2022*, Humanitarian Law & Policy Blog (Jan 12., 2023), https://blogs.icrc.org/law-and-policy/2023/01/12/icrc-engagement-armed-groups-2022/.

86. Henckaerts & Doswald-Beck, *supra* note 18, Rule 150; *see also* Ron Dudai, *Closing the Gap: Symbolic Reparations and Armed Groups*, 93 International Review of the Red Cross 783 (2011).

87. Henckaerts & Doswald-Beck, *supra* note 18, Rule 158.

88. Group of Eminent Experts, *Situation of human rights in Yemen, including violations and abuses since September 2014, Report of the United Nations High Commissioner for Human Rights containing the findings of the Group of Eminent International and Regional Experts and a summary of technical assistance provided by the Office of the High Commissioner to the National Commission of Inquiry*, U.N. Doc. A/HRC/39/43, ¶ 111(b) (Aug. 17, 2018).

89. Independent International Commission of Inquiry on the Syrian Arab Republic, *Report*, U.N. Doc. A/HRC/27/60, ¶ 142(a) (Aug. 13, 2014); Independent International Commission of Inquiry on the Syrian Arab Republic, *Rule of Terror: Living under ISIS in Syria*, U.N. Doc. A/HRC/27/CRP.3, ¶ 74 (Nov. 19, 2014); Independent International Commission of Inquiry on the Syrian Arab Republic, *Report*, U.N. Doc. A/HRC/28/69, ¶ 143(a) (Feb. 5, 2015); Independent International Commission of Inquiry on the Syrian Arab Republic, *Report*, U.N. Doc. A/HRC/34/64, ¶ 106(a) (Feb. 3, 2017).

including by issuing clear and public orders to troops to comply with IHL and IHRL,[90] to conduct investigations to ensure accountability,[91] and to make reparation.[92]

The Group of Experts on Yemen, when calling on the Houthi to comply with their obligations under IHL and IHRL, recommended, among other things, that they pursue "all credible allegations" of violations of IHRL, IHL, and crimes under international law "through prompt, effective and thorough, credible, independent and impartial gender-sensitive investigations, bringing perpetrators to account in line with international human rights norms and standards."[93] Likewise, the Syria Commission recommended that armed groups discipline or dismiss individuals under their command who are found responsible for violations of IHL and IHRL.[94]

The Group of Experts on Yemen also addressed lists of issues to the Houthi/Ansar Allah on four different occasions to further clarify information and verify facts relevant to the Group's mandate. The questions concerned, among other

90. Commission on Human Rights in South Sudan, *Conference Room Paper. Conflict-Related Sexual Violence against Women and Girls in South Sudan*, U.N. Doc. A/HRC/49/CRP.4, ¶ 226(a) (Mar. 21, 2022).

91. Group of Eminent Experts on Yemen, *supra* note 88, ¶ 111(k); Group of Eminent Experts on Yemen, *Situation of Human Rights in Yemen, Including Violations and Abuses Since September 2014. Report of the Group of Eminent International And Regional Experts as Submitted to the United Nations High Commissioner for Human Rights*, U.N. Doc. A/HRC/42/17, ¶ 98(g) (Aug. 9, 2019); Group of Eminent Experts on Yemen, *Situation of Human Rights in Yemen, Including Violations and Abuses since September 2014. Detailed findings of the Group of Eminent International and Regional Experts on Yemen*, U.N. Doc. A/HRC/45/CRP.7, ¶ 422(x) (Sept. 29, 2020); Group of Eminent Experts on Yemen, *Accountability Update*, U.N. Doc. A/HRC/48/CRP.4, ¶ 83(a)–(b) (Sept. 14, 2021); Independent International Commission of Inquiry on the Syrian Arab Republic, *Report*, U.N. Doc. A/HRC/36/55, ¶ 87(h) (Aug. 8, 2017); Independent International Commission of Inquiry on the Syrian Arab Republic, *Report*, U.N. Doc. A/HRC/34/64, *supra* note 89, ¶ 106(d); Independent International Commission of Inquiry on the Syrian Arab Republic, *Conference Room Paper. Human Rights Abuses and International Humanitarian Law Violations in the Syrian Arab Republic, 21 July 2016–28 February 2017*, U.N. Doc. A/HRC/34/CRP.3, ¶ 114(c) (Mar. 10, 2017).

92. Group of Eminent Experts on Yemen, *Situation of Human Rights in Yemen, Including Violations and Abuses since September 2014. Detailed Findings*, U.N. Doc. A/HRC/45/CRP.7, *supra* note 91, ¶ 422(y); Group of Eminent Experts on Yemen, *Accountability Update*, U.N. Doc. A/HRC/48/CRP.4, *supra* note 90, ¶ 83(d).

93. Group of Eminent Experts on Yemen, *Situation of Human Rights in Yemen, Including Violations and Abuses since September 2014. Report*, U.N. Doc. A/HRC/42/CRP.1, ¶ 930(d) (Sept. 3, 2019).

94. Independent International Commission of Inquiry on the Syrian Arab Republic, *Out of Sight, Out of Mind: Deaths in Detention in the Syrian Arab Republic*, U.N. Doc. A/HRC/31/CRP.1, ¶ 107(c) (Feb. 3, 2016); Independent International Commission of Inquiry on the Syrian Arab Republic, *Report*, U.N. Doc. A/HRC/36/55, *supra* note 91, at ¶ 89(c); Independent International Commission of Inquiry on the Syrian Arab Republic, *Report*, U.N. Doc. A/HRC/43/57, ¶ 102(d) (Jan. 28, 2020).

things, the groups' command and control structures and internal rules, their military operations and weaponry, their detention operations, the administration of justice, the recruitment and use of children, the protection of civil and political rights, reparations, and accountability mechanisms.[95] From the lists of issues and the recommendations included in its reports, it appears clear that the Group of Experts had quite extensive expectations in relation to what the rebel groups could and should do. For instance, in relation to detention, they asked if there was a procedure to review the legality of detention,[96] what measures the groups took to allow detainees to understand the reasons for their detention and to challenge any decision forming the basis of their detention,[97] and what process was in place to ensure that detainees receive a fair trial and legal counsel.[98] In a report, the Group of Experts also called on the Houthi to, among other things, establish a procedure for individuals to report disappearances and for disappearances to be investigated and perpetrators punished;[99] to adopt "a comprehensive policy and package of measures" to ensure the right to reparation of victims of IHL and IHRL violations and ensure compensation for wrongful civilian deaths;[100] to ensure medical and psychological support to survivors;[101] and to ensure access to healthcare, education, and all other essential public services to children.[102] The Syria Commission similarly recommended that armed groups take certain measures in relation to detainees in order to avoid enforced disappearances, including registering and holding them in recognized places of detention, promptly informing them of the reasons for their detention, and ensuring that they have contact with the exterior, including legal assistance.[103]

95. The lists of issues and the responses by the rebels (the latter only in Arabic) are available at https://www.ohchr.org/en/hr-bodies/hrc/yemen-gee/index (last visited May 3, 2023).

96. Group of Eminent Experts on Yemen, *List of Issues Addressed to the Houthi/Ansar Allah*, (2018), question no. 21.

97. Group of Eminent Experts on Yemen, *List of Issues Addressed to the Houthi/Ansar Allah*, (2019), question no. 26.

98. Group of Eminent Experts on Yemen, *List of Issues Addressed to the Houthi/Ansar Allah*, (2021), question no. 9.

99. Group of Eminent Experts on Yemen, *Situation of Human Rights in Yemen, Including Violations and Abuses since September 2014. Report*, U.N. Doc. A/HRC/42/CRP.1, *supra* note 93, ¶ 930(e).

100. *Id.*, ¶ 930(f).

101. *Id.*, ¶ 930(g).

102. *Id.*, ¶ 930(i).

103. Independent International Commission of Inquiry on the Syrian Arab Republic, *Without a Trace: Enforced Disappearances in Syria, Conference Room Paper*, at 10 (Dec. 19, 2013).

C. Appraisal

Both Special Rapporteurs and Independent Investigations seem to expect a lot from armed groups. This is justified from the perspective of victims. After all, whether a certain violation of IHL or IHRL is committed by a State or an armed group is immaterial from the point of view of the individuals who suffered that violation.[104] It makes sense, therefore, to ask that a party to the conflict—whether it is a State or an armed group—investigate and punish violations of IHL and IHRL, make reparation, and respect the fundamental rights of individuals under their control. Independent Investigations and Special Procedures are a reminder that human rights violations are not normalized and tolerated by the international community,[105] no matter the perpetrator.[106] From this point of view, the drawing of clear boundaries between different branches of law resulting in different rules applying to the same type of violations based on whether they were committed by a State or a non-State armed group is excessively legalistic and even artificial. Independent Investigations and Special Procedures allow victims and survivors to express themselves and explain what happened to them,[107] a particularly important feature in light of otherwise often scarce opportunities for the accountability of armed groups at the international level.

The intertwining of IHL, IHRL, and ICL in the findings, conclusions, and recommendations of the Human Rights Council's mechanisms should not be considered an accident or mistake of mechanisms that do not know any better. On the contrary, this seems to be a reasoned decision on their part. On the basis of extensive interviews with fact-finding practitioners, Rob Grace explains that they "offered several rationales for incorporating IHL and/or ICL when operating under human rights mandates," including that they "deemed these bodies of law to be closely related and not completely separable"[108] and that doing so was "necessary to undertake a comprehensive investigation."[109] Special Rapporteur

104. *See, e.g.*, Alston, *Report*, U.N. Doc. A/62/265, *supra* note 72, ¶ 41; and Callamard, *Report on armed non-State actors: the protection of the right to life*, U.N. Doc. A/HRC/38/44, *supra* note 74, ¶¶ 6–7.

105. Chinkin, *supra* note 59, at 496.

106. Philip Alston (Special Rapporteur on extrajudicial, summary or arbitrary executions), *Report. Addendum, Mission to Sri Lanka (28 November–6 December 2005)*, U.N. Doc. E/CN.4/2006/53/ADD.5, ¶ 27 (Mar. 27, 2006).

107. Chinkin, *supra* note 59, at 497; *see, e.g.*, Independent International Commission of Inquiry on the Syrian Arab Republic, *Rule of Terror: Living under ISIS in Syria*, U.N. Doc. A/HRC/27/CRP.3, *supra* note 89; Independent International Commission of Inquiry on the Syrian Arab Republic, *"They Came to Destroy": ISIS Crimes Against the Yazidis*, U.N. Doc. A/HRC/32/CRP.2 (June 15, 2016).

108. Rob Grace, *From Design to Implementation: The Interpretation of Fact-finding Mandates*, 20 JOURNAL OF CONFLICT AND SECURITY LAW 27, 40 (2015).

109. *Id.* at 41.

Callamard similarly expressed her dissatisfaction with considering only the IHL framework when it comes to arbitrary deprivation of life by armed groups. She pointed out, among other things, that IHL applies only to acts that have a nexus "or direct link to the conflict," that only States have the obligation to make reparation, and that IHL has weak enforcement mechanisms.[110]

On the other hand, some of the reports seem to ask too much of armed groups, even for those that have stable control over territory and State-like features. For instance, the identification of remains excavated from mass graves and the investigation and preservation of former Islamic State detention sites that the AANES was requested to perform[111] would require human and technical resources and expertise that can hardly be required as a matter of law from an armed group party to a NIAC, no matter how well organized or how stable its control over territory. Armed groups are also unlikely to be able to adopt "a comprehensive policy and package" for reparation and might not have at their disposal sufficient financial resources to ensure compensation or medical and psychological support to survivors, as was asked of the Houthi.[112] Some would also consider that the obligation to provide individuals deprived of liberty the opportunity to challenge their detention and with legal counsel, although filled with the best intentions, is unrealistic for armed groups.[113] One might also question whether it is desirable to require armed groups to punish perpetrators of international crimes, in light of the fact that they may have a hard time complying with applicable fair trial standards.[114]

Still, the far reaching obligations imposed on armed groups can also be taken as having an aspirational nature aimed at pursuing goals aligned with the expectations of the international community, concerning, for instance, the respect for human rights by any actor or organ of society[115] or the fight against impunity

110. Callamard, *Report on armed non-State actors: the protection of the right to life*, U.N. Doc. A/HRC/38/44, *supra* note 74, ¶ 28.

111. Letter by the Mandates of the Special Rapporteur on extrajudicial, summary or arbitrary executions; the Working Group on Arbitrary Detention; the Working Group on Enforced or Involuntary Disappearances and the Special Rapporteur on the promotion of truth, justice, reparation and guarantees of non-recurrence, AL OTH 28/2022, *supra* note 80, at 4.

112. Group of Eminent Experts on Yemen, *Situation of Human Rights in Yemen, Including Violations and Abuses since September 2014. Report*, U.N. Doc. A/HRC/42/CRP.1, *supra* note 93, ¶ 930(f) and (g).

113. Marco Sassòli, *Taking Armed Groups Seriously: Ways to Improve Their Compliance with International Humanitarian Law*, 1 Journal of International Humanitarian Legal Studies 5, 17 (2010).

114. *See* René Provost, Rebel Courts: The Administration of Justice by Armed Insurgents (2021) (for a recent and comprehensive study on courts of armed groups under international law).

115. Alston, *Report. Addendum, Mission to Sri Lanka (28 November–6 December 2005)*, U.N. Doc. E/CN.4/2006/53/Add.5, *supra* note 106, ¶¶ 25–27.

for international crimes.[116] These findings can also be seen as contributing to the clarification of norms whose applicability to armed groups in NIAC is highly contested, such as the prohibition of enforced disappearance[117] and the prohibition of arbitrary detention.[118] Because of the paucity or absence of other authoritative pronouncements on these matters, it is likely that the conclusions of Independent Investigations and Special Procedures will gain "semantic authority" or otherwise prompt the consideration and reaction of States and other interested actors. In this sense, the work of Special Procedures and Independent Investigations of the Human Rights Council contributes—or aims to contribute—to the process of shaping IHL in respect to the obligations of armed groups.

From a positivistic and voluntaristic perspective, the question arises as to whether the findings of the Human Rights Council's mechanisms in relation to the obligations of armed groups go beyond the international law rules to which States have agreed. Very often States do not react to the outputs of the Human Rights Council's mechanisms. They may not be aware of them or simply not have the interest or resources to do so.[119] The lack of reactions on the part of States is usually assumed to be a form of acquiescence to the output.[120] Conversely, if States did have a problem with Special Rapporteurs or Independent Investigations considering alleged violations of IHL and IHRL committed by armed groups and making extensive recommendations for armed groups to address them, they could say so, but they often do not. Their passive acquiescence may turn into active agreement if one considers that the renewal of mandates without excluding these matters from their purview may indicate agreement with past outputs. From this point of view, the process of shaping might be considered successful.

Even concerned States which are more likely to contest the work of these mechanisms end up reaffirming their authority to make findings about the obligations of armed groups. When the Syria Commission was first established and started taking IHL into account in its reports, the Syrian government was

116. *See* Hannes Jöbstl, *Bridging the Accountability Gap. Armed Non-State Actors and the Investigation and Prosecution of War Crimes*, 18 Journal of International Criminal Justice 567, 582–90 (2020) (on an emerging duty of armed groups to investigate and prosecute war crimes as opposed to individual obligations under the doctrine of command responsibility).

117. Andrew Clapham, *Armed Non-State Actors and the UN Convention on Enforced Disappearances, in* Réciprocité et universalité: sources et régimes du droit international et des droits de l'homme. Mélanges en l'honneur du Professeur Emmanuel Decaux 443 (2017).

118. Andrew Clapham, *Detention by Armed Groups under International Law*, 93 International Law Studies 1 (2017); Daragh Murray, *Non-State Armed Groups, Detention Authority in Non-International Armed Conflict, and the Coherence of International Law: Searching for a Way Forward*, 30 Leiden Journal of International Law 435 (2017).

119. Sivakumaran, *supra* note 23, at 382–84.

120. *Id.* at 384–86.

adamant that it was overstepping its mandate.[121] According to the Syrian government, rather than investigating IHL, the commission should have applied "international law on combating terrorism—including relevant United Nations Security Council Resolutions."[122] Yet, in subsequent diplomatic correspondence, the Syrian government started referring to "the responsibility borne by the armed terrorist groups for all the violations of human rights and war crimes..[123] For its part, the Group of Eminent Experts in Yemen was criticized by the Yemeni government and by the States supporting it for not paying sufficient attention to the violations of IHL and human rights committed by the Houthis[124] and other non-State actors.[125] Complaints that the Group exceeded its mandate by considering not only IHRL but also IHL were raised.[126] When it comes to specific findings in relation to the content and scope of the obligations of armed groups, time will tell whether the Human Rights Council's mechanisms have successfully shaped the understanding of States in relation to the application and interpretation of these rules.

121. *Note verbale dated 9 January 2013 from the Permanent Representative of the Syrian Arab Republic addressed to the Commission*, reproduced in Independent International Commission of Inquiry on the Syrian Arab Republic, *Report*, U.N. Doc. A/HRC/22/59, Annex I, at 31 (Feb. 5, 2013).

122. *Id.* at 32.

123. *Note verbale dated 15 August 2014 from the Permanent Mission of the Syrian Arab Republic to the United Nations Office and other International Organizations in Geneva Addressed to the President of the Human Rights Council*, U.N. Doc. A/HRC/27/G/2, at 4 (Aug. 26, 2014); the Syrian government also made reference to allegations of war crimes committed by opposing parties to the armed conflicts in, among others, *Note verbale dated 26 September 2018 from the Permanent Mission of the Syrian Arab Republic to the United Nations Office at Geneva addressed to the secretariat of the Human Rights Council*, U.N. Doc. A/HRC/39/G/7, at 2 (Nov. 16, 2018), and *Note verbale dated 5 March 2019 from the Permanent Mission of the Syrian Arab Republic to the United Nations Office at Geneva addressed to the secretariat of the Human Rights Council*, U.N. Doc. A/HRC/40/G/4, at 3 (Apr. 1, 2019).

124. *Note verbale dated 10 September 2018 from the Permanent Mission of Yemen to the United Nations Office at Geneva addressed to the secretariat of the Human Rights Council*, U.N. Doc. A/HRC/39/G/5, at 2 (Sept. 18, 2018); *Note verbale dated 28 March 2019 from the Permanent Mission of the United Arab Emirates to the United Nations Office at Geneva addressed to the Office of the United Nations High Commissioner for Human Rights*, U.N. Doc. A/HRC/40/G/9, at 9, 13–18 (Apr. 8, 2019).

125. *Note verbale dated 28 March 2019 from the Permanent Mission of the United Arab Emirates to the United Nations Office at Geneva addressed to the Office of the United Nations High Commissioner for Human Rights*, U.N. Doc. A/HRC/40/G/9, *supra* note 124, at 24–26; *Response of the Coalition Forces Supporting Legitimacy in Yemen to the Report of the Group of International and Regional Experts on Yemen for the year 2020*, at 16–17.

126. *Note verbale dated 19 September 2018 from the Permanent Mission of Saudi Arabia to the United Nations Office at Geneva addressed to the Office of the United Nations High Commissioner for Human Rights*, U.N. Doc. A/HRC/39/G/6, at 8 (Nov. 26, 2018).

IV. CONCLUSION

This chapter has sketched out the role of human rights mechanisms in shaping IHL. By understanding shaping both as a process and its results, the chapter showed that human rights mechanisms have played a role in shaping the scope of application of IHL, as well as the way that some IHL rules are interpreted and applied. The chapter also explored a relatively new area in which some human rights mechanisms might shape IHL, namely, the obligations of armed groups in NIACs.

The importance of the availability of these mechanisms cannot be ignored. While it is possible to bring violations of IHL and IHRL committed by States to the attention of UN treaty bodies, regional human rights courts, or inter-State dispute settlement mechanisms, very often victims of violations committed by armed groups have no other avenue of moral or legal accountability vis-à-vis these collective entities, and, at best, they can hope for the prosecution of individual perpetrators by an international criminal court or tribunal. The recourse of States to the Human Rights Council and its mechanisms to bring attention to violations committed by armed groups demonstrates that they believe this to be an appropriate forum for this kind of endeavor. Indeed, as the late Antonio Cassese wrote, "[m]onitoring and institutional fact-finding are . . . the best way of bringing the weight of the community to bear on each member state (and other international legal subjects)."[127] Although the entrenching of IHL with IHRL and ICL, which is prominent in the outputs of the Human Rights Council mechanisms addressed in this chapter, can be questioned in terms of its appropriateness and of leading to unrealistic obligations for armed groups, the continuum between these branches of international law contributes to the further "humanization" of IHL, ensuring the complementarity of these branches and of the different sensibilities underpinning them.

127. Antonio Cassese, *Fostering Increased Conformity with International Standards: Monitoring and Institutional Fact-Finding*, *in* Realizing Utopia: The Future of International Law 295, 303 (Antonio Cassese ed., 2012).

11

Applying and Interpreting the Law of Armed Conflict: Contributions by the UN Commissions on the Syrian Arab Republic and the Republic of South Sudan

YOUSUF SYED KHAN*

I. INTRODUCTION

Since its creation by the UN General Assembly in 2006,[1] the UN Human Rights Council (HRC) has convened some forty mandated mechanisms comprising commissions, fact-finding missions, and other ad hoc investigations to cover sudden events or protracted situations deemed sufficiently grave to warrant the Council's attention.[2] Year after year, these mechanisms continue to be established

* Yousuf Syed Khan is a Senior Lawyer with Global Rights Compliance. Previously, he was Reporting Officer/Analyst, UN International Commission of Human Rights Experts on Ethiopia; Reporting Officer/Analyst, OHCHR examination of the human rights situation in Belarus; Legal/Reporting Officer, UN Commission on Human Rights in South Sudan; and Reporting Officer/Analyst, UN Independent International Commission of Inquiry on the Syrian Arab Republic. The views expressed herein are those of the author and do not necessarily reflect the views of the United Nations.

1. G.A. Res. 60/251 (Apr. 3, 2006).

2. For an overview of the structure and functions of the HRC, *see generally*, Eric Tistounet, The UN Human Rights Council: A Practical Anatomy (2020); *see also* UN Library & Archives Geneva, *International Commissions of Inquiry, Fact-finding Missions: Chronological List*, UNOG,

Yousuf Syed Khan, *Applying and Interpreting the Law of Armed Conflict: Contributions by the UN Commissions on the Syrian Arab Republic and the Republic of South Sudan* In: *Making and Shaping the Law of Armed Conflict*. Edited by: Sandesh Sivakumaran and Christian R. Burne, Oxford University Press. © Yousuf Syed Khan 2024. DOI: 10.1093/oso/9780197775134.003.0011

at significant cost, with various staff compositions, while being ascribed an array of names. Their establishment generally fulfills the desire of member States to appoint investigative bodies that will report publicly on human rights violations or possible crimes against humanity committed in peacetime.

In respect of situations of armed conflict, HRC investigative mandates often contain explicit language recognizing violations of international humanitarian law (IHL) or the perpetration of "war crimes."[3] When they are established prior to the outbreak of an armed conflict which later emerges, the mandate holders have regularly determined the existence of the armed conflict(s), made findings of IHL violations, or of war crimes, and interpreted these tasks as falling within their respective purviews.[4]

In August 2011 and at least six-months prior to the outbreak of armed conflict in Syria,[5] the HRC established the Independent International Commission of Inquiry on the Syrian Arab Republic (Syria Commission), with a mandate focused on the pre-conflict uprising.[6] Similarly, in March 2016, the HRC established the Commission on Human Rights in South Sudan (South Sudan Commission). Despite the outbreak of the ongoing armed conflict in South Sudan over two years

https://libraryresources.unog.ch/factfinding/chronolist [hereinafter *UNOG Chronological list*]; UN Human Rights Council, *Human Rights Council-mandated Investigative Bodies*, OHCHR, https://www.ohchr.org/en/hr-bodies/hrc/list-hrc-mandat.

3. *See, e.g.*, Human Rights Council Res. 45/15, U.N. Doc. A/HRC/RES/45/15, at 2 (Oct. 12, 2020); *see also* Human Rights Council Res. S-28-1, U.N. Doc. A/HRC/RES/S-28-1, ¶ 5 (May 22, 2018).

4. For example, the preliminary mandates of the UN Commissions of Inquiry on Libya (2011–2014) and Syria (2011–Present) referred only to IHRL, though both Commissions later interpreted their mandates to include IHL based (initially) on NIAC threshold analyses. *See, e.g.*, Rep. of the International Commission of Inquiry to investigate all alleged violations of international human rights law in the Libyan Arab Jamahiriya, Human Rights Council, A/HRC/17/44, ¶¶ 55–56 (Jan. 12, 2012) [hereinafter Libya CoI Jan. 2020 report]; Rep. of the independent international commission of inquiry on the Syrian Arab Republic, Human Rights Council, A/HRC/21/50, annex II ¶ 3 (Aug. 16, 2012) [hereinafter Syria CoI Aug. 2012 report]. Indeed, the mandate holders determine the geographic scope (*ratione loci*), temporal mandate (*ratione temporis*), subject-matter mandate (*ratione materiae*), and the actors investigated (*ratione personae*). *See, e.g.*, OHCHR, Commissions of Inquiry and Fact-finding Missions on International Human Rights and Humanitarian Law, Guidance and Practice 37 (2015) [hereinafter OHCHR CoI Guidance].

5. The Syria Commission first determined that a NIAC emerged in February 2012. *See, e.g.*, Syria CoI Aug. 2012 report, *supra* note 4, annex II ¶ 3. Four months later, in June 2012, President Bashar al-Assad acknowledged in a televised address that Syria was indeed in a state of war. *Syria in State of War, Says Bashar al-Assad*, BBC (June 27, 2012), https://www.bbc.com/news/world-middle-east-18598533. The International Committee of the Red Cross (ICRC) determined a NIAC in July 2012. *Syria: ICRC and Syrian Arab Red Crescent Maintain Aid Effort amid Increased Fighting*, ICRC (July 17, 2012), https://www.icrc.org/en/doc/resources/documents/update/2012/syria-update-2012-07-17.htm.

6. Human Rights Council Res. 17-1, U.N. Doc. A/HRC/RES/17-1 (July 6, 2011).

prior, its initial mandate focused largely on human rights violations, as suggested by its very title, and acknowledged anticipated government cooperation.[7] In addition to findings and recommendations related to international human rights law (IHRL), however, and given the levels of hostilities in both States, the UN Commissions on Syria and South Sudan interpreted their mandates to cover IHL and reached a broad range of factual and legal findings, including of war crimes, during the prevailing armed conflicts in both States.[8]

Notably, these two UN investigative mechanisms were the first to consider a number of IHL issues. Concerning the Syria Commission, emblematic examples include: (a) the forced displacement of unsympathetic populations as a warring strategy after prolonged siege warfare; and (2) unlawful internment through battlefield detention perpetrated by a non-State armed group under the guise of camps for internally displaced persons. Similarly, after the Rome Statute of the International Criminal Court (ICC) was amended to include the starvation of civilians as a war crime in non-international armed conflicts (NIACs),[9] the South Sudan Commission was the first UN-mandated mechanism to dedicate a comprehensive report to starvation as a method of warfare during a NIAC.[10]

These findings have had a discernable impact on the conflict-related discourse. Often viewed as authoritative sources equipped with (quasi-)accountability mandates,[11] both independent Commissions have required member States and the international community at-large to grapple in real time with emerging and complex situations on the ground. Stated another way, among the most prominent contributions by these two UN Commissions has been their investigation of novel issues in real time and publication of their findings in brief public reports. By the same token, reactions to some of their findings have been a mix between international headlines and delayed acceptance by the international community, with the latter perhaps at least partly the consequence of latent factual understanding.

7. South Sudan has been involved in NIACs since Dec. 2013. *See* Human Rights Council Res. 31/20, U.N. Doc. A/HRC/RES/31/20, ¶ 21 (Apr. 27, 2016).

8. *See, e.g.*, Syria CoI Aug. 2012 report, *supra* note 4, annex II ¶ 3; *see also* Rep. of the Commission on Human Rights in South Sudan, Human Rights Council, A/HRC/37/71, ¶¶ 14 and 16 (Mar. 14, 2018). Regarding the Syria Commission, the HRC also noted in Oct. 2012 the need to investigate war crimes. Human Rights Council Res. 21/26, U.N. Doc. A/HRC/RES/21/26, ¶ 10 (Oct. 17, 2012).

9. Rome Statute of the International Criminal Court art. 8(2)(e)xix, July 17, 1998, 2187 U.N.T.S. 90 [hereinafter Rome Statute].

10. *See* "There is nothing left for us": starvation as a method of warfare in South Sudan, Conference room paper of the Commission on Human Rights in South Sudan, Human Rights Council, A/HRC/45/CRP.3 (Oct. 5, 2020) [hereinafter South Sudan starvation paper].

11. On criminal justice and the contemporary accountability landscape, this piece refers to HRC investigative mechanisms with accountability or "preservation-accountability" mandates as "(quasi)-accountability" bodies, and to the three investigative mandates that focus on criminal case-building (the IIIM, the Independent Investigative Mechanism for Myanmar (IIMM), and

Increasingly, HRC investigative mechanisms are additionally mandated to support criminal accountability, including both individual criminal and State responsibility, by collecting, consolidating, preserving, and analyzing information and evidence, and where possible, identifying those responsible ("preservation-accountability" mandates). While such mandated language signals the collective will of member States to combat impunity, the factual and legal findings contained in brief public reports cannot be, by their very nature, as well-reasoned as judicial decisions.

Despite this inherent limitation, by applying the law of armed conflict (LOAC (used interchangeably with IHL)), HRC investigative mechanisms necessarily have to interpret it. And "[t]he role of interpretation in the making and shaping of international law is significant, as the law develops incrementally through interpretation and the line between development through interpretation and creation of new law is a fine one."[12] Under the UN Charter, the United Nations should prioritize strengthening and enforcing *jus contra bellum*, though the United Nations has "become today the place where international law is developed."[13] As (quasi-)accountability bodies, when any such HRC investigative mechanism is the first major entity to apply and interpret a particular rule (sections III and IV), and/or share its underlying information and evidence with (quasi-)judicial bodies, their findings and underlying evidence have the potential to shape and influence the law (section V).

As non-adversarial "human rights fact-finding" conducted by (quasi-)accountability bodies, the value of HRC investigative mechanisms toward shaping and influencing the LOAC is therefore twofold: first, it lies in their ability to investigate and identify emerging and complex patterns and outcomes—often in real time. Second, these mechanisms then apply and interpret the LOAC, and increasingly serve as a precursor to distinct and complementary criminal investigations by cooperating with (quasi-)judicial bodies that can credibly advance prosecutions.

II. THE EVOLUTION, COMPOSITION, AND PRACTICE OF UN INVESTIGATIVE MECHANISMS

Over the past twenty-two years, the United Nations has relied on a series of mandated mechanisms to investigate and respond to periods of uprising, conflict, and post-conflict contexts ("atrocity inquiries").[14] These mechanisms regularly

UNITAD) as "(quasi-)judicial" bodies. Domestic prosecutorial authorities/courts, the Hybrid Court for South Sudan, ad hoc tribunals, and the ICC are referred to as judicial bodies. *See infra* section II.C.

12. Sandesh Sivakumaran, *Beyond States and Non-State Actors: The Role of State-Empowered Entities in the Making and Shaping of International Law*, 55 Columbia Journal of Transnational Law 343, 347 (2017) (internal citation omitted).

13. Marco Sassòli, *How Will International Humanitarian Law Develop in the Future?*, 104 International Review of the Red Cross 2052, 2060 (2022).

14. *See* Yousuf Syed Khan & Charles Majinge, *Advancing the Rule of Law and Human Rights Protection through United Nations Mandated Mechanisms, The Cases of the Syrian Arab Republic*

consider questions of law and, although their findings are not legally binding, through their growing application and interpretation of the LOAC, their work is becoming increasingly juridified.[15] Since its reconstitution from the Commission on Human Rights in 2006, the HRC has taken center stage among UN bodies to mandate atrocity inquiries with increased frequency.[16] Beyond the obvious interplay between IHRL and IHL, the favoring by the principal intergovernmental human rights body of nonbinding inquiries to respond to armed conflicts is likely part of a growing response to Security Council inefficacy and *realpolitik*, including the geopolitical interests at play for Syria and South Sudan.[17]

A. Composition

Ad hoc investigations mandated by the HRC are typically composed of three pro bono independent, international experts appointed by the HRC president, with one designated as chairperson.[18] They are supported by secretariats comprised of Office of the UN High Commissioner for Human Rights (OHCHR) staff or external consultants with varied professional backgrounds, who provide administrative and logistical support and expertise, and carry out field missions as required.[19] Although their mandates often necessitate reaching legal conclusions including of IHRL and IHL violations, or war crimes, appointed experts are not required to have a legal background nor specialization in the LOAC, and in several instances do not.[20] In practice, and especially for "preservation-accountability" mandates (section II.C), this may highlight the important role of the secretariat staff.

and the State of Libya, in 24 MAX PLANCK YEARBOOK OF UNITED NATIONS LAW 327, 336–39 (2021).

15. Juridification in this sense may be defined as "relying on legal process and legal arguments, using legal language, [and] substituting or replacing ordinary politics with judicial decisions and legal formality." GORDON SILVERSTEIN, LAW'S ALLURE: HOW LAW SHAPES, CONSTRAINS, SAVES, AND KILLS POLITICS 5 (2009). *See also* Larissa Van den Herik, *An Inquiry into the Role of Commissions of Inquiry in International Law: Navigating the Tensions between Fact-Finding and Application of International Law*, 13 CHINESE JOURNAL OF INTERNATIONAL LAW 507, 508 (2014).

16. *See UNOG Chronological list*, *supra* note 2.

17. *See, e.g.*, Steven J. Rapp, *Bridging The Hague-Geneva Divide: Harmonizing Multiple Investigations of International Crimes*, THE HAGUE INSTITUTE FOR GLOBAL JUSTICE, INTERSECTIONS (Oct. 2016), at 11; *see also* Van den Herik, *supra* note 15, at 528.

18. TISTOUNET, *supra* note 2, at 17; *see also* M. CHERIF BASSIOUNI, INTRODUCTION TO INTERNATIONAL CRIMINAL LAW 943 (2d ed. 2013).

19. OHCHR, HUMAN RIGHTS COUNCIL, 17 (2020), https://www.ohchr.org/sites/default/files/Documents/HRBodies/HRCouncil/HRC_booklet_EN.pdf.

20. Some resolutions have requested the investigative mechanism include experts in both IHL and IHRL. *See, e.g.*, S.C. Res. 2127, ¶ 24 (Dec. 5, 2013); *see also* OHCHR COI GUIDANCE, *supra* note 4, at 19–20.

B. Investigations and Standards of Proof

The proliferation and growing juridification of ad hoc atrocity inquires[21] over the past two decades has prompted closer scrutiny of the methodologies they employ.[22] Per the guidance and practice of the OHCHR on how HRC mechanisms conceptualize the law and apply it to their investigative mandates, they are supposed to develop an applicable legal framework at the outset of their work.[23] Given the pace of many conflict scenarios, however, this exercise is rarely feasible. In the case of Syria, as an example of the infeasibility of the Commission developing the legal framework at the outset of its work, the Commission would have had to assess anticipatorily the steady proliferation of belligerents over time, including: the proliferation of armed groups and extremist elements, with some operating under the aegis of third States; the classification of conflict(s) including via third-State intervention with or without the consent of the Syrian government, such as extraterritorial operations against non-State armed groups; and/or belligerent occupation.

Notably, there is also no universal standard of proof to which HRC investigative mechanisms must adhere.[24] As to the standard applied to make a finding of fact, HRC investigative mechanisms do not apply the criminal law standard of "beyond reasonable doubt," but rather have generally adopted "reasonable suspicion" or "reasonable grounds to believe," and less commonly "balance of probabilities."[25] Though uncommon, a UN-mandated mechanism's methodology or standard of proof may have to be adapted from mandate to mandate. Altering the methodology of an investigative mechanism could make its findings and evidence less useful for (quasi-)judicial bodies that operate to higher, criminal accountability standards, such as the International Impartial and Independent Mechanism (IIIM), the UN Investigative Team to Promote Accountability for Crimes Committed by Da'esh/ISIL (UNITAD), and judicial bodies such as the envisaged Hybrid Court for South Sudan (HCSS), ad hoc tribunals, or the ICC.[26]

21. The terms "investigations" and "fact-finding" are used interchangeably throughout this chapter.

22. *See, e.g.*, Théo Boutruche, *Credible Fact-Finding and Allegations of International Humanitarian Law Violations: Challenges in Theory and Practice*, 16 Journal of Conflict & Security Law 105 (2011).

23. OHCHR CoI Guidance, *supra* note 4, at 65.

24. *See generally* Stephen Wilkinson, *Standards of Proof in International Humanitarian and Human Rights Fact-Finding and Inquiry Missions*, Geneva Academy of International Humanitarian Law and Human Rights, https://www.geneva-academy.ch/joomlatools-files/docman-files/Standards%20of%20Proof%20in%20Fact-Finding.pdf.

25. OHCHR CoI Guidance, *supra* note 4, at 65.

26. *See, e.g.*, *id.*, at 62.

C. Collection, Consolidation, and Preservation

Beyond investigations and public reporting, some HRC investigative mechanisms are additionally tasked to support criminal accountability by collecting, consolidating, preserving, and analyzing information and evidence, and where possible, identifying those responsible ("preservation-accountability" mandates).[27] Assigned with increased frequency,[28] these functions may be particularly relevant to the notion of "law-making."

The application of the LOAC appears not only in the applicable legal framework of many of these mechanisms, and later, in the legal findings reached in their periodic public reports, but also ostensibly throughout the life cycle of the investigation stage. Once incidents or patterns of conduct related to violations of IHRL or IHL even seem to emerge, they are inevitably viewed and investigated through the prism of the law in order to inform the investigations and to juxtapose the gathered facts with the requisite elements of established violations or crimes. In practice, this means that much of the information being collected, consolidated, and preserved by these mechanisms has been gathered to prove or disprove violations of the law. To give an example, if the launching of an indiscriminate attack resulting in death or injury to civilians may have occurred as a war crime under customary IHL,[29] that attack—after preliminary analysis—would inevitably be investigated as such, and therefore the underlying information collected, consolidated, and preserved would be viewed through that prism. It is through this prism, then, that (quasi-)judicial bodies may later receive the gathered information. Therefore, as it concerns shaping and influencing the law of armed conflict more concretely (beyond applying and interpreting it), equal emphasis could be placed on the underlying information gathered by UN investigative mechanisms as on the findings reached in these mechanisms' brief public reports (section V).

1. Accountability and "Preservation-Accountability" Mandates

The contemporary wave of accountability mandates—which has aptly been described as part of an overall "accountability turn" in human rights fact-finding[30]—has been evolving gradually in the post–Cold War era, mainly since

27. *See, e.g.*, Human Rights Council Res. 34/25, U.N. Doc. A/HRC/RES/34/25 (Apr. 5, 2017), ¶ 16(b); Human Rights Council Res. S-30/1, U.N. Doc. A/HRC/RES/S-30/1 (May 28, 2021), ¶ 2(b); and Human Rights Council Res. 46/20, U.N. Doc. A/HRC/RES/46/20 (Mar. 29, 2021), ¶ 13(a).

28. This has been the case, for example, with the South Sudan Commission (2017–Present); the Independent International Commission of Inquiry on the Occupied Palestinian Territory and Israel (2021–Present); and the OHCHR examination of the human rights situation in Belarus (2021–Present). *Id.*

29. 1 Customary International Humanitarian Law (Jean-Marie Henckaerts & Louise Doswald-Beck eds., 2005), r. 156 [hereinafter ICRC Customary Rules].

30. *See generally* Federica D'Alessandra, *The Accountability Turn in Third Wave Human Rights Fact-Finding*, 33(84) Utrecht Journal of International & European Law 59 (2017).

the UN established a commission of experts in 1992 to investigate the situation in the former Yugoslavia.[31] Since 2017 in particular, this "accountability turn" has been further bifurcated between accountability and "preservation-accountability" mandates. Accountability mandates contain language to establish the facts and circumstances of violations and crimes perpetrated and to identify those responsible.[32] "Preservation-accountability" mandates go a step further, by tasking the mechanism to collect and preserve evidence.[33] For HRC atrocity inquiries, the latter practice of "preservation-accountability" functions first emerged in 2017 via the HRC's resolution renewing the South Sudan Commission.[34]

Established in August 2011, the Syria Commission preceded the "preservation-accountability" development of the "accountability turn."[35] Rather, and likely given the scope and scale of violations perpetrated during the Syrian conflict, the UN General Assembly adopted Resolution 71/248 in December 2016, establishing the IIIM[36] with a mandate in part to collect, consolidate, preserve, and analyze evidence of IHL violations and human rights abuses. Finally, other HRC investigative mechanisms have been tasked to collect and preserve information for a preexisting accountability body. In such instances, these mandates have focused on preparing information to pass on to that body.[37]

III. THE UN INDEPENDENT INTERNATIONAL COMMISSION OF INQUIRY ON THE SYRIAN ARAB REPUBLIC

The Syria Commission was established in August 2011.[38] Formed in the aftermath of the "Arab Spring" spate of pro-democracy protests that erupted in the Middle East and North Africa in early 2010, its first mandate centered upon the pre-conflict uprising.[39] At the time of writing in its twelfth year, the Syria Commission has

31. *See generally* Commissions of Inquiry: Problems and Prospects (Christian Henderson ed., 2017); *see also* S.C. Res. 780, ¶ 2 (Oct. 6, 1992).

32. U.N. Doc. A/HRC/RES/S-17/1, ¶ 13; U.N. Doc. A/HRC/RES/S-21/1, ¶ 13.

33. U.N. Doc. A/HRC/RES/34/25, ¶ 16(b).

34. *Id.*

35. Rather, in its initial resolution, the Syria Commission was tasked by the HRC "to identify those responsible with a view of ensuring that perpetrators of violations . . . are held accountable." U.N. Doc. A/HRC/RES/S-17/1, ¶ 13.

36. U.N. Doc. A/RES/71/248.

37. *See, e.g.*, U.N. Doc. A/HRC/RES/39/2, ¶ 30.

38. *See* U.N. Doc. A/HRC/RES/S-17/1, ¶ 13.

39. *Id.*

served as the longest running body among all UN investigate mechanisms and has interviewed over 10,000 witnesses and victims.[40]

A. Siege Warfare: Forced Displacement as a War Crime

Between November 2012 and April 2018, both Syrian government forces and organized armed groups waged siege warfare in at least seven governorates.[41] In one emblematic example, in July 2016, Syrian aerial and ground forces and allied Russian Aerospace Forces had intensified their efforts to recapture eastern Aleppo City. The offensive was characterized by encirclement, siege, and daily airstrikes that persisted for over five months.[42] Between July and December 2016, in order to force the surrender of armed groups controlling eastern Aleppo City, the Syria Commission found that Syrian and/or Russian forces used prohibited means and methods of warfare by deliberately bombing hospitals, schools, and markets, while Syrian forces also employed "weapons delivering toxic industrial chemicals, including chlorine."[43]

In December 2016, government forces negotiated the signing of a local truce with armed groups in eastern Aleppo City, which included an agreement to evacuate all residents.[44] Over 30,000 people were evacuated from eastern Aleppo over the period of a few days, and the evacuations were overseen by humanitarian organizations including the International Committee of the Red Cross (ICRC).[45]

Among the most debated legal conclusions of the Syria Commission was its qualification of the evacuation of eastern Aleppo as the war crime of forced displacement.[46] First published in its "special inquiry into the events in Aleppo" report, the Syria Commission found:

40. *About the Commission of Inquiry*, OHCHR, https://www.ohchr.org/en/hr-bodies/hrc/iici-syria/about-co-i.

41. *See, e.g.*, *Sieges as Weapons of War: Encircle, Starve, Surrender, Evacuate*, Int'l Comm'n of Inquiry on the Syrian Arab Republic (May 29, 2018), https://www.ohchr.org/Documents/HRBodies/HRCouncil/CoISyria/PolicyPaperSieges_29May2018.pdf [hereinafter *Syria Sieges paper*].

42. Rep. of the Independent International Commission of Inquiry on the Syrian Arab Republic, Human Rights Council, A/HRC/34/64, ¶¶ 8 and 14 (Feb. 2, 2017) [hereinafter Syria CoI Aleppo report].

43. *Id.*, ¶ 14.

44. *See Syria Sieges paper*, *supra* note 41, at 5.

45. Areeb Ullah, *Red Cross Defends Role in Aleppo Evacuations after Damning UN Report*, Middle East Eye (Mar. 2, 2017), https://www.middleeasteye.net/news/red-cross-defends-role-aleppo-evacuations-after-damning-un-report [hereinafter Red Cross Defends].

46. *See, e.g.*, Elvina Pothelet, *The Evacuation of Eastern Aleppo: Humanitarian Obligation or War Crime?*, EJIL:Talk! (Mar. 14, 2017), https://www.ejiltalk.org/the-evacuation-of-eastern-aleppo-humanitarian-obligation-or-war-crime; Kai Ambos, *Evacuation of Civilian Populations and*

> After the Government reached an evacuation agreement with armed groups in mid-December, residents of eastern Aleppo were transported from the city in government buses and private vehicles to Idlib, while others fled to western Aleppo. None had the option to remain in their home. As part of the agreement, more than 1,000 people were evacuated from Foah and Kafraya and went to Aleppo, Tartous, Homs and Latakia governorates. As warring parties agreed to the evacuation of eastern Aleppo for strategic reasons—and not for the security of civilians or imperative military necessity, which permit the displacement of thousands—the Aleppo evacuation agreement amounts to the war crime of forced displacement.[47]

The finding of forced displacement as the result of a humanitarian evacuation during a NIAC was the first of its kind by the United Nations, and, given the situation in Aleppo at the time, it garnered considerable media attention.[48] A series of discussions also emerged as to the validity and legal accuracy of the conclusion.[49] In reaching its findings, the Syria Commission relied primarily on customary IHL, and largely by citing the ICRC Customary IHL Study.[50] Pursuant to Rule 129(B) of the Study, "[p]arties to a non-international armed conflict may not *order* the displacement of the civilian population, in whole or in part, for reasons related to the conflict, unless the security of the civilians involved or imperative military reasons so demand."[51]

Criminal Complicity: A Critical Appraisal of the February 2017 Report of the Syria Commission of Inquiry, EJIL:Talk! (May 24, 2017), https://www.ejiltalk.org/evacuation-of-civilian-populations-and-criminal-complicity-a-critical-appraisal-of-the-february-2017-report-of-the-syria-commission-of-inquiry; and Matt Brown, *The Evacuation of Eastern Aleppo: Forced Displacement under International Law?*, ICD Brief 25 (Jan. 2019), https://www.internationalcrimesdatabase.org/upload/documents/20190109T160612-ICD%20Brief_Dec2018Forced%20Displacement%20in%20Syria%20as%20a%20Crime%20Under%20International%20Law.pdf.

47. U.N. Doc. A/HRC/RES/S-25/1; *see also* Syria CoI Aleppo report, *supra* note 42, ¶ 93.

48. *See, e.g.*, Martin Chulov, *Forced Evacuation of East Aleppo Was War Crime, Says UN*, The Guardian (Mar. 1, 2017), https://www.theguardian.com/world/2017/mar/01/syrian-regime-aleppo-airstrike-aid-convoy-united-nations-report; *Syria Conflict: All Parties Committed War Crimes in Aleppo—UN*, BBC (Mar. 1, 2017), https://www.bbc.com/news/world-middle-east-39126653; *All Sides Committed War Crimes in Aleppo, Says UN Probe*, France 24 (Mar. 1, 2017), https://www.france24.com/en/20170301-syria-all-sides-committed-war-crimes-aleppo-says-un-united-nations-probe; and Alison Meuse, *U.N. Report Says Syrian Forces and Rebel Factions Committed Aleppo "War Crimes,"* NPR (Mar. 3, 2017), https://www.npr.org/sections/parallels/2017/03/03/518134951/u-n-report-says-syrian-forces-and-rebel-factions-committed-aleppo-war-crimes.

49. *See supra* note 46.

50. For a detailed analysis of the authority of the ICRC Customary IHL Study, *see* Marko Milanovic & Sandesh Sivakumaran, *Assessing the Authority of the ICRC Customary IHL Study*, 104 International Review of the Red Cross 1856 (2022).

51. Emphasis added.

In finding that the residents who were evacuated from eastern Aleppo City were forcibly displaced, the Syria Commission did not reference an "order" to displace them. Comprised of two constituent elements, customary international law necessitates: (1) consistent and general practice by States, and (2) a subjective acceptance of the practice as law (*opinio juris*).[52] Although the ICRC Customary IHL Study references an "order" to displace,[53] State practice and *opinio juris* demonstrate that the customary prohibition of forced displacement also covers displacement which is not the result of an "order."[54]

As Syria is neither a State party to Additional Protocol II (APII) nor the Rome Statute, the "order" requirement is only addressed as a matter of customary IHL. Customary IHL notwithstanding, construing the act of ordering to displace broadly, as the involuntary movement of the civilian population, is consistent with the original proposal at the 1972 Conference of Government Experts relating to displacement being "ordered or compelled."[55] A similar position was also affirmed by the ICC in the *Ntaganda* Appeal, which upheld the order requirement as being satisfied when instruction(s) were given to perform acts, the result of which the displacement of a significant proportion of the civilian population "would necessarily occur."[56] In its finding, the Syria Commission found that the evacuation agreement meant that none of the residents in eastern Aleppo City "had the option to remain in their home" and were transported "in government buses and private vehicles,"[57] likely indicating that civilians were not displacing themselves.

Given the levels of devastation wrought upon eastern Aleppo during the prolonged siege and the means and methods of warfare employed, besieged residents were rendered extremely vulnerable and endured complex fatigue. While it remains ambiguous in the NIAC context whether the obligation to evacuate certain vulnerable groups (e.g., the wounded and sick) can be deduced from Common

52. North Sea Continental Shelf (F.R.G. v. Den., F.R.G. v. Neth.), Judgment, 1969 I.C.J. Rep. 3, ¶ 77 (Feb. 20).

53. *See* ICRC Customary Rules, *supra* note 29, at r. 129(B).

54. *See* Jan Willms, *Without Order, Anything Goes? The Prohibition of Forced Displacement in Non-international Armed Conflict*, 91 INTERNATIONAL REVIEW OF THE RED CROSS 547, 561 (2009).

55. SANDESH SIVAKUMARAN, THE LAW OF NON-INTERNATIONAL ARMED CONFLICT 285 (2012). On the voluntariness of displacement in the analogous context of crimes against humanity (deportation or forcible transfer), *see also, e.g.*, Prosecutor v. Blagojević & Jokić, Case No. IT-02-60-T, Judgment, ¶ 596 (Int'l Crim. Trib. for the former Yugoslavia Jan. 17, 2005) (citing, inter alia, Prosecutor v. Krnojelac, Case No. IT-97-25-A, Appeals Judgment, ¶ 229 (Int'l Crim. Trib. for the former Yugoslavia Sept. 17, 2003).

56. Prosecutor v. Ntaganda, ICC-01/04-02/06 A A2, Appeal Judgment, ¶¶ 544–45 (Mar. 30, 2021).

57. U.N. Doc. A/HRC/RES/S-25/1; *see also* Syria CoI Aleppo report, *supra* note 42, ¶ 93.

Article 3,[58] the Fourth Geneva Convention (GC IV) provides explicitly for evacuation agreements in encircled or besieged areas for certain vulnerable groups. Parties to IACs must "endeavor to conclude local agreements for the removal of wounded, sick, infirm, and aged persons, children and maternity cases, and for the passage of ministers of all religions, medical personnel and medical equipment on their way to such areas."[59] As noted in the Commentary to GC IV, however, there is an underlying temptation for the besieging forces "to oppose evacuation in order to avoid relieving the besieged forces of their supply difficulties and with the idea of inducing them to capitulate sooner."[60] Having deliberately rendered entire populations extremely vulnerable, and analogously in the NIAC context, the Syria Commission documented several sieges, including that of eastern Aleppo, appearing to have been laid with and characterized by this underlying temptation.[61]

In early March 2017, the ICRC reportedly defended its role in the evacuations publicly, by stating that the evacuations "helped avoid an even greater humanitarian catastrophe in Aleppo, at a time when people playing no part in the violence were trapped . . . and had literally nowhere to run."[62] The Syria Commission elaborated on how it viewed the finding in its next report,[63] including by providing detail on how, in the context of sieges, both government forces and armed groups routinely denied humanitarian evacuations for both wounded and sick civilians and fighters until after surrender, local truces, and subsequent evacuations (i.e., the above-mentioned underlying temptation).[64] To analyze the legitimacy of the evacuation agreements in the NIAC context, the Commission relied on: (1) ICTY case law dealing with displacement for humanitarian reasons; the actors that may lawfully consent to evacuation agreements; and (2) the ICRC Commentary on the

58. J.P. Benoit posits that ICRC Customary Rule 109 regarding the search for, collection, and evacuation of the wounded, sick, and shipwrecked may not actually be customary in nature. *See Mistreatment of the Wounded, Sick and Shipwrecked by the ICRC Study on Customary International Humanitarian Law*, 11 YIHL 175, 199–203 (2008) (internal citations omitted); *cf.* SANDESH SIVAKUMARAN, THE LAW OF NON-INTERNATIONAL ARMED CONFLICT 277 (2012).

59. Convention (IV) Relative to the Protection of Civilian Persons in Time of War art. 17, Aug. 12, 1949, 6 U.S.T. 3516, 75 U.N.T.S. 287 [hereinafter GC IV]. The removal of civilians to places of refuge from besieged or encircled places is further contemplated by arts. 14 and 15.

60. OSCAR M. UHLER ET AL., COMMENTARY TO GENEVA CONVENTION IV RELATIVE TO THE PROTECTION OF CIVILIAN PERSONS IN TIME OF WAR art. 17(2(B)) (1958).

61. *See, e.g.*, Syria CoI Aleppo report, *supra* note 42, ¶ 93; Rep. of the Commission on Human Rights in South Sudan, Human Rights Council, A/HRC/36/55, ¶ 35 (Aug. 8, 2017) [hereinafter Syria CoI Aug. 2017 report]; and *Syria Sieges paper*, *supra* note 41.

62. *See* RED CROSS DEFENDS, *supra* note 45.

63. Syria CoI Aug. 2017 report, *supra* note 61, 5–8 and annex III.

64. *Id.*, ¶ 27.

Additional Protocols.[65] The Commission concluded that post-siege evacuations enabled "government forces . . . to serve a calculated warring strategy" and that "the pattern of evacuations occurring throughout the country appears intended to engineer changes to the political demographies of previously besieged enclaves, by redrawing and consolidating bases of political support."[66] Such conduct is addressed in the Commentary to APII, which determines that "imperative military reasons cannot be justified by political motives."[67]

Notably, the Syria Commission reintroduced the "order" language in its reports following the Aleppo finding, signifying that it may deem the "order" requirement to in fact apply as an element of the customary IHL prohibition and corresponding war crime of forced displacement during NIACs.[68] In one such finding, the Commission stated that "[f]or each civilian who was unable to freely decide on his or her movement or destination, the agreement to evacuate him or her amounts to an unlawful order."[69] Over the course of its thirteen successive mandates,[70] and in the context of siege warfare, the Commission found reasonable grounds to believe that parties to the conflict committed the war crime of forced displacement of civilians seven times between 2016 and 2017.[71] Aside from the Aleppo finding, each subsequent finding of forced displacement made reference to an "order" and cited the ICRC Customary IHL Study to reach the conclusion. At the time of writing, it appears that the Commission has never addressed this discrepancy.

Prior to the Syria Commission's finding of forced displacement in Aleppo, the default presumption and dominant narrative were that post-siege evacuations in Syria were strictly a humanitarian imperative and unrelated to analysis of war crimes. The Syria Commission's finding therefore had significant impact on the discourse surrounding the conflict, including subsequent agreement from the

65. *Id.*, ¶¶ 24 and 30.

66. *Id.*, ¶ 31. On the logic of coordinated population transfers in Syria, *see* Yousuf Syed Khan, *Pandemic of Hunger Symposium: Population Transfers and the Civilian Toll of Starvation as a Method of Warfare in Syria and South Sudan*, Opinio Juris (May 20, 2021), http://opiniojuris.org/2021/05/20/pandemic-of-hunger-symposium-population-transfers-and-the-civilian-toll-of-starvation-as-a-method-of-warfare-in-syria-and-south-sudan; *see also Syria Sieges paper*, *supra* note 41.

67. Commentary on the Additional Protocols of 8 June 1977 to the Geneva Conventions of 12 August 1949, ¶ 4854 (Yves Sandoz, Christophe Swinarski, & Bruno Zimmermann eds., 1987). Though Syria is not a State party to APII, the majority of APII rules reflect CIL.

68. *See* ICRC Customary Rules, *supra* note 29, at rr. 129(B) and 156.

69. Syria CoI Aug. 2017 report, *supra* note 61, ¶ 35 and n. 3.

70. As of April 2023.

71. Syria CoI Aleppo report, *supra* note 42, ¶ 93 and *id.*, ¶ 35.

highest echelons within the United Nations. One month after the Commission's finding was made public, the UN Secretary-General stated:

> The United Nations has not been involved in the negotiations or evacuations around such [local] agreements, which do not appear to meet international legal standards or adhere to humanitarian principles. The United Nations has repeatedly expressed its concern at any local agreement that is preceded by the decimation of an area and results in the forced displacement of some parts of the civilian population. I would like to remind parties involved in such agreements that, under [IHL], the forced displacement of civilians for reasons relating to the conflict is permissible solely in order to guarantee their security or for imperative military necessity. Forced displacement for any other reason relating to the conflict is prohibited and may constitute a war crime.[72]

The same month, the UN Under-Secretary-General for Humanitarian Affairs and Emergency Relief Coordinator affirmed that the "process of evacuation [throughout Syria] must [not] be misconstrued as a positive development. These evacuations are not in line with humanitarian principles, and are not conducted in consultation with the people affected."[73] Similarly, the following November (2017), Amnesty International dedicated a thorough report to post-siege evacuations in Syria, in which it echoed the Commission's finding of forced displacement under customary IHL.[74]

B. Battlefield Detention: Displacement Camps and Unlawful Internment

Over approximately the past two decades, the number of NIACs has more than doubled,[75] and, as a corollary, there has been a marked proliferation of non-State armed groups. For UN investigative mechanisms that apply and interpret the

72. U.N. Doc. S/2017/339, ¶ 52.

73. Under-Secretary-General for Humanitarian Affairs and Emergency Relief Coordinator, Stephen O'Brien, Statement to the S.C. on the Humanitarian Situation in Syria (Apr. 27, 2017), https://www.unocha.org/sites/unocha/files/statement-and-speech/ERC_USG%20Stephen%20OBrien%20Statement%20to%20the%20SecCo%20on%20Syria%20-%2027April2017%20FINAL_0.pdf.

74. Amnesty International, Syria: "We Leave or We Die": Forced Displacement under Syria's "Reconciliation" Agreements 76 (2017), https://www.amnesty.org/en/documents/mde24/7309/2017/en.

75. ICRC, Allies, Partners and Proxies: Managing Support Relationships in Armed Conflict to Reduce the Human Cost of War 16 (Mar. 2021).

LOAC in NIAC contexts, reporting on the conduct of armed groups can raise any number of disputed or unaddressed legal issues.[76] Aside from the two UN-designated terrorist groups in Syria, namely, the Islamic State of Iraq and the Levant (ISIL)[77] and Hay'at Tahrir al-Sham,[78] one armed group that had received considerably less attention was the Syrian Democratic Forces (SDF). In response to the rise and subsequent expansion of ISIL in northern Syria in 2015, the SDF emerged by way of an alliance comprising primarily forces of the Kurdish People's Protection Units (YPG), alongside allied Arab, Assyrian, and other armed groups.[79] By late 2015, the SDF had gained control over indigenous Kurdish territory in northeast Syria along the border with the Republic of Türkiye, including in Aleppo and Raqqah governorates.[80]

As the SDF grew steadily in strength and captured territory from ISIL, they began overseeing a number of desert camps for internally displaced persons in Aleppo, Raqqah, and Hasakah governorates who had fled the previously ISIL-held territory. At the time of writing, these camps continue to comprise tens of thousands of women and children including Syrians, Iraqis, and third-State nationals.[81] Three such camps, including the sprawling and now ill-famed al-Hol camp,[82] are located in Hasakah governorate, and another two in Raqqah governorate.[83]

Beginning in May 2017, the SDF—alongside Kurdish civilian police (Asayish) and Kurdish military intelligence—conducted a systematic vetting procedure to assess the threat of women, men, and children fleeing into Kurdish-held territory from Raqqah and Dayr al-Zawr governorates, for their potential connections to ISIL. Just under a year later, in February 2018, the Syria Commission found that the civilians fleeing ISIL were forced by the SDF into the camps, amounting to de facto detention from the moment of capture.[84] The Commission concluded that the camps for internally displaced persons administered by the SDF were in fact serving

76. Sandesh Sivakumaran, *Making and Shaping the Law of Armed Conflict*, 17 CURRERNT LEGAL PROBLEMS 119, 133 (2018).

77. S.C. Res. 2170 (2014).

78. *Id.*

79. Rep. of the Independent International Commission of Inquiry on the Syrian Arab Republic, Human Rights Council, A/HRC/31/68, ¶ 11 (Feb. 11, 2016).

80. *Id.*, ¶ 30.

81. *See, e.g.*, Launch of the Global Framework for United Nations Support on Syria/Iraq Third Country National Returnees (Sept. 29, 2021), https://www.un.org/counterterrorism/events/launch-global-framework-united-nations-support-syria-iraq-third-country-national-returnees.

82. *See generally* U.N. News, *Al-Hol Camp*, https://news.un.org/en/tags/al-hol-camp.

83. Rep. of the Independent International Commission of Inquiry on the Syrian Arab Republic, Human Rights Council, A/HRC/37/72, annex III ¶ 3 (Feb. 1, 2018) [hereinafter CoI Syria Feb. 2018 report].

84. *Id.*, annex III ¶ 4.

as de facto detention facilities, and that the SDF was committing blanket unlawful internment of these internally displaced persons,[85] a conclusion it has regularly reaffirmed.[86] Specifically, the Commission established:

> In northern Raqqah and Hasakah, the [SDF] have interned 80,000 internally displaced persons in order to vet them for possible connections to ISIL. Irrespective of the legitimacy of a security threat, the blanket internment of all internally displaced persons from Raqqah and Dayr al-Zawr by the [SDF] cannot be justified. Among the civilians currently interned are women, children, the elderly and infirm, disabled persons and others who do not represent any imperative security threat and whose continued detention is manifestly unnecessary on any grounds. In many instances, the ongoing internment of those individuals amounts to arbitrary deprivation of liberty and the unlawful detention of thousands of individuals.[87]

In reaching the finding that a non-State armed group was engaging in arbitrary deprivation of liberty and unlawful detention (internment), the Commission concurred with the ICRC that "both customary and treaty [IHL] contain an inherent power to intern" during NIACs and found this "inherent power" to be applicable to armed groups.[88]

The Geneva Conventions contain over 175 rules regulating deprivation of liberty in IACs,[89] and GC IV recognizes expressly the authority of parties to IACs to detain individuals who do not benefit from prisoner-of-war privileges for security reasons.[90] During NIACs, Common Article 3 contemplates that both States and non-State actors will detain (or intern), though it is silent on the procedural principles and safeguards. As the LOAC rules governing the procedural aspects of administrative detention and the rights owed to internees in NIACs are extremely

85. *Id.*, ¶ 59 and annex III, at 27–30.

86. Most recently in February 2023. Rep. of the Independent International Commission of Inquiry on the Syrian Arab Republic, Human Rights Council, A/HRC/52/69, ¶¶ 121 and 124(a) (Feb. 7, 2023).

87. CoI Syria Feb. 2018 report, *supra* note 83, ¶ 59.

88. *See id.*, annex III, at n. 5. Notably, the most recent ICRC study of April 2023, "Detention by Non-State Armed Groups: Obligations under International Humanitarian Law and Examples of How to Implement Them," no longer refers to the existence of an "inherent power to detain" in NIACs. *Available at* https://shop.icrc.org/download/ebook?sku=4687/002-ebook. The broader debate surrounding the existence of a legal basis to detain in NIACs is beyond the scope of this section.

89. Tilman Rodenhäuser, *Strengthening IHL Protecting Persons Deprived of Their Liberty: Main Aspects of the Consultations and Discussions since 2011*, 98 International Review of the Red Cross 941, 943, 951 (2016).

90. GC IV, *supra* note 59, at arts. 41, 68, 70, 77–78, and 84.

thin, States parties to NIACs necessarily pivot to IHL, their domestic laws, and international human rights standards such as those derived from, inter alia, the International Covenant on Civil and Political Rights (ICCPR).[91]

Regarding the permissible grounds for detention for the SDF as an armed group party to a NIAC, the Commission found that internment may only be justified when absolutely necessary to address "imperative reasons of security."[92] It further stated that a case-by-case evaluation must take place in relation to every individual prior to detaining him or her, that all internees must have been informed promptly, in a language he or she understands, of the reasons for internment, and underscored the right to challenge, with the least possible delay, the lawfulness of the detention, the review of which it stated must be carried out by an independent and impartial body.[93]

On the broader application of human rights obligations to non-State actors, or armed groups, the Syria Commission adopted the position early on that non-State actors that cannot formally become parties to international human rights treaties must nevertheless respect the fundamental human rights of persons in areas where they exercise de facto control.[94] In so doing, the Commission underscored implicitly the complementary application of human rights and IHL, with LOAC applying as *lex specialis* in relation to the conduct of hostilities.[95] Aside from vague references to peremptory norms (*jus cogens*), throughout the course of its thirteen successive mandates, the Commission has never laid out the range of human rights obligations that it deems applicable to armed groups which exercise de facto control over territory.[96]

Rather, it has articulated some of these obligations on an ad hoc basis: in the case of the SDF and its finding of unlawful internment, the Commission established the SDF's manifestations of administrative control and drew on what it referred to as "core human rights obligations,"[97] in that, when conducting battlefield detention, armed groups exercising such control must respect certain minimum human rights obligations, including the rights to an adequate standard of living, which includes the rights to food and water, as well as the right to health.[98] The

91. International Covenant on Civil and Political Rights arts. 9 and 14(1), Dec. 16, 1966, 999 U.N.T.S. 171.

92. CoI Syria Feb. 2018 report, *supra* note 83, at annex III ¶ 13 (internal citations omitted).

93. *Id.*

94. *See, e.g.*, Syria CoI Aug. 2012 report, *supra* note 4, at annex II ¶ 10; Syria CoI Aleppo report, *supra* note 42, at annex I ¶ 5.

95. U.N. Doc. A/HRC/S-17/2/Add.1, ¶ 97.

96. *See generally* WILLIAM A. SCHABAS, THE CUSTOMARY INTERNATIONAL LAW OF HUMAN RIGHTS (2021); *see also* A/HRC/19/69, ¶ 106.

97. CoI Syria Feb. 2018 report, *supra* note 83, at 29, n. 8.

98. *Id.*, at annex III, at n. 9.

Commission therefore resorted to IHRL where it perhaps deemed IHL silent on a particular issue. In so doing, it relied upon the ICCPR and the UN Standard Minimum Rules for the Treatment of Prisoners, in effect applying the rubric of the "Nelson Mandela Rules" to regulate the behavior of an organized armed group engaged in civilian detention during a NIAC.[99] Moreover, the Commission relied on Inter-American Court of Human Rights (IACtHR) case law to find that the SDF could not transfer its human rights obligations onto international humanitarian aid organizations, irrespective of the SDF's "economic situation or budgetary considerations."[100] Similarly, the Commission relied on the case law of the IACtHR, European Court of Human Rights, and the African Commission on Human and Peoples' Rights to find that the SDF's failure to provide adequate food, water, and living conditions to its internees meant that the SDF, as a duty-bearer, was violating their human rights.[101]

Since the Syria Commission's finding of unlawful internment in February 2018, the camps for internally displaced persons in northeast Syria have gradually commanded the world's attention, particularly as several States had initially refused to repatriate their nationals from them.[102] Three years after the Commission's initial finding, the UN Counter-Terrorism Committee Executive Directorate,[103] Human Rights Watch,[104] Amnesty International,[105] and Médecins Sans Frontières[106] reached similar conclusions regarding the SDF interning or detaining civilians in these camps. These institutions have not, however, addressed the legal basis of the detention nor made mention of the SDF as a duty-bearer of human rights obligations.

99. *Id.*, at annex III, at nn. 8–11. The Mandela Rules are silent on whether or not they apply in times of armed conflict and focus rather on law enforcement and how States operate their regular penitentiary institutions. Rodenhäuser, *supra* note 89, at 951.

100. CoI Syria Feb. 2018 report, *supra* note 83, at annex III ¶ 16.

101. *Id.*, at annex III, at n. 11.

102. *See, e.g.*, Alessandra Spadaro, *Repatriation of Family Members of Foreign Fighters: Individual Right or State Prerogative?*, 70 International & Comparative Law Quarterly 251 (2021).

103. *CTED Analytical Brief, The repatriation of ISIL-associated children*, U.N S.C., Counter-Terrorism Committee Executive Directorate (Jan. 2021), at 3, *available at* https://www.un.org/securitycouncil/ctc/sites/www.un.org.securitycouncil.ctc/files/files/documents/2021/Jan/cted-analytical-brief-repatriation-of-children.pdf.

104. *Thousands of Foreigners Unlawfully Held in NE Syria*, Human Rights Watch (Mar. 23, 2021), https://www.hrw.org/news/2021/03/23/thousands-foreigners-unlawfully-held-ne-syria.

105. *Syria: Repatriate at Least 27,000 Children Held in Dire Conditions in North-East Syria*, Amnesty International (Nov. 30, 2021), https://www.amnesty.org/en/latest/news/2021/11/syria-repatriate-at-least-27000-children-held-in-dire-conditions-in-north-east-syria.

106. *A Lost Generation Live in Fear Inside Syria's Al-Hol Camp*, MSF (Nov. 7, 2022), https://www.msf.org/generation-lost-danger-and-desperation-syria%E2%80%99s-al-hol-camp.

Notably, in November 2022, the OHCHR also stated for the first time that, given their exercise of de facto control, the SDF had obligations "to ensure children are provided a safe and healthy environment, including access to education and recreational activities, and together with the rest of the population in the camps access to humanitarian assistance."[107] No legal basis was offered for these obligations.

Meanwhile, the operational environment in the camps remains extremely complex with both the security situation and living conditions continuously deteriorating. In both qualifying these sites as internment camps and ascribing certain minimum human rights obligations to the SDF as a duty-bearer in relation to encamped detainees whom they oversee, the Syria Commission was several years ahead of the broader international community in its legal analysis, risk assessment, and prevention through early warning. As with its findings on forced displacement, the Syria Commission has shaped the legal discourse on the issue.

IV. THE UN COMMISSION ON HUMAN RIGHTS IN SOUTH SUDAN

The HRC established the South Sudan Commission in March 2016[108] and subsequently extended its ongoing mandate seven times.[109] Fewer belligerents, no (explicit) third-State intervention, and the absence of aerial warfare has meant that it has thus far not faced the same legal issues as the Syria Commission. Having interviewed over 1,000 witnesses and victims,[110] the South Sudan Commission has nevertheless made several significant contributions to the interpretation of the LOAC.

A. Starvation as a Method of Warfare

Among the most visible of these contributions was perhaps its conference room paper dedicated to starvation as a method of warfare perpetrated by both State forces and non-State armed groups.[111] Released in October 2020, it served as the

107. *Syria: UN Human Rights Chief Condemns Brutal Killing of Two Girls, Alarmed by Sharp Rise in Violence at Al-Hol Camp* (Nov. 18, 2022), https://www.ohchr.org/en/press-releases/2022/11/syria-un-human-rights-chief-condemns-brutal-killing-two-girls-alarmed-sharp.

108. U.N. Doc. A/HRC/RES/31/20.

109. As of April 2023.

110. *UN Experts Call on South Sudan to Investigate Top Government Officials for Their Role in Sexual Violence* (Nov. 28, 2022), https://www.ohchr.org/en/press-releases/2022/11/un-experts-call-south-sudan-investigate-top-government-officials-their-role.

111. South Sudan starvation paper, *supra* note 10. The Commission first mentioned that starvation was occurring as a war crime in a NIAC in January 2020. A/HRC/43/56, ¶ 71.

first such report by a UN-mandated mechanism to deal with the prohibition of starvation in a NIAC after the amendment of Article 8 of the Rome Statute in December 2019.[112] The South Sudan Commission was thus able to make a significant contribution to the developing discussion on starvation in NIAC contexts.

At the outset, the Commission defined "starvation" and the contours of the crime of starvation as:

> [The] deprivation not just of food and water but also of other goods essential for survival in a particular context. The crime of starvation does not require that victims die from starvation, only that they should intentionally be deprived of objects indispensable to their survival. This may include depriving individuals of their ability to obtain food, degrading public health, and disrupting access to clean water, or deliberate denial of food and arbitrarily refusing to allow relief operations where the survival of the civilian population is threatened.[113]

In its factual analysis, the Commission documented how, between January 2017 and November 2018, government forces intentionally deprived Fertit and Luo communities living under the control of the opposition in Western Bahr el Ghazal State of critical resources, in acts amounting to collective punishment under customary IHL, Article 4(2)(b) of APII, and Article 4(b) of the Draft Statute of the Hybrid Court for South Sudan.[114] The Commission also found that government forces had "*deliberately* and systematically attacked, destroyed, and rendered useless objects indispensable to the survival of the civilian population in Jonglei State"[115] as an instrument to target and punish non-aligning communities, citing Rule 54 of the ICRC CIHL Study and Article 18(2) of APII as being applicable in the South Sudan context. Noting that the Rome Statute criminalizes "*intentionally* using starvation of civilians as a method of warfare," including by "willfully impeding relief supplies," the addition of the word "deliberately" by the Commission to the otherwise plain wording of Rule 54 appears to have been a way to address the intention requirement.[116]

As the ICC would likely not have subject-matter jurisdiction to consider the starvation crimes identified by the South Sudan Commission, due to the principle of non-retroactivity (*nullum crimen sine lege*),[117] nor personal jurisdiction as South Sudan is not a State party to the Rome Statute, the South Sudan Commission

112. *See* Rome Statute, *supra* note 9, at art. 8(2)(e)(xix).

113. South Sudan starvation paper, *supra* note 10, ¶ 36.

114. *Id.*, ¶ 9.

115. *Id.*, ¶¶ 123 and 146 (emphasis added).

116. Rome Statute, *supra* note 9, at art. 8(2)(e)(xix) (emphasis added).

117. *Id.*, art. 22.

further highlighted the possibility of a Security Council referral.[118] Moreover, the Commission dedicated legal analysis to the envisaged HCSS's draft statute,[119] as a Court with which it would share its underlying information and evidence, including on starvation. Overall, as with the Syria Commission, the South Sudan Commission was the first UN-mandated mechanism to consider a widened aperture through which it applied and interpreted the LOAC, and, in turn, may be credited with having a discernable impact on the conflict-related discourse.[120]

V. HRC INVESTIGATIVE MECHANISMS AND PATHWAYS TO ACCOUNTABILITY

The growing juridification of HRC investigative mechanisms is highlighted in part by the advent and proliferation of both accountability and "preservation-accountability" mandates that regularly apply and interpret the law, including the LOAC. As evidenced by their mandates and factual and legal conclusions, such bodies "can also play a crucial role in attributing criminal responsibility and laying the groundwork for subsequent prosecutions at the domestic and/or international levels."[121] The overlap in investigative and collection and preservation functions of (quasi-)accountability mandates and (quasi-)judicial bodies such as the IIIM, IIMM, and UNITAD,[122] however, raises several questions as to the role of the former in the international legal order, particularly concerning the interplay between atrocity inquiries and actionable criminal accountability. Implicit in this interplay is a tripartite spectrum of international criminal justice, where (quasi-)accountability mechanisms lie at the foot of a vertical hierarchy, beneath (quasi-)judicial mechanisms, both of which are essentially subordinated by judicial entities—be they domestic, ad hoc tribunals,[123] or the ICC.[124]

118. South Sudan starvation paper, *supra* note 10, ¶ 89.

119. *Id.*, ¶¶ 47, 94, and 145.

120. *See, e.g.*, the prominent work of Global Rights Compliance building upon the South Sudan starvation paper, including vis-à-vis an Article 15 Communication to the ICC: https://globalrightscompliance.com/wp-content/uploads/2022/11/FINAL-No-Choice-But-To-Flee-NO-EDIT.pdf.

121. Philip Alston & Sarah Knuckey, *The Transformation of Human Rights Fact-Finding: Challenges and Opportunities*, *in* THE TRANSFORMATION OF HUMAN RIGHTS FACT-FINDING 3, 7 (Philip Alston & Sarah Knuckey eds., 2016).

122. *See supra* note 11.

123. The creation of an ad hoc tribunal based on the preparatory work of UN investigative mechanisms is not always realistic nor suitable. Micaela Frulli, *Fact-Finding or Paving the Road to Criminal Justice?: Some Reflections on United Nations Commissions of Inquiry*, 10 JOURNAL OF INTERNATIONAL CRIMINAL JUSTICE 1323, 1328 (2012).

124. On the improbability of S.C. referrals to the ICC, *see, e.g.*, *supra* note 17.

It has been noted that "international criminal investigators and prosecutors cannot afford to ignore information from UN human rights sources."[125] The question then turns to the probative value that may be attached to "human rights fact-finding" mechanisms that apply and interpret the law, that is, whether and to what extent their legal findings, or the evidence they collate and preserve, may be relevant or admissible for competent jurisdictions.[126] Regarding the Syria and South Sudan Commissions, both mechanisms have ongoing or envisaged cooperation with the IIIM and the HCSS, respectively. Though by no means exhaustive,[127] such relationships demonstrate how the findings reached and information or evidence collected by both an accountability and a "preservation-accountability" mechanism may ultimately be drawn upon in practice.

As noted earlier, the growing trend of "preservation-accountability" mechanisms tasked by the HRC began just over six years ago.[128] This nascence has meant that the relationship between atrocity inquiries and their evidence sharing remains underresearched. In the case of Syria, the IIIM's constitutive resolution specifically instructs it to "closely cooperate" with the Syria Commission.[129] With regard to bringing war crimes to trial before national courts, as of August 2020, the Syria Commission has and continues to provide the IIIM with most of the information it has collected since its inception and by contacting and liaising with sources and potential witnesses.[130] For its part, as of January 31, 2023, the IIIM has received 242 requests for assistance from 15 jurisdictions and assisted 130 distinct national investigations,[131] several of which it has processed and closed.[132] The IIIM has also shared at least 23 analytical products with competent jurisdictions, including with national war crimes units in support of ongoing investigations.[133]

125. Lyal S. Sunga, *Can International Criminal Investigators and Prosecutors Afford to Ignore Information from United Nations Human Rights Sources?*, *in* Quality Control in Fact-Finding 375, 416 (Morten Bergsmo & Carsten Stahn eds., 2d ed. 2020).

126. *See generally* Carsten Stahn & Dov Jacobs, *Human Rights Fact-finding and International Criminal Proceedings: Towards a Polycentric Model of Interaction*, Grotius Centre Working Paper 2014/017-ICL, Leiden Law School Research Paper (Jan. 31, 2014).

127. The Syria Commission "has [also] provided information directly to the national prosecution authorities of third-party State national jurisdictions for over 60 national criminal investigations . . . comprising more than 300 discrete requests . . . ." *See* Rep. of the Independent International Commission of Inquiry on the Syrian Arab Republic, Human Rights Council, A/HRC/46/54, ¶ 89 (Jan. 21, 2021) [hereinafter Syria CoI Jan. 2021 report].

128. U.N. Doc. A/HRC/RES/34/25, ¶ 16(b).

129. U.N. Doc. A/RES/71/248, ¶ 4.

130. U.N. Doc. A/75/311, ¶ 13; *see also* U.N. Doc. A/77/751, ¶ 11.

131. U.N. Doc. A/77/751, ¶ 4.

132. U.N. Doc. A/76/690, ¶ 34.

133. *Id.*, ¶ 35.

In addition to cooperating with the IIIM and sharing most of its information, the Syria Commission's reports have themselves been relied upon by national jurisdictions. For example, on February 24, 2021, in a landmark verdict and the first of its kind to convict a Syrian government official for committing crimes under international law, the Higher Regional Court in Koblenz, Germany, sentenced a Syrian security officer to four-and-a-half years in prison for perpetrating crimes against humanity in aiding and abetting the torture of detained protesters in Damascus. Three reports released by the Syria Commission in 2011 and 2012 were reportedly read into evidence during the trial.[134] While the Syria Commission has further asserted that its "reports have also been used as evidence in numerous other proceedings,"[135] it has not provided further information publicly.

Regarding the South Sudan Commission, and in line with its "preservation-accountability" mandate to clarify responsibility for alleged IHRL violations and abuses and related crimes, and to collect and preserve evidence for future accountability purposes, it has compiled case files and dossiers on at least 142 individuals who it deems "warrant further investigation."[136]

The standards of proof employed by HRC investigative mechanisms are not suited to judicial evidentiary standards.[137] The reports by atrocity inquiries specifically—as potential sources of information and evidence—are not generally relevant or admissible in criminal proceedings, pursuant to their laxer evidentiary rules and lower standard of proof. Indeed, as commented by Judge Ušacka of the ICC, their legal conclusions "may be relevant only by analogy."[138] Therefore, the information and evidence gathered by these mechanisms may be most valuable when used contextually—for example, to identify patterns and the possible objectives underlying criminal conduct.

As it concerns shaping and influencing the LOAC, beyond simply applying and interpreting it publicly, when HRC mechanisms share their underlying information with (quasi-)judicial bodies and/or courts, where appropriate,[139] the underlying information "shows their work" and can serve as a rubric for how the HRC

134. *See* Syria CoI Jan. 2021 report, *supra* note 127, ¶ 89.

135. *Id.*

136. Yasmin Sooka, Chair of the Commission on Human Rights in South Sudan, Statement to the Human Rights Council (Mar. 18, 2022), https://www.ohchr.org/en/statements/2022/03/statement-yasmin-sooka-chair-commission-human-rights-south-sudan-human-rights.

137. *See supra* section II.B.

138. Prosecutor v. Al Bashir, Case No. ICC-02/05–01/09, Pre-Trial Chamber I, Decision on the Prosecution's Application for a Warrant of Arrest against Omar Hassan Ahmad Al Bashir, Separate and Partially Dissenting Opinion of Judge Anita Ušacka, ¶ 6 (Mar. 4, 2009) (internal citations omitted).

139. *E.g.*, subject to the informed consent of each individual and in accordance with confidentiality measures ensuring source protection.

mechanism had viewed the elements of crimes and therefore how it viewed application of the LOAC. Upon receiving this underlying information and evidence, and in particular interviews conducted during investigations, judicial verdicts may later be reached relying on this information. Through judicial decisions and their status as subsidiary means for the determination of rules of law,[140] it is by sharing their underlying work that atrocity inquires have the potential to shape and influence the LOAC more concretely.

VI. CONCLUSION

Having witnessed a rapid rise since 2006, the work of HRC investigative mechanisms has clearly made contributions to the development of the LOAC. Contributions of the Syria Commission include clarifications around forced displacement and unlawful internment by armed groups during NIACs. Similarly, the South Sudan Commission has contributed significantly to interpreting the prohibition of starvation as a method of warfare in a NIAC.

Moreover, UN-mandated mechanisms, and particularly those with accountability and "preservation-accountability" mandates, serve as a credible and complementary response to international criminal processes[141] and can lay the necessary groundwork for future accountability. Despite the myriad difficulties associated with adjudicating battlefield evidence,[142] the reports of HRC investigative mechanisms and their underlying information and evidence, have and can continue to support criminal accountability. They can serve as a basis to nurture prosecutorial interest at the domestic level, including pursuant to the principle of universal jurisdiction.[143] In this way, beyond applying and interpreting the LOAC, through cooperating and sharing their underlying information and evidence, their work may ultimately lead, albeit indirectly, to making and shaping of the law, especially if and when judicial decisions rely on the investigative mechanism's information and evidence. With the Syria and South Sudan Commissions, this exercise has primarily entailed cooperation with the (quasi-)judicial IIIM, and packaging information and evidence for anticipated cooperation with the envisaged HCSS, respectively.

140. Statute of the International Court of Justice art. 38, June 26, 1945, 59 Stat. 1055, 33 U.N.T.S. 993.

141. Larissa van den Herik, *Accountability Through Fact-finding: Appraising Inquiry in the Context of Srebrenica*, 62 NETHERLANDS INTERNATIONAL LAW REVIEW 295, 310 (2015).

142. *See, e.g.*, U.N. Human Rights Special Procedures, *Position of the UN Special Rapporteur on the promotion and protection of human rights and fundamental freedoms while countering terrorism on the use of "Battlefield" or military produced evidence in the context of investigations or trials involving terrorism offences* (Apr. 2021), https://www.ohchr.org/sites/default/files/Documents/Issues/Terrorism/SR/UNSRCT_Position_Battlefield-evidence-2021.pdf.

143. *See, e.g.*, BASSIOUNI, *supra* note 18, at 942.

The reports prepared by atrocity inquiries "are often considered the highlights of the [HRC] session and the subject of intense media reporting with specific focus on their conclusions."[144] It has been rightly observed that "the harshest criticised reports have been the ones that featured questions of law and fact related to international crimes within the findings."[145] As the examples in this chapter demonstrate, both the Syria and South Sudan Commissions have reported on IHRL and IHL violations and war crimes that may have otherwise been overlooked or insufficiently documented. In doing so, they have also shaped the discourse surrounding those violations and crimes. As noted by Dapo Akande and Hannah Tonkin, "[i]n the absence of any court that has compulsory and universal jurisdiction with respect to the determination of violations of human rights, IHL and other rules of international law, international commissions of inquiry may be one of the best ways of obtaining authoritative pronouncements on these legal issues."[146]

144. TISTOUNET, *supra* note 2, at 17.

145. D'Alessandra, *supra* note 30, at 70 (emphasis removed) (citing Alston & Knuckey, *supra* note 121, at 5).

146. Dapo Akande & Hannah Tonkin, *International Commissions of Inquiry: A New Form of Adjudication?*, EJIL:TALK! (Apr. 6, 2012), https://www.ejiltalk.org/international-commissions-of-inquiry-a-new-form-of-adjudication.

12

Non-State Armed Groups, Law-Making, and the Shaping of International Law in Armed Conflict

EZEQUIEL HEFFES*

I. INTRODUCTION

International organizations, the humanitarian community, scholars, and States are well aware that non-State armed groups (NSAGs) are involved in the majority of armed conflicts and this has humanitarian consequences for civilian populations.[1] It is also widely acknowledged that these non-State entities present specific challenges for the application of international humanitarian law (IHL) in non-international armed conflicts (NIACs)[2]—or at least some of the rules

* Ezequiel Heffes is the Director of Watchlist on Children and Armed Conflict in New York. The author would like to thank Katharine Fortin and Ioana Cismas for their feedback on earlier versions. This chapter has been written in his personal capacity and in no way represents the views of any institution.

1. The ICRC recently recognized that "the number of armed groups that are of humanitarian concern has remained consistently between 500–600 over the last three years." Matthew Bamber-Zryd, *ICRC Engagement with Armed Groups in 2022*, ICRC Humanitarian Law & Policy Blog (2023), https://blogs.icrc.org/law-and-policy/2023/01/12/icrc-engagement-armed-groups-2022/. In 2022, the same organization had noted that 100 NSAGs were parties to armed conflicts. Bruno Demeyere, *Editorial*, 102 International Review of the Red Cross 979, 679 (2021).

2. The International Criminal Tribunal for the former Yugoslavia (ICTY) has noted that there is a NIAC "wherever there is [. . .] protracted armed violence between governmental authorities

Ezequiel Heffes, *Non-State Armed Groups, Law-Making, and the Shaping of International Law in Armed Conflict* In: *Making and Shaping the Law of Armed Conflict*. Edited by: Sandesh Sivakumaran and Christian R. Burne, Oxford University Press.
 DOI: 10.1093/oso/9780197775134.003.0012

pertaining to this legal regime[3]—and that there is a need for greater engagement to increase their knowledge and understanding of, and respect for, this body of law.[4] A growing number of publications also describe how NSAGs deal with individuals living in territories under their control, a dynamic described as "rebel governance"[5] and how they may be bound by regimes different to IHL, notably international human rights law (IHRL).[6]

In spite of this exponential interest, the impact of NSAGs on the shaping of the law of armed conflict seems to have been overlooked. This is despite the fact that non-State actors (NSAs) more broadly have played active roles in influencing, to various degrees, the ways in which IHL is understood, how other NSAs and States apply the rules contained therein, and how this normative framework has continued to develop, evolve, and interact with other sets of rules.[7] The International Committee of the Red Cross (ICRC), for instance, has promoted the conclusion of international treaties and identified customary IHL rules. Nongovernmental organizations (NGOs) have publicly advocated for the respect of IHL and IHRL in

and organized armed groups or between such groups within a State." Prosecutor v. Dusko Tadić a/k/a "Dule," Decision on the Defence Motion for Interlocutory Appeal on Jurisdiction, IT-94-1-T, T.Ch. II 70 (1995).

3. Geneva Call has published various reports in this regard. *See, e.g.*, GENEVA CALL, *Administration of Justice by Armed Non-State Actors. Report from the 2017 Garance Talks* (2018), https://www.genevacall.org/wp-content/uploads/2023/06/GaranceTalks_Issue02_Report_2018_web-1.pdf ; GENEVA CALL, *Conduct of Hostilities by Armed Non-State Actors. Report from the 2020 Garance Talks* (2020), https://www.genevacall.org/wp-content/uploads/2023/06/Garance-Series-Issue-3.pdf .; GENEVA CALL, *Positive Obligations of Armed Non-State Actors: Legal and Policy Issues. Report from the 2015 Garance Talks* (2016), https://www.genevacall.org/wp-content/uploads/2023/06/GaranceTalks_Issue01_Report.pdf .

4. *See generally* ICRC, *ICRC Engagement with Non-State Armed Groups: Why, How, for What Purpose, and Other Salient Issues*, ICRC POSITION PAPER (2021), https://www.icrc.org/sites/default/files/wysiwyg/Activities/Humanitarian-diplomacy/icrc_engagement_with_non-state_armed_groups_position_paper.pdf.

5. Fortin has defined this as "the manner in which an insurgent group regulates life within a defined territory and provides public services." KATHARINE FORTIN, THE ACCOUNTABILITY OF ARMED GROUPS UNDER HUMAN RIGHTS LAW 40 (2017). *See also* ZACHARIAH CHERIAN MAMPILLY, REBEL RULERS: INSURGENT GOVERNANCE AND CIVILIAN LIFE DURING WAR (2011).

6. FORTIN, *supra* note 5; DARAGH MURRAY, HUMAN RIGHTS OBLIGATIONS OF NON-STATE ARMED GROUPS (2016); TILMAN RODENHÄUSER, ORGANIZING REBELLION: NON-STATE ARMED GROUPS UNDER INTERNATIONAL HUMANITARIAN LAW, HUMAN RIGHTS LAW AND INTERNATIONAL CRIMINAL LAW (2018); EZEQUIEL HEFFES, DETENTION BY NON-STATE ARMED GROUPS UNDER INTERNATIONAL LAW (2022).

7. Ezequiel Heffes, Marcos D. Kotlik, & Manuel J. Ventura, *Introduction: The Functions and Interactions of Non-State Actors in the Realm of International Humanitarian Law*, *in* INTERNATIONAL HUMANITARIAN LAW AND NON-STATE ACTORS 1, 10 (Ezequiel Heffes, Marcos D. Kotlik, & Manuel J. Ventura eds., 2020).

armed conflict and directly engaged with States and NSAGs to increase their level of compliance with the law. International judicial and quasi-judicial bodies, notably the UN Commissions of Inquiry and Panels of Experts, have also interpreted and applied international law in armed conflict. NSAGs have also been involved in these normative dynamics, at least to some extent.

Evidently, given the current State-centric system, coupled with the unlawful nature of NSAGs under States' domestic law, the capacity of these non-State entities to fully participate in the creation of international law is still not recognized.[8] Indeed, such entities are actively prevented from becoming parties to international treaties, at least from a traditional perspective,[9] and their behavior does not constitute "practices" for the purposes of creating a customary rule.[10] This, however, does not necessarily mean that NSAGs are excluded from *every* process with a normative value. As this chapter shows, NSAGs do participate in such activities, either on their own or with the support of external entities such as the ICRC, Geneva Call, and the United Nations. Drawing on concrete examples, the following pages argue that these activities actually shape the legal landscape in which NSAGs operate and that these entities are not merely passive observers but actual participants in such interactive processes.

The analysis as presented in this chapter is structured as follows. Section II presents the different law-making endeavors in which NSAGs play an active role. It identifies and examines two types of process: (1) "domestic" law-making efforts which take the form of NSAGs' laws and other regulations addressing the activities of their own fighters, individuals living in territories under their control, and even their enemies; and (2) "quasi-international" law-making efforts that include, for instance, the conclusion of agreements by NSAGs with third parties and the adoption of other normative tools with the support of humanitarian and international organizations. Section III discusses how these law-making activities shape the applicable law in NIACs. It explores two scenarios, focusing first on *small-scale* effects in specific armed conflicts, and then on *large-scale* ones vis-à-vis the

8. This is despite the fact that efforts have been made within the legal literature to push for a more inclusive environment. In this regard, *see* Marco Sassòli, *How Will International Humanitarian Law Develop in the Future?*, 104 International Review of the Red Cross 2052, 2072–2076 (2022); Annyssa Bellal & Ezequiel Heffes, *"Yes, I Do": Binding Armed Non-State Actors to IHL and Human Rights Norms through Their Consent*, 12 Human Rights & International Legal Discourse 120 (2018).

9. Although the Vienna Convention on the Law of Treaties recognizes that there may be agreements concluded between States and "other subjects of international law or between such other subjects of international law, it defines 'treaty' as an international agreement concluded between States in written form and governed by international law, whether embodied in a single instrument or in two or more related instruments and whatever its particular designation." Vienna Convention on the Law of Treaties 1969, 1155 U.N.T.S. 331, art. 1(a).

10. This has been explicitly acknowledged in the ICRC Customary IHL Study. *See* Customary International Humanitarian Law, xlii (Jean-Marie Henckaerts & Louise Doswald-Beck eds., 2005).

broader international legal architecture. The first scenario evaluates how some of the normative processes highlighted in section II have been used in specific NIACs to bring into force previously non-applicable provisions and thereby alter the regulation of the activities of the parties to the conflict. The second scenario extends beyond the IHL realm (and also the dynamics of specific armed conflicts) to assess how NSAGs' law-making efforts have influenced views related to the application of IHRL to these non-State entities. Although this is still disputed in certain circles,[11] various international institutions and scholars have made reference to NSAGs' normative practices and commitments in this field and even encourage their adoption of legal frameworks to ensure that IHRL is respected. The concluding remarks of this chapter are presented in section IV.

II. NON-STATE ARMED GROUPS' LAW-MAKING ACTIVITIES: DOMESTIC AND QUASI-INTERNATIONAL EFFORTS

As is the case with other entities in the international realm, NSAGs often make statements related to their ideology, goals, justification for the use of force, and other aspects concerned with their own existence. They also adopt legal frameworks regulating the activities of their own fighters and the individuals living in territories under their control, and even criminalize the behavior of enemy fighters. Contrary to commonly held perceptions, NSAGs are sometimes able to offer a degree of stability, subjecting people to their laws and regulations and acting as de facto authorities. In numerous NIACs, these actors have also concluded agreements with States, other NSAGs, and international and humanitarian actors. Some of these documents have included explicit commitments to apply a set of international rules.[12] This section examines the various forms these law-making activities have taken, distinguishing between those adopted by the groups themselves, which are categorized for the purposes of this chapter as "domestic" normative efforts, and those involving other parties (e.g., States, international organizations, international NGOs, and even other NSAGs), which are classified as "quasi-international."[13]

11. The ICRC has noted, in this sense, that "[t]he question whether and to what extent human rights law applies to non-State armed groups is not settled." ICRC, COMMENTARY ON THE FIRST GENEVA CONVENTION. CONVENTION (I) FOR THE AMELIORATION OF THE CONDITION OF THE WOUNDED AND SICK IN ARMED FORCES IN THE FIELD 517 (2016).

12. Ezequiel Heffes & Marcos D. Kotlik, *Special Agreements as a Means of Enhancing Compliance with IHL in Non-international Armed Conflicts: An Inquiry into the Governing Legal Regime*, 96 INTERNATIONAL REVIEW OF THE RED CROSS 1195, 1198 (2014).

13. Of course, NSAGs' law-making activities could be categorized in different ways, for example, differentiated according to their content (i.e., whether they deal with purely local matters, with international law or both), and not based on the actors involved in their process of adoption. In

A. Non-State Armed Groups' "Domestic" Law-Making Activities

When evaluating "domestic" law-making endeavours of NSAGs, it is important to leave aside the idea that the adoption of rules regulating certain activities, such as those of civilians living in a given territory, is the exclusive prerogative of States. Certainly, the predominant State-centric system of international law presents obstacles in this regard, as these "domestic" law-making prerogatives are inherently related to the attributes of sovereignty.[14]

Lawyers and anthropologists have nonetheless examined the existence and adoption of norms prevailing in groups within States since at least the late 1960s under the heading of "legal pluralism," a school of thought that offers relevant tools for the study of "domestic" law-making activities of NSAG. According to Margaret Davies, "legal pluralism" claims that "in any one geographical space defined by the conventional boundaries of a nation state, there is more than one 'law' or legal system."[15] Based on this understanding, René Provost has argued that NSAGs' legal frameworks appear as "legal pluralism incarnate."[16] Recent discussions in the context of the administration of justice by NSAGs in the IHL, IHRL, and international criminal law (ICL) realms seem to support such views,[17] with the ICRC stating that NSAGs' laws could be used by these non-State entities to establish "regularly constituted" courts.[18]

There are two "domestic" law-making activities that are frequently undertaken by NSAGs. The first of these is the adoption of written documents that are similar to States' laws. Their passage is designed to regulate the everyday life of

any case, it should be noted that several NSAGs' "domestic" law-making processes have been supported by external actors.

14. James Crawford, Brownlie's Principles of Public International Law 448 (8th ed. 2012).

15. Margaret Davies, *Legal Pluralism*, *in* The Oxford Handbook of Empirical Legal Research 805, 805 (Peter Cane & Herbert M. Kritzer eds., 2010).

16. René Provost, Rebel Courts: The Administration of Justice by Armed Insurgents 12 (2021).

17. The 2004 UK Manual of the Law of Armed Conflict also considers that the word "law" contained in Article 6 of the 1977 Additional Protocol II could also be wide enough to cover "laws" passed by an insurgent authority. UK Ministry of Defence, *The Joint Service Manual of the Law of Armed Conflict*, 404, fn. 94 (2004), https://assets.publishing.service.gov.uk/government/uploads/system/uploads/attachment_data/file/27874/JSP3832004Edition.pdf. Similarly, the Commentary to the same Protocol II affirms "the possible co-existence of two sorts of national legislation, namely, that of the State and that of the insurgents." Commentary on the Additional Protocols of 8 June 1977 to the Geneva Conventions of 12 August 1949, at 1339 (Yves Sandoz, Christophe Swinarski, & Bruno Zimmermann eds., 1987).

18. icrc, *supra* note 11, at 692. *See also* Heffes, *supra* note 6, at 170–72.

individuals living in territories controlled by NSAGs.[19] Numerous NSAGs, in particular those with a high degree of organization and which exercise de facto control over a territory, have promulgated laws, including penal ones, that apply to the inhabitants of those regions.[20] NSAGs have also modified and adapted rules already applicable in the territory under their control.[21] The specific law-making process as well as the sophistication of these laws varies depending on different factors, notably whether there is external support and the level of organization of the NSAG. Important determinants in regard to the latter include the existence or not of a "legislative" body of the NSAG, whether the law-making activity is undertaken by a civilian wing or military commanders, and the legal knowledge of the individual(s) leading the process. These factors will also be influenced by the NSAG's goals, objectives, and the moment in which they are adopted. As is the case with States during NIACs, the "domestic" law-making activities of NSAGs and their content respond to social processes and conflict realities that are dynamic in nature.

There are several examples of NSAGs enacting domestic laws. In Colombia, the *Fuerzas Armadas Revolucionarias de Colombia–Ejército del Pueblo* (FARC-EP) enacted laws on issues such as taxation and "administrative corruption."[22] In Nepal, the Communist Party of Nepal-Maoist (CPN-M) had its own "wartime and transitional" comprehensive public legal code, which covered civil provisions as well as penal ones.[23] In Syria, the Autonomous Administration of North-East Syria adopted a Charter of the Social Contract in 2014, which was later reformed in 2016, and enacted various laws to be applied in the territory under its control,[24] including to criminalize the activities of enemy

19. As Sivakumaran has explained, "just as states enact legislation, so too do armed groups." Sandesh Sivakumaran, *Lessons for the Law of Armed Conflict from Commitments of Armed Groups: Identification of Legitimate Targets and Prisoners of War*, 93 International Review of the Red Cross 463, 467 (2011). *See also* sandesh sivakumaran, the law of non-international armed conflict 140 (2012).

20. heffes, *supra* note 6, at 179.

21. Prosecutor v. Omar Haisam Sakhanh, 31 (2017), https://casebook.icrc.org/case-study/swedensyria-can-armed-groups-issue-judgments (last visited May 22, 2020). *See also* Katharine Fortin, *The Procedural Right to a Remedy When the State Has Left the Building? A Reflection on Armed Groups, Courts and Domestic Law*, 14 Journal of Human Rights Practice 387, 400 (2022).

22. FARC-EP, *Ley 002: Sobre la Tributación*, 002 (2000), http://www.cedema.org/ver.php?id=4354; FARC-EP, *Ley 003: Sobre la Corrupción Administrativa*, 003 (2000), http://www.cedema.org/ver.php?id=7956.

23. Jonathan Somer, *Jungle Justice: Passing Sentence on the Equality of Belligerents in Non-international Armed Conflict*, 89 International Review of the Red Cross 655, 681 (2007); Sivakumaran, The Law of Non-international Armed Conflict, *supra* note 19, at 140.

24. Charter of the social contract in Rojava (Syria).

forces[25] and to regulate the "freedom of opinion and expression" and activities of the media.[26] In Sri Lanka, the Liberation Tigers of Tamil Eelam (LTTE) also engaged in a process of parallel State building,[27] which consisted of enacting the Tamil Eelam Penal and Civil codes, based on a mix of Sri Lankan, Indian, and British law.[28] Importantly, some of these laws include explicit references to international law. For example, through the aforementioned Charter of the Social Contract and its subsequent version, the 2016 Social Contract of the Democratic Federation of Northern Syria, the administration pledged to respect various IHRL safeguards.[29]

The second "domestic" law-making endeavor undertaken by NSAGs consists of the development of internal codes of conduct and other rules.[30] Such efforts are undertaken to address and regulate the behavior and interactions of their members with civilians and enemy fighters. Numerous examples have been collected,[31] and Olivier Bangerter has suggested on the basis of available evidence that "codes of conduct are the internal regulations most commonly used by armed groups to shape the behaviour of their members."[32] The FARC-EP's political and military activities were indeed ruled by three internal documents: the Statute (*Estatuto*), the Rules of the Disciplinary Regime, and the Internal Rules of Command.[33] It has also been reported that the Taliban issued its first *Layha* in 2006 to "control fighter behaviour and begin to build clear command structures and normative boundaries

25. Democratic Autonomous Administration of Rojava, *Translation: North and East Syria's Anti-Terrorism Act Used to Try Local ISIS Suspects* (2014), https://rojavainformationcenter.com/2020/05/translation-north-and-east-syrias-anti-terrorism-act-used-to-try-local-isis-suspects/ (last visited Nov. 20, 2020).

26. General Council of the Autonomous Administration of North and East Syria, *Media Law of the Autonomous Administration of North and East Syria* (2021), https://rojavainformationcenter.com/storage/2021/07/Media-Law-2021.pdf (last visited Jan. 31, 2023).

27. Kristian Stokke, *Building the Tamil Eelam State: Emerging State Institutions and Forms of Governance in LTTE-controlled Areas in Sri Lanka*, 27 Third World Quarterly 1021, 1022 (2006).

28. *Thamil Eelam Judiciary Said a Basis for Rebuilding Northeast*, TamilNet, Oct. 30, 2003, https://www.tamilnet.com/art.html?artid=10277 (last visited May 22, 2020).

29. Heffes, *supra* note 6, at 195.

30. This chapter does not differentiate between codes of conduct and other internal regulations for the purposes of examining NSAGs' "domestic" law-making activities. These sources can nonetheless be differentiated for operational purposes. *See* Olivier Bangerter, Internal Control: Codes of Conduct within Insurgent Armed Groups 9–10 (2012).

31. Bangerter, *supra* note 30.

32. *Id.* at 10.

33. Heffes, *supra* note 6, at 205–06.

as the movement gained greater military capacity and presence."[34] The text of the *Layha* would be later modified in consultation with scholars, muftis, experts, and specialists,[35] with new editions (2009 and 2010) incorporating "policies and directives on a range of new issues, from taxation to education to the execution of 'spies,'"[36] thus adopting the form of a "values-based operational framework" instead of a simple code of conduct.[37] In Mali, the *Mouvement National de Libération de l'Azawad* (MNLA) drafted a military code of conduct in 2012 that "affirms the basic rules of warfare to which MNLA soldiers must abide,"[38] guiding the group's fighters on "the standards and behaviour that must be respected."[39] Interestingly, some NSAGs have developed their own codes of conduct based on other groups' norms. For example, the Revolutionary United Front (RUF) of Sierra Leone, the National Resistance Army (NRA) of Uganda, the New People's Army (NPA) of the Philippines, the CPN-M in Nepal, and the Naxalities in India all have (or have had) internal codes based on the Three Main Rules of Discipline and Eight Points for Attention of the Chinese People's Liberation Army.[40] Other NSAGs, such as the *Conseil National de Libération* of the Democratic Republic of the Congo (DRC), have adapted these rules to their own realities.[41]

Importantly, NSAGs' codes of conduct and other internal regulations may draw exclusively from international legal rules, or incorporate other frameworks, such as local traditions, religious,[42] or cultural

34. Ashley Jackson & Rahmatullah Amiri, *From Words to Deeds: A Study of Armed Non-State Actors' Practice and Interpretation of International Humanitarian and Human Rights Norms: The Taliban-Afghanistan*, 14 (2022), https://words2deeds.org/wp-content/uploads/2022/09/Taliban_Case-Study.pdf.

35. Muhammad Munir, *The Islamic Emirate of Afghanistan. The Layha [Code of Conduct] for Mujahids*, 93 International Review of the Red Cross 103, 85 (2011).

36. Jackson & Amiri, *supra* note 34, at 15.

37. *Id.*

38. Pascal Bongard, *From Words to Deeds: A Research Study of Armed Non-State Actors' Practice and Interpretation of International Humanitarian and Human Rights Norms. The National Movement for the Liberation of Azawad (Mouvement National de Libération de l'Azawad, MNLA), Mali*, 14 (2021), https://words2deeds.org/wp-content/uploads/2021/07/Case-Study-MNLA.pdf.

39. *Id.* Interestingly, the code was drafted by lawyers, who were mandated by MNLA for several activities related to international law. *Id.*

40. Bangerter, *supra* note 30 at 70.

41. *Id.*

42. On the influence of religious values on parties to armed conflict, including NSAGs, *see* Ioana Cismas et al., *Considerations and Guidance for the Humanitarian Engagement with Religious Leaders* (2023), https://static1.squarespace.com/static/5e624fe7ac1bea36a064929c/t/63c532089f167c409eb8649e/1673867787947/Religious+Leaders+%26+Humanitarian+Norms_Considerations+and+Guidance.pdf.

elements,[43] some of which may have a more direct effect on these entities' members than international legal rules. As is the case with NSAGs' laws, the process through which these sources are adopted is dynamic in nature, and groups may modify their content depending on social interactions and conflict realities.

B. Non-State Armed Groups' "Quasi-International" Law-Making Activities

In addition to their "domestic" endeavors, NSAGs have also been involved in certain law-making activities categorized for the purposes of this chapter as "quasi-international" in nature. Such classification relates to the actors involved and the framework under which they are undertaken. As a caveat, these "quasi-international" activities should not be equated with the possible participation of NSAGs in the creation of international law, an issue that remains beyond the scope of this chapter.

Broadly speaking, these law-making activities either restate IHL rules that are already applicable in a specific conflict or go beyond such legal frameworks,[44] bringing into force other international obligations. Some law-making activities have been encouraged or facilitated by third parties interested in ensuring compliance with the law applicable in armed conflict, notably States, international organizations, the ICRC, and humanitarian NGOs. Three such normative processes are: (1) special agreements as envisaged in Common Article 3 (CA3) of the 1949 Geneva Conventions (GCs); (2) Geneva Call's *Deeds of Commitment*; and (3) UN Action Plans dealing with child protection issues.[45] The following paragraphs will examine these examples.

As mentioned earlier, a NSAG may rely on different means to express its views on the rules applicable to them during armed conflict. Of these means, special agreements are of particular importance, as they are the only tool explicitly mentioned in the 1949 Geneva Conventions available to NSAGs and States parties to NIACs. CA3 affirms that "[t]he Parties to the conflict should further

43. ICRC, *Increasing Respect for International Humanitarian Law in Non-international Armed Conflicts*, 23 (2008), https://www.icrc.org/sites/default/files/topic/file_plus_list/0923-increasing_respect_for_international_humanitarian_law_in_non-international_armed_conflicts.pdf.

44. In NIACs, the parties' obligations include CA3, the 1977 Additional Protocol II to the GCs (taking into account its more restricted scope of application), and those rules that have over time become applicable as customary international law.

45. Of course, a historical example that could be mentioned is the one of the national liberation movements (NLMs) that were invited to participate in the negotiation and drafting of the 1977 Additional Protocols, with some of them even signing the Final Act of the Diplomatic Conference. At the Conference, NLMs were nonetheless refused voting power. This case is not further explored in this chapter as it would entail NSAGs being involved in the development of international law, which lies beyond the scope of this study.

endeavour to bring into force, by means of special agreements, all or part of the other provisions of the present Convention." These agreements have been defined as "explicit commitments between two or more parties to a NIAC to comply with certain rules of IHL, and they may be expressed in a signed document, a joint declaration, or any other form. They are essentially public expressions of a concurrent will to abide by IHL."[46] Special agreements have been concluded in numerous NIACs, including in Angola, Bosnia and Herzegovina, El Salvador, the DRC, Indonesia, Liberia, the Philippines, Sierra Leone, Somalia, and Sudan.[47] Special agreements can emphasize some rules that are already binding upon the parties that States and NSAGs may consider of relevance or in need of further reinforcement or clarification, as well as bring into force provisions that may not otherwise be applicable to that specific conflict. The ICRC has affirmed that

> [a] special agreement might either create new legal obligations by going beyond the provisions of IHL already applicable in the specific circumstances (a "constitutive" agreement), or it might simply restate the law that is already binding on the parties, independent of the agreement (a "declaratory" agreement). It may also be limited to specific rules that are particularly relevant to an ongoing conflict.[48]

Special agreements under CA3 often include both declaratory and constitutive clauses, and the process that leads to their conclusion serves to demonstrate the parties' concurrent will to comply with international law.

The second type of "quasi-international" law-making process involves a NSAG becoming a signatory to *Deeds of Commitment* under the auspices of Geneva Call.[49] This humanitarian NGO was created after members of the International Campaign to Ban Landmines (ICBL) realized that a ban on antipersonnel mines would not be effective unless NSAGs could also be persuaded to renounce

46. Heffes & Kotlik, *supra* note 12, at 1198.

47. These examples have been referred to in *id.*

48. ICRC, *supra* note 43, at 16.

49. Instead of referring to "non-State armed groups," Geneva Call uses "armed groups and *de facto* authorities" to describe the actors to be engaged. This section deliberately continues to use the term "NSAG" to avoid any confusion. For further information on Geneva Call's terminology, *see* Geneva Call, *Armed Groups and De Facto Authorities (AGDA): Geneva Call Adapts Its Engagement Terminology* (2022), https://www.genevacall.org/armed-groups-and-de-facto-authorities-agda-geneva-call-adapts-its-engagement-terminology/#:~:text=Founded%20in%202000%2C%20Geneva%20Call,offices%20in%2016%20conflict%20areas. For more information about Geneva Call and its approach, *see* Ezequiel Heffes, *Non-State Actors Engaging Non-State Actors: The Experience of Geneva Call in NIACs, in* International Humanitarian Law and Non-State Actors 427 (Ezequiel Heffes, Marcos D. Kotlik, & Manuel J. Ventura eds., 2020); Geneva Call, *How We Work*, https://www.genevacall.org/how-we-work/ (last visited Jan. 27, 2024).

their use.[50] NSAGs were not formally bound by the 1997 Convention on the Prohibition of the Use, Stockpiling, Production and Transfer of Anti-Personnel Mines and on their Destruction (Ottawa Convention) and thus necessitated a different approach. Geneva Call developed an innovative tool that would allow these non-State entities to commit to this treaty's core obligations. The *Deed of Commitment for Adherence to a Total Ban on Anti-Personnel Mines and for Cooperation in Mine Action* recognizes the importance of NSAGs' consent to international obligations and aims to develop a sense of ownership over the humanitarian rules these non-State actors undertake to respect and be held accountable for. Geneva Call has since expanded its thematic work, developing four additional Deeds: the *Deed of Commitment for the Protection of Children from the Effects of Armed Conflict* (2010), the *Deed of Commitment for the Prohibition of Sexual Violence in Situations of Armed Conflict and Towards the Elimination of Gender Discrimination* (2012), the *Deed of Commitment for the Protection of Health Care in Armed Conflict* (2018), and the *Deed of Commitment for the Prevention of Starvation and Addressing Conflict-Related Food Insecurity* (2021).[51] These five *Deeds of Commitment* mirror international rules applicable to States and include both negative and positive obligations. While some of the provisions may reflect existing obligations for NSAGs, others would otherwise not be applicable.

Crucially, the drafting process for each *Deed* involved discussions with NSAGs as well as scholars and other humanitarian organizations.[52] NSAGs were allowed to go through their content before they were adopted, discuss them with Geneva Call and provide input, through face-to-face meetings and written exchanges and based on real-life scenarios they would face on the battlefield.[53] For instance, NSAGs could inform Geneva Call if a specific provision was unclear, if it was inapplicable in their specific context, or if additional information was needed. This process sought to ensure that the final text of the *Deeds* is realistic, and thus more likely to be respected by those (and other) groups. As stated elsewhere, "[i]ncluding NSAGs' views in these processes serves as a 'reality check,' as these actors will be in charge of their implementation on the ground."[54] Since its creation,

50. Pascal Bongard & Jonathan Somer, *Monitoring Armed Non-State Actor Compliance with Humanitarian Norms: A Look at International Mechanisms and the Geneva Call Deed of Commitment*, 93 International Review of the Red Cross 673, 684–85 (2011); Heffes, *supra* note 49; Sivakumaran, The Law of Non-international Armed Conflict, *supra* note 19, at 538.

51. Geneva Call also works on other thematic areas, such as the prohibition of forced displacement and the protection of cultural heritage.

52. Ezequiel Heffes & Jonathan Somer, *Inviting Non-State Armed Groups to the Table. Inclusive Strategies towards a More Fit for Purpose International Humanitarian Law*, 8 ODI Briefing Note (2020), https://www.odi.org/sites/odi.org.uk/files/resource-documents/odi-ec-nonstatearmed grioups-briefingnote-dec20-proof01a.pdf.

53. *Id.*

54. *Id.*

Geneva Call has engaged with more than 180 NSAGs worldwide, and as of early 2023, more than 65 have signed one or more *Deeds of Commitment*.

The final illustration of NSAGs participating in a form of "quasi-international" law-making process is that of groups signing so-called UN Action Plans on child protection issues. The provisions of these Plans are rooted in IHL and IHRL, and the conclusion and subsequent implementation of the Plan can lead to the removal of the NSAG from the UN Secretary General's (UNSG's) list of actors that commit grave violations of children's rights.[55] These documents "outline specific, time-bound measures in order to comply with international law" and achieve the party's removal from the list.[56] To date, thirty-eight Action Plans have been concluded, including with twenty-seven NSAGs,[57] although they have not systematically been made public.[58]

The system was established by UN Security Council (UNSC) Resolution 1261 concerning children and armed conflict, which called on the parties to armed conflicts to respect their legal obligations. In 2001, the UNSC, through Resolution 1379, required the UNSG to submit reports to the UNSC including an annex listing parties that recruit and use child soldiers, with the goal of "naming and shaming" perpetrators.[59] In 2005, following a suggestion of the UNSG to establish a mechanism based on IHL and IHRL to monitor grave violations of children's rights,[60]

55. A UN action plan is a "written, signed commitment between the United Nations and those parties who are listed." For further information, *see* UN Office of the Special Representative of the Secretary General for Children and Armed Conflict, *Action Plans*, https://childrenandarmedconflict.un.org/tools-for-action/action-plans/#:~:text=An%20action%20plan%20is%20a,on%20Children%20and%20Armed%20Conflict (last visited Jan. 27, 2024); Marcos D. Kotlik, *Compliance with Humanitarian Rules on the Protection of Children by Non-State Armed Groups: The UN's Managerial Approach*, *in* International Humanitarian Law and Non-State Actors 387 (Ezequiel Heffes, Marcos D. Kotlik, & Manuel J. Ventura eds., 2020), http://link.springer.com/10.1007/978-94-6265-339-9_14..

56. Kotlik, *supra* note 55, at 407.

57. UN Office of the Special Representative of the Secretary General for Children and Armed Conflict, *supra* note 55.

58. Two Action Plans between the UN and NSAGs are nonetheless public, namely, between the United Nations and the Moro Islamic Liberation Front (MILF), from the Philippines, and the United Nations and the Justice and Equality Movement, from Sudan. *See* Action Plan between the Moro Islamic Liberation Front (MILF) and the United Nations in the Philippines regarding the Issue of Recruitment and Use of Child Soldiers in the Armed Conflict in Minadao (2009), http://theirwords.org/media/transfer/doc/1_ph_milf_biaf_2009_13-d74703efad5c37df5ab9842bc87e67a2.pdf; Action Plan—Operational Mechanism to Prevent and End Recruitment and Use of Child Soldiers (2012), http://theirwords.org/media/transfer/doc/sd_jem_2012_55-b4f6cb533f33a9415cc738069a0efee6.pdf.

59. Sivakumaran, The Law of Non-international Armed Conflict, *supra* note 19, at 533–34.

60. These include: (1) killing and maiming of children; (2) recruiting or using children as soldiers; (3) attacks against schools or hospitals; (4) sexual violence against children; (5) abduction of children; and (6) denial of humanitarian access. Although, as mentioned, the focus started with the prohibition of use and recruitment of children, the UNSG includes in his

the UNSC adopted Resolution 1612, allowing for the creation of the Working Group on Children and Armed Conflict. According to Andrew Clapham, "[t]he mechanism vis-à-vis the non-state actors works not only through naming and shaming, but by encouraging the armed groups to submit an 'action plan' to the Security Council. In this way, the groups can eventually be removed from the list of violators."[61]

Two conclusions can be drawn from these three examples. First, they demonstrate that the involvement of NSAGs in "quasi-international" law-making processes is accepted, at least to some degree, by various institutions, including the UNSC and States, which were responsible for the creation of the aforementioned UN framework and who also may be parties to special agreements concluded with NSAGs – this is the case, in particular, of States. Second, the content of these normative efforts is not necessarily restricted to the rules already binding upon these NSAs. Special agreements, Geneva Call's *Deeds of Commitment*, and UN Action Plans often extend beyond the applicable IHL and may contain provisions belonging to other legal frameworks, notably IHRL,[62] thereby modifying and clarifying the regulatory framework of conflicts in which those NSAGs operate.

III. HOW NSAGS' LAW MAKING ACTIVITIES SHAPE INTERNATIONAL LAW IN ARMED CONFLICT

As noted earlier, the law-making activities of NSAGs encompass both "domestic" and "quasi-international" processes. This raises the question as to whether these normative efforts affect the law of armed conflict and how it is shaped. It is useful to consider two scenarios in this regard, both of which imply that NSAGs may have an impact on the legal framework applicable to the specific NIACs in which they operate as well as on the broader international legal architecture:

reports "those parties to armed conflict that engage, in contravention of applicable international law," in violations of (1)–(5). Security Council Resolution 1882. For further information on the IHL and IHRL sources relied upon for these grave violations, *see* UN Office of the Special Representative of the Secretary General for Children and Armed Conflict, *Working Paper No. 1, The Six Grave Violations Against Children During Armed Conflict: The Legal Foundation*, https://childrenandarmedconflict.un.org/publications/WorkingPaper-1_SixGraveViolationsLegalFoundation.pdf.

61. Andrew Clapham, *Non-State Actors*, *in* International Human Rights Law 557, 573 (Daniel Moeckli, Sangeeta Shah, & Sandesh Sivakumaran eds., 3rd ed. 2018).

62. For instance, Geneva Call's *Deed of Commitment for the Protection of Children from the Effects of Armed Conflict*, through which NSAGs commit not to use and recruit children in hostilities, defines "children" as "persons under the age of 18," which is based on IHRL standards. Also, in the Action Plan signed with the United Nations, the MILF openly accepted and committed "to the obligations under International Humanitarian Law, International Human Rights Law, specifically the Optional Protocol to the Convention on the Rights of the Child (CRC) on the involvement of children in armed conflict, and relevant UN Security Council Resolutions [. . .]." Government of the Republic of the Philippines and the MILF, *supra* note 58, at 4.

(1) *NSAGs' law-making activities shape the international law applicable in specific armed conflicts.* This scenario occurs when the scope of an NSAG's normative effort is limited to the specific armed conflict to which the group is a party. These efforts could serve to restate a norm already applicable, clarify and interpret its content (thus shedding some light on the legal framework), or apply additional international legal provisions.

(2) *NSAGs' law-making activities shape broader considerations about the application of IHRL to these non-State entities.* Indeed, various institutions have made reference to the norm-development activities of an NSAG to support the view that IHRL is binding upon them. These institutions have even encouraged NSAGs to include IHRL provisions in their normative frameworks.

A. NSAGs' Law-Making Activities: Shaping the International Law in Specific NIACs

The examples included in section II show that NSAGs have been directly involved in different law-making activities. Some of these concern the regulation of their own fighters' behavior and that of the civilian population living in territories under their control. In some such instances, for example, many codes of conduct and internal regulations of NSAGs, there are no references to international law. In other instances, these actors have actively intervened in norm-development processes that included rules pertaining to various international law regimes. These processes have restated provisions already applicable to specific NIACs, such as CA3 and customary IHL, which the groups consider to be of relevance or in need of further clarification.[63] They have also brought into force rules that might otherwise not be applicable to these specific conflicts, notably from IHRL, the 1977 Additional Protocol II to the GCs (APII) (if not applicable)[64] and the 1977 Additional Protocol I (API) to the GCs, which is envisaged for application only in international armed conflicts. In doing so, these NSAGs' law-making endeavors have shaped the law applicable in those specific armed conflicts. By including bodies of law which otherwise would not apply, NSAGs have expanded the rules regulating their behavior in the respective NIACs and also, when special agreements are involved, that of States.

63. Anthea Roberts & Sandesh Sivakumaran, *Lawmaking by Nonstate Actors: Engaging Armed Groups in the Creation of International Humanitarian Law*, 37 Yale Journal of International Law 107, 149–50 (2012).

64. APII has a more restricted scope of application than CA3. It applies to those conflicts "which take place in the territory of a High Contracting Party between its armed forces and dissident armed forces and other organized armed groups which, under responsible command, exercise such control over a part of its territory as to enable them to carry out sustained and concerted military operations and to implement" APII.

Among the various law-making activities and processes that were explored, one that can be used to exemplify the application of additional international rules to specific NIACs is the case of special agreements under CA3. This is because the provision envisaging their conclusion refers explicitly to the possibility of bringing into force IHL obligations that would otherwise not apply. Special agreements may include both declaratory and constitutive clauses. The importance of the former relates to the fact that parties to a conflict, whether States and NSAGs, or exclusively NSAGs, have an opportunity to publicly express their intention to comply with existing IHL obligations.[65] For instance, the 1992 Agreement on the application of IHL between the parties to the NIAC in Bosnia-Herzegovina, concluded at the invitation of the ICRC, contained a commitment to respect and to ensure respect for CA3.[66] The 1985 Nairobi Agreement between the military government of Uganda and the National Resistance Movement noted in its Article 1(i) that CA3 was applicable, and repeated the full text of this provision in its Appendix D.[67]

By agreeing to incorporate constitutive clauses (i.e., those that go beyond the applicable IHL provisions), the parties to special agreements may decide to be bound by additional obligations, for instance, obligations from all the GCs (beyond CA3) and API. The ICRC has even stated that States and NSAGs "should be encouraged to include both treaty and customary rules."[68] They could also commit to apply rules belonging to other regimes, such as those of IHRL and weapons' law.[69] Special agreements containing these types of clauses have been concluded in Afghanistan, Angola, Liberia, the DRC, Tajikistan, and Uganda.[70] The 1991 Memorandum of

65. Heffes & Kotlik, *supra* note 12, at 1205.

66. Bosnia and Herzegovina, Agreement No. 1 of May 22, 1992, at 1, https://casebook.icrc.org/case-study/former-yugoslavia-special-agreements-between-parties-conflicts. It shall be noted that the parties also agreed to apply provisions concerning the protection of the wounded, sick, and shipwrecked, of hospitals and other medical units, and of the civilian population, the treatment of captured fighters, the conduct of hostilities, assistance to the civilian population, and respect for the Red Cross and Red Crescent emblems. It goes without saying that the 1992 Agreement did not have the expected effect of preventing violations. *See* Lindsay Moir, The Law of Internal Armed Conflict 127 (2002).

67. The Nairobi Peace Agreement (1985), http://theirwords.org/media/transfer/doc/ug_nrm_nra_1985_07-4a3f4fc1ec1f7f088e9669480d8c54ff.pdf.

68. ICRC, *supra* note 43, at 16.

69. There are different views on whether agreements including IHRL can be considered as special agreements under CA3. For an affirmative view, *see* Heffes & Kotlik, *supra* note 12. The ICRC has varied its position on this issue. Back in 2008, it noted that "[s]ome agreements between the parties to a non-international armed conflict refer to both IHL and human rights law and are therefore not common Article 3 agreements in the strict sense." ICRC, *supra* note 43 at 18. In its recent Commentary to CA3, it affirmed that special agreements "may contain obligations drawn from human rights law and help to implement humanitarian law." ICRC, *supra* note 11, at 851.

70. Heffes & Kotlik, *supra* note 12, at 1206.

Understanding between the parties to the NIAC in the former Yugoslavia is also worth mentioning, due to the multiple references to rules of the GCs and API, applicable to international armed conflicts, and the Protocol on Prohibitions or Restrictions on the Use of Mines, Booby Traps and Other Devices annexed to the 1980 Weapons Convention.[71] The 2004 Humanitarian Ceasefire Agreement on the Conflict in Darfur was supplemented by a Protocol on the Establishment of Humanitarian Assistance, through which the parties agreed to apply rules enshrined in the GCs, API, APII, and a series of IHRL instruments.[72] The 1998 Comprehensive Agreement on Respect for Human Rights and International Humanitarian Law (CARHRIHL) between the government of the Philippines and the National Democratic Front of the Philippines (NDFP) also contains a number of human rights and IHL guarantees.[73] In Sierra Leone, the parties agreed

> that the basic civil and political liberties which are recognized by the Sierra Leone legal system and are contained in the Declarations and Principles on Human Rights adopted by the United Nations and the Organization of African Unity, especially the Universal Declaration of Human Rights and the African Charter on Human and People's Rights, shall be fully guaranteed and promoted within Sierra Leone society.[74]

As can be seen, NSAGs' law-making activities can shape and affect the international law applicable in specific NIACs. This occurs in particular when these groups agree with the other parties involved, either States or other NSAGs, to expand the number of applicable binding rules, which may also include other international legal regimes, such as IHRL.

Importantly, agreements concluded within the framework of CA3 cannot be used to diminish the safeguards and obligations enshrined in that same provision. This is because, as the International Court of Justice in its *Nicaragua* judgment has asserted, CA3 constitutes "a minimum yardstick" that reflects "elementary considerations of humanity."[75] It also flows from the text of CA3, which states that

71. Yugoslavia/Croatia, Memorandum of Understanding of November 27, 1991, https://casebook.icrc.org/case-study/former-yugoslavia-special-agreements-between-parties-conflicts.

72. Protocol on the Establishment of Humanitarian Assistance in Darfur (2004), http://peacemaker.un.org/sites/peacemaker.un.org/files/SD_040408_Humanitarian%20Ceasefire%20Agreement%20on%20the%20Conflict%20in%20Darfur.pdf.

73. Comprehensive Agreement on Respect for Human Rights and International Humanitarian Law between the Republic of the Philippines and the National Democratic Front of the Philippines (1998), http://www.incore.ulst.ac.uk/services/cds/agreements/pdf/phil8.pdf.

74. Peace Agreement between the Government of the Republic of Sierra Leone and the Revolutionary United Front of Sierra Leone, 19 (1996), http://theirwords.org/media/transfer/doc/1_sl_ruf_1996_03-e377977056bb4bc499dfaa 593507511d.pdf.

75. International Court of Justice, Military and Paramilitary Activities in and against Nicaragua (Nicaragua v. United States of America), 218 (1986), https://www.icj-cij.org/public/files/case-related/70/070-19860627-JUD-01-00-EN.pdf.

"each Party to the conflict shall be bound to apply, as a minimum," this article.[76] As a result, if a special agreement were concluded, CA3 would still continue to apply, as "its rules constitute a minimum standard that protect individuals against any attempt to implement a lower threshold of protection."[77] Furthermore, the ICRC has also noted that special agreements cannot derogate from obligations under customary IHL, "nor from the provisions of Additional Protocol II where it is applicable, or other humanitarian law treaties applicable" in NIACs.[78]

B. NSAGs' Law-Making Activities and Their Impact on the International Legal Architecture

In addition to shaping the international law applicable in specific NIACs, the law-making activities of NSAGs have affected the broad international ecosystem. One example is the increase in discussions related to the application of IHRL to NSAGs' activities. It is nowadays undisputed that NSAGs have obligations under IHL and that there is no significant distinction between the applicability of this legal regime to these non-State actors and to States alike in NIACs, based on the so-called principle of equality of belligerents.[79] However, the last few decades have seen extensive debate about whether NSAGs are also bound by IHRL. Given that the wording of the main IHRL treaties addresses only States,[80] such discussions are often justified by the existence of protection gaps left by IHL, and the wider range of accountability mechanisms embedded in IHRL compared to those contained in IHL.[81] Based on these two arguments, scholars, UN bodies and agencies, the ICRC, and NGOs have proposed that, under certain circumstances, NSAGs could be bound by IHRL, or at least incur responsibilities under this legal regime.[82]

76. The ICRC has also shared this interpretation. ICRC, *supra* note 11, at 854.

77. Heffes & Kotlik, *supra* note 12, at 1209.

78. ICRC, *supra* note 11, at 854, fn. 808.

79. *Id.* at 503–04.

80. There are nonetheless two exceptions. The first is the Optional Protocol to the Convention on the Rights of the Child, which governs the involvement of children in armed conflict, and in Article 4 establishes that "[a]rmed groups that are distinct from the armed forces of a State should not, under any circumstance, recruit or use in hostilities persons under the age of 18 years." The second exception is the 2009 Convention for the Protection and Assistance of Internally Displaced Persons in Africa (Kampala Convention), whose Article 7(5) creates obligations for "armed groups."

81. Ezequiel Heffes, *International Human Rights Law and Non-State Armed Groups: The (De) Construction of an International Legal Discourse*, *in* Research Handbook on Human Rights and Humanitarian Law 265 (Robert Kolb, Gloria Gaggioli, & Pavle Kilibarda eds., 2022).

82. ICRC, *supra* note 11, at 517.

Some NSAGs have also taken an active role in this regard by incorporating explicit references to IHRL in the regulations they adopt. In so doing, they have actively influenced the perspectives of other actors operating within the international realm. Sandesh Sivakumaran has argued that the fact that agreements by NSAGs contain IHRL norms lends support to the view that they may indeed be bound by this legal regime.[83] For instance, the Special Rapporteur on the right of everyone to the enjoyment of the highest attainable standard of physical and mental health stated:

> [A]rmed groups have been held accountable for obligations voluntarily assumed through agreements, unilateral statements and monitoring systems under the Security Council [. . .], which have included both obligations to respect human rights and to protect or fulfil them where armed groups exercise the control and authority to do so. Armed groups must therefore, at the minimum, respect human rights, including the right to health, and may assume further obligations to protect or fulfill human rights.[84]

As can be observed from this, the Special Rapporteur considers the various frameworks adopted by NSAGs, and the inclusion of IHRL provisions therein, to affirm that they should indeed respect this international legal regime. He even went a step further by encouraging States to facilitate agreements on IHRL and humanitarian issues with NSAGs:

> States, civil society and international organizations have successfully facilitated agreements on human rights and humanitarian issues with non-State armed groups, including agreements to provide "days of tranquillity" for health workers to safely provide vaccinations. States should adopt, support and expand these initiatives to protect and fulfil the right to health in conflict and minimize the impact of conflict on vulnerable groups.[85]

Other special procedures have shared a similar view, also recommending that NSAGs adopt norms including IHRL. For instance, the former UN Special Rapporteur on extrajudicial, summary or arbitrary executions claimed in a 2018 report that NSAGs "can be accommodated as subjects of IHRL," and that despite not being bound by "the full range of human rights law," they have obligations

83. Sandesh Sivakumaran, *Implementing Humanitarian norms through Non-State Armed Groups*, *in* Inducing Compliance with International Humanitarian Law 125, 130 (Heike Krieger ed., 2015).

84. Anand Grover (Special Rapporteur on the Right of Everyone to the Enjoyment of the Highest Attainable Standard of Physical and Mental Health), *Report*, ¶ 57, U.N. Doc. A/68/297 (Aug. 9, 2013).

85. *Id.* at ¶ 58.

that follow a threshold "derived from the nature of their control and degree of organization, or capacity."[86] In the recommendations provided by the former Special Rapporteur, she affirmed that States should "[e]ncourage [NSAGs'] adoption of policies, practices, and codes of conduct of human rights protection," that NSAGs should "[a]dopt and implement policies, practices, and codes of conduct to protection human rights; [d]raft or contribute to the drafting of commitments," and that UN bodies should "[e]ncourage and support [NSAGs'] development of written commitments of human rights protection, including oversight monitoring mechanisms."[87] A similar position was reached in 2021 by numerous UN human rights experts.[88] In a joint statement, they highlighted the "far-reaching negative human rights impacts of [NSAGs] on rights' holders and human rights defenders," and recommended that States should "encourage the adoption by [NSAGs] of policies, practices and codes of conduct for human rights protection."[89] They also asserted that NSAGs should "implement their human rights responsibilities in their codes of conduct or other internal documents," and that "[o]ther stakeholders should [. . .] encourage and support [NSAGs] in adopting and adhering to international human rights standards."[90] Prior to this, in 2013, the Committee on the Elimination of all Forms of Discrimination against Women (CEDAW) in its General Recommendation 30 had also urged NSAGs "to commit themselves to abide by codes of conduct on human rights and the prohibition of all forms of gender-based violence."[91] Finally, the UN Special Rapporteur on the promotion of truth, justice, reparation, and guarantees of nonrecurrence recognized that the inclusion of IHRL (and IHL) in NSAGs' codes of conduct may "provide a useful framework to encourage non-State armed groups' engagement with transitional justice."[92]

These examples show that NSAGs' law-making activities in the field of IHRL are increasingly recognized and encouraged as a way to ensure respect for this

86. Agnès Callamard (Special Rapporteur on Extrajudicial, Summary or Arbitrary Executions), *Report on Armed Non-State Actors: the Protection of the Right to Life*, ¶ 19, U.N. Doc. A/HRC/38/44.

87. *Id.* at ¶¶ 20–21.

88. OHCHR, *Joint Statement by independent United Nations human rights experts on human rights responsibilities of armed non-State actors* (2021), https://www.ohchr.org/EN/NewsEvents/Pages/DisplayNews.aspx?NewsID=26797&LangID=E (last visited Feb. 26, 2021).

89. *Id.*

90. *Id.*

91. Committee on the Elimination of Discrimination against Women, *General recommendation No. 30 on women in conflict prevention, conflict and post-conflict situations*, 5 (2013), https://www.ohchr.org/sites/default/files/Documents/HRBodies/CEDAW/GComments/CEDAW.C.CG.30.pdf.

92. Fabián Salvioli (Special Rapporteur on the Promotion of Truth, Justice, Reparation and Guarantees of Non-Recurrence), *Role and Responsibilities of Non-State Actors in Transitional*

legal regime. While an assessment of these non-State entities' level of compliance with international law is beyond the scope of this chapter, it suffices to note that these views are influenced by past experiences of NSAGs incorporating IHRL into their codes of conduct, laws, and agreements, and respecting such commitments. In so doing, it is argued that NSAGs are shaping the broad international legal architecture in multiple ways. First, by shaping the public perception of themselves as duty-bearers and responsible actors, they are not being considered as entities created to exclusively conduct military operations in violation of States' domestic law. Some NSAGs provide services in the territories they control and adopt laws to regulate these activities. Second, it is argued that the content of their law-making activities has influenced the discourse related to the application of IHRL to NSAGs, as nowadays there is an increasing number of actors convinced that this is indeed the case. This exceeds the immediate circumstances of a specific law-making effort and creates a sense of expectation within the broad international architecture. Finally, these NSAGs' law-making efforts focused on IHRL may serve to take on a precedent setting role for future NSAGs on similar legal issues.

IV. CONCLUDING REMARKS

This chapter demonstrates that the law-making activities of NSAGs are shaping the international law applicable in armed conflict. The chapter first explored the various forms these activities can take and proposed a differentiation between "domestic" and "quasi-international" law-making efforts. The former category includes NSAGs' codes of conduct and laws, while the latter comprises special agreements concluded with third parties under CA3, UN Action Plans, and Geneva Call's *Deeds of Commitment*. The chapter then explored how these documents shape the legal landscape in which NSAGs operate, focusing on (1) specific NIACs, through the conclusion of special agreements; and (2) the growing view that IHRL is applicable to their actions. Interestingly, human rights bodies have encouraged NSAGs to adopt norms, including from international human rights law, and also recommended that States support these efforts.

Two final remarks are important for the purposes of this chapter. First, the armed conflict ecosystem currently consists of several entities, including States and NSAGs, which are involved in numerous law-making and law-enforcement dynamics in various settings with different degrees of (in)formality.[93] Accordingly,

Justice Processes, ¶ 20, U.N. Doc. A/HRC/51/34 (July 12, 2022). The original text, instead of referring to the "inclusion" of IHL and IHRL provisions as a way of encouraging NSAGs to engage with transitional justice processes, mentions that that their codes of conduct should be in compliance with such legal frameworks. For the purposes of this chapter, it is submitted that both should be considered in a similar manner, and the inclusion of these legal regimes can serve to indeed assess NSAGs' commitment to comply with them.

93. Heffes, Kotlik, & Ventura, *supra* note 7, at 2.

any examination of NSAGs' activities should accept that conflict-based and conflict-related scenarios are no longer exclusively State-centric in nature. NSAGs do exist and shape what individuals and entities do; they do not operate in isolation but instead are part of a wider net of players that affect and are affected by the law of armed conflict. This chapter has attempted to tackle some of these interactions. It has explained, in this regard, that some NSAGs' normative activities have been encouraged and facilitated by third parties. Second, there is always a temptation to neglect NSAGs and their norm-development process due to their unlawful domestic nature under States' law. For the millions of people living in territories under NSAGs' control, these legal regimes have often allowed them to continue with their life, sometimes without noticing that the authority in charge was not a sovereign State but a non-State entity. Although there is a commonly held view that the existence of a State provides a certain order, and that the absence of State institutions in certain territories results in chaos and disorder, this is not always the case. This observation does not attempt to romanticize NSAGs or to deny their humanitarian impact on individuals; rather, it provides a countervailing view that such situations are more complex than might be assumed, and that there is more to them than meets the eye.

PART FOUR

Spaces

13

The Role of Regionalism in the Making and Shaping of the Law of Armed Conflict

GUS WASCHEFORT*

I. INTRODUCTION

In its most acute and rare form regionalism in international law speaks to substantially self-contained regional systems of law, such as European Union law. Other less acute forms of regionalism include the development of regional human rights systems, regional security frameworks, regional treaty-based organizations, and so forth.[1] These regional arrangements share the feature that they are regionally selective not only in their development but also in membership. Less prominent, though not altogether absent, from the discussion is the impact of regionalism on international law of universal application.[2] In the international human rights law (IHRL) discourse, the tension between universality and regional particularism is a perennial debate that strikes at the very heart of the theory of human rights.[3] In contrast, the law of armed conflict (LOAC) is cast as a regime of super

* Gus Waschefort is Associate Professor at Essex Law School and Armed Conflict Hub, and Barrister at Guernica 37 Chambers, London.

1. For general discussion of regionalism in international law, *see* JÁN KLUČKA, REGIONALISM IN INTERNATIONAL LAW (2019).

2. *See, e.g.*, Michael Salter & Yinan Yin, *Analysing Regionalism within International Law and Relations: The Shanghai Cooperation Organisation as a Grossraum?*, 13 CHINESE JOURNAL OF INTERNATIONAL LAW 819 (2014).

3. For a classic contribution that defines the contours of the debate, *see* Jack Donnelly, *Cultural Relativism and Human Rights*, 6(4) HUMAN RIGHTS QUARTERLY 400 (1984).

Gus Waschefort, *The Role of Regionalism in the Making and Shaping of the Law of Armed Conflict* In: *Making and Shaping the Law of Armed Conflict*. Edited by: Sandesh Sivakumaran and Christian R. Burne, Oxford University Press.
 DOI: 10.1093/oso/9780197775134.003.0013

universality, negating regional or local study.[4] It is only recently that any regard has been paid to David Kennedy's claim that international law is "different in different places," which has resulted in a growing body of scholarship on "comparative international law."[5] Broader appreciation of this reality allows for a departure from orthodoxy and opens the possibility for greater engagement with regionalism in the study of LOAC, already evident through recent publications such as Suzannah Linton, Tim McCormack, and Sandesh Sivakumaran's edited volume *Asia-Pacific Perspectives on International Humanitarian Law*,[6] as well as the emergence of region-specific LOAC periodicals, such as the *African Yearbook on International Humanitarian Law* and the *Asia-Pacific Journal of International Humanitarian Law*.

This chapter follows the ebb and flow of regionalism in the making and shaping of LOAC. The first section sets the scene by conceptualizing regionalism and determining the temporal scope of the development of modern LOAC for purposes of the present enquiry. Thereafter, the contribution of regionalism to the making and shaping of contemporary conventional and customary LOAC is considered. The third section reconsiders and critiques the prevailing narrative of LOAC as a regime of super universality, which emerged in response to a period of increased regional impact in the development of LOAC. Finally, a call is made for increased accommodation of regional approaches and perspectives in the making and shaping of LOAC as a regime of universal application. This will enhance the legitimacy of LOAC, expand ownership of the regime (which may positively impact compliance), and insulate LOAC from separate regional developments, for example, an African LOAC regime, which would be deeply problematic. In keeping with the theme of this volume, this chapter considers a broader set of factors than simply the formal development of the law, and extends to the "shaping" of LOAC, which often takes place in informal settings.

II. SITUATING THE DEBATE

To conduct an inquiry into the role of regionalism in the development of LOAC we must define terms and establish parameters. In particular, the term "regionalism"

4. For limited treatment of regional particularism in LOAC, *see* René Provost, *The International Committee of the Red Widget? The Diversity Debate and International Humanitarian Law*, 40(2) Israel Law Review 614 (Summer 2007); Richard Burchill, *Regional Approaches to International Humanitarian Law*, 41 Victoria University of Wellington Law Review 205 (2010).

5. David Kennedy, *The Disciplines of International Law and Policy*, 12 Leiden Journal of International Law 9, 17 (2008); *see also* Martti Koskenniemi, *The Case for Comparative International Law*, Finnish Yearbook of International Law 1 (2009). In her seminal study, Anthea Roberts poses and addresses the question: "is international law international?" Anthea Roberts, Is International Law International? (2017).

6. Asia-Pacific Perspectives on International Humanitarian Law (Suzannah Linton, Tim McCormack, & Sandesh Sivakumaran eds., 2020).

lacks clarity and the continuum on which modern LOAC developed needs to be established.

A. Conceptualizing Regionalism

In conceptualizing regionalism in the context of international law, there is a clear tension between geography on the one hand, and political, social, cultural, and historical elements on the other. We thus see overlapping conceptions of regions aimed at defining the same geographic space, but often with materially different results, such as the Americas, North America, South America, and Latin America.

Linton, McCormack, and Sivakumaran took a purely geographic approach to define the Asia-Pacific region.[7] Accordingly, States close in geography, but remote in a political, social, cultural, and historical context, such as Australia and Bhutan, are grouped together. Such an approach is well suited to studies that focus on a single region, as the political and social outliers in such studies adds to the richness of the region's engagement with LOAC. However, the present contribution engages with regionalism as antithetic to Western or Eurocentric dominance in the development of LOAC. This premise is shared with a range of critics, particularly those who identify with critical legal studies (CLS) and Third World approaches to international law (TWAIL). Yet the aim of this chapter is not to build on existing critical scholarship but rather to engage in a more narrow, doctrinal critique.

Increased engagement and participation in the making of LOAC from States within a given region is important. More significantly though, States close in geography often share a range of characteristics that creates a regional cohesiveness and identity. Regionalism in this sense speaks to a collective contribution from several States within a region that is reflective of the shared characteristics of these States. For example, Judge Yusuf of the International Court of Justice, who is of Somali origin, has recognized the significance of Pan-Africanism to international law in an African context, commenting that "Pan-Africanism offers a unique vantage point to study Africa's encounters with international law."[8] To this end, the preamble to the Constitutive Act of the African Union provides:

> Inspired by the noble ideas which guided the founding fathers of our Continental Organization and generations of Pan-Africanists in their determination to promote unity, solidarity, cohesion and cooperation among the peoples of Africa and African states.

7. Tim McCormack, *Introduction: Asia-Pacific Perspectives on International Humanitarian Law*, *in* Asia-Pacific Perspectives on International Humanitarian Law 1, 1 (Suzannah Linton, Tim McCormack, & Sandesh Sivakumaran eds., 2020).

8. Abdulqawi A. Yusuf, Pan-Africanism and International Law 1 (2014).

> [. . .] the Organization for African Unity has played a determining and invaluable role in the liberation of the continent, the affirmation of a common identity and the process of attainment of the unity of our continent and *has provided a unique framework for our collective action and in our relations with the rest of the world.* (own emphasis)[9]

Finally, diverse regions are drawn upon in the present chapter, necessitating a macro rather than micro level of engagement with specific regions. As such, a geopolitical conception of regionalism is better suited to this discussion. The UN Regional Groups (UNRG) are premised on geopolitical groupings of States.[10] In terms of that approach, Australia and Bhutan belong to different groups—the Western European and Others Group and the Asia and the Pacific Group, respectively.[11] While significant critique can be leveled at the groupings defined in the UNRG, it provides a useful geopolitically infused baseline from which to proceed. To facilitate the analysis, this chapter places emphasis on the Latin American and Caribbean; African; and Asia and the Pacific Groupings of the UNRG.

A feature that complicates a macro-level enquiry into the role of regionalism in the development of LOAC is the fact that different regions decolonized at different moments in history. For example, much of South America decolonized within the first decade of the nineteenth century, whereas by 1945 Africa had only four independent States. The result is that each region has a unique history in contributing to the development of LOAC. Nevertheless, as will be seen in this chapter, there are several overarching features to regional contributions to the development of LOAC.

B. Determining the Continuum of Modern LOAC

Contemporary LOAC is cast as a patently universal and homogenous regime that forms part of a globally inclusive international legal order. Even to the extent that this characterization is accurate, this has not always been the case. Moreover, as we shall see, regionalism plays a pivotal role in the constructed narrative that presents LOAC as a particularly universal regime of international law.

Pictet suggests that "the laws of war are as old as war itself, and war is as old as life on earth."[12] The beginning of human history is certainly not an appropriate starting point for this enquiry. While law develops incrementally, several

9. Constitutive Act of the African Union preamble, July 11, 2000, 2158 U.N.T.S. 3 [hereinafter Constitutive Act of the AU].

10. Regional groups of Member States, United Nations Department for General Assembly and Conference Management, https://www.un.org/dgacm/en/content/regional-groups.

11. *Id.*

12. Jean Pictet, Development and Principles of International Humanitarian Law 6 (1985).

moments in history redefined the international legal order. The great international law jurists of the sixteenth and seventeenth centuries, Gentili, de Vitoria, and Grotius, all dedicated significant portions of their hugely influential writings to the laws of war.[13] The Peace of Westphalia, signed during 1648—three years after Grotius's death—is often identified as the starting point of modern international law.[14] However, this chapter aims to advance the discussion of regionalism in modern LOAC. Modern LOAC, in its international law incarnation, found its genesis in the adoption of the 1864 Geneva Convention.[15] While this convention is no longer in force, it forms part of the Geneva Convention regime that is significantly constitutive of LOAC as we know it. As such, 1864 forms the starting point of the substantive enquiry.

Although international law today bears little resemblance to the international law of 1864, reflection on the place of LOAC in international law of that period is needed to frame the broader discussion. The legal order within which the 1864 Geneva Convention was adopted was the *ius publicum Europaeum*. Martti Koskenniemi identifies two dimensions to this legal order.[16] In the internal dimension, Europe was divided into nation-States which recognized each other's equal sovereignty. In the external dimension, it distinguished a non-European space, which was free for appropriation. Nico Krisch has noted that in time, the internal dimension expanded beyond the territory of Europe.[17] However, this happened on a highly selective basis, at the full discretion of the existing subjects of the *ius publicum Europaeum*.[18] Even then, influential opinion at the time suggested that these new members of the club of States were inferior. In response to China, Siam, and Persia's participation at the 1907 Hague Conference, John Westlake commented that their admission into the "system" fell short of "recognizing [their] voices as of equal importance with those of the European and American Powers."[19] Yet expansion of the club inevitably eroded the Eurocentric

13. Most notable works include, Francisco de Vitoria, De Jure belli Hispanorum in Barbarous (1532); Francisco de Vitoria, Relectiones Theologicae (1557); Alberico Gentili, De Jure Belli Libri Tres (1598); Hugo Grotius, De iure belli ac pacis (1625).

14. *See, e.g.*, Leo Gross, *The Peace of Westphalia 1648–1948*, 42 American Journal of International Law 20 (1948).

15. Convention for the Amelioration of the Condition of the Wounded in Armies in the Field, Aug. 22, 1864, 22 Stat. 940, 129 Consol. T.S. 361.

16. Martti Koskenniemi, The Gentle Civilizer of Nations: The Rise and Fall of International Law 1870–1960, at 416 (2001).

17. Nico Krisch, *International Law in Times of Hegemony: Unequal Power and the Shaping of the International Legal Order*, 16 European Journal of International Law 369, 386 (2005).

18. For my more detailed thoughts on this issue, *see* Gus Waschefort, *Africa and the Law of Armed Conflict: The More Things Change, the More They Stay the Same*, 902 International Review of the Red Cross 593, 600–03 (2016).

19. John Westlake, *The Native State of India*, *in* The Collected Papers of John Westlake on Public International Law 623 (Lassa Oppenheim ed., 1914).

order. There is significant theoretical and historical complexity to the transition from the *ius publicum Europaeum* to international law as we know it, and though it happened rapidly, there is no single event or date that marks the completion of this process.

LOAC terminology follows a similar contour, and this is no coincidence. Much has been made recently about the shift of terminology from law of armed conflict to international humanitarian law.[20] Indeed, it has been argued convincingly that the shift in terminology came about as a conscious and successful effort to expand the scope of the *jus in bello* to include a greater variety of purely humanitarian norms.[21] This body of law was known as "the laws and customs of war" until the adoption of the Geneva Conventions of 1949.[22] As with the *ius publicum Europaeum* and international law, the shift from the laws and customs of war to LOAC is one of great significance. Indeed, at the outset the laws and customs of war properly belonged to the *ius publicum Europaeum*. This had two significant consequences: only those States that were on the inside were able to participate in the development of the law; and, perhaps more significantly, the laws and customs of war did not apply to violence between a subject of the *ius publicum Europaeum* and a nonsubject.[23] Both the Hague Convention regime and the Geneva Convention regime developed as part of the *ius publicum Europaeum*. Indeed, that the Hague Regime was steeped in the *ius publicum Europaeum* is well illustrated by Boyd van Dijk:

> Building upon racial and other types of hierarchies within the existing law of nations, international jurists in fact widely accepted that indigenous populations deemed not "civilized" were to be excluded from international law's shield of protection. Rather than a universalizing language applying to the whole of humanity, the laws of war in this increasingly violent period excluded a whole range of non-European victims of war.[24]

20. Amanda Alexander, *A Short History of International Humanitarian Law*, 26 European Journal of International Law 109 (2015); Page Wilson, *The Myth of International Humanitarian Law*, 93 International Affairs 563 (2017).

21. *Id.*

22. Convention (I) for the Amelioration of the Condition of the Wounded and Sick in the Armed Forces in the Field, Aug. 12, 1949, 6 U.S.T. 3114, 75 U.N.T.S. 31; Convention (II) for the Amelioration of the Condition of the Wounded, Sick, and Shipwrecked Members of Armed Forces at Sea, Aug. 12, 1949, 6 U.S.T. 3217, 75 U.N.T.S. 85; Convention (III) Relative to the Treatment of Prisoners of War, Aug. 12, 1949, 6 U.S.T. 3316, 75 U.N.T.S. 135; Convention (IV) Relative to the Protection of Civilian Persons in Time of War, Aug. 12, 1949, 6 U.S.T. 3516, 75 U.N.T.S. 287.

23. I expand upon this at Waschefort, *supra* note 18, at 599–600.

24. Boyd van Dijk, *Human Rights in War: On the Entangled Foundations of the 1949 Geneva Conventions*, 112 American Journal of International Law 553, 559 (2018).

In 1900, Field Marshal Lord Wolseley expressed his views as to whether British forces should have observed the laws and customs of war during the Boer War in South Africa as follows: "To attempt to tie our hands in any way, no matter how small, by the 'Laws and Customs of War' *proposed for civilized nations* at the peace Conference, would be in my opinion suicidal, for the Boers would not be bound by any such amenities."[25] Such violence, mostly colonial wars, was unrestrained and significantly asymmetrical. A striking example is the Anglo-Zulu War where British forces armed with Martini-Henry rifles, canons, and Gatling guns faced off against Zulu forces, whose equipment was described by John Shepstone, Acting Secretary for Native Affairs at the time, thus: "Each man carries his shield and *assegais* [an iron-tipped spear], and a kaross or blanket if he possesses one, he may also have a war dress of monkey skins or ox tails, this is all."[26]

The period of the *ius publicum Europaeum* excluded regional (other than European) contributions to the development of LOAC. But this history is highly relevant to understanding the significance of regionalism in the prevailing theoretical narrative of LOAC as a universal regime of international law.

III. REGIONALISM IN THE HISTORICAL DEVELOPMENTAL OF THE LAW OF ARMED CONFLICT: 1864 TO THE PRESENT

The primary sources of LOAC are treaty law and customary international law. Prior to the adoption of the 1977 Additional Protocols to the Geneva Conventions, a distinction was often observed between those parts of LOAC that dealt with the regulation of the conduct of hostilities on the one hand, and the protection of victims of war on the other.[27] The former emanated in large part from the Hague Conventions and Declarations of 1899 and 1907,[28] and the latter from the Geneva Conventions, most recently updated in 1949 and augmented in 1977.

25. Lord Wolseley to Parliamentary Under-Secretary, War Office 32/850, Feb. 14, 1900, as quoted in Andries W.G. Raath & Hennie A. Strydom, *The Hague Conventions and the Anglo-Boer War*, 24 South African Yearbook of International Law 149, 156 (1999) (emphasis added).

26. Ron Lock & Peter Quantrill, Zulu Victory: The Epic of Isandlwana and the Cover-up 62 (2005).

27. Protocol Additional to the Geneva Conventions of 12 August 1949, and Relating to the Protection of Victims of International Armed Conflicts, June 8, 1977, 1125 U.N.T.S. 3 [hereinafter API]; Protocol Additional to the Geneva Conventions of August 12, 1949, and Relating to the Protection of Victims of Non-international Armed Conflicts, June 8, 1977, 1125 U.N.T.S. 609 [hereinafter APII].

28. Convention No. II with Respect to the Laws and Customs of War on Land, July 29, 1899, 32 Stat. 1803, T.S. No. 403; Convention No. III for the Adaptation to Maritime Warfare of the Principles of the Geneva Convention of 22 August 1864, July 29, 1899, 32 Stat. 1827, T.S. No. 396; Declaration (IV, 1) to Prohibit for the Term of Five Years, the Launching of Projectiles and Explosives from Balloons, and other Methods of Similar a Nature, July 29, 1899, 32 Stat. 1839,

This distinction is now defunct, yet it illustrates that the normative framework of modern LOAC was established by 1977 through the adoption of broad-spectrum multilateral treaties enjoying wide ratification.

The Geneva regime provides the richest source for analysis of the transition from the *ius publicum Europaeum* to a more inclusive international legal order. This is so because formal development of the Geneva regime occurred over a much more expansive time period than the Hague regime. Both Hague Conferences took place during a time when the international legal order was characterized by hegemony and exclusion, with no indication of decolonization. In contrast, the development of the Geneva regime spans the period 1864 to 1977, which included the principal period of decolonization. As such, the Geneva regime is singled out in the following section.

A. The Geneva Convention Regime

The first Geneva Convention for the Amelioration of the Condition of the Wounded in Armies in the Field was negotiated and adopted during 1864 by fifteen Western European States and the United States.[29] Four years later, the Additional Articles relating to the Condition of the Wounded in War was adopted primarily to clarify some provisions of the 1864 Convention and to extend their application to naval warfare.[30] However, the Additional Articles of 1868 never entered into force. This Convention was superseded by the 1906 Geneva Convention bearing the same title.[31] In 1929, a Diplomatic Conference was again convened in Geneva, resulting in yet another update to the Convention for the Amelioration of the Condition of the Wounded in Armies, as well as the elaboration of the 1929 Convention

T.S. No. 393; Declaration (IV, 2) Concerning Asphyxiating Gases, July 29, 1899, 187 Consol. T.S. 453; Declaration (IV, 3) Concerning Expanding Bullets, July 29, 1899, 187 Consol. T.S. 459, 26 Martens Nouveau Recueil; Convention No. I for the Pacific Settlement of International Disputes, Oct. 18, 1907, 32 Stat. 2199, T.S. No. 536; Convention No. II Respecting the Limitation of the Employment of Force for the Recovery of Contract Debts, Oct. 18, 1907, 36 Stat. 2241, T.S. No. 537; Convention No. III Relative to the Opening of Hostilities, Oct. 18, 1907, 36 Stat. 2259, T.S. No. 538 Convention No. IV Respecting the Laws and Customs of War on Land, Oct. 18, 1907, 36 Stat. 2227, T.S. No. 539; Regulations Respecting the Laws and Customs of War on Land, annexed to Convention No. IV Respecting the Laws and Customs of War on Land, Oct. 18, 1907, 36 Stat. 2227, T.S. No. 539 [hereinafter Hague Regulations]; Convention No. V Respecting the Rights and Duties of Neutral Powers and Persons in Case of War on Land, Oct. 18, 1907, 36 Stat. 2310, T.S. No. 540.

29. *Conférence internationale pour la neutralisation du Service de santé militaire en campagne, Conférence de Genève* (1864), https://library.icrc.org/library/docs/AF/AF_0688_01.pdf.

30. Additional Articles relating to the Condition of the Wounded in War, Oct. 20, 1868, 18 Martens Nouveau Recueil (ser.1) 612, 138 Consol. T.S. 189.

31. Convention for the Amelioration of the Condition of the Wounded and Sick in Armies in the Field, July 6, 1906, 35 Stat. 1885, 202 Consol. T.S. 144.

Table 1 Participation at the Diplomatic Conferences at which the Geneva Conventions were negotiated.

	1864	1868	1906	1929	1949	1977
Total Participants	16	14	35	47	59	132
Western European & Others[b]	16	14	16	22	23	30
Latin American and Caribbean Group	0	0	9	10	16	19
African Group	0	0	1	2	2	40
Eastern European Group	0	0	5	8	8	10
Asia and the Pacific Group	0	0	4	5	10	33

[a]The data in respect of each conference was sourced from the following sources: *Conférence internationale*, *supra* note 29; Schindler & Toman, *supra* note 32, at 285–88, 309–10, and 323; I Final Record of the Diplomatic Conference of Geneva of 1949, at 158–70; 2 Official Records, Diplomatic Conference on the Reaffirmation and Development of International Humanitarian Law Applicable in Armed Conflicts 40-363 (1978).

[b] The Western European and Others Grouping includes the United States, Australia, New Zealand, and Israel.

relative to the Treatment of Prisoners of War.[32] These conventions were, respectively, superseded by the 1949 Geneva Conventions I and III. Moreover, the scope of the Geneva regime was expanded through the addition of two further conventions, one focusing on the Amelioration of the Condition of Wounded, Sick and Shipwrecked Members of Armed Forces at Sea (Convention II) and the other on the Protection of Civilian Persons in Time of War (Convention IV). Most recently, the Geneva regime was significantly supplemented through the adoption of the two Additional Protocols of 1977 (Table 1).

Starting in 1906, there was a noticeable increase in participation from the Latin America and Caribbean Group, as well as the Eastern European Group. Ostensibly, this is owed to the dual factors of early decolonization in Latin America together with the incremental transition from the *ius publicum Europaeum* to a more inclusive international legal order, thus allowing non-Western States into the club. Participation from the African Group as well as the Asia and the Pacific Group, jointly accounting today for 55.44 percent of UN membership, remained low until 1977. While the shift is most acute between 1949 and 1977, there is a clear incremental progression in regional presence across the spectrum between 1906 and 1977.

32. The 1906 Convention remained in force until 1970, when Costa Rica acceded to the Geneva Conventions of 1949. For participation in the 1929 Conference, *see* Dietrich Schindler & Jiri Toman, The Laws of Armed Conflicts—A Collection of Conventions, Resolutions and Other Documents, 321–24 (1988).

At the diplomatic conference of 1949 there were examples of tangible contributions to the development of conventional LOAC from the Asia and the Pacific Group.[33] However, these were largely based on individual State contributions rather than any truly regional critical mass. As discussed in detail later, during the diplomatic conference of 1974–1977, regional participation led to a dramatic expansion of the material scope of the notion of international armed conflict (IAC), which remains the apex of regional contribution to the development of LOAC.

There is a significant disparity in the extent of engagement between delegations, which is informed by aspects such as the size of the delegation and the expertise within the delegation.[34] Cape Verde provides a striking example—it only gained independence on July 5, 1975, thus participating only in the fourth session in 1977, and was represented by a single accredited delegate.[35] David Forsythe, who was an observer at the conference, commented that a rift existed between the approaches of Western States and that of Third World States.[36] The former premised their arguments on legalism, whereas the latter took a non-legal approach, addressing themselves to political concerns.[37] He observed that this was to some extent, "a reflection of the lack of legally trained people in delegations from Third World states," and he shared that an important Third World delegate had commented to him in private, "many of the delegates in his caucus just did not understand the difference between a UN resolution and a draft treaty."[38] Fritz Kalshoven's observation that a smaller percentage of Third World delegations took part in the committee phase of the conference is thus not surprising.[39] Discussion during the committee phase tends to focus more narrowly on legal-technical precision in language. Forsythe's observation is likely too dismissive of the contributions made by the Third World and the extent to which such contributions were legalistic. What it does point to is that Western and Third World groupings of States were primarily concerned by slightly different issues and considerations, leading to distinct forms of legalism.

33. Sandesh Sivakumaran, *Asia-Pacific States and the Development of International Humanitarian Law*, *in* Asia-Pacific Perspectives on International Humanitarian Law 119 (Suzannah Linton, Tim McCormack, & Sandesh Sivakumaran eds., 2020).

34. *Id.* at 119.

35. 2 Official Records, Diplomatic Conference on the Reaffirmation and Development of International Humanitarian Law Applicable in Armed Conflicts 79 (1978).

36. David P. Forsythe, *The 1974 Diplomatic Conference on Humanitarian Law: Some Observations*, 69 American Journal of International Law 77, 78–84 (1975).

37. *Id.* at 80–81.

38. *Id.* at 82.

39. Fritz Kalshoven, *The Diplomatic Conference on Reaffirmation and Development of International Humanitarian Law Applicable in Armed Conflicts, Geneva, 1974–1977*, 8 Netherlands Yearbook of International Law 107 (1977).

By the mid-1970s the world had changed dramatically. Regional groupings for the first time managed to significantly influence the content and scope of the conventional LOAC under negotiation in a manner that reflected a cohesive regional position. A key example of this regionalism was Pakistan, a member of the Asia and the Pacific Group, effectively saving Additional Protocol II to the Geneva Conventions (APII).[40] Perhaps more strikingly, cumulatively the groups representing the "Third World," with particularly strong influence from the Africa group, successfully expanded the material scope of application of Additional Protocol I to the Geneva Conventions (API) to include, inter alia, "armed conflicts in which peoples are fighting against colonial domination and alien occupation and against racist regimes in the exercise of their right of self-determination."[41] The position preferred by Western States was for API to follow the scope of application of Common Article 2 of the Geneva Conventions.[42] The magnitude of this contribution to the development of LOAC is illustrated jointly by the vote for adoption in committee and the extraordinary measures that were taken to avoid the adoption of such an expansion in the scope of IAC.[43] The amendment passed in committee with seventy votes to twenty-one against and thirteen abstentions.[44] Strikingly, the twenty-one votes against included thirteen Western European States, as well as Canada, the United States, and New Zealand. The thirteen abstentions included a further four Western European States as well as Australia. The only African State that voted against was, predictably, South Africa, and the rest of the Africa group voted in favor.[45] In response, the Western States successfully orchestrated a procedural move to avoid a vote being taken in plenary, allowing further future opportunity to lobby and negotiate on this matter.[46] We

40. Sivakumaran, *supra* note 33, at 119.

41. API art. 1(4).

42. Forsythe, *supra* note 36, at 80–84.

43. *Id.* at 78–80.

44. Against: Belgium; Canada; Denmark; Federal Republic of Germany; France; Israel; Italy; Japan; Liechtenstein; Luxembourg; Monaco; Netherlands; New Zealand; Portugal; Republic of South Korea; South Africa; Spain; Switzerland; United Kingdom; United States of America; and Uruguay. Abstentions: Australia; Austria; Brazil; Burma; Chile; Colombia; Greece; Guatemala; Holy See; Ireland; Philippines; Sweden; and Turkey.

45. South Africa would not ratify API until November 21, 1995 (as it did APII). The National Party Government grappled with the implications of the African National Congress's (ANC) commitment, deposited as a declaration to the president of the ICRC, to "respect and be guided by the general principles of international humanitarian law" and undertaking to respect the rules of the four Geneva Conventions of 1949 and Protocol I of 1977 "wherever practically possible." The matter was further complicated by the argument that the expanded scope of IAC per API Article 1(4) had reached the status of customary international law. As such, ANC detainees were, it was suggested, to be treated as prisoners of war under GCIII. *See* John Dugard, *The Conflict between International Law and South African Law: Another Divisive Factor in South African Society*, 2 South African Journal on Human Rights 1 (1986).

46. Forsythe, *supra* note 36, at 79–80.

know now that this came to no effect, as API reflects the exact language adopted in committee in 1974.[47]

Forsythe identifies the expansion of IAC to include wars of national liberation as "the most important of all actions taken by any of the four Conference committees."[48] This was indeed the apex of regional particularism in the development of LOAC.

B. The Post-1977 Landscape

Conventional LOAC is a regime that develops at a relatively slow pace, particularly in comparison to IHRL. This has limited the scope for regional contributions to the development of conventional LOAC. Moreover, those treaty developments that have occurred post-1977 largely fall into one of two categories: firstly, treaties on narrow or niche aspects of LOAC, which often include non-LOAC *sui generis* elements, such as the Protocol on the protective emblem[49] and the Convention on Certain Conventional Weapons (CCW) of 1980, which incorporates elements of LOAC proper as well as arms control;[50] and secondly, human rights treaties with LOAC components, such as the restriction on the use and recruitment of children in armed conflict.[51]

J. Ashley Roach, who was a member of the U.S. Delegation to the Conference on Prohibitions or Restrictions on the Use of Certain Conventional Weapons which may be Deemed to be Excessively Injurious or to have Indiscriminate Effects (1979–1980) provides insight into those negotiations, of which no detailed record exists.[52] Roach laments the divergence of African delegates from the Western delegates on several issues during the negotiations.[53] Building on the momentum from the 1974–1977 Diplomatic Conference, the African delegates advanced regional priorities in a manner that impacted on the ultimate terms of the treaty. Again, a key example relates to the scope of application of the Convention to wars

47. API art. 1(4).

48. Forsythe, *supra* note 36, at 79.

49. Protocol Additional to the Geneva Conventions of 12 August 1949, and Relating to the Adoption of an Additional Distinctive Emblem, Dec. 8, 2005, 2404 U.N.T.S. 261.

50. Convention on Prohibitions or Restrictions on the Use of Certain Conventional Weapons Which May Be Deemed to Be Excessively Injurious or to Have Indiscriminate Effects, Oct. 10, 1980, 1342 U.N.T.S. 137 [hereinafter CCW].

51. Convention on the Rights of the Child, Nov. 20, 1989, 1577 U.N.T.S. 3 [hereinafter CRC]; and the African Charter on the Rights and Welfare of the Child, July 1, 1990 [hereinafter African Children's Charter].

52. J. Ashley Roach, *Certain Conventional Weapons Convention: Arms Control or Humanitarian Law*, 105 Military Law Review 3 (1984).

53. *Id.*

of national liberation.[54] The United States, supported by other Western States, proposed that the Convention's scope of application to wars of national liberation, as envisaged in Article 1(4) of API, be restricted such that it only applied once "the authority representing the people in question had accepted and applied the rules of warfare which already applied to States as a result of various international agreements."[55] African delegates were of the view that such an additional requirement places an unfair burden on national liberation movements.[56] In the end, the African delegates succeeded and the adopted provision provides simply:

> This Convention and its annexed Protocols shall apply in the situations referred to in Article 2 common to the Geneva Conventions of 12 August 1949 for the Protection of War Victims, including any situation described in paragraph 4 of Article 1 of Additional Protocol I to these conventions.[57]

C. Indirect Contributions through International Human Rights Law Conventions

The space in which regional groupings, particularly the African Group, have recently made the most significant, albeit indirect, contribution is the elaboration of regional human rights treaties that include a LOAC element. The inclusion of LOAC-esque provisions in IHRL treaties is not unique to regional systems and was in fact pioneered by the UN human rights treaty framework.[58] However, reflecting continental needs and priorities, African regional human rights treaties characteristically make reference to LOAC and provide for a range of obligations related to the protection of victims of armed conflict.[59] For example, the African Charter on the Rights and Welfare of the Child provides:

> 1. States Parties to this Charter shall undertake to respect and ensure respect for rules of international humanitarian law applicable in armed conflicts which affect the child.

54. CCW art. 1.

55. Roach, *supra* note 52, at 19.

56. *Id.* at 24.

57. CCW art. 1.

58. *See* CRC art. 38(1).

59. *See* the African Children's Charter art. 22; the Protocol to the African Charter on Human and Peoples' Rights on the Rights of Women in Africa art. XI, July 11, 2003 [hereinafter African Women's Protocol]; and African Union Convention for the Protection and Assistance of Internally Displaced Persons in Africa art. 7, Oct. 23, 2009 [hereinafter Kampala Convention].

2. States Parties to the present Charter shall take all necessary measures to ensure that no child shall take a direct part in hostilities and refrain in particular, from recruiting any child.
3. States Parties to the present Charter shall, in accordance with their obligations under international humanitarian law, protect the civilian population in armed conflicts and shall take all feasible measures to ensure the protection and care of children who are affected by armed conflicts. Such rules shall also apply to children in situation of internal armed conflicts, tension and strife.[60]

This provision amounts to a significant regional contribution to the standard of protection afforded to children affected by armed conflict, as it remains the only widely ratified treaty that protects all children younger than eighteen against use for direct participation in hostilities recruitment. Essentially, the provision consists of two types of obligations: those that reaffirm the State's IHL obligations, and those that are legislative in that they create norms of international law. There are differing views as to the nature of the obligation States incur in undertaking "to respect and ensure respect for rules of international humanitarian law applicable in armed conflicts" through ratification of IHRL treaties. Commenting on the comparable provision of the Convention on the Rights of the Child (CRC), Mark Drumbl and John Tobin argue that "article 38 does not import the entire corpus of international humanitarian law. It only uploads those rules that are 'relevant to children' and only when those rules are 'applicable' to states."[61] They clarify that for a rule to be applicable, it must either be ratified by the State in question or be of a customary nature. This suggests that those subsets of rules that are applicable in a given case and which affect children are incorporated by reference. This proposition is problematic, not least because the nature and scope of obligations of individual States will depend significantly on the scope of LOAC obligations to which the given State has subscribed at that point in time. It is indeed doubtful that incorporation by reference can take place without a greater degree of precision in identifying the incorporated material, as well as a more explicit articulation of the intention to incorporate by reference.[62] Conceptually, it is difficult to see what normative value there is in incorporating preexisting LOAC obligations on a wholesale basis into an IHRL treaty, for the quality of the obligation is not enhanced simply through its repetition. Brett's position is certainly

60. African Children's Charter art. 22.

61. Mark A. Drumbl & John Tobin, *Article 38: The Rights of Children in Armed Conflict*, *in* The UN Convention on the Rights of the Child: A Commentary 1503, 1507 (John Tobin ed., 2019).

62. I discuss this issue in more detail elsewhere. *See* Gus Waschefort, *The Subject-Matter Jurisdiction and Interpretive Competence of the African Court on Human and Peoples' Rights in Relation to International Humanitarian Law*, 20 African Human Rights Law Journal 41, 46–53 (2020).

to be preferred: "[t]he logical interpretation . . . is that it simply reinforces the obligations of states to abide by the humanitarian law by which they are already bound."[63]

In the context of conventional law, the legislative component of contributions such as the African Children's Charter does not contribute directly to the development of LOAC. The norms in question are of an IHRL nature. This has far-reaching implications for the normative framing and scope of application of the underlying obligation to respect, protect, and fulfill the rights in question. There is, however, at least one example of an African regional treaty that effectively incorporates LOAC by reference and which erodes the space between the distinct normative framings of IHRL and LOAC. The provision dealing with armed conflict of the Kampala Convention provides that "the protection and assistance to internally displaced persons under this article shall be governed by international law and in particular international humanitarian law."[64] The provision further prohibits "members of armed groups" distinct from the State from engaging in nine activities, the nature of which is a combination of human rights and LOAC issues.[65] This provision of the Kampala Convention is noteworthy, as it goes further in bridging the design gap between IHRL and IHL than any other treaty provision. It is an IHRL convention that relies on IHL to expand its scope of application *ratione personae* to non-State entities.[66]

D. Regional Contribution to the Development of the Customary LOAC

Customary international law (CIL) consists of two components: State practice (*usus*) and *opinio juris*.[67] In 2005, the International Committee of the Red Cross (ICRC) published its much awaited and significantly influential study on customary international humanitarian law.[68] The Study comprises of two volumes in three parts. Volume I contains the defined rules of customary humanitarian law and Volume II, Parts 1 and 2 are compilations of material reflecting State practice. The project was launched following a 1995 recommendation by the Intergovernmental Group of Experts for the Protection of War Victims:

63. Rachel Brett, *Child Soldiers: Law, Politics and Practice*, 4 INTERNATIONAL JOURNAL OF CHILDREN'S RIGHTS 115, 116 (1996).

64. Kampala Convention art. 7(3).

65. *Id.*, art. 7(5).

66. For further discussion, *see* Waschefort, *supra* note 62, at 51–54.

67. Statute of the International Court of Justice, Apr. 18, 1946, art. 38(1)(b) ("international custom, as evidence of a general practice accepted as law").

68. 1 & 2 CUSTOMARY INTERNATIONAL HUMANITARIAN LAW (Jean-Marie Henckaerts & Louise Doswald-Beck eds., 2005) [hereinafter Customary IHL Study].

> The ICRC be invited to prepare, with the assistance of experts in IHL . . . *representing various geographical regions and different legal systems*, and in consultation with experts from governments and international organisations, a report on customary rules of IHL applicable in international and non-international armed conflicts. . . .[69]

The process that led to the adoption of the Study advances inclusivity. On the face of it, the twelve-member steering group, the grouping of academic and government experts, and the forty-seven States included in the State practice case studies are largely representative.[70] However, the long-term effect of past exclusion from formal and informal spaces in which LOAC is made and shaped still has a very real impact on the study.

For a State to be included in the case studies, a substantial body of State practice, as defined by the methodology of the Study, had to exist and be accessible. The Study provides that such State practice includes physical and verbal acts of States.[71] Physical acts relate to behavior, such as the use of specific weapons or the treatment of individuals. Verbal acts include a range of written or spoken acts, including legislation, case law, standing orders, official legal advice, and so forth. Where such information is not accessible, the relevant State cannot feasibly be included as a case study.

Such information is often not readily accessible for certain States due to a range of factors, including court cases not being universally reported or publicly available, no reliable source of official information existing or accessible, laws on confidentiality prohibiting publication, and so forth. Language and online availability may also be inhibiting factors. Francophone and civil law African countries are grossly underrepresented. Such limitations are exacerbated by lack of resources. It is thus no surprise that the nine African States included in the case studies represent the four largest GDPs, as well as the seventh and ninth largest GDP in Africa. Practical considerations thus limited the scope of States that could be included, and particularly acted as a bar to poorer States with underdeveloped communications infrastructure.

Where the information is accessible, lack of capacity and IHL expertise in many countries in the developing world creates a further barrier to inclusion. Even among States that are included in the case studies, a significant disparity in the size and level of LOAC expertise is noticeable among the national research teams that developed the case studies. The average size of research teams from the nine African States is 1.22 people per team.[72] In contrast, Spain sent the largest

69. Meeting of the Intergovernmental Group of Experts for the Protection of War Victims, Geneva, Jan. 23–27, 1995, Recommendation II, 310 International Review of the Red Cross 55, 84 (1996) (emphasis added).

70. 1 Customary IHL Study, at xxv–xxviii.

71. *Id.* at xxxviii.

72. *Id.* at xxv–xxvii.

team with fourteen members.[73] However, some teams from the developing world fielded particularly high-profile international law specialists as members, the most notable examples being Antônio Augusto Cançado Trindade, Maurice Kamto, and Raúl Emilio Vinuesa.[74] In contrast, the high-profile members of Western teams tended to be better known for their more narrow LOAC expertise rather than public international law expertise. They include Theodor Meron, Francoise Hampson, Yoram Dinstein, Horst Fischer, and Fritz Kalshoven.[75]

The national practice that underpins the Study as a whole includes the practice of all the States included in the national State practice case studies, as well as the State practice of other States. The defined rules are thus underpinned by State practice inclusive of a relatively representative cross-section of States globally. There are no clearly noticeable regional trends that emerge. Treaties are relied upon both in the context of State practice, as well as in the commentary to the defined rules. These treaties include IHRL treaties, and the Study clarifies that "human rights law has been included in order to support, strengthen and clarify analogous principles of international humanitarian law."[76] For example, the African Children's Charter is widely referenced on provisions that relate to children.[77]

Unfortunately, in instances where regional IHRL conventions provide for better protection than their equivalent universal level conventions as well as conventional LOAC, proper account was not taken of these more protective regional norms. A key example is Rule 137 of the Study, which provides that "Children must not be allowed to take part in hostilities." The commentary specifically states that the African Children's Charter provides a minimum age for participation of eighteen.[78] Furthermore, the expressed dissatisfaction of several States with the threshold of fifteen years of age found in Additional Protocols I and II is noted.[79] None of the forty-seven States whose practice was surveyed allows for the use of children younger than eighteen in hostilities and not a single example of practice or *opinio juris* is cited that justifies such use of children younger than eighteen. Yet the commentary concludes, "although there is not, as yet, a uniform practice regarding the minimum age for participation in hostilities, there is agreement that it should not be below 15 years of age."[80] It appears as though conventional LOAC rules significantly determined the protective threshold of norms in the Study. This is not consistent with the notion of customary international law, and given the

73. *Id.* at xxvi.

74. *Id.* at xxv–xxvii.

75. *Id.* at xxv–xxvii.

76. *Id.* at xxvi.

77. *Id.* at 479–85, in particular Rules 135 & 136 together with their commentary.

78. *Id.* at 488, in particular Commentary to Rule 137.

79. *Id.*

80. *Id.*

hugely influential nature of the study,[81] this may inhibit the development of customary norms for years to come.

IV. REGIONALISM IN THE CONSTRUCTED UNIVERSALITY OF THE LAW OF ARMED CONFLICT

Koskenniemi observes, "European stories, myths and metaphors continue to set the conditions for understanding international law's past *as it does for outlining its futures*."[82] In the context of LOAC, the Eurocentrism endemic to the Hague and Geneva treaty regimes not only significantly determines the scope and tone for further refinement and development, but it does so by design. The prevailing narrative advances the universal legitimacy and associated homogeneity of LOAC on a two-step basis: the first step identifies the early development of LOAC in diverse, generally non-Western codifications that span the history of human civilization.[83] This acknowledgment is accurate and unproblematic. In his powerful and fascinating dissent in the Nuclear Weapons Advisory Opinion, Judge Weeramantry invoked such a historical claim:

> It greatly strengthens the concept of humanitarian laws of war to note that this is not a recent invention, nor the product of any one culture. The concept is of ancient origin, with a lineage stretching back at least three millennia. As already observed, it is deep-rooted in many cultures—Hindu, Buddhist, Chinese, Christian, Islamic and traditional African. These cultures have all given expression to a variety of limitations on the extent to which any means can be used for the purposes of fighting one's enemy.[84]

The issue arises with the second step in the narrative, which suggests that there is a tangible nexus between this open-ended historical claim and modern LOAC as a

81. Marko Milanovic & Sandesh Sivakumaran, *Assessing the Authority of the ICRC Customary IHL Study*, 920–21 International Review of the Red Cross 1856 (2022).

82. Martti Koskenniemi, *Histories of International Law: Dealing with Eurocentrism*, 19 Zeitschrift des Max-Planck-Instituts für europäische Rechtsgeschichte 152, 155 (2011) (emphasis added).

83. Most commonly these include: the Code of Hammurabi (17th century BC); the Laws of Manu (1500 BC); the law of the Hittites (13th century BC); the Hindu Mahabharata (5th century BC); Sun Tsu (Warring States period—476–221 BC); the orders of Islam's first caliph, Abu Bakr (632); and codes of chivalry (1170–1220). *See, e.g.*, Mary Ellen O'Connell, *Historical Development and Legal Basis*, *in* The Handbook of International Humanitarian Law 10, 26 (Dieter Fleck ed., 4th ed. 2021).

84. Legality of the Threat or Use of Nuclear Weapons, Advisory Opinion, Dissenting Opinion of Judge Weeramantry, 1996 I.C.J. 226, 478, 41 (July 8).

defined regime of international law, endowing LOAC with universal legitimacy.[85] For example, in reflecting on LOAC, Antony Anghie and B.S. Chimni opine:

> Simply, it greatly facilitates the creation of a culture of compliance if the rules in question have been established through an open process which has received the broad approval of the international community as a whole. Thus, for example, the recognition of the multicultural basis of the laws of war is particularly relevant to improving compliance with the law of war. The point is relevant even from the point of view of the issue of the enforcement of international humanitarian laws in internal conflicts.[86]

As discussed at length previously, both the Hague and Geneva treaty regimes came about through closed and exclusionary processes. Thus, Anghie and Chimni are conflating the existence of LOAC-esque norms and philosophy in diverse cultures and traditions with the process that led to the development of modern LOAC as a regime of law. The approach is even more apparent in Christopher Greenwood and Mary Ellen O'Connell's assertion that "the theory that humanitarian law is essentially 'Eurocentric' is in reality more a criticism of most literature on the subject than a reflection of historical fact."[87]

In constructing this narrative during 1985, Pictet, its architect, commented:

> The roots of humanitarian law are very much deeper than some European authors with a narrow view of matters had long believed, content as they were to situate its origins in the Middle Ages. In reality, the laws of war are as old as war itself, and war is as old as life on earth.[88]

This narrative was carefully and purposefully crafted, co-opting "history" to serve three interrelated ends: (1) to stop the cultural relativist debate in the LOAC context in its tracks; (2) to close the chasm between Third World States and Western States that became evident during the Diplomatic Conference of 1974–1977; and

85. Jean Pictet, *Humanitarian Ideas Shared by Different Schools of Thought and Cultural Traditions, in* International Dimensions of Humanitarian Law 1, 6 (1988).

86. Antony Anghie & B.S. Chimni, *Third World Approaches to International Law and Individual Responsibility in Internal Conflicts*, 2 Chinese Journal of International Law 77, 95 (2003).

87. This sentence has been repeated in each of the four editions of the publication. Authorship of this chapter passed from Greenwood to O'Connell as of the third edition; the statement is thus attributable to both authors. *See* Christopher J. Greenwood, *Historical Development and Legal Basis, in* The Handbook of International Humanitarian Law in Armed Conflict 1, 13 (Dieter Fleck ed., 1st ed. 1995); Christopher J. Greenwood, *Historical Development and Legal Basis, in* The Handbook of International Humanitarian Law 10, 16 (Dieter Fleck ed., 2d ed. 2008); Mary Ellen O'Connell, *Historical Development and Legal Basis, in* The Handbook of International Humanitarian Law 1, 16 (Dieter Fleck ed., 3d ed. 2013); and Mary Ellen O'Connell, *supra* note 83, at 26.

88. Pictet, *supra* note 12, at 6.

(3) to redeem the Eurocentric history of the development of modern LOAC, while staying the course that had been set by the West.

Somewhat in the tradition of Johann Bluntschli's "organic" understanding of the development of law,[89] Jean Pictet invoked human nature as the basis for LOAC: ". . . in an international environment, man's rights can only be on what is universal, on ideas capable of bringing together men of all races. [...] Similarity alone can be the basis for universality and, although men are different, human nature is the same the world over."[90] Rather paradoxically, Pictet endeavored to illustrate the universality of LOAC by reference to "the study of savage tribes existing in our own time," which he argued, "gives some insight into the nature of primitive man at the dawn of society."[91] Conveniently, the practice of the single "savage tribe" discussed accorded well to established notions of LOAC. This speaks to a general fallacy in the direct link often drawn between traditional practice in diverse geographical and cultural settings and modern LOAC. The use of handpicked confirmatory examples has little actual probative value upon which to conclude that modern LOAC is reflective of "human nature" and thus universal. Surely such conclusions can only be supported if robust methodology employing proper sampling techniques are used to investigate the extent of consistency between the practices of the mentioned "tribes" and modern LOAC. Pictet makes no mention of the extent to which contrary practice can be found.

The entrenchment of Pictet's narrative is well illustrated by leading contemporary authorities on LOAC.[92] The influential ICRC publication *How Does Law Protect in War?* adds some nuance to Pictet's narrative, acknowledging that modern rules of LOAC "are not universal by birth" as they were crafted and formalized in the European tradition; but they are "universal by nature, since the principles they codify can be found in most non-European systems of thought."[93] Notwithstanding this modest development in argumentation, the contribution to the same text by Louis Lafrance builds very directly on Pictet's narrative.[94] Like Pictet, Lafrance invokes human nature as the root for the universality of LOAC:

> Is the whole of international humanitarian law universal? The foundations of that law certainly are, since they derive from natural law. The fact that

89. Johann C. Bluntschli, Das moderne Völkerrecht der zivilisierten Staaten, als Rechtsbuch dargestellt (1868).

90. Pictet, *supra* note 12, at 6.

91. *Id.*

92. *See, e.g.*, Greenwood & O'Connell, *supra* note 87; *see also* Dissenting Opinion of Judge Weeramantry, *supra* note 84.

93. 1 Marco Sassóli, Antoine A. Bouvier, & Ann Quintin, How Does Law Protect in War?: Cases, Documents and Teaching Materials on Contemporary Practice in International Humanitarian Law 139–40 (3d ed. 2011).

94. *Id.* at 98–99, contribution to text by Louis Lafrance.

> fundamental legal rules exist is based on an intuitive force and can even be said to be a requirement of the human condition, which causes killing, torture, slavery and unfair judgement to arouse repulsion not only among the vast majority of intellectuals but among ordinary people as well. Whether attributed to reason, universal harmony or the divine origin of mankind, sound assertions are made about human nature. International humanitarian law therefore attains a universal dimension by symbolizing common human values.[95]

The invocation of natural law, the human condition, and the divine origin of mankind as the source of the universality of LOAC is at odds with the dire need for the very existence of LOAC, not to mention the widely acknowledged compliance deficit that exists within the field. Indeed, Lafrance accounts for the lack of constant application of LOAC by conceding, rather bluntly, that "[n]on-Western cultures cannot escape the steamroller of modern life, and the hybridization of human societies is very real. In a number of African countries, for example, three legal systems operate side by side: a modern system, an Islamic system and a customary system."[96] A tension emerges between the proposed natural law underpinning of LOAC and the forced standardization that is a consequence of "modern life." Reference to "modern [legal] system," as opposed to "an Islamic system and a customary system," further betrays Lafrance's own Eurocentric bias.[97]

This argument is tantamount to suggesting that the recognition of the sanctity of life in cultures and tribes the world over finally settles the universality versus cultural relativism debate. It is true that a lot of practice can be discerned throughout human history that resembles notions of modern LOAC, such as distinction and proportionality. However, reliance on selective confirmatory examples fails to meet even the most elementary standards of scientific argumentation. Yet it has become part and parcel of the dogma of LOAC. More strikingly, regionalism, in the form of practice from the non-Western world, is co-opted with the purpose of inhibiting true regionalism in the development and discourse on LOAC. It can hardly be a coincidence that Pictet constructed this narrative at a time when the 1974–1977 Diplomatic Conference, the apex of regional contribution to conventional LOAC, was fresh in memory. The universality of LOAC, premised on sameness in human nature, fails altogether to take account of the massive divide between Western and Third World States that emerged at the

95. *Id.* at 99.

96. *Id.*

97. For detailed discussion of the notion of modernity in international law, *see* John Haskell, *The Traditions of Modernity within International Law and Governance: Christianity, Liberalism and Marxism*, Howard Human and Civil Rights Law Review 1 (2016). The framing of modern versus Islamic and customary alludes to a conception of modernity as a form of Western liberalism rather than history. Many aspects of Lafrance's modern systems predate the Islamic and customary systems.

conference. It is more likely that this narrative was constructed as a counterbalance to regional particularism, rather than failing to take account of one of the major developments of the time. Narrative alone, however, could not sustain the sanctity of the established LOAC framework.

As noted, Western States suffered a major setback at the outset of the 1974–1977 Diplomatic Conference in the form of the inclusion of wars of national liberation in the scope of IACs. According to Forsythe, Third World States were able to achieve this through a non-legal approach, addressing themselves to political concerns rather than competing with Western States in arguments steeped in legalism.[98] He identifies the contributions by Georges Abi-Saab, member of the Egyptian delegation, as a lone exception.[99] Forsythe's observations in this regard are certainly subject to debate. However, the lack of strong LOAC expertise among some delegates of developing world States, together with a lack of diplomatic experience, particularly among the recently decolonized States, feasibly impacted upon the ability of several delegations from developing countries to engage fully on highly technical features of the law.

Treaty negotiations are a quintessential form of diplomacy in which States use all that is at their disposal to advance their own interests and mitigate their losses—such means include the rules of the game itself. Sivakumaran analyzes the "making and shaping" of LOAC by considering the LOAC community and communities within the community. He notes:

> Membership of the community "entails the internalisation of a common set of background assumptions and disciplinary rules which are accepted by other . . . [members of the community] as valid". There is a shared vocabulary and shorthand (LOAC, NIAC, API, DPH, CCF, Pictet), an accepted set of documents, and set roles and procedures. There are also tacit rules, including subtle clues, untold rules of thumb, and underlying assumptions.[100]

Military lawyers comprise one such community within the LOAC community, and they are hugely influential actors in this space. The divisiveness of politics and conflict extend to the range of fora within which LOAC is discussed and often shaped. For example, in the era of coalition warfare, which extends back to the Korean War, a given State's military doctrine and operational practice is influenced by that of other members of the coalition. By contrast, the coalition's adversaries may be excluded from these formal and informal fora.

Naz Modirzadeh further posits:

98. Forsythe, *supra* note 36, at 82.

99. *Id.*

100. Sandesh Sivakumaran, *Making and Shaping the Law of Armed Conflict*, 71 Current Legal Problems 119, 129–30 (2018).

> IHL lawyers, as a whole, are very fond of rules and rules-talk. For other international lawyers, IHL lawyers often seem remarkably positivist: They spend a great deal of time debating and discussing black-letter rules, their interpretation, their manifestation, and the consequences of their violation. . . . Rules and their perceived realness can also function as a guardian to membership in the discipline and its society; hardcore IHL lawyers not only know many, many articles from memory, but they can recite key points from the famous commentaries, know the seminal debates by the leading figures, contribute to the same Festschrifts, and speak about armed violence in a certain clinical, sombre, and respectful way. Rules help to separate IHL lifers from dilettantes . . .[101]

Thus, the LOAC space is dominated by those who are expertly versed in legalism. Gone are the days where LOAC dilettantes could sway the debate based on the advancement of the political concerns of their States and regions, regardless of the intrinsic importance of these concerns. The Western LOAC community has long been preoccupied with legalism, and a particular type of legalism at that, but what has changed is the extent to which this community is receptive of the contributions of other communities. This, together with Pictet's constructed universalist narrative has dramatically and purposefully shrunk the space for true regionalism in the debate and development of LOAC. It is notable that through such gatekeeping, the space has also been shrunk for effective contribution for individual States that do not possess the level of technical expertise to participate.

V. REGIONALISM AND THE FUTURE OF LOAC

There is no doubt that the legitimacy of international law is currently hanging in the balance. There is a paradox in the fact that Western dominance in international law is at odds with the dominant liberal philosophical understanding of inclusiveness and accommodation within the West. Yet the international legal order has not yet rid itself completely of systemic bias, as illustrated by the permanent membership of the UN Security Council.[102] Moreover, the West plays a dominant role in the theorization, understanding, and indeed making and shaping of substantive international law. LOAC, as a subregime of international law, is similarly afflicted with legitimacy deficits. The constructed narrative of super universality

101. Naz Modirzadeh, *Folk International Law: 9/11 Lawyering and the Transformation of the Law of Armed Conflict to Human Rights Policy and Human Rights Law to War Governance*, 5 Harvard National Security Journal 225, 235 (2014).

102. For a full account of the implications of the lack of regional representation in the Security Council, the need for reform, and the various proposals for reform, *see* Sabine Hassler, Reforming the UN Security Council Membership: The Illusion of Representativeness (2013).

and the resulting lack of regional contribution to development is an acute legitimacy deficit in the context of LOAC. Much of the importance of regional contributions to the development of LOAC lies in ensuring and maintaining the health of LOAC as a regime of international law.

All the subregimes of international law most closely related to LOAC have experienced forms of regionalization in the African context. These developments cover the spectrum from being highly valuable, such as the African human rights system, to being no more than knee-jerk forms of backlash, such as the Malabo protocol relating to an African international criminal chamber.[103] Indeed, like LOAC, the law on the use of force (*jus ad bellum*) is an area of international law traditionally seen as falling exclusively within the province of international law of universal application. Yet the Constitutive Act of the African Union bestows the authority upon its Assembly to authorize military intervention in member States in response to the commission of war crimes, genocide, and crimes against humanity.[104] There is thus a clear trend toward regionalization of international in the African context.

The essence of LOAC does not lend itself to separate regional development. Unlike IHRL, there is no space for an African, European, or American convention on LOAC, reflecting the values, aspirations, and needs of the peoples of a given region.[105] Still, nothing in the architecture of international law prevents States within a region from constructing a regional system for the regulation of armed conflict. Such a development will cause a great many problems, as the operation of LOAC is premised on the equality of belligerents, a notion incompatible with the development of different regional standards. The regionalization of LOAC should be avoided at all costs. The best way to avoid it is by being responsive to regional contributions in the development and discourse of LOAC. Ironically, the reason why such regional developments have not yet occurred in LOAC in the African context, when they have in all other related fields, is likely because of the regional marginalization of LOAC.[106]

While universal participation in the making and shaping of LOAC has a legitimizing function, a deficit remains as a result of past exclusion and hegemony. However, the importance of regional contributions goes beyond legitimizing LOAC. Human suffering because of armed conflict is highly concentrated outside

103. Protocol on Amendments to the Protocol on the Statute of the African Court of Justice and Human Rights, June 27, 2014.

104. Constitutive Act of the AU art. 4(h).

105. For a compelling account of the value of regional development in IHRL, which includes, values, aspirations, and needs of the peoples of the region, *see* former Senegalese President Leopold S. Senghor's address delivered at the opening of the Meeting of African Experts preparing the draft African Charter in Dakar, Senegal, November 28 to December 8, 1979, *reprinted in* Issa G. Shivji, The Concept of Human Rights in Africa 121 (1989).

106. For a fuller account of the regional marginalization of LOAC in Africa, *see* Waschefort, *supra* note 18.

of the West. Yet the marginalization of the developing world in the making, shaping, and cutting-edge discourse of LOAC, results in a lack of ownership and dissonance from some regions toward LOAC.[107] This likely has a negative impact on compliance.[108] LOAC is less frequently invoked, and there is certainly less compliance with LOAC, particularly as it relates to the protection of victims of armed conflict, in much of the developing world.[109] Juxtaposing this reality with the super universality narrative leads to uncomfortable questions: If LOAC is reflected in cultures across the globe, and is indeed premised on human nature, why is LOAC less frequently invoked and less complied with in some parts of the world than others? The implication is that such divergence is necessarily contra–human nature and contra-civilization.

As the developmental pace of conventional LOAC is slow compared to that of other subregimes of international law, the opportunity for regional contributions to the formal development of the law is limited. The call for greater accommodation of regional perspectives in the making and shaping of LOAC is not a radical call for any form of regionalization of LOAC. However, merely being more inclusive in participation and processes does not in itself amount to any form of increased regional impact in the development of LOAC—the universalist narrative is designed to be all-inclusive and to safeguard the established framework. Indeed, CLS and TWAIL perspectives are virtually absent within the LOAC discourse.[110] More strikingly, the limited engagement with LOAC from TWAIL and CLS critics tends to focus on issues such as the overlap between traditional custom or Sharia law and LOAC. This has the effect of reinforcing Pictet's universalist narrative, as these works evoke yet more selective confirmatory examples of the overlap between LOAC and traditional approaches.[111]

The debate and development of LOAC remains a highly technical space in which high-level expertise and vernacular fluency are *sine quo non* to effective participation. There is much value in such proficiency and expertise. As Michael Schmitt and Sean Watts observe, "[t]hose with the expertise and experience to fully appreciate the fragile IHL balance between military necessity and humanity that provides its foundational raison *d'etre* have been the key drivers of this

107. *Id.*

108. *Id.*

109. *See, e.g.*, Heike Krieger, *Introduction*, *in* Inducing Compliance with International Humanitarian Law: Lessons from the African Great Lakes Region 1, 1 (Heike Krieger ed., 2015).

110. For exceptions, *see* Anghie & Chimni, *supra* note 86; Karolina Aksamitowska, *Traditional Approaches to the Law of Armed Conflict: Disseminating IHL through the Receptor Approach*, 11 Journal of International Humanitarian Legal Studies 5 (2020); Corri Zoli, *Islamic Contributions to International Humanitarian Law: Recalibrating TWAIL Approaches for Existing Contributions and Legacies*, 109 AJIL Unbound 271 (2015).

111. *See, e.g.*, Aksamitowska, *supra* note 110; Zoli, *supra* note 110.

process of change."[112] The goal ought to be the balancing of high-quality technical expertise with greater accommodation of regional perspectives in the making and shaping of LOAC. To achieve this goal, more effort must be made to develop high-level LOAC expertise globally; to mainstream LOAC in regions where it is marginalized; to ensure inclusive participation; and to be receptive to different approaches and perspectives. Conceivably, there will not be that many issues in relation to which clear regional perspectives will emerge. Nevertheless, where such issues do emerge, they should be taken seriously in the LOAC discourse and, where appropriate, accommodated in the development of LOAC.

VI. CONCLUSION

The historical record is clear. By definition, the "laws and customs of war," which formed part of the *ius publicum Europaeum*, did not allow for regional influence. The subsequent transition to a more geographically inclusive public international law together with the effects of decolonization increasingly provided for regional contributions to the making and shaping of LOAC. This reached its apex with the negotiation of the 1977 Additional Protocols and carried through to the conclusion of the 1980 Convention on Certain Conventional Weapons. The post-1980 ebb in regional impact is no coincidence. Rather it is a calculated response designed in large part by Pictet to safeguard the hold of the old guard—the original members of the *ius publicum Europaeum*—on the making and shaping of LOAC. The project was so successful that today this narrative is enshrined in the dogma of LOAC such that it is hard to identify Provost's comment with LOAC, that "the evolution of public international law as a whole has been marked by the ebb and flow of universalist aspirations and claims of cultural particularism."[113]

The super-universalist perspective of LOAC has been successful in maintaining the influence of a select group of States and actors in the making and shaping of the law. But it has also produced a sense of apathy if not hostility toward LOAC in parts of the developing world. This is well illustrated by the fact that IHL is largely omitted from consideration in the African Union's Agenda 2063, which serves to provide a "shared strategic framework for inclusive growth and sustainable Development and a global strategy to optimize the use of Africa's Resources for the benefit of all Africans."[114] This, in turn, challenges the legitimacy of LOAC

112. Michael N. Schmitt & Sean Watts, *State Opinio Juris and International Humanitarian Law Pluralism*, 91 International Law Studies 171, 174 (2015). I am, however, more skeptical of Schmitt and Watts's implicit suggestion that armed forces legal advisers are superior to civilian lawyers in their ability to make and shape LOAC.

113. René Provost, *The International Committee of the Red Widget? The Diversity Debate and International Humanitarian Law*, 40 Israel Law Review 614, 615 (2007).

114. *A.U., Agenda 2063: The Africa We Want, Framework Document* (Sept. 2015), https://au.int/sites/default/files/documents/33126-doc-framework_document_book.pdf.

and likely impacts adversely on compliance. However, critique of the super-universalist perspective of LOAC must not be confused with critique of the goal of regulation of armed conflict through international law of universal application. The real impact of increased accommodation of regional approaches and perspectives in the making and shaping of LOAC will have a modest impact on the actual understanding and normative development of the law. It will, however, have a drastic impact on the legitimacy and shared ownership of LOAC and, in time, may have a positive impact on compliance.

14

Between War and the Text: The Pedagogical Life of International Humanitarian Law

REBECCA SUTTON* ■

I. INTRODUCTION

How do international humanitarian law (IHL) rules circulate "down" from normative sites like The Hague and "up" from conflict settings like the Central African Republic (CAR), and where does IHL pedagogy fit in? What happens to the life and the meaning of a given legal rule as it travels back and forth across different domains, shifting between contexts such as: the Geneva Conventions and military manuals; competing interpretations among lawyers and policy makers; teaching, trainings, and peacetime dissemination initiatives; and actual armed conflicts? Finally, how are these dynamics shaped by the perceptions, attitudes, behavior, and interactions of differently situated actors who engage with IHL to their own ends?

Addressing these questions invites us to devote attention to practice[1] and to adopt a pluralistic understanding[2] of who makes and shapes IHL. This necessitates

* Rebecca Sutton is Senior Lecturer in International Law, School of Law, University of Glasgow. Field research in the Central African Republic received funding from the European Research Council under the European Union's Seventh Framework Programme (FP/2007-2013)/ERC Grant Agreement n. [340956 – IOW].

1. Lianne M. Boer, *The Greater Part of Jurisconsults: On Consensus Claims and Their Footnotes in Legal Scholar*ship, 29 Leiden Journal of International Law 1021 (2016).

2. Sally Engle Merry, *International Law and Sociolegal Scholarship: Towards a Spatial Global Legal Pluralism*, *in* 21 Special Issue: Law and Society Reconsidered 149 (Austin Sarat ed., 2007).

Rebecca Sutton, *Between War and the Text: The Pedagogical Life of International Humanitarian Law* In: *Making and Shaping the Law of Armed Conflict*. Edited by: Sandesh Sivakumaran and Christian R. Burne, Oxford University Press.
 DOI: 10.1093/oso/9780197775134.003.0014

that we cast our gaze beyond the usual actors and the typical settings in which we tend to seek out IHL's meaning. Taking a sociolegal approach[3] and collapsing the doctrine-practice divide, this chapter proposes that law can be found in very different kinds of settings and that it is being constituted and reconstituted on a daily basis by those we might not tend to think of as legal actors. Building on a six-year project that involved empirical research in South Sudan, the Central African Republic, and at civil-military trainings,[4] the discussion focuses on IHL engagement by international military, peacekeeping, and humanitarian actors, as well as lawyers and judges. What we discover through this granular investigation of the "everyday life" of IHL is that core IHL rules and norms take on a multiplicity of forms as they travel across various domains. As differently situated actors enact, engage with, and contest IHL rules, they individually and collectively forge IHL's (multiple) meaning(s).

To elucidate the everyday life, or rather *lives*, of IHL, the chapter introduces three distinct but interrelated realms in which a foundational IHL rule—the principle of distinction—circulates. First, the Pedagogical realm is a sphere of practice with a strong normative aspect, in which legal rules are taught, learned, and brought into question through teaching and training. Second, the Kinetic realm is where we find IHL rules in motion in operational contexts where active hostilities are underway. Third, the Intellectual realm encompasses more traditional legal settings such as courts or Geneva-based conferences in which lawyers, academics, policy makers, and judges theorize and adjudicate IHL rules. While each of the three realms constitutes a valid site of study for the everyday life of IHL, it is the Pedagogical realm that I want to bring to the fore in the present discussion. This is for the simple reason that so many accounts of how IHL works in the world overlook what happens in between "war and the text." Top-down legal academic accounts of IHL that revolve around some version of the Intellectual realm often obscure the relevance of teaching and trainings, and bottom-up approaches focusing on the operational context are just as likely to do so. In centering the Pedagogical realm, this chapter adopts a "middle-out" approach. Beginning with an examination of how the principle of distinction circulates at civil-military trainings attended by international military and peacekeeping actors, the discussion then follows distinction "down" to the armed conflict in the Central

3. *See also* Sarah H.M. Nouwen, Complementarity in the Line of Fire: The Catalysing Effect of the International Criminal Court in Uganda and Sudan (2013).

4. I thank Oxford University Press for allowing me to reproduce here some of the findings discussed in Rebecca Sutton, The Humanitarian Civilian: How the Idea of Distinction Circulates within and beyond International Humanitarian Law (2021). Research from CAR is addressed in more detail in Rebecca Sutton, *Who Is Civilian? Perceptions of "Civilianness" in the Central African Republic*, Research Brief 1 for the Individualization of War Project (July 2019), https://iow.eui.eu/wp-content/uploads/sites/20/2019/07/IOW-Policy-Brief-1-Sutton-Full-Brief-070719.pdf.

African Republic and "up" to the prosecution of crimes against humanity at the International Criminal Tribunal for the former Yugoslavia (ICTY).[5]

Drawing on the empirical findings, I advance a broader argument about who might be considered a "lawmaker" and who "makes" IHL. The international actors considered here are treated as lawmakers in the broadest sense of the word. The chapter does not assert the claim that these actors are (always) enacting positive law in the conventional sense, but rather that they are constituting, producing, and disseminating law's meaning(s) through their everyday practices.[6] At the same time, we can also say that these actors are unmaking IHL. I do not mean this in the narrow sense that they are "breaking" the rules through their (mis) interpretations and interventions. Rather, my contention is that as these actors make judgments, articulate competing perspectives, and puzzle through various ways of seeing civilians and combatants, they unmake IHL as we conventionally understand it. Their everyday practices produce civilians who creep too close to the fight, for example, and fighters who display quintessential civilian characteristics like vulnerability. As these actors redefine concepts and introduce the prospect of new categories, this unmaking is at the same time, irrefutably, a form of making IHL.

II. THE EVERYDAY LIFE OF IHL: THREE REALMS

This section of the discussion introduces the Pedagogical realm and its Kinetic and Intellectual counterparts. By treating the Pedagogical realm as its own domain, I make the case that training reveals something new about IHL—something that can be gleaned neither from the Geneva Conventions and the Additional Protocols of 1977, nor from the day-to-day routines of operational settings.

Across all three realms, international actors can be found producing, contesting, and giving meaning to foundational IHL rules such as the principle of distinction. This principle is articulated in Article 48 of the First Additional Protocol (API) to the Geneva Conventions, as follows:[7]

5. Prosecutor v. Milan Martić, Case No. IT-95-II-A, Appeal Judgment (Int'l Crim. Trib. for the former Yugoslavia Oct. 8, 2008) ("*Martić* Appeal Judgment"); Prosecutor v. Dragomir Milošević, Case No. IT-98-29/1-T, Trial Judgment (Int'l Crim. Trib. for the former Yugoslavia Dec. 12, 2007) ("*Milošević* Trial Judgment").

6. This brings an IHL focus to the literature on the everyday life of international law. *See, e.g.*, Luis Eslava, Local Space, Global Life: The Everyday Operation of International Law and Development (2015).

7. Article 48 of Protocol Additional to the Geneva Conventions of 12 August 1949, and Relating to the Protection of Victims of International Armed Conflicts, 8 June 1977, 1125 UNTS 3 ("API"). Article 50 of API further defines the civilian as follows: "1. A civilian is any person who does not belong to one of the categories of persons referred to in Article 4 A (1), (2), (3) and (6) of the Third Convention and in Article 4 of this Protocol. . . ."

> In order to ensure respect for and protection of the civilian population and civilian objects, the Parties to the conflict shall at all times distinguish between the civilian population and combatants and between civilian objects and military objectives and accordingly shall direct their operations only against military objectives.

While the main onus for upholding distinction lies with the parties to the conflict,[8] international actors like peacekeepers and judges also have a stake in, and routinely engage with, the civilian-combatant distinction. As the distinction concept travels across the Pedagogical, Kinetic, and Intellectual realms, competing ideas circulate about what I will call "civilianness" and "combatantness." *Civilianness* refers to a set of qualities that are perceived to be linked to civilian identity—such as harmlessness, innocence, and nonparticipation in fighting. *Combatantness* captures an opposing set of qualities, namely, dangerousness, participation, and complicity. This framing distills the essential features that allow someone to be perceived as civilian-*like* or combatant-*like*, moving us away from attachment to distinction as a bright-line rule. This might seem anathema from an IHL perspective, but it reflects the way in which distinction materializes in everyday practice: as a fuzzy and nebulous idea that often bears little resemblance to a bright-line civilian-combatant binary.

A. The Pedagogical Realm

The Pedagogical realm is a middle zone that lies in between the conflict zone and the legal text—a space between theory and practice. To showcase how IHL rules circulate here, I present empirical research findings from civil-military training programs in Sweden, Germany, and Italy. These training programs are explicitly designed to prepare international military and peacekeeping actors to participate in the comprehensive and integrated missions that have been in ascendancy since the end of the Cold War.[9] One aim of the trainings is to familiarize participants with the foundational rules of IHL, with a focus on how these rules work in practice. These trainings are especially relevant to IHL's principle of distinction because they are specifically designed to help military (and peacekeeping) actors navigate their relationships with different types of civilian actors in operational settings. While some of the trainers are of a more academic bent, the emphasis is on practical preparation for deployment and a minority of trainers have formal legal training. After outlining the three training sites and research methods in

8. *See, e.g.*, art. 51(7) and art. 58(b) of API.

9. Joanna Macrae & Nicholas Leader, *Shifting Sands: The Search for "Coherence" between Political and Humanitarian Responses to Complex Emergencies*, Humanitarian Policy Group Report No. 8, 9 (Aug. 2000).

more detail, I will articulate a broader rationale for paying close attention to the Pedagogical realm.

1. Three Civil-Military Training Sites

First, the Comprehensive Approach in Multi-Dimensional Peace Operations (CAMPO) training is a week-long program run by the German Centre for International Peace Operations (Zif),[10] and it takes place at the Akademie Schmöckwitz outside of Berlin. It is facilitated by training staff from Zif and the Command and Staff College of the German Armed Forces in Hamburg, and it involves guest lectures by high-level actors such as UN diplomats. The stated aim of the CAMPO training program is to prepare trainees to follow a comprehensive approach when deploying as members of multidimensional peacekeeping operations. Participants include a mixture of civilian and military actors, most of whom are engaged in EU or UN missions.

Second, the Swedish Armed Forces offers a two-week training program on Civil-Military Relations (CMR) at the Swedish Armed Forces International Centre (SWEDINT), located on a military base an hour outside of Stockholm. The course prepares international civilian, military, and police actors to cooperate and coordinate with each other in international crisis response and peace support operations under the aegis of the United Nations, the European Union, or NATO. The relations of interest in this training program are those between soldiers or peacekeepers working for an international mission, on the one hand, and the wide array of civilian actors present in the conflict context, on the other. This training makes use of innovative "mixed reality" simulation exercises which bring together virtual reality exercises with other forms of simulation, such as live role play.

Third, the one-week Functional Specialist Civil-Military Cooperation (CIMIC) course is run by the NATO Multi-National Civil-Military Cooperation Group and takes place in Motta di Livenza, Italy. Its goal is to provide trainees with a basic understanding of NATO CIMIC policies, principles, and tasks.[11] The training is specifically geared toward "functional specialists"—soldiers with a civilian area of expertise, such as medicine or psychology. Serving as "CIMIC personnel" in NATO missions, these individuals bridge the gap between military institutions and civilian organizations. CIMIC, or civil-military cooperation, is the main rubric under which NATO soldiers engage with civilian actors. CIMIC presupposes cooperation between the relevant actors and is organized around the achievement of military goals.[12] Military actors learn about, and work closely with, civilian

10. In German: *Zentrum fur Internationale Friedenseinsatz* (Zif). English description of the course: Zif, *Comprehensive Approaches to Multi-Dimensional Peacekeeping Operations*, http://www.zif-berlin.org/en/training/zif-training-courses/specialization-courses/campo.html.

11. NATO Multi-National CIMIC Group, *Functional Specialist Course*, https://www.cimic-coe.org/branches/training-education/course-landscape/NATO_CIMIC_Functional_Specialist_Course/.

12. CIMIC approaches overlap somewhat with COIN, which marshals civilian and military players to address the root causes of insurgencies, in hopes of appeasing, marginalizing, or

actors in order to fulfill the military mission.[13] The broad aim of CIMIC is to "create civil-military conditions that will offer the Commander the greatest possible moral, material and tactical advantages."[14]

In 2015 and 2016, I conducted thirty-eight interviews across the abovementioned training grounds, mostly in the form of small focus group discussions. I administered seventeen perception surveys to trainees, to supplement interview findings and inform interview planning. In addition, I logged over 200 hours of participant observation hours at the training sites. The technique of participant observation is particularly valuable in a practice-oriented project like this one, as it enables the researcher to learn things that come up in natural conversation. This research method is especially useful when seeking to make sense of complex social relationships or patterns of interaction.[15] As participant observation also gives the researcher access to practical nonverbal knowledge, it can reveal disconnects between what people claim to do and what they actually do.[16] This illuminates the tacit practices and assumptions of international actors, including those relating to IHL rules.

2. Why Study (Civil-Military) Trainings?

Three benefits of studying trainings in general—and civil-military trainings in particular—will be highlighted here.

First, civil-military training grounds are venues where overt attempts are made to disseminate international rules and norms and to shape the behavioral ideals of international actors. Ideas from the Intellectual realm circulate down to trainings in the form of classroom sessions, which draw on military manuals, institutional policies, best practice guidelines, and international legal instruments. Given that the training programs are explicitly designed to address the contact point between civilian and military actors, they inevitably put IHL's principle of distinction—and broader ideas about the civilian and combatant categories—in issue.

The second reason to examine civil-military training spaces is that doing so enriches and complements the investigation of civil-military interaction in operational contexts. While places such as South Sudan or the Central African Republic might more obviously appear to be sites of everyday life—albeit conflict-affected

defeating insurgents. *See* Austin Long, *Counter Insurgency*, *in* The Oxford Handbook Of International Security (Alexandra Gheciu & William Wohlforth eds., 2018).

13. Western European Union, WEU 1999–WEU (1999), *WEU Draft Concept on Civil-Military Cooperation (CIMIC)*, WEU-DMS 99246 (WEU Brussels, Feb. 17, 1999).

14. *Id.*

15. Alan Bryman, *The Debate about Quantitative and Qualitative Research: A Question of Method or Epistemology*, 35 The British Journal of Sociology 75, 81 (1984).

16. Michael Burawoy et al., Ethnography Unbound: Power and Resistance in Modern Metropolis, 2 (1991).

ones—professional training spaces are also venues where everyday life unfolds.[17] Almost all the participants who attend civil-military training programs are returning from frontline work in the field, on a break between stints, or preparing for a new mission. At their most useful, the programs establish a temporary space where these international actors can take stock of and make sense of their time in the field. Trainees bring their knowledge and experiences with them from the operational context, and their unique individual experiences also shape their engagement with the lessons. There is some natural overlap with the Kinetic realm, as trainees' firsthand accounts of their experiences in deployment zones offer granular, thick descriptions of the operational context. To varying degrees, these training grounds also bring civilian and military actors together in face-to-face interaction.

Third, rather than measuring how well the training programs mimic the "real" world, the artificial aspects of the training are valuable in their own right—particularly as they showcase facets of distinction that are often hidden from view. Simulation exercises, for example, afford an opportunity to observe complex patterns of interaction as if in slow motion. Trainees can literally pause the action as a role-play exercise unfolds, and they might even be granted a chance at a do-over. This kind of iterative process is rarely witnessed in other contexts. It is also through these types of exercises that tensions between competing ideals start to emerge. Commitments that seem possible to uphold simultaneously in the relevant texts, or in the classroom, suddenly rub up against each other, and trainees must negotiate this friction. This aspect of training again edges closer to the operational context.

B. The Kinetic Realm

Of all three realms, Kinetic practices tend to be the most practical—and potentially reactive. As the Kinetic realm is where one finds legal rules in motion, it sheds light on the way in which IHL is enacted as a day-to-day matter on the ground. Here, official policies and normative debates are brought into contact with the mundaneness of daily decision-making, revealing the nuances of what international actors actually do.

My own investigations of the Kinetic realm have focused on the practices and interactions of international humanitarian actors and international military and peacekeeping actors. The field of humanitarian studies has substantiated the need to attend to grounded practices, and these insights apply equally to the military and peacekeeping spheres. Alex de Waal entreats us to consider "actually existing humanitarianism,"[18] for example, and Zoe Marriage instructs us to look beyond

17. Bureaucratic conferences and meetings are treated as a site of everyday life in LAW IN EVERYDAY LIFE (Austin Sarat & Thomas R. Kearns eds., 1993).

18. ALEX DE WAAL, FAMINE CRIMES: POLITICS AND THE DISASTER RELIEF INDUSTRY IN AFRICA 66 (1997).

official discourse: humanitarian actors may invoke rules or principles at the same time as they ignore or breach them, in practice.[19] It was with the aim of better understanding how the civilian-combatant distinction circulates in operational settings that I embarked on research in CAR in April–May 2019.

1. The Central African Republic

Conflict in CAR has been characterized by a fragmentation of armed actors, lack of cohesive command structures, generalized criminality and banditry, and localized conflict dynamics.[20] The nature of French colonial rule of CAR is described by many analysts as a facilitating factor in ongoing State weakness and instability, and there is a lengthy history of intervention in CAR by other regional and international players.[21] CAR is also entangled in decades-long regional conflict cycle involving other countries such as Uganda, Chad, and Sudan.[22] December 10, 2012, is often viewed as the starting point of the most recent iteration of armed conflict in CAR. Broadly speaking, the international community has framed the conflict in CAR as a battle between Muslim (ex-Seleka)[23] actors and Christian and animist (Anti-Balaka) actors. Those who are more familiar with the country vigorously dispute the preceding paradigm,[24] pointing to the importance of reaching further back into history.[25]

The classification of an armed conflict in CAR, and equally the determination that there is *not* an armed conflict, will depend upon the facts on the ground. From an international law perspective this classification is crucial: the legal obligations (and protections) of States, non-State actors, and international actors such as humanitarians and peacekeepers will flow from it.[26] From approximately

19. Zoe Marriage, Not Breaking the Rules, Not Playing the Game: International Assistance to Countries at War 10 (2006).

20. Emma Fanning, *Safeguarding Distinction in the Central African Republic*, Humanitarian Exchange Magazine No. 62 (Sept. 2014).

21. UK Foreign and Commonwealth Office ("UK Briefing Note"), *Central African Republic: Background Brief and Analysis of the Crisis* (Dec. 2013).

22. *Id.* Many (ex-)Seleka fighters are from Chad or Sudan.

23. The coalition of Seleka rebels originates primarily from the northern part of CAR, and they are primarily Muslim. They have been formally demobilized, so members are often referred to as the ex-Seleka. The Anti-Balaka were initially formed as civilian defense forces in response to the violence by Seleka, but Anti-Balaka have subsequently engaged in large-scale attacks that included civilians.

24. Louisa Lombard & Sylvain Batianga-Kinzi, *Violence, Popular Punishment, and War in the Central African Republic*, 114 African Affairs 52 (2014); Babatunde Olugboji, *This Is Not a Religious War: What the Fight Is Really About*, Human Magazine No. 1, 10 (Summer 2014).

25. *See* Louisa Lombard, State of Rebellion: Violence and Intervention in the Central African Republic (2016) (addressing the "meta conflict" in CAR).

26. Classification also matters for assessments of whether MINUSCA has become a party to the conflict by using force.

December 2012 onward, international observers have generally described the situation in CAR as a non-international armed conflict (NIAC)—or more precisely a set of multiple, overlapping NIACs.[27] As armed groups in CAR have increasingly fragmented, however, it has become less evident where the conflicts are and who the parties to the conflict(s) are. There was further uncertainty regarding the presence of an armed conflict following the 2019 Khartoum peace agreement.[28]

With this uncertainty in the background, we find among operational actors significant disagreements about IHL's application and whether there is an armed conflict. Two groupings of international actors are of interest here: *international humanitarian actors* working for UN humanitarian agencies like UNHCR, non-governmental organizations (NGOs) like the Oxford Committee for Famine Relief (Oxfam) and Médecins Sans Frontières (MSF), as well as the International Committee of the Red Cross (ICRC); and *international peacekeeping actors* working for the UN mission in CAR, MINUSCA. These two sets of actors are worthy of scrutiny because their perceptions of civilian identity inform their protection activities.[29] In 2019, I engaged seventy-one respondents through semistructured interviews and focus group discussions in the capital Bangui, the town of Bria in Haute-Kotto Prefecture, and the "PK3" Internally Displaced Persons (IDP) site which lies three kilometers outside of Bria.[30] As of 2022, a full quarter of the population in CAR is displaced—many having moved multiple times over to flee violence and insecurity. At the time of fieldwork in 2019, many of the IDPs residing in PK3 had fled violence in central Bria in the two years prior. A pressing issue at the time was the active presence of Anti-Balaka fighters within the site, raising questions about the site's civilian character.

When discussing the relevance of law to their everyday work, the humanitarians and MINUSCA staff that I spoke with in CAR fluidly move back and forth between armed conflict scenarios in which IHL is the governing regime, and peacetime scenarios in which international human rights law (IHRL) is the main point of reference. This is not to say that IHL rules are a habitual topic of conversation for most international actors in CAR: much of the discussion of governing

27. Discussed in Patryk I. Labuda, *The UN Goes to War in the Central African Republic: What Are the Limits of Peacekeeping*, Just Security (Mar. 23, 2017), https://www.justsecurity.org/39151/war-central-african-republic-limits-peacekeeping/.

28. Political Agreement for Peace and Reconciliation in the Central African Republic (Khartoum Accord) (Feb. 5, 2019), https://www.peaceagreements.org/wview/2147/Political%20Agreement%20for%20Peace%20and%20Reconciliation%20in%20the%20Central%20African%20Republic%20(Khartoum%20Accord) [hereinafter "Khartoum Peace Agreement"].

29. Interview respondents in CAR in 2019 included, with some overlap due to IDPs working for local NGOs: 29 humanitarians (UN, international and local NGO, ICRC); 18 MINUSCA and UN Police (UNPOL) staff; 19 IDPs; and 5 members of armed groups.

30. As of May 2022, there were 37,000 IDPs living in PK3. A UN-led "durable solutions" project has been launched to oversee the return of IDPs to Bria as the security situation had been improving over time.

regimes is indirect or implicit, and the most overt engagements with law were often elicited through my own prompts in interviews. My empirical research in CAR also uncovers a broader practice whereby international actors draw on practical reasoning in their engagement with armed groups, instead of citing legal rules and principles. When entreating armed actors to spare local populations, for example, they will emphasize concerns of reciprocity or accessing the benefits of the peace process—rather than IHL targeting rules such as distinction or precautions in attack. While some international actors—humanitarians in particular—believe that clarifying the relevant law is crucial, others question whether it would make a difference for daily operations and engagement with armed elements. In section III we will see how these dynamics play out with respect to perceptions of "civilianness" in CAR.

C. The Intellectual Realm

The Intellectual realm encompasses a collection of sites more traditionally associated with law-making, and it is the most normative of the three realms. This is a domain in which lawyers, legal officials, judges, and (legal) academics, formally trained in international law, codify, adjudicate, and theorize the principle of distinction. It is also a domain in which policymakers and practitioners devise soft law guidelines and rules for civilian-military interaction. When the Intellectual realm is saved for last, one might expect that here, finally, we will find IHL rules as we know them. This is not to be. Instead, we discover that a rule like the principle of distinction is disrupted historically, doctrinally, and in practice. The fact that this murkiness and uncertainty prevails in the most normative of realms should inform our thinking about contemporary practices that impugn the idea of a bright-line binary and a mythically pure civilian. While it is perhaps easier to see the judges and lawyers of the ICTY, rather than their counterparts in the Pedagogical and Kinetic realms, as lawmakers, this study puts all of these actors on the same plane. The courtrooms of The Hague are thus treated as simply one more site at which the everyday life of IHL is enacted.

In contrast to research in the Pedagogical and Kinetic realms, my investigation of the Intellectual realm did not involve field research or the gathering of primary materials. Instead, I relied on historical materials on the civilian concept, publicly available legal judgments, and secondary sources that engaged with the historical and legal documents.

1. Crimes against Humanity at the ICTY

International criminal law (ICL) plays an important role in interpreting and enforcing IHL.[31] International criminal tribunals are significant forums where

31. Sandesh Sivakumaran, *Re-Envisaging the International Law of Internal Armed Conflict*, 22 European Journal of International Law 219, 232–33 (2011) ("Re-Envisaging"); *see also* Sivakumaran, in this volume.

the figure of the civilian is constituted, articulated, produced, and disseminated. In section III of this discussion, the *Martić* appeal judgment and the *Milošević* trial judgment at the ICTY will be used to show how ideas about "civilianness" circulate in the Intellectual realm. While *Martić* introduces a potentially vulnerable combatant who might be protected like a civilian, *Milošević* places a high burden on civilians to demonstrate that they are worthy of protected status. Taken together, these cases challenge the idea of a bright-line distinction and a stable civilian category.

Although the ICL courtroom will be the focus of the Intellectual realm discussion, a few words are merited on two other sites in this realm in which the civilian-combatant distinction circulates. First, there are the legal rules encoded in the Geneva Conventions and the Additional Protocols of 1977. While we find the clearest articulation of the principle of distinction in API, this legal instrument also contains targeting rules that call into question a binary formulation. In particular, the "direct participation in hostilities," or DPH, concept impugns the idea of a bright-line distinction by introducing a moment in which certain civilians can be intentionally targeted.[32] Consider also historical approaches to legal protection in war. When we revisit past conceptualizations of who was to be shielded from war's violence and on what basis, we find that the idea of a stable distinction—and the related notion of a unified civilian category populated by (equally) protected civilians—is constantly troubled.[33] Along with the goings on at the ICTY, these historical approaches affirm that the civilian concept is, and has always been, contested. The notion of an innocent, harmless, and nonparticipating figure cleanly separated from fighting is in many respects more myth than reality.

The third section of the discussion deepens the engagement with the Pedagogical life of IHL, examining how the civilian-combatant distinction travels to and from this middle domain of practice.

III. THE PEDAGOGICAL LIFE OF IHL

This section presents empirical findings from three civil-military trainings to showcase how IHL's civilian-combatant distinction circulates in this middle realm. It then moves outward to the other domains, painting a picture of how IHL concepts travel "down" to the Kinetic realm and "up" to the Intellectual realm.

32. Discussed in SUTTON, THE HUMANITARIAN CIVILIAN, *supra* note 4, ch. 5.

33. *Id.*, ch. 4; and *see generally* HELEN KINSELLA, THE IMAGE BEFORE THE WEAPON: A CRITICAL HISTORY OF THE DISTINCTION BETWEEN COMBATANT AND CIVILIAN (2015).

A. The Pedagogical Life of IHL: Three Civil-Military Trainings

"You're either a combatant or you're not."
–Trainer, Swedish Armed Forces International Centre

"Not all civilians are civilians. There are different kinds."
--Trainee, Swedish Armed Forces International Centre

Civil-military training spaces serve as sites where struggles over distinction naturally arise, whether they materialize face to face, virtually, or in the form of stories shared from the operational context.

Beginning with the CAMPO training in Germany, military and peacekeeping trainees try to discern the boundaries of the civilian category in a role-play exercise. IHL's principle of distinction is explicitly engaged here, presenting an opportunity to investigate how various international actors understand this legal rule. When international actors reach for a bright-line civilian-combatant distinction—and they do reach for it, repeatedly—what they tend to find in its place is a confused, fuzzy, and fragmented idea.

Trainees are introduced at the CAMPO training to the elaborate fictional land of the Batari people, where an armed conflict is being fought between State armed forces and the Batari Liberation Army fighters. Members of the Batari civilian population are caught in between, and they are in urgent need of life-saving humanitarian services as well as protection from the ongoing violence. It is into this context that the CAMPO trainees are plunged, tasked with designing and implementing an international response to the unfolding crisis. Each group of trainees is instructed to identify who is a civilian in the land of Batari. Remarks on the haziness of the civilian category fly around the room, as trainees struggle in earnest to come to a consensus. In an earlier training session, the CAMPO trainees have learned that "It's very rough to say 'civilians,'" and that the civilian is "not that easy to describe." Now, they wonder: Is it only the members of the local Batari population who are truly civilians under international law? What about individuals belonging to the non-Batari population who also reside in the area? Might some of the Batari Liberation Army fighters who do not carry weapons be civilians? To cope with this complexity, one group establishes different compartments in the civilian category. They differentiate unarmed liberation fighters from members of the local population, labeling them as different kinds of civilians. The other groups mostly arrive at indeterminate answers to this question.

Moving "up" briefly now to the Intellectual realm, the scholarly literature on civil-military relations generally treats civilian actors as a bounded group, juxtaposed with military actors as their "other." This is not to say that there is a complete lack of nuance: some scholars and practitioners of civil-military relations nod to plurality within the civilian and military categories.[34] In the preceding account from the CAMPO training program, trainees grapple with IHL's civilian category in different ways. When the trainees are immersed in the fictional land of the Batari, they strain to fit every actor on the ground into the civilian-combatant binary. The move by some groups to delineate subcategories of civilians does not contravene the formal lessons of the CAMPO training, but instead amplifies a trainer's earlier observation during a classroom session that the civilian category is something of an approximation.

The main point being stressed here is that CAMPO participants treat IHL's civilian-combatant distinction merely as a point of departure that is both unsatisfactory and malleable. We see how blurry the vision of distinction is when trainees import this understanding into subsequent training tasks—as when they are asked to situate humanitarian actors in relation to the civilian category. Here again the Pedagogical realm reaches over to, and is permeated by, the other domains. As noted previously, the ideas disseminated in classroom lessons are informed by civil-military guidelines from the Intellectual realm. Some of these guidelines treat humanitarians as members of the civilian category and, at the same time, suggest that humanitarians are somehow set apart from other civilians. For example, the UN Office for the Coordination of Humanitarian Affairs (OCHA) Guidelines[35] appeal to a civilian-combatant binary while introducing a humanitarian-military distinction that enacts a carveout for humanitarians from the civilian category. The Kinetic realm also reaches into the training sessions here (and vice versa) as trainers and trainees mine their own diverging experiences in the Kinetic realm. In operational contexts such as Afghanistan and South Sudan, military and peacekeeping actors have observed humanitarians seeking different treatment from the general civilian population—as though they do not all belong to a unified civilian category. Even where the trainees reject the notion of a carveout that affords humanitarians special protections and privileges, it is possible to entertain the thought because their interpretation of the civilian category is so shaky.

The civilian-combatant distinction also circulates at SWEDINT, where a military trainer asks trainees what they would do in situations of hybrid warfare where they cannot discern between civilians and combatants. A UN civilian trainee responds that, following the UN Department of Peacekeeping Operations (DPKO)[36] policy for UN missions, "when in doubt, assume someone is civilian."

34. *See* Hugo Slim, *The Stretcher and the Drum: Civil-Military Relations in Peace Support Operations*, 3 International Peacekeeping 123, 128 (1996).

35. UN-OCHA, Guidelines on the Use of Military and Civil Defence Assets to Support United Nations Humanitarian Activities in Complex Emergencies (Mar. 2003), https://docs.unocha.org/sites/dms/Documents/01.%20MCDA%20Guidelines%20March%2003%20Rev1%20Jan06.pdf.

36. Now Department of Peace Operations, DPO.

When the same question arises with respect to international actors, a military trainee proposes dividing international actors into armed versus unarmed categories. He points out that this fits with the framework of civil-military relations and "it's the best term we have." He goes on to note the difficulty of drawing this line when civilian security actors are armed, or when politicians and donors take on the appearance of military actors. Still, he believes that the preferred approach is to situate all international civilians together in one unified category; he includes humanitarian actors in this category, as well.

Later, during a chat in the hallway outside the classroom, a civilian trainer at SWEDINT reflects on these exchanges. He proposes that, in theory, anyone should be able to look at international actors and say: "You're either a combatant or you're not." This is in many respects the official line at the SWEDINT training. But the trainer's ambivalence about this is also evident, as he draws on his observations of international interventions in the Kinetic realm. He laments that there are blurred lines in practice: military forces engage in humanitarian activities, and humanitarian actors who use military assets start to resemble a military force.

Similar tensions arise when different trainees at SWEDINT are canvassed about their understanding of the civilian-combatant distinction. One military trainee pronounces: "Not all civilians are civilians. There are different kinds." Another military trainee vociferously opposes this splitting, appealing to a bright-line distinction and a civilian category that contains everyone who is not a combatant or a fighter. The Intellectual, Pedagogical, and Kinetic realms intersect again here, as trainees draw partly on what they have just heard in the classroom and partly on their experiences of past deployments.

At the NATO CIMIC training, trainees also learn about what NATO terms the "civil dimension" of the operational context. They are taught that it encompasses a plethora of actors, including NGOs, governmental organizations, donors, international organizations, media, IDPs, refugees, civilian populations, and local authorities. One NATO military trainer sorts actors into good and bad—leaving room for a disorderly in-between. In conflict zones, he proposes, "We have good guys and bad guys. Everything in the middle is a mess, including NGOs." Contemplating who is civilian among international actors, one NATO trainer reaches for a bright-line binary that positions civilians who DPH on the combatant side. He asserts: "It is very simple. You're civilian if you are not carrying a weapon and you're not participating in hostilities."[37] When I ask him in a subsequent interview how this perspective translates in comprehensive international missions, he struggles to delineate a distinction and emphasizes the importance of perceptions.

At another point in the NATO training, international civilian actors are configured similarly to Russian nesting dolls. First there are international humanitarian actors, who are nestled within international civilian actors, who are nestled

37. Civilians who DPH do not forfeit their civilian status in IHL, but they are treated differently from civilians who do not directly participate.

within the larger civilian landscape. In this conceptualization, humanitarian actors are depicted as a subcategory of civilian actors, much as in the conceptualization at CAMPO described previously. Intriguingly, one of the military trainers at NATO also refers to humanitarian actors as "*civilian* civilians." Expanding on this, she says that when military actors use the word "civilian" in the context of a UN peacekeeping mission, they typically use it as shorthand for UN police; they do not digest it as a reference to humanitarian actors. Another military trainer at NATO counters that the term "civilian" is meant to capture all international civilian actors. He appeals to international law's authority to state: "[H]umanitarians are just civilians. There is no other kind of civilian." Of any claims to the contrary, he says: "[T]hat's not the law."

In these brief accounts from the civil-military trainings, we get a glimpse of how a legal rule like IHL's principle of distinction travels into, and out from, training spaces. The next two sections will further contextualize IHL's Pedagogical life, examining how distinction circulates upward and downward to other domains.

B. Circulation Down to the Kinetic Realm

Moving on to the Kinetic realm, this section of the discussion considers what it means to say that a particular actor is "civilian" in CAR: Who is seen to possess qualities of "civilianness," and who is perceived to fit into the civilian category? The discussion centers the perspectives of international humanitarian actors (working for the UN, NGOs, ICRC) and peacekeeping actors (working for MINUSCA). Particular attention is paid to the practice of identifying civilians for the purpose of discerning who merits (UN) protection—rather than, say, who constitutes a legitimate target under IHL. Many of these humanitarian and peacekeeping actors cite a civilian-combatant distinction in their routine operations, implying that there is an armed conflict and IHL is governing law.[38] As the discussion in section II attests, however, there is no consensus among these actors regarding IHL's application in CAR.

The first subsection scrutinizes perceptions of the civilian character of CAR's IDP sites, focusing on the "PK3" IDP site near Bria town. The second subsection considers who is understood to be a bona fide civilian in CAR more broadly. As humanitarians and peacekeepers adopt competing perspectives on "civilianness," we sense that their claims are informed as much by their own worldviews and the pressures of their mandates as they are by IHL.

38. While there is no civilian-combatant distinction as such in NIACs, the civilian-combatant distinction applies as a matter of customary IHL. *See* Customary International Humanitarian Law, Rule 1 (Jean-Marie Henckaerts & Louise Doswald-Beck, 2005).

1. The Civilian Character of the IDP Sites in CAR

"The Character of the IDP camps here is not civilian."
–MINUSCA protection actor, Bangui

"Every day and night, armed groups can come. There's no fence or gate and we aren't protected . . ."
–IDP residing in the cathedral site, Bria

Humanitarians and peacekeepers in CAR routinely speak of the importance of guarding or maintaining the civilian character of IDP sites. The terminology of "maintaining" is somewhat misleading, however, as it suggests the sites are, presently, populated exclusively by civilians. On the contrary, representatives from international organizations and NGOs seem to agree that armed actors are present in and around most (if not all) of the IDP sites throughout the country. A humanitarian actor in Bangui speaks of the PK3 site as follows: "For some of these armed guys it's a shelter. They are in the middle of thousands of people, knowing they won't be harmed while they're there."[39] A MINUSCA protection actor in Bangui puts it bluntly: "The character of the IDP camps here is not civilian."[40]

Many international actors also remark that armed groups in CAR are harming "their own" populations inside the IDP sites. This refers to local populations considered loyal to a particular armed group due to religious or ethnic ties; for example, the Christian community in the case of Anti-Balaka. From the vantage point of a humanitarian actor in Bria, "the PK3 site is not purely civilian, because the armed groups are there and they are doing things to the population."[41]

It is well known that Anti-Balaka actors maintain an active presence in PK3, despite the efforts that international actors make to enforce the site's civilian character. One international humanitarian actor describes the routine efforts that humanitarians make in this respect, effectively putting the onus on site residents. "We have relationships with community leaders . . . If someone in your family is Anti-Balaka, you need to tell them not to come here. The community thinks Anti-Balaka protects them, but Anti-Balaka causes problems and is taxing them."[42] Dynamics of reprisal and revenge attacks are particularly difficult to thwart. For example, Anti-Balaka residing inside the IDP site try to tax or launch attacks against ex-Seleka affiliates outside PK3, and those targeted respond by attacking

39. Interview with Humanitarian actor, Bangui, Apr. 18, 2019.

40. Interview with MINUSCA actor, Bangui, Apr. 12, 2019.

41. Focus group with humanitarian actors, Bria, Apr. 24, 2019.

42. Interview with humanitarian actor, Bria, Apr. 25, 2019. A similar point is made in Interview with humanitarian actor, Bangui, Apr. 23 2019.

IDPs inside the site—whether the latter are Anti-Balaka or not.[43] Anti-Balaka fighters are also likened to a band of youth, with some interviewees rejecting the "self-defence" posture claimed by these fighters. Armed actors formerly affiliated with ex-Seleka forces, such as the Mouvement pour l'Unité et la Paix en Centrafrique (UPC), also make much of the fact that certain IDP sites host Anti-Balaka elements. The subtext of these claims is that those residing in the sites are potentially "fair game" for targeted violence.

Although CAR's IDP sites are meant to be free of weapons, it is widely known that there are weapons held inside. These are often "artisanal" or homemade weapons.[44] One MINUSCA actor describes the futility of weapons collections in this way: "In [Disarmament, Demobilization and Reintegration] you collect the weapons. They'll give you two and keep the others. They can make good machetes and they can make modern Kalashnikovs. They will go and kill and come back to the IDP site."[45] MINUSCA staff also point out that weapons searches in Bria are made difficult by the fact that: there are up to 55,000 IDPs residing in the PK3 site, with no fence around the perimeter; alert networks enable armed actors to hide their weapons when a search is underway; and armed actors are increasingly retreating further inside the site to avoid detection along the main road.[46] More and more, the notion of "maintaining" the civilian character of IDP sites offers a poor descriptor of the nature of international engagement in CAR.

IDPs in CAR also express anxieties about the porousness of the sites.[47] A focus group discussion with IDPs residing in the cathedral area revealed that although things have calmed down somewhat since the Khartoum[48] and Bria[49] peace agreements, the inhabitants do not feel protected in this setting. "Every day and night, armed groups can come. There's no fence or gate and we aren't protected. They take the children, and sometimes adults, to their base. You can't do anything to stop it."[50] Connecting back to the problem of civilian-combatant muddling, a humanitarian actor cites such fears as a central reason for which displaced populations are loath to give up (all of) their weapons.[51]

43. Interview with MINUSCA actor, Bangui, Apr. 14, 2019.

44. Interview with MINUSCA actor, Bangui, Apr. 12, 2019.

45. *Id.*

46. Interview with MINUSCA actor, Bria, Apr. 25, 2019.

47. Focus groups with IDPs in PK3, Cathedral Area and Hospital Area in Bria, Apr. 26, 2019.

48. *See* "Khartoum Peace Agreement," *supra* note 28.

49. *Central African Republic: Six Armed Groups Sign Peace Agreement in Bria*, Centre For Humanitarian Dialogue Report (Apr. 11, 2019), https://reliefweb.int/report/central-african-republic/central-african-republic-six-armed-groups-sign-peace-agreement-bria. The agreement can be accessed here: https://www.peaceagreements.org/viewmasterdocument/2350.

50. Focus group with IDPs in Cathedral Area, Bria, Apr. 26, 2019.

51. Interview with humanitarian actor, Bangui, Apr. 23, 2019.

2. Discerning Who Is Civilian in CAR

> *"You figure it out in the moment that they begin to act violently, take some kind of action."*
>
> –INGO actor, Bria

> *". . . public opinion is MINUSCA is firing at civilians. MINUSCA is killing civilians."*
>
> –INGO actor, Bangui

When asked how one might discern who is civilian inside the PK3 site, officials from MINUSCA and humanitarian organizations indicate that distinguishing civilians from members of armed groups is a difficult task. Often the "moment of truth" comes only when a particular actor begins to act violently. This challenge appears to be particularly acute with respect to Anti-Balaka, as they are so embedded in the IDP sites. One NGO actor in Bangui describes CAR as "a place where *everyone* is civilian. Even if you have a weapon, wear a uniform and are attached to an armed group, you would claim you are a civilian."[52] If a person is killed by international forces, armed groups will often claim that such forces are "killing our people," suggesting that members of these groups are civilians.

In April 2018, MINUSCA carried out an operation with CAR Armed Forces and Internal Security Forces to "flush out" armed groups from PK5—a predominantly Muslim neighborhood in the capital, Bangui. As "Operation Sukula" got underway, locals attempted to thwart MINUSCA's progress.[53] When MINUSCA reportedly returned fire after shots came from a group gathering around MINUSCA tanks, a number of local people died and MINUSCA was accused of killing civilians.[54] In connection with that incident, interviewees for this research openly mused as to whether those killed were "real" combatants or "real" civilians.

Other actors in CAR speak of the challenges of determining who is civilian in a setting in which armed groups are "making use" of civilians. Some interviewees take the view that it is one thing if civilians are used involuntarily—as in a human shield scenario—but another if civilians voluntarily decide to participate in fighting. The difference is not always obvious: "But often civilians sympathize with armed groups and can become 'active' . . . If conscious, and not under duress, they

52. Interview with humanitarian actor, Bangui, Apr. 13, 2019.

53. *See Security Council Press Statement on Attack against United Nations Multidimensional Integrated Stabilization Mission in Central African Republic*, SC/13291-PKO/724 (Apr. 11, 2018), https://www.un.org/press/en/2018/sc13291.doc.htm.

54. *Id.* (referring to the death of civilians and reminding all parties of their IHL obligations); Leger Serge Kokopakpa, *Civilians Killed in Central African Republic Were "Manipulated": UN*, REUTERS (Apr. 12, 2018), https://uk.reuters.com/article/uk-centralafrica-un/civilians-killed-in-central-african-republic-were-manipulated-u-n-idUKKBN1HJ3FS (reporting that MINUSCA actors emphasize that the armed actors in PK5 were criminal gangs).

are combatants in my view. But it's so hard to know."[55] Another MINUSCA actor puts the term "civilian" in air quotes for local populations that are used as human shields.[56] In such accounts, no mention tends to be made of the direct participation in hostilities, or DPH, concept in IHL.

The issue of military uniforms has also proven vexing for international actors. This is especially the case with Anti-Balaka, as they do not typically wear any uniforms or insignia. A humanitarian actor in Bangui elaborates:[57]

> Usually we cannot say who is in a group. . . . It depends what distinction we want to make: civilian, armed civilian or member of an armed group. I could be part of an armed group, and just be the "papa" protecting the house with a weapon. So we can't look at the weapon to determine the civilian character of a person. In periods of tension, it can become a bit more clear: groups might put on uniforms and identify themselves more.

A MINUSCA official further explains: "Most of the armed groups are civilians with arms. When they don't have the arms, you don't have the right to consider them armed groups. We have to call them civilians then."[58] A practical implication of this fluidity is the difficulty of counting deaths and casualties, as noted earlier. In CAR, it is also sometimes the case that *not* wearing a uniform can amount to a sort of uniform. Actors on the ground explain how the lack of uniforms for the Anti-Balaka enables ex-Seleka and affiliated actors to make accusations that anyone who is not in uniform is Anti-Balaka.[59]

As muddled as these dynamics are, some local interviewees (who are themselves from CAR) voice skepticism of international actors' claims that they can't delineate a civilian-combatant distinction. One IDP *chef de bloque* (i.e., leader of a block within the site) says of internationals based in field offices that they "know everyone," including those who are part of armed groups, simply because "they are here."[60]

Tensions also arise between humanitarians and MINUSCA staff about the UN mission's categorization of actors in CAR. Humanitarians fault MINUSCA for associating ethnicity with combatant status, for example.[61] Pointing to the mission's treatment of the Fulani, a nomadic people who roam Central and West

55. Interview with MINUSCA actor, Bangui, Apr. 15, 2019.

56. Interview with MINUSCA actor, Bangui, Apr. 17, 2019.

57. Interview with humanitarian actor, Bangui, Apr. 16, 2019.

58. Interview with MINUSCA actor, Bangui, Apr. 18, 2019. It is worth pointing out here that under IHL, being armed does not, in and of itself, disqualify an individual from civilian status.

59. Interview with humanitarian actor, Bangui, Apr. 16, 2019.

60. Interview with IDP, PK3 IDP site, Apr. 26, 2019.

61. Interview with humanitarian actor, Bangui, Apr. 16, 2019.

Africa, humanitarians submit that some UN actors do not comprehend the nuances of transhumance in the region.[62] Humanitarians further emphasize that conflict parties instrumentalize allegations of non-civilianness to justify violent attacks, as was the case with respect to two widely publicized incidents in 2018. First, in three IDP sites in the town of Batangafo in northern CAR, armed groups deliberately targeted civilians and threatened an MSF hospital they claimed was "sheltering enemies."[63] When UN peacekeepers failed to respond, 15 people reportedly died and more than 20,000 were displaced from IDP camps.[64] Second, there was a violent attack by fighters from the Seleka offshoot UPC, accompanied by armed Muslim "civilians," on an IDP camp in Alindao town in the Basse-Kotto region.[65] On the pretext that Anti-Balaka fighters were using the site as a refuge, these armed elements killed 70 to 100 women, children, older people, and people with disabilities as UN peacekeepers guarding the site looked on.[66] Humanitarians also perceive MINUSCA's tendency to view residents of the PK5 neighborhood in Bangui not as combatants participating in an armed conflict, but rather as criminals carrying out opportunistic acts, as an outgrowth of the mission's stated objective of bringing peace to CAR. That is, a criminal gang paradigm suits MINUSCA because it conforms to a peacetime rather than a wartime scenario. Higher-level MINUSCA actors counter that violence in IDP sites—which is often perpetrated with artisanal weapons and hunting rifles—should indeed be understood as criminal and a symptom of law-and-order problems.[67]

These accounts from the Kinetic realm give an impression of how the civilian-combatant distinction circulates in a context in which intervenors cannot even agree on whether an armed conflict exists. Although we see few obvious references in CAR to the more normative Pedagogical and Intellectual realms, views on civilianness are shaped by each actor's (lack of) familiarity with international law and the training they have (not) received before deployment.

62. Interview with humanitarian actors, Bangui, Apr. 19, 2019.

63. *Unprotected: Report on Violence and Lack of Protection for Civilians in CAR*, Médecins Sans Frontières (Feb. 19, 2019), https://www.msf.org/unprotected-report-violence-and-lack-protection-civilians-car-central-african-republic.

64. Ibid.

65. *CAR: Attacks on an IDP Camp in Alindao*, ACAPS Briefing Note (Nov. 30, 2018), https://www.acaps.org/sites/acaps/files/products/files/20181130_acaps_briefing_note_attacks_on_an_idp_camp_in_alindao_car_0.pdf.

66. *Central African Republic: "Everything Was in Flames": The Attack on a Displaced Persons Camp in Alindao*, Amnesty International (Dec. 14, 2018), https://www.amnesty.org/en/documents/afr19/9573/2018/en/.

67. For more on this claim, *see* Rebecca Sutton, *Everyday Criminal Justice and Civilian Protection in the Central African Republic*, Policy Brief 2 for the Individualization of War Project (Oct. 2019), https://iow.eui.eu/wp-content/uploads/sites/20/2019/10/IOW-Policy-Brief-2-Sutton-Full-Brief-151019.pdf.

C. Circulation Up to the Intellectual Realm

Traveling to the Intellectual realm, this section demonstrates that "civilianness" is pushed in two directions at the *Milošević* trial and the *Martić* appeal. As a caveat for what follows, the "civilian" protected under ICL from offenses such as crimes against humanity is not necessarily the API civilian accorded with immunity from attack in the conduct of hostilities.[68] It should thus be kept in mind that the civilian figure circulating in the ICTY courtrooms is not always one and the same as that in IHL.

1. The Case of *Martić*

Milan Martić had held various governmental positions within the Serbian Autonomous Region of Krajina, and subsequently became Commander of the Republic of Serbian Krajina (RSK) forces. Among other offenses perpetrated individually or as a member of a Joint Criminal Enterprise, he was accused of planning and ordering the shelling of civilian areas and the civilian population of Zagreb in May 1995. Some of the victims of these attacks were soldiers *hors de combat*, and the main point of interest from the *Martić* appeal is that these individuals were found to be victims of crimes against humanity. The implication was that qualities associated with contemporary civilianness—particularly harmlessness and vulnerability—could attach to individuals who would otherwise be categorized as combatants, entitling them to be protected like civilians. What is more, ICTY judges entertained the possibility that solders *hors de combat* could also be classified as "civilians" for the purpose of crimes against humanity. While the ICTY Appeals Chamber ultimately rejected this latter proposition, it may yet see the light of day in other international tribunals.

A preliminary issue to consider here is the breadth of the civilian category in the context of crimes against humanity. While war crimes as a category of offense explicitly protect combatants, those rendered *hors de combat*, and civilians, crimes against humanity are primarily designed to protect civilians. In brief, crimes against humanity are systematic crimes that are committed as part of a general policy of attacking a civilian population.[69] In Article 5 of the ICTY Statute, this category of crime is constructed in such a way that certain underlying offenses (i.e., murder) must be committed in the context of an attack directed against "any civilian population."[70] This latter requirement is referred to as the *chapeau*

68. On different definitions of terms in IHL and ICL, *see* Sivakumaran, *Re-Envisaging*, *supra* note 31, at 239. On why transposing the API definition of the civilian in ICL is potentially problematic, *see* An Introduction to International Criminal Law and Procedure 231 (Robert Cryer et al. eds., 3rd ed. 2014).

69. Statute of the International Criminal Tribunal for the former Yugoslavia art. 5, S.C. Res. 827 (May 25, 1993), adopting The Secretary-General Report Pursuant to Paragraph 2 of Security Council Resolution 808 ("ICTY Statute").

70. Ibid.

element, and it designates an attack that is widespread or systematic in nature.[71] Neither the nationality nor the ethnicity of the civilians against whom the attack is directed are relevant.[72]

The *Martić* trial and appeal chambers grappled with the definition of "civilian" in Article 5 of the ICTY Statute. In the trial judgment, the ICTY Trial Chamber had found that defining the civilian too expansively would "impermissibly blur" the distinction between combatant and non-combatant.[73] Following suit, the Appeals Chamber applied the narrow API definition of the civilian,[74] citing the "fundamental character of the notion of the civilian" in both IHL and ICL.[75] The Chamber also noted that the API definition accords with the ordinary meaning of the term "civilian" as a person who is not a member of the armed forces.[76] The ICTY had not consistently applied such a narrow definition of the civilian in past cases, however.[77]

Another question of interest in the *Martić* appeal was whether all individual victims of crimes against humanity must be civilians. Article 5 of the ICTY statute is silent on this point.[78] While retaining the *chapeau* requirement of "any civilian population," the Appeals Chamber found that, within the wider civilian population, each individual victim does not have to be a civilian in the IHL sense.[79] Accordingly, members of armed forces who have been rendered *hors de combat*

71. Prosecutor v. Duško Tadić, Opinion and Judgment, Case No. IT-94-I, Trial Judgment, ¶ 727 (Int'l Crim. Trib. for the former Yugoslavia May 7, 1997) ("*Tadic* Trial Judgment").

72. William J. Fenrick, *The Crime against Humanity of Persecution in the Jurisprudence of the ICTY*, 32 Netherlands Yearbook of International Law 81, 86 (2001).

73. Prosecutor v. Milan Martić, Case No. IT-95-11, Trial Judgment, ¶ 56 (Int'l Crim. Trib. for the former Yugoslavia June 12, 2007) ("*Martić* Trial Judgment"). A similar approach is followed in Prosecutor v. Tihomir Blaškić, IT-95-14-A, Appeal Judgment, ¶¶ 113–14 (Int'l Crim. Trib. for the former Yugoslavia July 29, 2004); Prosecutor v. Stanislav Galić, IT-98-29-A, Appeal Judgment, fn. 437 (Int'l Crim. Trib. for the former Yugoslavia Nov. 30, 2006), fn. 437 (members of armed forces cannot claim civilian status); Prosecutor v. Mrkšić et al., Case No. IT-95-I3/I-T, Trial Judgement, 461 (Int'l Crim. Trib. for the former Yugoslavia ICTY Sept. 27, 2007).

74. *Martić* Appeal Judgment, *supra* note 5, ¶ 299. Following Prosecutor v. Dragoljub Kunarac et al., Case No. IT-96-23/IT-96-23/I-A, Appeal Judgment, ¶ 91 (Int'l Crim. Trib. for the former Yugoslavia June 12, 2002).

75. *Martić* Appeal Judgment, *supra* note 5, ¶ 299.

76. *Id.*, ¶ 297.

77. *See, e.g.*, Prosecutor v. Dario Kordić and Mario Cerkez, Case No. IT-95-14/2-A, Appeal Judgment, ¶¶ 421–22 (Int'l Crim. Trib. for the former Yugoslavia ICTY Dec. 17, 2004); Prosecutor v. Kupreškić et al., Case No. IT-95-16-T, Trial Judgment (Int'l Crim. Trib. for the former Yugoslavia ICTY, Jan. 14, 2000).

78. Joakim Dungel, *Defining Victims of Crimes against Humanity:* Martić *and the International Criminal Court*, 22 Leiden J. of Int'l L. 727, 736.

79. *Martić* Appeal Judgment, *supra* note 5, ¶ 307.

may also be victims of crimes against humanity.[80] One question that *Martić* left unresolved is what would happen in a scenario where every single individual targeted in an attack failed to meet the API definition of a civilian. This was addressed in the *Mrkšić* appeal, wherein the Appeals Chamber found that a population composed (almost) entirely of those who were *hors de combat*—in that case, prisoners of war—did not meet the criteria of "any civilian population."[81] To date, most international tribunals have followed *Martić* in excluding soldiers *hors de combat* from the civilian population.[82]

Reflecting on *Martić*, this is an instance where the ICTY Appeals Chamber established the category of a suddenly vulnerable combatant who merits civilian-like protection, albeit for the purposes of crimes against humanity. This was the case, even if the Appeals Chamber did not go so far as to include soldiers *hors de combat* in the civilian population. The treatment of soldiers *hors de combat* as vulnerable figures worthy of special protection offers a striking counterpoint to the beleaguered civilian figure in CAR, whose civilianness is doubted at every turn. Next, the *Milošević* trial suggests that presenting as the combatant's opposite is not enough to establish civilian bona fides.

2. The Case of *Milošević*

In the *Milošević* trial, the issue of attacks directed at a civilian population arose in the context of crimes against humanity and the war crime of terrorizing the civilian population.[83] In this case, the ICTY imposed a heavy burden on civilians to demonstrate their worthiness of civilian status. They not only had to show that qualities of "combatantness"—that is of danger, complicity, and participation in fighting—did not attach to them at the time of the attack, but they also had to make the case that qualities of civilianness did. The *Milošević* trial thus introduces further instability to the civilian-combatant distinction, setting high standards for appearance, comportment, and behavior for those claiming civilian status.

In *Milošević*, the Trial Chamber explained that the term "civilian" is defined negatively to include any person who is not a member of the armed forces or an organized military group belonging to a party to the conflict.[84] The Trial Chamber also noted that, in some circumstances, it may be difficult to ascertain whether

80. *Id.* The Appeals chamber found this to reflect customary international law (¶ 309).

81. Prosecutor v. Mrkšić et al., Case No. IT-95-13/1-A, Appeal Judgment, ¶¶ 27–44 (Int'l Crim. Trib. for the former Yugoslavia ICTY May 5, 2009). The same attack was still prosecuted as a war crime.

82. *See, e.g.*, Prosecutor v. Germain Katanga, Case No. ICC-01/04-01/07, Judgment pursuant to Article 74 of the Statute, ¶ 1102 (Mar. 7, 2014); Prosecutor v. Issa Hassan Sesay, Morris Kallon and Augustine Gbao, Case No. SCSL-04-15-T, Trial Judgment, ¶ 82 (Mar. 2, 2009).

83. *Milošević* Trial Judgment, *supra* note 5, ¶¶ 875, 882, 921–24.

84. *Id.*, ¶ 945. Citing Prosecutor v. Stanislav Galić, IT-98-29-T, Trial Judgment, ¶ 47 (Int'l Crim. Trib. for the former Yugoslavia ICTY Dec. 5, 2003).

a given individual is a civilian.[85] The Chamber highlighted the general requirement that combatants distinguish themselves by wearing a uniform (or distinctive sign) and carrying weapons openly.[86] It went on to list other factors that may be helpful in identifying civilians, such as the activities they were engaging in at the relevant time, their age, and their sex.[87] When considering the legal status of one particular victim, the Trial Chamber cited an expert report stating that the victim's clothing "would have enabled the shooter to identify her as civilian."[88] The Chamber proceeded to comment on the victim's age (thirteen years) and height, concluding that these characteristics gave "no reason to identify the victim as a combatant."[89]

When seeking to establish the civilian status of a particular witness, the prosecution in *Milošević* routinely emphasized victim characteristics such as age, occupation, clothing, and other aspects of appearance, as well as the individual's actions at the relevant time.[90] As Claire Garbett notes, the defense rarely interrogated the civilian status of the witnesses who testified, except when they were young males—insinuating that their male gender and youthful age gave rise to the possibility that they could have been combatants.[91] Significantly, the civilians who testified as witnesses at the *Milošević* trial also claimed that they had not worn a military uniform or military insignia (as a combatant would have). They asserted civilian status in three further ways: emphasizing their choice to not engage in military conduct or operations; recounting their efforts to go about their everyday lives as normally as possible during the conflict; and speaking of a shared experience of the conflict, connecting themselves to others who were beset by the same threats of harm.[92]

The vision of civilianness established at the *Milošević* trial required something more than presenting as the combatant's opposite. The emphasis on characteristics such as age, sex, and conduct summoned signifiers of harmlessness, nonparticipation, and vulnerability. When attention was drawn to the fact that a particular victim had been wearing a woman's dress, for example, these signifiers

85. *Milošević* Trial Judgment, *supra* note 5, ¶ 945.

86. *Id.*, ¶¶ 945–46.

87. *Id.* The Appeals Chamber in the *Milošević* appeal found no error with this approach. Prosecutor v. Dragomir Milošević, Case No. IT-98-29/1-A, Appeal Judgment, ¶ 198 (Int'l Crim. Trib. for the former Yugoslavia Nov. 12, 2009) ("*Milošević* Appeal Judgment").

88. *Milošević* Trial Judgment, *supra* note 5, ¶ 353, citing P514, Expert report by Lt. Patrick van der Weijden, at 43.

89. *Id.*

90. As observed in Claire Garbett, The Concept of the Civilian: Legal Recognition, Adjudication and the Trials of International Criminal Justice 109 (2015).

91. *Id.* at 110–12.

92. *Id.* at 105–07.

were grounded in femaleness.[93] Based on her observations of this trial, Garbett finds that international actors at the ICTY delineate a positive definition of the civilian to supplant IHL's negative one.[94] To do so, they introduce clear markers of civilian identity and draw on social characteristics of group membership.[95] Yoram Dinstein, for his part, characterizes the attempt to identify unequivocal civilian markers as "chimerical"; he emphasizes the difficulty of ascertaining what constitutes normal life in times of armed conflict.[96] While Dinstein's point about the elusiveness of definitive markers is well taken, it is still noteworthy that international actors cast about for such markers.

In addition to troubling a bright line civilian-combatant distinction, *Milošević* reaches down to the Kinetic realm to grapple with how civilianness materializes in war. As the ICTY Trial Chamber ratchets up what is required in terms of civilian credentials, we detect echoes of the operational context in CAR. The vision of civilianness that emerges in *Milošević* also stands in stark contrast to that in the *Martić* appeal, which contemplated an opening up of the category to accommodate vulnerable former fighters. Taken together, the two cases support Garbett's argument that the navigation of the civilian concept at the ICTY undermines the IHL premise "that all persons are either civilian or combatant."[97]

IV. CONCLUSION: THE MAKING AND SHAPING OF IHL

A NATO functional specialist attending a pre-deployment training, a MINUSCA official overseeing a weapons search of an IDP site, and a lawyer furnishing details of a victim's clothing in The Hague. Are these actors, individually and collectively, making or unmaking IHL? To draw this discussion to a close, I want to suggest that they are doing both.

If we place the Pedagogical, Kinetic, and Intellectual realms on the same plane and treat them all as settings in which legal rules circulate, then we come to understand that myriad actors are making and shaping IHL through their everyday practices. This is so, I would argue, even if they cannot discern whether they are operating within the context of an armed conflict. Humanitarians, soldiers, peacekeepers, judges, and lawyers alike can be considered "lawmakers," in the

93. On gender and the principle of distinction, *see* Orly Stern, Gender, Conflict and International Humanitarian Law: A Critique of the Principle of Distinction (2019); Kinsella, *supra* note 33.

94. Garbett, *supra* note 90, at 98.

95. *Id.*

96. Yoram Dinstein, The Conduct of Hostilities Under the law of International Armed Conflict 143 (2004).

97. Garbett, *supra* note 90, at 149.

sense that their engagement with the distinction concept constitutes, produces, and breathes life into how this idea circulates. At the same time as these actors play a crucial role in shaping the everyday meaning(s) of IHL, it has also been shown that they unmake IHL in daily practice. This is to say that the things these actors are doing with ideas like distinction often upend conventional understandings of legal rules. Within this multiplicity there also lies a "making" element: as we confront these competing and unorthodox perspectives, we come to appreciate IHL rules in new dimensions and in greater depth.

As this discussion has centered the Pedagogical realm and explored how ideas circulate down to CAR and up to the ICTY, I have argued that there is an important space in between war and the text in which the everyday life of IHL unfolds. The civilian-combatant distinction is a particularly fruitful rule to track in this manner: debates about civilianness in war are widespread and have high material stakes; non-lawyers routinely participate in these debates and evince some familiarity with the general civilian concept; IHL's negative definition of the civilian is almost begging to be fleshed out, so that we might recognize the civilian when we see it. Having highlighted distinction's amenability to a middle-out approach, nothing should confine this type of analysis to any specific IHL rule. One could just as easily investigate trainings on means and methods of warfare, for example, or dealing with the dead in war, and follow the thread to operational contexts as well as more normative domains. In doing so, we could further elucidate the Pedagogical life of IHL—and, indeed, the many lives of IHL rules and norms—to enrich our understanding of how IHL works in the world.

PART FIVE

Unmaking

15

A Prologue to Law of War Unmaking

SEAN WATTS*

I. INTRODUCTION

As this volume attests, the law of war has seen a marked increase in attention not only to its content, implementation, and enforcement but also to its methodology. A growing body of academic work addresses questions of law of war formation, interpretation, and development.[1] Even work styled chiefly as descriptive or oriented toward practitioners has provoked pressing questions of methodology.[2]

* Sean Watts is a Professor in the Department of Law at the United States Military Academy at West Point, where he co-directs the Lieber Institute for Law and Warfare.

1. *See, e.g.*, Law-Making and Legitimacy in International Humanitarian Law (Heike Krieger ed., 2021); Bruno Demeyere, *The Power of Asking "How"—A Key to Understanding the Development of IHL?*, 104 International Review of the Red Cross 1507 (2022); Adil Ahmad Haque, *Indeterminacy in the Law of Armed Conflict*, 95 International Law Studies 118 (2019).

2. *See* International Committee of the Red Cross, Commentary on the First Geneva Convention (2016) [hereinafter GC I Commentary]; International Committee of the Red Cross, Commentary on the Second Geneva Convention (2017); International Committee of the Red Cross, 1 Commentary on the Third Geneva Convention (2021) [hereinafter 1 GC III Commentary]; International Committee of the Red Cross, 2 Commentary on the Third Geneva Convention (2021); Eric Talbot Jensen & Carolyn Sharp, *Non-State Commentaries: Law-Making or Law-Suggesting*, Articles of War (Apr. 8, 2021), https://lieber.westpoint.edu/non-state-commentaries-law-making-law-suggesting/; Michael W. Meier, *The Updated GCIII Commentary: A Flawed Methodology?*, Articles of War (Feb. 3, 2021), https://lieber.westpoint.edu/updated-gciii-commentary-flawed-methodology/; Sean Watts, *Interpretation in the Updated GCIII Commentary*, Articles of War (Dec. 15, 2020), https://lieber.westpoint.edu/interpretation-updated-gciii-commentary/.

Sean Watts, *A Prologue to Law of War Unmaking* In: *Making and Shaping the Law of Armed Conflict.*
Edited by: Sandesh Sivakumaran and Christian R. Burne, Oxford University Press.
DOI: 10.1093/oso/9780197775134.003.0015

That is not to say that attention to law of war methodological issues is new.[3] Disputes over legal process have long separated various camps of the law of war community.[4] Methodological differences have been at the heart of some of the most contentious law of war products and projects.[5] But no period of law of war history has tackled methodological questions more pervasively and intently than the present one.

As part of this effort, scholarship has been eager to addresses the formation or "making" of the law of war.[6] Yet very little attention has been devoted to its repeal or its "unmaking."[7] It is an analytical gap found not only in the law of war but in the study of public international law generally.[8] But because the law of war is touted simultaneously as the most codified[9] and as an especially reactive regime

3. *See, e.g.*, John B. Bellinger III & William J. Haynes II, *A US Government Response to the International Committee of the Red Cross Study Customary International Humanitarian Law*, 89 International Review of the Red Cross 443 (2007).

4. *See* David Luban, *Military Necessity and the Cultures of Military Law*, 26 Leiden Journal of International Law 315 (2013).

5. Methodological differences concerning interpretation of Additional Protocol I, Article 51(3) including the meaning of the term "take a direct part in hostilities" were pronounced and even inspired members of a working group to withdraw from an ICRC project. International Committee of the Red Cross, Interpretive Guidance on the Notion of Direct Participation in Hostilities under International Humanitarian Law (2009); Forum, *Direct Participation in Hostilities: Perspectives on the ICRC Interpretive Guidance*, 42 New York University Journal of International Law & Policy 637 (2010).

6. *See, e.g.*, Gilad Ben-Nun, The Fourth Geneva Convention for Civilians: The History of International Humanitarian Law (2020).

7. Though inelegant, I have adopted the term "unmaking" as a counterpart to frequent references to law "making." The term has been used in prior scholarship. *See* Usha Natarajan & Kishan Khoday, *Locating Nature: Making and Unmaking International Law*, 27 Leiden Journal of International Law 573 (2014); Philip Allott, *State Responsibility and the Unmaking of International Law*, 29 Harvard International Law Journal 1 (1988). Other terms such as "exit," "denunciation," "repeal," "excise," "voiding," "expunging," or "rescindment" may be more descriptive or doctrinally accurate in some instances.

8. *See* Laurence R. Helfer, *Terminating Treaties*, *in* The Oxford Guide to Treaties 624 (Duncan B. Hollis ed., 2d ed. 2020) [hereinafter Helfer (2020)]. *But see* Michael Glennon, *How International Rules Die*, 93 Georgetown Law Journal 939 (2005); Herbert W. Briggs, *Unilateral Denunciation of Treaties: The Vienna Convention and the International Court of Justice*, 68 American Journal of International Law 51 (1974).

9. Surepalli Prashanth, *The International Court of Justice and International Humanitarian Law: A Critical Study*, 4 International Journal of Law Management & Humanities 482 (2021); Vincent Chetail, *The Contribution of the International Court of Justice to International Humanitarian Law*, 85 International Review of the Red Cross 235 (2005). Professor Colonel Draper also observes, "the law of war was the first part of [international law] to receive codification." Gerald Draper, *The Development of International Humanitarian Law*, *in* Reflections on Law and Armed Conflicts: The Selected Works on the Laws of War by the Late Professor Colonel G.I.A.D. Draper, OBE, 69, 69 (Michael A. Meyer & Hilaire McCoubrey eds., 1998).

of international law,[10] it is surprising that repeal does not feature more conspicuously in its discourse than in that of general international law. The sheer volume of law of war treaty provisions, combined with the exceptionally dynamic character of warfare suggest that law of war unmaking might be a far more common phenomenon of law development and of scholarship than it has been. Uneven implementation and spotty practice concerning notorious law of war provisions further suggests a more prominent role for unmaking than is apparent.

This chapter offers a preliminary exploration of law of war unmaking. It places alongside the chapters of this volume that address formation and interpretation, a discussion of mechanisms for repeal, revocation, or abandonment of law of war treaties or provisions thereof. A brief outline of the international law of treaties that bears on unmaking reveals relatively clear, if guarded, procedures for treaty termination. It also identifies provisions of the law of war itself that address denunciation, withdrawal, or termination by States. A selective survey of the law of war offers examples of unmaking and provisions that show signs of informal repeal or such disuse that repeal may be in order. Then, the chapter preliminarily identifies forces that may explain why States and other actors involved in law of war formation have not seized on unmaking with either the zeal or comparative rigor they have applied to its making and development. The chapter seeks to spur greater attention to law of war unmaking and to encourage steps toward a more refined and rigorous methodology and practice by States.

II. FORMAL MEANS OF UNMAKING

Multilateral treaties form the backbone of the modern law of war.[11] Although customary international law remains relevant to the regulation of armed conflict, attempts at its modern expression are based largely on the texts of law of war treaties.[12] Formerly, custom—consistent, prolonged, and nearly universal State practice undertaken from a sense of legal obligation—had largely informed major law of war codifications and treaty formation. However, the reverse may now be true.[13] Following the twentieth century's proliferation of multilateral law of war treaties, identifying the customary law of international armed conflict now seems to start and end with determining whether a given treaty or its various provisions

10. *See* Michael Howard, *Constraints on War*, *in* The Laws of War: Constraints on Warfare in the Western World 2 (Michael Howard et al. eds., 1994). *See also* Laurie R. Blank & Gregory P. Noone, International Law and Armed Conflict 78 (2013); Stephen C. Neff, War and the Law of Nations: A General History 2 (2005).

11. *See* Robert Kolb & Richard Hyde, An Introduction to the International Law of Armed Conflicts 51–53 (2008).

12. Yoram Dinstein, The Conduct of Hostilities under the Law of International Armed Conflict 20–21 (4th ed. 2022).

13. *See* 1 The Law of War: A Documentary History 151–55 (Leon Friedman ed., 1972).

have or have not crystallized into custom.[14] It now seems that few, if any, putative customary rules of the law of war governing international armed conflict find form or are derived independently of treaties.[15]

The international law of treaties is found largely in the 1969 Vienna Convention on the Law of Treaties[16] and in customary international law that is thought to track the Vienna Convention in significant part.[17] This generally applicable body of law addresses treaties from cradle to grave. In addition to treaty formation, adoption, ratification, and interpretation, the law of treaties includes elaborate rules on treaty termination, suspension, and modification.[18]

A. Treaty Termination

Treaty termination reflects a drastic, though relatively rare method of legal exit or law unmaking. The legal effect of treaty termination is to extinguish all of the withdrawing State's obligations flowing from the treaty in question.[19] In light of its stark legal effects, the Vienna Convention does not admit treaty termination lightly.[20] It provides that treaties may only be terminated according to their expressed terms or in accordance with the Vienna Convention itself.[21] The

14. *See* Elizabeth Wilmshurst, *Conclusions*, *in* Perspectives on the ICRC Study on Customary International Humanitarian Law 401 (Elizabeth Wilmshurst & Susan Breau eds., 2007).

15. Professor Stephan has observed that many law of war treaties "frame propositions at such a high level of abstraction that a [customary international law] overlay is required to give the rule any meaning." Paul B. Stephan, *Disaggregating Customary International Law*, 21 Duke Journal of Comparative & International Law 191, 201 (2010). While he identifies an important role for custom, the overlay function does not seem to identify customary rules that are independent of law of war treaties. Rather, Professor Stephan illustrates that a great deal of current customary law of war is closely tied to conventional laws of war.

16. Vienna Convention on the Law of Treaties, May 23, 1969, 1155 U.N.T.S. 331 [hereinafter Vienna Convention]. *See also* The Oxford Guide to Treaties vii (Duncan B. Hollis ed., 2d ed. 2020).

17. President of the United States, Letter of Transmittal to United States Senate, Vienna Convention on the Law of Treaties, Nov. 22, 1971; United States Dep't of State, Letter of Submittal to the President, Vienna Convention on the Law of Treaties, Oct. 18, 1971; U.S. Dep't of State, *Vienna Convention on the Law of Treaties* (last visited Mar. 21, 2023), http://www.state.gov/s/l/treaty/faqs/70139.htm.

18. Vienna Convention, *supra* note 16, Part V, § 3.

19. Vienna Convention, *supra* note 16, art. 70(1). *But see id.*, art. 43.

20. *See, e.g.*, Lea Brilmayer & Isaias Yemane Tesfalidet, *Treaty Denunciation and "Withdrawal" from Customary International Law: An Erroneous Analogy with Dangerous Consequences*, 120 Yale Law Journal Forum (Jan. 5, 2011).

21. Vienna Convention, *supra* note 16, art. 42(2).

Convention regulates the processes of treaty termination in a series of articles that addresses both bilateral and multilateral treaties.[22]

It is important to realize that the Vienna Convention operates largely as a default regime for treaty termination. Its termination provisions apply chiefly when a treaty does not include its own, specific provisions on termination, a case that is reportedly rare.[23] It is also important to realize that the Vienna Convention is entirely forward-looking. Its regime, including its provisions on treaty termination, is expressly inapplicable to treaties concluded prior to its entry into force for a given State party.[24] Many significant law of war treaties, including the 1899 and 1907 Hague Conventions, the 1949 Geneva Conventions, the 1954 Hague Cultural Property Convention, and the 1977 Additional Protocols to the Geneva Conventions (for some early Additional Protocol ratifying States or States that were late to ratify the Vienna Convention) predate the Vienna Convention's entry into force and are not regulated by its provisions as a technical matter. Nonetheless, some commentators have effectively read out the non-retroactivity clause by regarding the Vienna Convention as reflective of custom international law applicable in a retroactive sense or having crystallized by the time of these earlier treaties.[25]

When applicable, the Convention expresses a presumption in favor of continuation and even a bias against termination.[26] Treaty denunciation or withdrawal is not permitted under the Vienna Convention unless:

22. Although outside literature and even other treaties do not do so consistently, the Vienna Convention uses the term "denunciation" to refer to unilateral termination of a bilateral instrument. Vienna Convention, *supra* note 16, art. 56. Meanwhile, it uses the term "withdrawal" to refer to a State's effort to terminate its obligations under a multilateral treaty. Vienna Convention, *supra* note 16, art. 56. Professor Helfer concludes that the terms "denunciation" and "withdrawal" are used interchangeably in much treaty practice. Helfer (2020), *supra* note 8, at 625, n.8.

23. *See* Helfer (2020), *supra* note 8, at 624, 632; Anthony Aust, *Treaties, Termination*, *in* Max Planck Encyclopedias of Public International Law ¶ A.3. (Anne Peters & Rüdiger Wolfrum eds., June 2006); Cong. Research Serv., RL 44761, Withdrawal from International Agreements: Legal Framework, the Paris Agreement, and the Iran Nuclear Agreement 4 (2018), *available at* https://crsreports.congress.gov.

24. Vienna Convention, *supra* note 16, art. 4. The Vienna Convention entered force on January 27, 1980.

25. *See, e.g.*, 1 GC III Commentary, *supra* note 2, ¶ 75.

26. *See* Brilmayer & Tesfalidet, *supra* note 20. A noteworthy example is the International Covenant on Civil and Political Rights, which has no withdrawal clause. International Covenant on Civil and Political Rights, Dec. 16, 1966, 999 U.N.T.S. 171 (1967). In 1997, North Korea purported to withdraw nonetheless, provoking the UN Human Rights Committee and the UN Secretary General to conclude the withdrawal was without legal effect. *See* Helfer (2020), *supra* note 8, at 629–30.

(a) it is established that the parties intended to admit the possibility of denunciation or withdrawal; or
(b) a right of denunciation or withdrawal may be implied by the nature of the treaty.[27]

Under the Vienna Convention's general regime, States need not provide a cause or express a particular justification to terminate a treaty. A State's intention to revoke the consent that gave rise to the treaty obligation in the first place—which remains at the core of positive international legal obligations—is usually sufficient.[28] Treaty withdrawals or denunciations are often simple affairs. Most withdrawing States submit only a line or two on a single-page notification to the treaty depository or other States parties.[29]

Notice to other States parties is the essential element of treaty termination under the Vienna Convention's default withdrawal regime.[30] Article 65 requires a denouncing or withdrawing State to notify the treaty's other parties twelve months in advance of a denunciation or withdrawal taking effect.[31] Parties objecting to the withdrawal then have a period of "not less than three months following receipt of notification" to do so.[32] Although the Convention does not limit or regulate a State's reasons for termination, Article 65 requires notice of denouncement or withdrawal to include "the reasons therefore."[33]

A UN Office of Legal Affairs handbook on final clauses of treaties—the concluding articles usually relating to the administration and functioning of a treaty—intended for use by treaty drafters identifies five types of withdrawal clauses including:

(1) treaties that may be denounced at any time; (2) treaties that preclude denunciation for a fixed number of years, calculated either from the date

27. Vienna Convention, *supra* note 16, art. 56(1).

28. *See* VASSILIS PERGANTIS, THE PARADIGM OF STATE CONSENT IN THE LAW OF TREATIES: CHALLENGES AND PERSPECTIVES 154–73 (2017); Duncan Hollis, *Why State Consent Still Matters—Non-State Actors, Treaties and the Changing Sources of International Law*, 23 BERKELEY JOURNAL OF INTERNATIONAL LAW 137 (2005).

29. *See, e.g.*, *Depositary Notifications (CNs) by the Secretary-General*, UNITED NATIONS TREATY COLLECTION, https://treaties.un.org/Pages/CNs.aspx?cnTab=tab2&clang=_en; Laurence Helfer, *Taking Stock of Three Generations of Research on Treaty Exit*, 52 ISRAEL LAW REVIEW 103, 105 (2019) [hereinafter Helfer (2019)].

30. Notice and especially notice periods have been observed to minimize opportunities for States to game and exploit other States' investments in compliance by withdrawing early and suddenly from treaties. *See* Barbara Koremenos & Allison Nau, *Exit, No Exit*, 21 DUKE JOURNAL OF COMPARATIVE & INTERNATIONAL LAW 81, 82–83 (2010).

31. Vienna Convention, *supra* note 16, art. 56(2).

32. *Id.*, art. 65(2).

33. *Id.*, art. 65.

> the agreement enters into force or from the date of ratification by the State; (3) treaties that permit denunciation only at fixed time intervals; (4) treaties that may be denounced only on a particular occasion, identified either by a time period or upon the occurrence of a particular event; and (5) treaties whose denunciation occurs automatically upon the State's ratification of a subsequent agreement.[34]

Many law of war instruments incorporate one of these specific termination schemes. For instance, each of the four universally ratified 1949 Geneva Conventions indicates that States parties are "at liberty to denounce the present Convention."[35] Written notification to the Swiss Federal Council, in its capacity as treaty depository, signals a State's intention to withdraw from the Geneva Conventions.[36] The Federal Council must then notify the other States parties of the withdrawing party's intentions.

Withdrawal from the Geneva Conventions takes effect one year after notification unless the withdrawing State is involved in an armed conflict regulated by the Conventions at the time of the denunciation. In that case, termination takes effect when "peace has been concluded and . . . after operations connected with release, repatriation and re-establishment of the persons protected by the . . . Convention have been terminated."[37] The withdrawal provisions of the 1977 Additional Protocols I and II to the 1949 Geneva Conventions largely track the 1949 provisions, although neither protocol repeats the Conventions' reference to "liberty to denounce" and Additional Protocol II, applicable to certain non-international armed conflicts, reduces the one-year tolling of termination to six months.[38]

34. Laurence R. Helfer, *Exiting Treaties*, 91 Virginia. Law Review 1579, 1597 (2005) (citing UN Office of Legal Affairs, Final Clauses of Multilateral Treaties Handbook (2003)) [hereinafter Helfer (2005)].

35. Convention (I) for the Amelioration of the Condition of the Wounded and Sick in Armed Forces in the Field, Aug. 12, 1949, art. 63, 75 U.N.T.S. 31 [hereinafter GC I]; Convention (II) for the Amelioration of the Condition of Wounded, Sick and Shipwrecked Members of Armed Forces at Sea, Aug. 12, 1949, art. 62, 75 U.N.T.S. 85 [hereinafter GC II]; Convention (III) Relative to the Treatment of Prisoners of War, Aug. 12, 1949, art. 142, 75 U.N.T.S. 135 [hereinafter GC III]; Convention (IV) Relative to the Protection of Civilian Persons in Time of War, Aug. 12, 1949, art. 158, 75 U.N.T.S. 287 [hereinafter GC IV].

36. *See* GC I, *supra* note 35, art. 63; GC II, *supra* note 35, art. 62, GC III, *supra* note 35, art. 142; GC IV, *supra* note 35, art. 158.

37. *See* GC I, *supra* note 35, art. 63; GC II, *supra* note 35, art. 62, GC III, *supra* note 35, art. 142; GC IV, *supra* note 35, art. 158.

38. Protocol Additional to the Geneva Conventions of Aug. 12, 1949, and Relating to the Protection of Victims of International Armed Conflicts, June 8, 1977, art. 99, 1125 U.N.T.S. 3 [hereinafter API]; Protocol Additional to the Geneva Conventions of Aug. 12, 1949, and Relating to the Protection of Victims of Non-international Armed Conflicts, June 8, 1977, art. 25, 1125 U.N.T.S. 609 [hereinafter APII].

As noted, most treaties' withdrawal provisions do not require the withdrawing State to justify its decision.[39] However, not all law of war treaties leave reasons for withdrawal unaddressed or unregulated. The 1993 Chemical Weapons Convention (CWC)[40] reflects an effort by States to fill perceived gaps in the preceding 1925 Geneva Protocol on Asphyxiating Gases.[41] The CWC does not terminate the Geneva Gas Protocol. Instead, its obligations are "complementary" to the Protocol. In fact, the Geneva Protocol remains in force for its States parties and includes no provisions for termination, denunciation, or withdrawal, presumably leaving the issue to the customary international law of treaties.[42]

The CWC addresses termination by its States parties at Article XVI.[43] Identifying withdrawal as an aspect of "national sovereignty," the CWC indicates that States parties may withdraw upon ninety days' notification to all other States parties. Interestingly, and departing from the Vienna Convention and most other treaties' cause-ambivalent approach, the CWC limits States parties' withdrawal to what is reminiscent of a termination-for-cause limitation. According to Article XVI(1), a party's withdrawal notification must include "the extraordinary events it regards as having jeopardized its supreme interests."[44] The CWC does not elaborate on or illustrate what might constitute "extraordinary events," leaving the withdrawing State significant discretion on the question. Though taking a rare approach, the CWC is not alone in limiting reasons for withdrawal. The bilateral U.S.-U.S.S.R. Anti-Ballistic Missile Treaty similarly conditioned a party's withdrawal on the treaty having "jeopardized its supreme interests."[45]

B. Treaty Duration

Finally with respect to representative termination clauses, there is the matter of duration. Some law of war treaties express that they remain in force indefinitely. For

39. Helfer (2020), *supra* note 8, at 633; Helfer (2019) *supra* note 29, at 105.

40. Convention on the Prohibition of the Development, Production, Stockpiling and Use of Chemical Weapons and on Their Destruction, Jan. 13, 1993, 1974 U.N.T.S. 45 [hereinafter CWC].

41. 1925 Geneva Protocol of the Prohibition of the Use in War of Asphyxiating, Poisonous or Other Gases, and of Bacteriological Methods of Warfare, June 17, 1925, 26 Martens NRG 3ème sér. 643.

42. CWC, *supra* note 40, pmbl., ¶ 6; William Boothby, Weapons and the Law of Armed Conflict 130 (2009). Recall that the Vienna Convention would not apply to the 1925 Geneva Protocol by virtue of the former's non-retroactivity clause. Vienna Convention, *supra* note 16, art. 4. *See supra* text accompanying notes 24–25.

43. CWC, *supra* note 40, art. XVI.

44. *Id.*, art. XVI.

45. Treaty on the Limitation of Anti-Ballistic Missile Systems, U.S.-U.S.S.R., art. XV, May 26, 1972, 944 U.N.T.S. 13.

example, the 1997 Ottawa Convention on Anti-Personnel Landmines provides, "This Convention shall be of unlimited duration."[46] Other law of war treaties limit their duration after entry into force. As part of the 1899 Hague Peace Conference, States adopted a Declaration on Balloons that prohibited aerial bombing.[47] The Declaration included a sunset clause in its single substantive article stating, "The Contracting Powers agree to prohibit, *for a term of five years*, the launching of projectiles and explosives from balloons, or by other new methods of a similar nature."[48] The Declaration also included a denunciation provision—what today would be called a withdrawal clause—permitting termination of obligations upon one year's notice communicated to the Declaration's other States parties.

States later abandoned the 1899 Balloon Declaration's term-of-years approach. After the Declaration expired, the next Hague Conference adopted the 1907 Declaration (XIV) on Balloons.[49] That instrument reinstated the prohibition on aerial bombing of its predecessor. However, rather than renew the 1899 Declaration's five-year term, drafters set its duration to run "for a period extending to the close of the Third Peace Conference." Almost 120 years later, that conference has still not taken place and almost surely never will. The plainest result is that the 1907 Balloon Declaration remains in force for its remaining thirty-three States parties.[50] To that end, the Declaration's most recent accession was by Fiji in 1973.[51]

Nonetheless, the near impossibility of a Third Hague Peace Conference taking place suggests to some that the Declaration has effectively been terminated. Few, if any, expressions of targeting law include reference to the Declaration. A prolonged and consistent course of practice, or more specifically lack of practice, seems to have voided the Balloons Declaration. The U.S. War Department expressed this view already during the Second World War.[52] And although the United States is technically still a State party, the current U.S. Department of Defense Law of War

46. Convention on the Prohibition of the Use, Stockpiling, Production and Transfer of Anti-Personnel Mines and on their Destruction, art. 20(1), Sept. 18, 1997, 2056 U.N.T.S. 211.

47. Declaration (IV, 1), to Prohibit, for the Term of Five Years, the Launching of Projectiles and Explosives from Balloons, and Other Methods of Similar Nature, July 29, 1899, 1 Bev. 270.

48. *Id.* (emphasis added).

49. Declaration Prohibiting the Discharge of Projectiles and Explosives from Balloons, Oct. 18, 1907, 36 Stat. 2439 [hereinafter 1907 Balloons Declaration].

50. Dietrich Schindler & Jiri Toman, The Laws of Armed Conflicts: A Collection of Conventions, Resolutions and Other Documents 309 (4th ed. 2004).

51. *Id.* at 313.

52. United States, Dep't of Defense, Law of War Manual § 19.7.3 (Dec. 2016) (citing United States, War Dep't, Circular No. 136, § 1 (May 7, 1942) [hereinafter U.S. Manual]. As the DoD Manual notes, operation of the 1907 Balloons Declaration is further unlikely owing to its *si omnes*, or all participation, clause which requires that all parties to a conflict also be parties to the Declaration for it to operate. *Id.*

Manual does not list the 1907 Balloon Declaration among its "Treaties to Which the United States is a Party." Instead, the Manual lists it as a treaty "of Mainly Historical Value."[53] Still, it does not appear the United States, or any other State for that matter, has fully followed the Declaration's clearly prescribed termination provision.[54]

C. Treaty Withdrawals

By contrast, four recent episodes of expressed withdrawal have concerned the Rome Statute of the International Criminal Court.[55] Although more precisely regarded as an international criminal law treaty, the Rome Statute bears an important relationship to the law of war. In addition to providing an important enforcement regime, the Statute's war crimes provisions reflect rarely achieved common ground among States. They offer detailed expressions and elements of prohibited conduct during armed conflict.[56] But in October 2016, South Africa submitted a notification of withdrawal from the Rome Statute, followed by Burundi and The Gambia.[57] In 2018, the government of the Philippines also withdrew from the Rome Statute.[58]

Each State notified the United Nations in accordance with Article 127 of the Statute.[59] The withdrawals would undoubtedly reduce their exposure to

53. U.S. Manual, *supra* note 52, §§ 19.2.1, 19.2.5.

54. The Declaration's denunciation provision provides:

> In the event of one of the high Contracting Parties denouncing the present Declaration, such denunciation shall not take effect until a year after the notification made in writing to the Netherlands Government, and forthwith communicated by it to all the other Contracting Powers.
>
> This denunciation shall only have effect in regard to the notifying Power.

1907 Balloons Declaration, *supra* note 49.

55. Statute of the International Criminal Court, July 17, 1998, 2187 U.N.T.S. 90 [hereinafter Rome Statute].

56. *Id.* art. 8.

57. South Africa, Withdrawal Depository Notification, C.N.786.2016.TREATIES-XVIII.10, Oct. 25, 2016; Burundi, Withdrawal Depository Notification, C.N.805.2016.TREATIES-XVIII.10, Oct. 28, 2016; The Gambia, Withdrawal Depository Notification, C.N.862.2016.TREATIES-XVIII.10, Nov. 11, 2016.

58. Philippines, Withdrawal Depository Notification, C.N.138.2018.TREATIES-XVIII.10, Mar. 17, 2018 (citing a "principled stand against those who politicize and weaponize human rights . . . .").

59. Rome Statute, *supra* note 55, art. 127. Article 127 prescribes an effective date of not less than one year following notification of intent to withdraw. *Id.*, art. 127(1). The article also indicates that withdrawal has no effect on proceedings commenced prior to the effective date of withdrawal. *Id.*, art. 127(2).

international criminal law enforcement of these States' law of war obligations. But their motives for withdrawal appear to have been related to political considerations concerning the Court's recent exercises of its jurisdiction rather than to disagreement with the Rome Statute's law of war provisions.[60] And none of the withdrawals reduced or terminated any of these States' substantive law of war obligations in armed conflict. Ultimately, only the Burundi and Philippines withdrawals took effect. South Africa revoked its withdrawal pursuant to a domestic court judgment.[61] Meanwhile, The Gambia rescinded its withdrawal notification after a change of government.[62]

More recently and reflecting termination concerning what is more clearly a law of war provision, the Russian Federation withdrew a prior declaration that had accepted the competence of the 1977 Additional Protocol I, Article 90 International Fact-Finding Commission.[63] The Fact-Finding Commission's competence extends, among other matters, to convening inquiries to determine whether grave and other breaches of the Conventions can be established in fact.[64] News media and commentators have occasionally mischaracterized the Russian act as withdrawal from the Additional Protocol entirely.[65] It is clear, however, that the Russian Federation remains a State party to the Additional Protocol. After Russia's withdrawal from the Article 90 process, seventy-six States parties to Additional

60. Manisuli Ssenyonjo, *State Withdrawal Notifications from the Rome Statute of the International Criminal Court South Africa, Burundi and The Gambia*, 29 CRIMINAL LAW FORUM 63, 68 (2018).

61. *See* South Africa, Withdrawal of Notification of Withdrawal, C.N.121.2017-TREATIES-XVIII.10, Mar. 7, 2017. *See also* Democratic Alliance v. Minister of International Relations and Cooperation and Others, Case No. 83145/2016 (High Court of South Africa), Feb. 22, 2017.

62. The Gambia, Withdrawal of Notification of Withdrawal, C.N.62.2017.TREATIES-XVIII.10, Feb. 16, 2017.

63. Russian Federation, Withdrawal of Declaration to Article 90(2) (Apr. 11, 2019), *available at* https://treaties.un.org/Pages/showActionDetails.aspx?objid=0800000280563aca; Switzerland, Federal Department of Foreign Affairs, Notification to Governments of the States Parties to the Geneva Conventions, *Withdrawal of a Declaration by the Russian Federation*, 413-04-01/2019/7056—GEN 2/19, Oct. 30, 2019, *available at* https://www.eda.admin.ch/eda/fr/dfae/politique-exterieure/droit-international-public/traites-internationaux/depositaire/protection-des-victimes-de-la-guerre/notifications-du-depositaire-communes-aux-conventions-de-gen%C3%A8ve-et-aux-protocoles-additionnels.html (last visited Mar. 16, 2023).

64. API, *supra* note 38, art. 90(2)I.

65. David Crane, *Russia's Snub of Geneva Convention Protocol Sets Dangerous Precedent*, THE HILL (Oct. 20, 2019, 2:00 PM), https://thehill.com/opinion/international/466531-russias-snub-of-geneva-convention-protocol-sets-dangerous-precedent (stating Russia "is pulling out of Protocol I . . . ."); Ryan Musto, *In Addressing Russia's Attack on Zaporizhzhia, Look to Africa*, LAWFARE (Jan. 4, 2023, 8:16 AM), https://www.lawfareblog.com/addressing-russias-attacks-zaporizhzhia-look-africa (claiming in error that Russia "pulled out of a protocol to the Geneva Conventions . . . .").

Protocol I still have active Article 90 declarations.[66] However, that figure amounts to well less than half the Protocol's States parties. More significantly, although the Commission has repeatedly proposed its services, belligerent States have never resorted to its procedures in relation to any international armed conflict.[67]

D. Grounds for Withdrawal

In addition to addressing general conditions and termination practices, the Vienna Convention on the Law of Treaties identifies select grounds or justifications for withdrawal, denouncement, or suspension. The Convention permits, though with significant procedural and substantive conditions, termination or suspension of a treaty or a provision thereof for the following reasons:

- "material breach";[68]
- "impossibility of performance";[69]
- "fundamental change of circumstances";[70] and
- emergence of "a new peremptory norm of general international law."[71]

None of these bases for termination or suspension has featured frequently in law of war treaty practice by States. It is a remarkable development merely considering the great number of law of war treaties and States parties to them, the dynamic character of armed conflict, and the frequency with which it is arguably breached.

However, the Vienna Convention's "material breach" provision addresses so-called "treaties of a humanitarian character" separately from other treaties. Article 60(5) indicates that the Convention's usual termination and suspension options "do not apply to provisions relating to the protection of the human person" in

66. International Humanitarian Fact-Finding Commission, *States Parties*, https://www.ihffc.org/index.asp?Language=EN&page=statesparties_list (last visited Mar. 16, 2023).

67. International Humanitarian Fact-Finding Commission, *Public Reports*, https://www.ihffc.org/index.asp?Language=EN&page=public_reports&listfilter=off (last visited Mar. 16, 2023); Charles Garraway, *The International Humanitarian Law Fact-Finding Commission*, 34 Commonwealth. Law Bulletin 813 (2008).

68. Vienna Convention, *supra* note 16, art. 60. *See generally* Bruno Simma & Christian J. Tams, *Reacting against Treaty Breaches*, *in* The Oxford Guide to Treaties 568, 574 (Duncan B. Hollis ed., 2d ed. 2020).

69. Vienna Convention, *supra* note 16, art. 61. *See* Malgosia Fitzmaurice, *Exceptional Circumstances and Treaty Commitments*, *in* The Oxford Guide to Treaties 595, 601 (Duncan B. Hollis ed., 2d ed. 2020).

70. Vienna Convention, *supra* note 16, art. 62. *See* Fitzmaurice, *supra* note 69, at 602–04.

71. Vienna Convention, *supra* note 16, art. 64. *See* Jan Klabbers, *The Validity and Invalidity of Treaties*, *in* The Oxford Guide to Treaties 545, 562–66 (Duncan B. Hollis ed., 2d ed. 2020).

such instruments.[72] It is widely thought that the provision is meant to apply to law of war treaties.[73] It is also thought that Article 60(5) removes reciprocity as a condition for law of war obligations.[74] That is, breach by another State does not permit a victim State to suspend or terminate its corresponding law of war treaty-based obligations to an offending or any other State.[75] There are reasons to question the integrity of the prevailing view.[76] But Article 60(5) may explain in part why so few law of war treaty terminations and suspensions of specific law of war obligations have resulted from material breach.

E. Subsequent Agreements

Additionally, agreements between States subsequent to a treaty entering into force may serve as a means to extinguish, or perhaps more often in practice to modify or preempt, a prior obligation. It is generally understood that a later-in-time treaty may extinguish a prior treaty. Article 59 of the Vienna Convention indicates that a later treaty "relating to the same subject-matter" concluded by all its States parties terminates an earlier treaty.[77] The Convention requires either that the intention to terminate the earlier treaty be apparent from the text of the later treaty or that the later treaty be "so far incompatible" with the earlier that the two "are not capable of being applied at the same time."[78]

Law of war instruments have approached the "later-in-time" issue differently from one another. The Geneva Convention series reflects an iterative effort to

72. Vienna Convention, *supra* note 16, art. 60(5).

73. *See* René Provost, International Human Rights and Humanitarian Law 173–74 (2002). *See also* Leslie S. Green, The Contemporary Law of Armed Conflict 58 (2d ed. 2000); Simma & Tams, *supra* note 68, at 578–79; Jérome de Hemptinne, *Prohibition of Reprisals*, *in* The 1949 Geneva Conventions: A Commentary 575, 579 (Andrew Clapham et al. eds., 2015).

74. Legal Consequences for States of the Continued Presence of South Africa in Namibia (South East Africa) notwithstanding Security Council Resolution 276, Advisory Opinion, 1971 I.C.J. 16, ¶ 94 (June 21); Prosecutor v. Kupreškić, Case No. IT-95-16-T, Judgment, ¶ 520 (Jan. 14, 2000); 1 Customary International Humanitarian Law: Rules 498 (Jean-Marie Henckaerts & Louise Doswald-Beck eds., 2005).

75. Marco Sassòli, International Humanitarian Law: Rules, Controversies, and Solutions to Problems Arising in Warfare 81 (2019).

76. *See* Sean Watts, *Reciprocity and the Law of War*, 50 Harvard International Law Journal 365, 418–25 (2009).

77. Vienna Convention, *supra* note 16, art. 59.

78. *Id.*

protect victims of war beginning in 1864 and extending to 2005.[79] Each successive round of the Geneva Conventions has updated and expanded the scope and protections of its predecessors. The First, Second, and Third 1949 Geneva Conventions address their relationships to the preceding Geneva Conventions on Wounded and Sick and on Prisoners of War, respectively.[80] The 1949 First Geneva Convention provides, "The present Convention replaces the Conventions of August 22, 1864, July 6, 1906, and July 1929, in relations between the High Contracting Parties."[81] Meanwhile, the 1949 Third Geneva Convention indicates, "The present Convention *replaces* the Convention of July 27, 1929 in relations between the High Contracting Parties."[82]

The 1949 Geneva Conventions address their relationship to the 1899 and 1907 Hague Conventions II and IV and their respective annexed Regulations separately.[83] Notwithstanding the field's general distinction between so-called Hague and Geneva traditions of the law of war, the Hague and Geneva Conventions have addressed many of the same subjects, including prisoner of war treatment and rules of belligerent occupation.[84] But rather than replace or terminate States parties' obligations under the earlier Hague Conventions, the 1949 Geneva Conventions are expressed as "complementary" or "supplementary" to the respective chapters of the former.[85] Thus, the Hague Conventions remain in force

79. *See* Amelioration of the Condition of the Wounded in Time of War, Aug. 22, 1864; Protocol Additional to the Geneva Conventions of Aug. 12, 1949, and Relating to the Adoption of an Additional Distinctive Emblem, Dec. 8, 2005, 2404 U.N.T.S. 261 [hereinafter APIII].

80. GC I, *supra* note 35, art. 59; GC II, *supra* note 35, art. 58; GC III, *supra* note 35, art. 134. The 1949 Fourth Geneva Convention had no preceding counterpart and therefore does not address its relationship to any preceding Geneva Convention.

81. GC I, *supra* note 35, art. 59.

82. GC III, *supra* note 35, art. 134 (emphasis added). Myanmar's 1992 accession to the 1949 Conventions seems to have finally terminated the 1929 Convention Relative to Prisoners of War. Some successor States to the Soviet Union and Yugoslavia had been States parties to the 1929 Convention. They acceded to the 1949 Conventions after regaining their status as States, arguably delaying the 1929 Conventions' termination in a technical sense until after the Myanmar accession. *See* Adam Roberts & Richard Guelff, Documents on the Laws of War 355–61 (3d ed. 2000). The extent to which these successor States were bound by their predecessor's ratifications of treaties is "not entirely settled in international law." Fausto Pocar, *Some Remarks on the Continuity of Human Rights and International Humanitarian Law Treaties*, *in* The Law of Treaties beyond the Vienna Convention 279 (Enzo Cannizzaro ed., 2011).

83. Hague Convention (II) Respecting the Laws and Customs of War on Land with Annex of Regulations, July 29, 1899, 32 Stat. 1803; Hague Convention (IV) Respecting the Laws and Customs of War on Land, Oct. 18, 1907, 36 Stat. 2277 [hereinafter Hague IV].

84. *See, e.g.*, Leslie C. Green, The Contemporary Law of Armed Conflict 31–32 (2d ed. 2000).

85. GC III, *supra* note 35, art. 135 (using the term "complementary"); GC IV, *supra* note 35, art. 154 (using the term "supplementary").

for their States parties, despite the Geneva Conventions providing more detailed regulations on many of their subjects.

Many prominent law of war treaties do not include any specific procedures for amendment. For instance, the 1949 Geneva Conventions include no prescribed procedures for their amendment, presumably leaving the matter to the general law of treaties as found in customary international law, including Article 31.[86] In 1977, States adopted two Additional Protocols to the 1949 Geneva Conventions, and in 2005, they added another protocol respecting protected emblems.[87] In some cases, these Protocols supplement or replace the obligations of their States parties under the prior Conventions. For example, the Fourth Convention's Article 6 indicates that the Convention's operation in occupied territory ceases "one year after the general close of military operations."[88] Additional Protocol I, applicable to international armed conflicts as well as to situations of occupation, abandons the one-year standard for its States parties indicating instead that the 1949 Conventions and the Additional Protocol cease to apply "on the termination of the occupation."[89] For their part, both Additional Protocols I and II include provisions prescribing procedures for their amendment, though States have not resorted to either protocol's procedures.[90] Yet neither protocol is an amendment to the base 1949 Geneva Conventions themselves. In fact, over twenty States that are parties to the 1949 Conventions are not parties to the Additional Protocols and are therefore unaffected as a matter of treaty law by the latter's entry into force.

F. Peremptory Norms

Finally, with respect to the Vienna Convention's formal provisions on termination, Article 64 addresses treaties' interactions with so-called peremptory or *ius cogens* norms. Peremptory norms are those that States accept as permitting no derogation or modification save by a norm of the same superseding character.[91] The Convention indicates that newly emerged peremptory norms render invalid treaties that are incompatible. Although law of war rules are increasingly alleged to constitute peremptory norms, perhaps to excess, few such norms are likely to

86. Recall that the Vienna Convention is not technically applicable to most States implementation of the 1949 Geneva Conventions because the latter predate the former instrument. *See* Vienna Convention, *supra* note 16, art. 4.

87. APIII, *supra* note 79.

88. GC IV, *supra* note 35, art. 6.

89. API, *supra* note 38, art. 3(b).

90. API, *supra* note 38, art. 97; APII, *supra* note 38, art. 24.

91. Vienna Convention, *supra* note 16, art. 53; Jochen A. Frowein, *Ius Cogens*, *in* Max Planck Encyclopedias of International Law ¶¶ 1, 6 (Anne Peters & Rüdiger Wolfrum eds., Mar. 2013).

conflict with the law of war treaties from which many are drawn.[92] The trend has been for commentators, if not necessarily States, to incorporate law of war treaties into *ius cogens* rather than for *ius cogens* norms to develop that conflict with existing law of war treaty provisions.

III. OTHER MEANS OF UNMAKING

It is widely assumed that adoption of text and the close of a diplomatic conference do not signal the end of a treaty's development. States have resorted to a variety of means to refine, alter, condition, or even to effectively terminate treaty obligations. These include subsequent agreements as well as post-adoption reservations submitted by ratifying States.

A. Subsequent Agreement

Included among its rules of treaty interpretation, the Vienna Convention indicates, "There shall be taken into account, together with the context: (a) any subsequent agreement between the parties regarding the interpretation of the treaty or the application of its provisions . . . ."[93] Thus treaty interpretation under the Convention involves not only examination of the adopted text and its originally agreed meaning to the parties but also must investigate whether the States parties' subsequent dealings include an agreement relevant to the meaning or condition of that text.

While more usually understood as a means to clarify or perhaps to expand on the meaning of treaty provisions, it is not difficult to imagine a situation in which States might subsequently agree to an interpretation of a treaty that effectively negates its prior legal force in some respect. For instance, a subsequent agreement might either create a substantially novel obligation, displacing another or effectively terminating a preceding obligation. Alternatively, an obligation stated as compulsory in treaty text may evolve through practice and agreement to have an advisory or hortatory character. However, and particularly with respect to a multilateral treaty, subsequent agreement by all States parties is likely to prove elusive or difficult. Thus, this approach does not offer the promise some suppose, nor has significant practice accumulated, to suggest it as a regular means of termination of law of war treaty obligations.

Still, like the Vienna Convention, some law of war treaties anticipate that States' subsequent agreements will modify their content. The most prominent example

92. *See* Prosecutor v. Kupreškić et al., Case No. IT-95-16, Trial Judgment, ¶ 520 (Int'l Crim. Trib. for the Former Yugoslavia Jan. 14, 2000); Int'l Law Comm'n, Peremptory Norms of General International Law (*jus cogens*), Draft Conclusion 23, U.N. Doc. A/CN.4/L.936 (May 29, 2019).

93. Vienna Convention, *supra* note 16, art. 31(3)(a).

may be the 1980 Convention on Conventional Weapons (CCW).[94] The CCW is best thought of as a treaty collection or framework. While a baseline convention briefly addresses administrative matters, the series' substantive regulations of various weapons appear in protocols, some of which were drafted well after the base convention entered into force.[95] Article 8 of the base CCW permits States parties to adopt subsequent protocols to regulate categories of weapons.[96] States parties to the CCW meet every five years to form such protocols or to amend the existing protocols. In a sense, each protocol to the CCW colloquially modifies its States parties' obligations under that series. Yet no protocol modifies the provisions of the base CCW itself. Therefore, the protocols do not reflect "subsequent agreements" in the Vienna Convention Article 31(3)(a) sense.

In addition to subsequent agreements as formal means for treaty modification or termination, it is increasingly clear that interpretation may prove an opportunity for law of war unmaking as well. A growing contingent of law of war scholars characterizes treaties as living documents.[97] Rather than simply reflecting records of agreement frozen in place at diplomatic conferences, this view urges that the meanings of the terms of treaties change with time. It is argued that their meaning and content regularly evolve through State practice and implementation, a notion usually associated with customary international law.

This view finds support in Article 31(3)(b) of the Vienna Convention addressing subsequent State practice that implements treaty obligations. Following its provisions on interpretation of treaties with reference to subsequent agreement, the Convention offers, "There shall be taken into account, together with the context: . . . (b) any subsequent practice in the application of the treaty which establishes the agreement of the parties regarding its interpretation . . . ."[98] The article has been associated with an evolutionary approach to treaty interpretation.[99]

94. Convention on Prohibitions or Restrictions on the Use of Certain Conventional Weapons Which May be Deemed to Be Excessively Injurious or to Have Indiscriminate Effects, Apr. 10, 1981, 1342 U.N.T.S. 137 [hereinafter CCW].

95. States adopted three original protocols at the same time as the CCW addressing non-detectable fragments, land mines, and incendiary weapons. Protocol I on Non-Detectable Fragments, Oct. 10, 1980, 1342 U.N.T.S. 168; Protocol II on Prohibitions or Restrictions on the Use of Mines, Booby Traps and Other Devices, Oct. 10, 1980, 1342 U.N.T.S. 168; Protocol III on Prohibitions or Restrictions on the Use of Incendiary Weapons art. 2(2), Oct. 10, 1980, 1342 U.N.T.S. 171. They later added protocols on blinding lasers and explosive remnants. Protocol IV on Blinding Laser Weapons art. 1, Oct. 13, 1995, 1380 U.N.T.S. 370; Protocol V on Explosive Remnants of War, Nov. 28, 2003, 2399 U.N.T.S. 100.

96. CCW, *supra* note 94, art. 8.

97. *See, e.g.*, Cordula Droege & Eirini Giorgou, *How International Humanitarian Law Develops*, 104 International Review of the Red Cross 1798, 1805 (2022).

98. Vienna Convention, *supra* note 16, art. 31(3)(b).

99. *See* Eirik Bjorge & Robert Kolb, *The Interpretation of Treaties over Time*, *in* The Oxford Guide to Treaties 494 (Duncan Hollis ed., 2d ed. 2020).

In practice, Article 31(3)(b) has been used chiefly to clarify obligations or to add nuance to their operation and particularly to keep them apace with the passage of time since their conclusion.[100] Whether such interpretation amounts to simply applying a treaty or instead to "*giving* a meaning to a text" has generated perennial debate in treaty law circles.[101]

But if treaties are indeed living documents, then perhaps there is also room to conceive of them as dying documents? That is, the State practice that modifies a treaty's meaning through interpretation and implementation might alternatively signify extinction of a treaty's obligations when States' agreed practices indicate its provisions are no longer binding in the sense originally agreed. For example, State practice and agreement might indicate that a treaty provision expressed as a strict obligation has matured to become hortatory. A "shall" might have been modified under Article 31(3)(b) to operate in fact, then later in law, as a "may" or a "should." In that case the compulsory aspects of the provision in question could be regarded as effectively terminated.

As with interpretation for purposes of modification, termination by interpretation would require not only very clear, consistent, and widespread practice but also practice that "establishes the agreement of the parties."[102] Ideally, an overwhelming number or even all of a treaty's States parties should concur in the interpretation that extinguishes the obligation in question.[103]

Article 31(3)(b) interpretive updates and modifications feature widely in a recent project to update previous private commentaries to the 1949 Geneva Conventions. The International Committee of the Red Cross (ICRC) showcases the article's subsequent practice provision as a major methodological component of its update project.[104] Throughout the updated Commentaries one finds argument that original meanings of the Conventions' text have been effectively modified in succeeding years of State practice. While in most cases, the project cites subsequent practice to augment, expand, or refine the Conventions obligations

100. Pierre-Marie Dupuy, *Evolutionary Interpretation of Treaties: Between Memory and Prophecy*, *in* The Law of Treaties beyond the Vienna Convention 124 (Enzo Cannizzaro ed., 2011).

101. Richard Gardiner, *The Vienna Convention Rules on Treaty Interpretation*, *in* The Oxford Guide to Treaties 461–62 (Duncan Hollis ed., 2d ed. 2020) (quoting II Yearbook of the International Law Commission 53 (1964) (citing a statement by the ILC projects Rapporteur H. Waldock) (emphasis in original)).

102. Vienna Convention, *supra* note 16, art. 31(3)(b).

103. *See* International Law Comm'n, *Report on the Work of Its Seventh Session*, U.N. Doc. A/73/10, commentary on draft conclusion 10.2, ¶ 13 (2018); Gardiner, *supra* note 101, at 468.

104. International Committee of the Red Cross, Commentary on the Third Geneva Convention (III) Relative to the Treatment of Prisoners of War ¶ 92 (2021) [hereinafter ICRC Commentary III]. *See* Jean-Marie Henckaerts et al., *ICRC Perspectives on the Interpretation of the Third Geneva Convention More than Seventy Years after Its Adoption*, *in* lieber studies volume 8: prisoners of war in contemporary conflict (Michael N. Schmitt & Christopher J. Koschnitzky eds., 2023).

and restraints, on occasion the Commentary's interpretations effectively terminate them, though the project often avoids saying so explicitly.

For instance, common Article 8/8/8/9 of the Geneva Conventions states, "The present Convention shall be applied with the cooperation and under the scrutiny of the Protecting Powers . . . ."[105] A longstanding concept borrowed from diplomacy law and practice, the protecting power system has classically involved a neutral State, representing the interests of a sending State in the territory of a receiving State, agreed to by each.[106] Evaluating Article 8, the original 1960 Commentary to the Third Geneva Convention by Dr. Jean Pictet, observed bluntly, "this is a command."[107] Yet despite several dozen or more armed conflicts having activated the Conventions since their entry into force, protecting powers have been appointed in only five such conflicts.[108] Accordingly, the ICRC's updated Commentary concludes:

> Practice since 1949 has not developed in the direction envisioned by the drafters of the Geneva Conventions: the appointment of Protecting Powers in case of an international armed conflict has been the exception rather than the rule. Seemingly, practice since 1949 has evolved to the point of considering the appointment of Protecting Powers as *optional* in nature. This does not preclude, however, that Protecting Powers may still be appointed in future international armed conflicts on the basis of Article 8.[109]

A scholarly commentary concludes similarly, observing, "the institution of Protecting Powers has fallen into disuse . . . state practice has turned the original duty to nominate a Protecting Power into a *mere option*."[110] Thus, in the judgment of these commentators, interpretation in light of subsequent practice and agreement by States compels the conclusion that the obligatory character of Article 8 is terminated or void.

105. GC I, *supra* note 35, art. 8; GC II, *supra* note 35, art. 8; GC III, *supra* note 35, art. 8; GC IV, *supra* note 35, art. 9. While common in text, the numbering of many of the common articles of the 1949 Geneva Convention is staggered owing to the addition of an intervening article in the Fourth Convention.

106. Commentary: III Geneva Convention relative to the Treatment of Prisoners of War 93 (Jean Pictet ed., 1960) (providing historical background on the Protecting Powers system).

107. *Id.*, at 93.

108. Robert Kolb, *Protecting Powers*, *in* The 1949 Geneva Conventions: A Commentary 550, 557 (Andrew Clapham et al. eds., 2015); *see* George A.B. Peirce, *Humanitarian Protection for the Victims of War: The System of Protecting Powers and the Role of the ICRC*, 90 Military Law Review 89, 91 (1980).

109. ICRC Commentary III, *supra* note 104, ¶ 1196 (emphasis added).

110. Kolb, *supra* note 108, at 558–59 (emphasis in original).

It is a stark repeal by States, particularly considering the originally critical character of the protecting power system. The 1949 diplomatic conference that produced the Conventions had judged protecting powers to be "the lynchpin of the system for monitoring compliance with the Geneva Conventions in international armed conflict."[111] The effects of its collapse have been mitigated somewhat by the willingness of the ICRC to perform the functions assigned by protecting powers as a substitute, a course envisioned in many respects by the Conventions.[112]

B. Treaty Reservations

A final means by which States may shape their treaty obligations, including those derived from law of war treaties, is the reservation. Generally speaking, reservations permit States selectively to opt out of the provisions of a treaty while otherwise ratifying the instrument as a whole. The Vienna Convention addresses reservations thoroughly and generally limits their use by States.[113] Reservations, by contrast with subsequent agreement, do not require unanimous consent among the States parties to a treaty. Rather, reservations may be accepted or rejected, with varying effects on the content of States' obligations under a treaty, on a case-by-case basis.[114] Reservations have featured somewhat regularly in law of war treaties although they may be waning in modern instruments.[115]

However, timing prevents reservations from serving as an effective means of termination of treaty obligations for States parties in the truest sense. Article 19 of the Vienna Convention indicates that a "State may, *when signing, ratifying, accepting, approving or acceding* to a treaty, formulate a reservation."[116] While a State may later withdraw its reservation, it may not formulate a new reservation post-ratification or accession.[117] Thus reservations, while an active part of law of war treaty formation, do not prove a particularly effective means for termination of a treaty or for withdrawal from any specific provision of a treaty once undertaken by a State.

111. ICRC Commentary III, *supra* note 104, ¶ 1186.

112. GC I, *supra* note 35, art. 10; GC II, *supra* note 35, art. 10; GC III, *supra* note 35, art. 10; GC IV, *supra* note 35, art. 11.

113. Vienna Convention, *supra* note 16, Part II, § 2.

114. *Id.*, arts. 20–21.

115. *See generally* Roberts & Guelff, *supra* note 82.

116. Vienna Convention, *supra* note 16, art. 19 (emphasis added).

117. Edward T. Swaine, *Treaty Reservations*, *in* The Oxford Guide to Treaties 285, 286 (Duncan B. Hollis ed., 2d ed. 2020).

IV. INFORMAL MEANS OF UNMAKING

In addition to the formal procedures of treaty termination and modification identified in the Vienna Convention, in the customary international law of treaties, and in law of war instruments themselves, public international law sometimes recognizes less formal means of unmaking . The concept or doctrine of desuetude is often linked to the notion of obsolescence as a basis for terminating an international legal obligation, including a treaty or provision thereof.[118] Obsolescence for purposes of desuetude is practice-focused and usually results from either extended and consistent noncompliance or nonenforcement by States.[119]

The International Court of Justice (ICJ) implicitly acknowledged the concept in an advisory opinion relating to the UN Charter, the foundational document of the *ius ad bellum*.[120] The Court noted that despite Article 27(3) of the Charter requiring nine affirmative votes, including all permanent members of the Security Council, to pass a resolution, practice established that abstention by a permanent member was not disqualifying and that a valid resolution could nonetheless result.[121] The Court observed:

> [T]he proceedings of the Security Council extending over a long period supply abundant evidence that presidential rulings and the positions taken by members of the Council, in particular its permanent members, have consistently and uniformly interpreted the practice of voluntary abstention by a permanent member as not constituting a bar to the adoption of resolutions.[122]

Other cases have also provided the Court opportunities to invoke or address the doctrine, though it has not done so explicitly.[123]

Like the ICJ, the Vienna Convention does not recognize desuetude explicitly. However, the concept has been linked to the Convention's recognition of subsequent agreements and modifications of treaties as well as to the principle *lex posterior derogate legi priori*.[124] Like subsequent agreements and practice, desuetude

118. Jan Wouters & Sten Verhoeven, *Desuetudo*, *in* Max Planck Encyclopedias of Public International Law ¶ 1 (Anne Peters & Rüdiger Wolfrum eds., Nov. 2008).

119. Wouters & Verhoeven, *supra* note 118, ¶ 1.

120. Legal Consequences for States of the Continued Presence of South Africa in Namibia (South West Africa) notwithstanding Security Council Resolution 276, Advisory Opinion, 1971 I.C.J. 16 (June 21).

121. Legal Consequences Advisory Opinion, ¶¶ 21–22.

122. Legal Consequences Advisory Opinion, ¶ 22.

123. Wouters & Verhoeven, *supra* note 118, ¶ 7 (citing Nuclear Tests Case (Austl.-Fr.), 1974 I.C.J. 253. (Dec. 20); Nuclear Tests Case (N.Z.-Fr.) 1974 I.C.J. 457 (Dec. 20); East Timor (Port.-Austl.) 1995 I.C.J. 90 (June 30)).

124. Wouters & Verhoeven, *supra* note 118, ¶ 1.

focuses on State conduct that follows a treaty's entry into force. Desuetude has also been linked to the doctrine of *rebus sic stantibus*, or as it is expressed in the Vienna Convention, "fundamental change of circumstances."[125] Desuetude is sometimes understood to operate more flexibly than both the former doctrine and the latter article.[126]

Recalling that the Vienna Convention does not recognize termination of treaties beyond its own and other treaties' expressed provisions, desuetude is unlikely to terminate a treaty or a provision thereof under the Convention's regime for treaties in a strictly legal sense.[127] The Convention's articulated bases, listed earlier, are understood by some, and indeed by the plain text of the Convention itself, to be its exclusive means of modification or termination.[128] Still, others have acknowledged the possibility that emergence of a new rule of customary international law could nonetheless modify or even terminate a State's treaty obligations or serve as a "factual cause for terminating treaties or conventional rules."[129] That method may amount to a sort of cross-source, that is, a custom-to-treaty means of modification or termination process. While still others consider that desuetude may survive as an aspect of the customary international law of treaties outside or in addition to the rules codified by the Vienna Convention.[130]

Early reports on the International Law Commission's (ILC) work on treaty law suggested that desuetude might involve State practice distinct from the later-in-time or changed-circumstances conditions ultimately codified in the Vienna Convention.[131] In addition to these bases, the ILC's rapporteur for the treaty project indicated that treaties may

> lapse by the mere passage of time as such, failure by both or all the parties over a long period to apply or invoke a treaty or other conduct evidencing a lack of interest in it, may amount to a tacit agreement by the parties to disregard the treaty, or to treat it as terminated.[132]

125. Vienna Convention, *supra* note 16, art. 62.

126. Wouters & Verhoeven, *supra* note 118, ¶ 2.

127. Vienna Convention, *supra* note 16, art. 42(2).

128. Mark E. Villiger, Commentary on the 1969 Vienna Convention on the Law of Treaties 541–47 (2009).

129. Wouters & Verhoeven, *supra* note 118, ¶¶ 9, 11.

130. Marcelo G. Kohen, *Desuetude and Obsolescence of Treaties*, *in* The Law of Treaties Beyond the Vienna Convention 351 (Enzo Cannizzaro ed., 2011).

131. *Id.*, at 352 (citing International Law Comm'n, Gerald Fitzmaurice, Second Report, 2 Yearbook of the International Law Commission 28 (1957)).

132. *Id.*, at 352 (quoting International Law Comm'n, Gerald Fitzmaurice, Second Report, 2 Yearbook of the International Law Commission 28 (1957)).

It has been argued that this conception better captures desuetude, both in its original legal sense and as a reflection of what States actually do as a matter of negative practice from time to time, than the Vienna Convention provisions on termination and interpretation.[133] As distinct from the "change of circumstances" situation resulting material impossibility of performance, classic desuetude does not envision impossibility of performance by States parties.[134] In fact, the opposite is true. Desuetude envisions that States parties are fully capable of performance but as a matter of policy then practice, routine then custom, agreement and then ultimately of law, excuse themselves from their obligations over an extended period.[135]

Understood in this sense, several law of war provisions may be candidates for having fallen into desuetude. As noted earlier, the 1949 Geneva Conventions regulate both situations of international armed conflict as well as belligerent occupation.[136] Eager to foreclose States from prematurely terminating situations of occupation to evade duties owed to the displaced regime and its population, States resolved to extend application of the Fourth Convention to "one year after the close of military operations . . . for the duration of the occupation."[137] Yet the one-year standard appears not to have been put into regular practice nor has it been deemed especially well-suited to its purpose. The 1977 Additional Protocol I to the Geneva Conventions effectively replaced the one-year standard for its States parties.[138] Meanwhile, for States parties to the Geneva Conventions that have not ratified the Additional Protocol, Article 6 of the Fourth Convention has arguably been judged to have fallen into desuetude.[139] A recent study of the law of belligerent occupation concludes that "the entire scope of the law of occupation remains applicable until the occupation is terminated" rather than according to the Article 6 one-year term.[140]

A further putative rule of the law of belligerent occupation may have suffered a similar fate. Regulations annexed to the 1907 Hague Convention IV include early regulations on occupation.[141] Most concern the relationship between the occupying power and the displaced sovereign. The Regulations devote particular attention to the occupying power's treatment of the occupied State's property and assets. Article 49 of the Hague Regulations restricts an occupying power's levies

133. *Id.*, at 353.

134. *Id.*, at 358.

135. *See* Wouters & Verhoeven, supra note 118, ¶ 10.

136. GC I, *supra* note 35, art. 2; GC II, *supra* note 35, art. 2; GC III, *supra* note 35, art. 2; GC IV, *supra* note 35, art. 2.

137. GC IV, *supra* note 35, art. 6.

138. API, *supra* note 38, art. 3(b).

139. Eliav Lieblich & Eyal Benvenisti, Occupation in International Law 28 (2022).

140. *Id.*, at 28.

141. Hague IV, *supra* note 83, § III.

of "money contributions" to fulfilling "the needs of the army or the administration of the territory in question."[142] The article's restraints clearly imply that the occupying power is authorized to levy military contributions in the first place. But that authority is increasingly regarded as both internally inconsistent with occupation law requirements of reimbursement and compensation as well as counter to "the spirit of the law of occupation."[143] It has been noted that recent occupations have not resorted to the military contributions envisioned by Article 49, and some have called for its repeal.[144] In light of these quite longstanding assessments and absence of its practice, it has been assessed as possibly falling into desuetude.[145]

Like the law of belligerent occupation, the law of neutrality saw early codification at the 1899 and 1907 Hague Peace Conferences. Also like the law of belligerent occupation, the law of neutrality has suffered uneven practice and enforcement since its early life.[146] An aspect of the international laws of war, and applicable only in case of international armed conflict, neutrality law seeks to regulate relations between belligerent and nonbelligerent States both to limit the spread of conflict and, as far as possible, to preserve international trade and economic relations.[147] Key aspects of neutrality law include the inviolability of neutral territory by belligerents and neutral States' obligations to remain impartial between belligerents.[148] Yet questions concerning its ongoing viability have swirled around it almost since its adoption at The Hague.[149]

To take just one of its many provisions, consider Article 11 of Hague Convention V. That article provides in part:

142. *Id.*, art. 49.

143. Lieblich & Benvenisti, *supra* note 139, at 209.

144. *Id.*, at 209 (citing Yoram Dinstein, The International Law of Belligerent Occupation 139 (2d ed. 2019)); Paul Fauchille, 2 Traite de Droit International Public 1224 (1921); Ernst H. Feilchenfeld, The International Economic Law of Belligerent Occupation 44 n. 4 (1942)).

145. Lieblich & Benvenisti, *supra* note 139, at 209.

146. Hague Convention (V) Respecting the Rights and Duties of Neutral Powers and Persons in Case of War on Land, Oct. 18, 1907, 36 Stat. 2310 [hereinafter Hague V]; Hague Convention (XIII) Concerning the Rights and Duties of Neutral Powers in Naval War, Oct. 18, 1907, 205 Consol. T.S. 395.

147. Michael Bothe, *The Law of Neutrality*, *in* The Handbook of Humanitarian Law in Armed Conflicts 486 (Dieter Fleck ed., 1999). The International Court of Justice identified neutrality as a "principle of fundamental character" in an advisory opinion. Legality of the Threat or Use of Nuclear Weapons, Advisory Opinion, 1996 I.C.J. 226, ¶¶ 88–89 (July 8).

148. Hague V, *supra* note 146, arts. 1–2, 9.

149. William H. Boothby & Wolff Heintschel von Heinegg, The Law of War: A Detailed Assessment of the U.S. Department of Defense Law of War Manual 371 (2018). *Contra* U.S. Manual, *supra* note 52, § 15.

> A neutral Power which receives on its territory troops belonging to the belligerent armies *shall intern them*, as far as possible, at a distance from the theatre of war.[150]

The obligation finds collateral support in the 1949 Third Geneva Convention which prescribes prisoner of war treatment for:

> The persons belonging to one of the categories in the present Article, who have been received by neutral or non-belligerent Powers on their territory and whom these Powers *are required to intern under international law . . . .*[151]

While some neutral States reportedly interned belligerent armed forces found on their territory during the Second World War, it seems that practice since has been nearly negligible, nor have what might be breaches of the obligation to intern been enforced by States.[152] States that are not belligerents and to which the law of neutrality apply routinely find on their territory armed forces of States that are engaged in international armed conflicts. These forces may be on their territory for a variety of reasons including for personal, professional, transit, or educational pursuits. Yet such receiving States seem to regularly permit these persons either to remain free from internment or parole while on their territory or to return to their States of origin.

A partial explanation for this practice may be found in the increasingly accepted status of a qualified neutral State. Some have held the view that all States that are not parties to an international armed conflict are neutral States.[153] That is, status under the law of neutrality is binary; a State is either a neutral or a belligerent. An alternative view, however, undertaken by both States and private commentators, particularly in the context of the ongoing armed conflict between Ukraine and the Russian Federation, has acknowledged a third status, that of qualified neutral or nonbelligerent.[154]

150. Hague V, *supra* note 146, art. 11 (emphasis added).

151. GC III, *supra* note 35, art. 4B(2) (emphasis added).

152. *See* U.S. Manual, *supra* note 52, § 15.16, n. 314 (citing 1 Report of the International Committee of the Red Cross on its Activities During the Second World War (September 1, 1939–June 30 1947) 557 (1948)).

153. *See, e.g.*, Sassòli, *supra* note 75, at 476.

154. *See* U.S. Manual, *supra* note 52, § 15.2.2; Wolff Heintschel von Heinegg, *Neutrality in the War Against Ukraine*, Articles of War (Mar. 1, 2022), https://lieber.westpoint.edu/neutrality-in-the-war-against-ukraine. *See also* Michael N. Schmitt, *Providing Arms and Materiel to Ukraine: Neutrality, Co-Belligerency, and the Use of Force*, Articles of War (Mar. 7, 2022), https://lieber.westpoint.edu/ukraine-neutrality-co-belligerency-use-of-force. *Contra* Raul Pedrozo, *Ukraine Symposium—Is the Law of Neutrality Dead?*, Articles of War (Mar. 31, 2022), https://lieber.westpoint.edu/is-law-of-neutrality-dead.

States regarding themselves as qualified neutral States or nonbelligerent States may regard many obligations of the law of neutrality not applicable to their relations with belligerent States. These have included most prominently neutral State obligations to maintain impartiality and not to arm either belligerent State. But the rationale could extend as well to the Article 11 internment obligation it seems. One of the "qualified" aspects of qualified neutrality may be relief from the obligation to intern belligerent States' armed forces. Still, it is unlikely that qualified neutrality or nonbelligerency explains fully the sparse practice and enforcement of Article 11 across the decades since the Second World War. A fuller account of State practice seems worthy of collection. Investigation whether the neutrality law internment rule has fallen into desuetude, at least with respect to its status as an unequivocal obligation, is worthy of examination and comment by States.

Finally, for purposes of this chapter's very preliminary consideration, some law of war provisions that amount to secondary rules may be worthy of consideration for desuetude. It is often helpful to categorize international law rules as being either primary or secondary in character.[155] Primary rules tend to directly prescribe conduct by States on a given subject. Whereas secondary rules concern the "creation, alteration, or extinction of the primary rules."[156] The Vienna Convention on the Law of Treaties is a prominent example of international law secondary rules. Secondary rules have also been conceived somewhat more broadly as "rules about rules."[157] In this sense they may also prescribe particular modes of application and compliance with or enforcement of primary rules.[158] By the latter half of the twentieth century, law of war treaties included increasingly elaborate primary rules, but also a growing collection of secondary rules that prescribed obligations concerning law of war implementation and enforcement.[159] In addition to regulating the actual conduct of hostilities, the law of war has increasingly regulated the *procedures* States used to apply the primary laws of war.[160]

155. *See* Sean D. Murphy, *The Concept of International Law*, 103 American Society of International Law Proceedings 165, 168 (2009) (citing H.L.A. Hart, The Concept of Law 222 (1961).

156. Murphy, *supra* note 155, at 168.

157. *See* Michael Beyers & Simon Chesterman, *Changing the Rules about Rules? Unilateral Humanitarian Intervention and the Future of International Law*, *in* Humanitarian Intervention: Ethical, Legal, and Political Dilemmas 177 (J.L. Holzgrefe & Robert O. Keohane eds., 2003).

158. Theresa Reinhold & Michael Zürn, *Rules about Rules and the Endogenous Dynamics of International Law: Dissonance Reduction as a Mechanism of Secondary Rule-Making*, 3 Global Constitutionalism 240 (2014) (quoting Thomas M. Franck, Fairness in International Law and Institutions 8 (1995)).

159. *See* Sean Watts, *Law-of-War Precautions: A Cautionary Note*, *in* Lieber Studies Volume 2: The Impact of Emerging Technologies on the Law of Armed Conflict 112 (Eric Talbot Jensen & Ronald T.P. Alcala eds., 2019).

160. *Id.*

One of the most prominent contributions of the 1949 Geneva Conventions to the law of war was their addition of an enforcement system. Preceding conventions had left enforcement largely unaddressed or had addressed it only vaguely.[161] Each 1949 Convention, as well as their Additional Protocol I, includes a so-called grave breach regime that compels States to enforce or support enforcement of certain of the Conventions' provisions against individual persons.[162] Article 129 of the Third Convention is representative. It requires all States parties to the Convention, whether parties to an armed conflict or not, to enact penal sanctions and to search for and bring before their courts or extradite persons responsible for certain breaches.[163] Although it resembles a primary rule in that it prescribes a course of conduct, Article 129 can be considered to have secondary elements in that it is a rule about implementation and enforcement of the rules of the Convention. It prescribes obligations with respect to implementation and especially enforcement of the Convention's rules for the treatment of prisoners of war.

Despite reflecting a long-sought improvement to the law of war, the grave breaches regime has underperformed significantly since its adoption. States have only sporadically implemented its provisions with respect to enacting laws to enforce the Conventions. And States have only rarely, and only recently at that, exercised the very extensive universal jurisdiction understood to have been compulsory under the grave breaches regime. By 1969, only 49 of 122 States parties to the Conventions had sent information indicating they had implemented any national legislation affecting any aspect of the grave breach regime.[164] Meanwhile, the ICRC project to update previous academic commentaries on the Geneva Conventions notes:

> A literal interpretation of Article 129(2) could therefore imply that each State Party must search for and prosecute any alleged perpetrators the world over, regardless of their nationality. Such a literal interpretation has not been widely shared by States Parties in the last 60 years. The practice since 1949 shows that some States, while having extended the principle of universal jurisdiction to grave breaches, have made prosecution conditional on the presence, temporary or permanent, of the alleged offender in the territory of the State Party.[165]

161. *See, e.g.*, Hague IV, *supra* note 83, art. 3. Meanwhile, States parties to the 1929 Geneva Convention Relative to Prisoners of War had merely agreed "to propose to their legislatures" measures to enforce its provisions. Convention Relative to the Treatment of Prisoners of War, art. 29, July 27, 1929, 47 Stat. 2021.

162. *See also* GC I, *supra* note 35, art. 49; GC II, *supra* note 35, art. 50; GC IV, *supra* note 35, art. 146; API, *supra* note 38, art. 85.

163. GC III, *supra* note 35, art. 129.

164. International Committee of the Red Cross, Respect of the Geneva Conventions: Measures Taken to Repress Violations, Report Prepared for the 21st International Conference of the Red Cross, Istanbul 1–2 (1969).

165. ICRC Commentary III, *supra* note 104, ¶ 5132.

Although the project avoids concluding the obligatory facets and character of the grave breaches regime have fallen into desuetude, it observes, "States Parties have made little use of this mechanism, which was ground-breaking at the time."[166] It later observes, "This has led many commentators to admit that, more than 40 years after the adoption of this innovative mechanism, prosecutions of grave breaches, in particular on the basis of universal jurisdiction, were almost unheard of."[167] And despite a thorough effort to discern State practice concerning the grave breaches regime, the project notes no evidence of any State enforcing failure to implement it against another State party.

The 1977 Additional Protocol I to the Geneva Conventions continued and perhaps expanded the latter's work on law of war procedural rules. In fact, alongside merger of the Hague and Geneva traditions of the law of war, procedural and secondary rules of enforcement may be the hallmarks of Additional Protocol I. Among the Protocol's rules supporting the prohibitions unnecessary suffering and indiscriminate attacks is a requirement to review the legality of weapons.[168] Article 36 of the Protocol provides:

> In the study, development, acquisition or adoption of a new weapons, means or method of warfare, a High Contracting Party is under an obligation to determine whether its employment would, in some or all circumstances, be prohibited by this Protocol or by any other rule of international law applicable to the High Contracting Party.[169]

Although the humanitarian and compliance benefits of such reviews are clear, State practice concerning their implementation has been exceptionally sparse. In 2006, the ICRC determined that as few as 8 of the then 164 States parties to Additional Protocol I had institutional review programs.[170] A more recent study determines that only 20 of 174 States parties have a weapons review procedure in place.[171] Moreover, there is no evidence that States have regarded other States parties failure to comply with Article 36 as an internationally wrongful act. Whether the legal review scheme still truly reflects a freestanding legal obligation or instead a matter of best practice—a secondary rule advisable for implementing the Protocol's other targeting rules—is worthy of consideration.

166. *Id.*, ¶ 5154.

167. *Id.*, ¶ 5154.

168. API, *supra* note 38, arts. 35, 48, 51.

169. *Id.*, art. 36.

170. International Committee of the Red Cross, A Guide to the Legal Review of New Weapons, Means and Methods of Warfare: Measures to Implement Article 36 of Additional Protocol I of 1977 5, n. 8 (2006).

171. *See* Natalia Jevglevskaya, *Weapons Review Obligation under Customary International Law*, 94 International Law Studies 186, 209 (2018).

There are doubtless other provisions of the law of war whose spotty records of implementation or enforcement by States call for evaluation for desuetude. The Hague Convention's all participation clause[172] and their strict conservationist rule for belligerent occupations come to mind. No doubt, the conclusions drawn from such study will vary according to the extent to which their authors accept or reject desuetude as a means of rule or treaty termination. And in the case of acceptance, variance in the evidentiary standards and span of time required to draw that conclusion and to assign it legal and factual effect can surely be expected. Still, such dialogue and attention to desuetude as a potential aspect of law of war unmaking would make welcome contributions not only to the content of States' law of war obligations but also to a better understanding of how informal procedures of termination, such as desuetude, shape or even work to unmake the law of war.

V. OBSTACLES TO UNMAKING

Despite the availability of clear doctrinal processes to do so, both general and specific to the law of war, as well as indications of routine departure, disregard, or neglect, States have only rarely terminated their law of war treaty obligations. Although a widely used compilation of law of war documents and treaties which also records States' signatures, ratifications, and accessions includes an entry for "denunciations," the entry for each treaty is "none."[173] And an influential textbook series acknowledges the withdrawal provisions of the four Geneva Conventions and their Protocols but observes, "In practice there has never been such a denunciation."[174]

Still, based on data reported by international organizations, a 2005 study "identified 1,546 instances of denunciation and withdrawal from 5,416 multilateral agreements registered with the UN between 1945 and 2004."[175] Evidence points toward perhaps increased resorts to withdrawals by States since that study.[176] And withdrawals are even frequent in specialized areas of law such as investment treaties.[177]

172. Hague IV, *supra* note 83, art. 2. Article 2 states, "The provisions contained in the Regulations referred to in Article 1, was well as in the present Convention, do not apply except between Contracting Powers, and the only if all the belligerents are parties to the Convention."

173. Roberts & Guelff, *supra* note 82.

174. Marco Sassòli et al., 1 How Does Law Protect in War?: Cases, Documents and Teaching Materials on Contemporary Practice in International Humanitarian Law 150, n. 77 (3d ed. 2011).

175. Helfer (2020), *supra* note 8, at 634 (citing Helfer (2005), *supra* note 34, at 1601–07).

176. Laurence R. Helfer, *Introduction to Symposium on Treaty Exit at the Interface of Domestic and International Law*, 11 American Journal of International Law Unbound 425 (2017).

177. Clint Peinhardt & Rachel L. Wellhausen, *Withdrawing from Investment Treaties but Protecting Investment*, 7 Global Policy 571 (2016).

So, if it is as reactive, as attuned to the imperatives of battlefield reality as claimed, why are there so few instances of recognized law of war unmaking? Major law of war treatises rarely catalog such formal repeals or even cases of desuetude. Projects to refine and clarify the law of war, such as the ICRC's updates to commentaries on the Geneva Conventions, seem loathe to conclude desuetude has attached even in the face of prolonged obsolescence or dormancy. Just as developments in the means and methods of warfare have inspired additions to the law of war, surely those same events should have proved at least some existing rules inapt or ineffectual and prompted their repeal.

That termination of law of war treaties or provisions thereof is so rare is surely attributable in part to their careful formation and resulting efficacy. There is no doubt a linkage between the forces and events that inspire States to make laws for war and to abandon them. Law of war treaties are not spontaneous or spur-of-the moment phenomena. Most involve long lead-up periods of consultations and iterative circulations of drafts, leading to widely attended and prolonged diplomatic conferences involving multiple rounds of reviews, amendments, and voting, culminating in adoption that often requires the consensus of all participant States. The results of such careful, deliberative, and increasingly pluralistic processes are highly likely to be fit for purpose as understood by the States that adopt them. Meanwhile, States that do not participate, do not adopt, or do so and later decline to ratify can be assured of having thoroughly considered the treaty in question and have not judged it suited to their interests or security needs. In light of the care with which law of war treaties are formed and adopted, their scant termination may not be surprising after all.

Further reluctance to withdraw from multilateral law of war treaties may be attributable to their simultaneous status as customary international law. That is, a State considering withdrawal may conclude that formal steps toward treaty termination would not fully extinguish its legal obligations. There are numerous claims, perhaps to excess, that many law of war treaties reflect customary international law. Moreover, many law of war treaties have included a residual clause purporting to ensure regulation of hostilities. As a representative example, the Geneva Conventions' termination scheme anticipates persistent legal obligations after withdrawal through the law of war Martens Clause.[178] Thus, even meticulous resort to treaty termination processes, either formal or informal, may not have the effect of freeing a State from a customary international restraint on its conduct of hostilities, a source of law that involves far more contested and murkier termination and exit procedures not addressed by this chapter, though no doubt worthy of consideration.[179]

178. *See* GC I, *supra* note 35, art. 63; GC II, *supra* note 35, art. 62; GC III, *supra* note 35, art. 142; GC IV, *supra* note 35, art. 158.

179. The late 2000s to early 2010s saw robust consideration of the possibility of a State's exit from customary international law, initiated by work of Professors Bradley and Gulati. Curtis A. Bradley & Mitu Gulati, *Withdrawing from International Custom*, 120 YALE LAW JOURNAL 202 (2010). *See generally* Stephan, *supra* note 15.

Other obstacles to unmaking may be the very same obstacles to making law of war treaties in the first place. That is, if States are reluctant to develop or adopt new law of war treaties on the basis of not fully understanding the subject in question, preferring to allow an issue to steep longer, they may be similarly hesitant to repeal or exit from treaties on the basis of new or very recent developments.

Meanwhile, access to the State practice that informs unmaking can be limited. Precisely how other States are implementing or failing to implement their law of war treaty obligations is not always easily discernable, even for States with robust intelligence-gathering capabilities. This is especially true with respect to practice during armed conflict, where secrecy and operational security cloud insight into State decision-making and execution. Even nongovernmental organizations play a role in restricting access to States' practice in treaty implementation. The reputedly extensive ICRC archives of State practice, gathered from its unique access to belligerents' activities, are largely closed for outside examination. The policy is entirely understandable in light of the organization's reliance on confidentiality to secure access to victims of war. But the resulting blind spots for the community of States hide the true character of State practice both for purposes of evaluating efficacy and the extent to which subsequent practice indicates alternation or even abandonment of extant law. Such secret practices of law of war treaty implementation are likely to skew understanding with respect to rules that are no longer supported by practice as originally adopted.

And even when practice can be clearly discerned, it can be difficult to interpret its meaning. A State's failure to observe a law of war obligation can be assigned a variety of meanings. Perhaps the failure was an oversight or unintentional, in which case it does not reflect a meaningful exercise of legal policy. But even if a breach is calculated, its significance may be unclear. For instance, a law of war breach may simply reflect the State's assessment that the cost of compliance exceeds the cost of breach—a case of efficient breach. Alternatively, breach may not in fact be a breach, reflecting a view that the State in question did not accept the rule in question as binding in the first place. Or, more significantly to the question of unmaking, the State may intend its breach to signal withdrawal of its support for the rule or as an intent to repeal.

Lack of resort to formal means of repeal may also be attributable to reluctance to convene or reconvene the diplomatic conferences that form treaties. Subsequent treaties may indeed replace preceding instruments on the same subject matter. But in addition to States' own reticence, there is also a subtle, though sometimes expressed, sense among the private actors that often support or initiate modern treaty efforts that States can no longer be trusted with the law of war. It is thought that reopening treaties, including efforts to repeal their predecessors, would risk backtracking on humanitarian advances.[180]

A recent examination of law of war formation dates the first appearance of the term "international humanitarian law," for many the modern pseudonym for the

180. Demeyere, *supra* note 1, at 1507.

law of war, to 1953.[181] Related and perhaps more fundamentally, repeal of a law that is conceived as chiefly or even exclusively humanitarian may be regarded as regressive or at minimum be a bad look for a State. Similarly, that the law of war is often characterized as born from "social pressure derived from moral force" may complicate its repeal.[182] Nonetheless, that such social pressure develops and manifests unevenly and undemocratically or out of proportion to the inherent weight of an issue should alleviate such misgivings. At minimum, many rules inspired by such forces should not be immune from review for signs of unmaking.

Law of war unmaking may also be unlikely to attract the sorts of advocacy projects that have resulted in new treaties and the replacement or repeal of preceding instruments. Victims of overly restrictive rules, often combatants, by contrast with victims of hostilities, don't often find a public voice. They chiefly rely on the governments for whom they fight, but that are subject to the restraints and obstacles to law-making and unmaking addressed in this chapter to represent their interests.

While none of the preceding conditions is singly responsible for inattention to law of war unmaking, collectively, they no doubt account for it in no small measure. However, neither singly nor collectively do they justify it. The same impulses and arguments that call for clarity and determinacy in law auger in favor of a clear picture of what law isn't or is no longer.

VI. CONCLUDING THOUGHTS

There is a symmetry between the study of the law of war and of war itself concerning termination. If law of war scholarship has dedicated significant study to the formation of treaties yet little to their termination, war studies also seem to have focused predominantly on beginnings rather than endings. From the latter field, one writer has offered, "Wars are unpleasant and much of the study of them has been motived by the practical question of how to prevent them. As a result the study of wars of all sorts focuses overwhelmingly on how they begin, rather than how they end."[183] Another has observed, perhaps apocryphally, "For every thousand pages published on the causes of wars there is less than one page directly

181. Antoon De Baets, *The View of the Past in International Humanitarian Law (1860–2020)*, 104 International Review of the Red Cross 1586, 1586 (2022) (citing International Committee of the Red Cross, Report on the Work of the International Committee of the Red Cross (Jan. 1 to Dec. 31, 1952) 67 (1953)).

182. Droege & Giorgou, *supra* note 97, at 1805.

183. Robert Harrison Wagner, *The Causes of Peace*, *in* Stopping the Killing 235, 241 (Roy Licklider ed., 1993).

on the causes of peace."[184] Without hazarding an empirical guess, it seems safe to say the ratio of writing on law of war formation greatly exceeds that on its termination.

All the same, the laws of war should be assessed with equal rigor for their unmaking as for their making. It is widely accepted that as much as any legal regime, the laws of war depend on their connections to context. While the effort has waned of late, law of war treaty formation has historically been a project committed to accounting for and incorporating the evolving realities of armed conflict. Just as the changing character of warfare calls for new rules, it surely calls for clear-eyed assessments whether existing rules should stand or be repealed and replaced. Law of war unmaking may in this sense even be conceived as preliminary and integral to law of war making.

As a preliminary and only brief work, this chapter has not addressed unmaking of customary international laws of war. It is a subject of equal importance and perhaps of exceeding doctrinal complexity.[185] Fuller treatment of law of war unmaking will no doubt call for attention to the subject, including questions relating to its repeal.

As stated at its outset,this chapter is not intended to occupy the field of law of war unmaking. Rather it hopes to inspire a more thorough survey of States' resorts to the means of unmaking. Perhaps its catalog of various mechanisms for unmaking, both formal and informal, will inspire further doctrinal work on the secondary rules of treaty termination and modification. And perhaps the chapter's initial effort at identifying treaties and provisions worthy of reconsideration or tidying up will inspire identification of others.

184. GEOFFREY BLAINEY, THE CAUSES OF WAR 3 (3d ed. 1988). *See* SIDNEY BAILEY, 1 HOW WARS END: THE UNITED NATIONS AND THE TERMINATION OF ARMED CONFLICT 1946–1964 (1982); COLEMAN PHILIPSON, TERMINATION OF WAR AND TREATIES OF PEACE (1916).

185. *See supra* discussion following note 174.

INDEX

For the benefit of digital users, indexed terms that span two pages (e.g., 52–53) may, on occasion, appear on only one of those pages.

Tables are indicated by *t* following the page number